THE TWILIGHT STRUGGLE

Other books by William Attwood

Making It Through Middle Age

The Fairly Scary Adventure Book (for children)

The Reds and the Blacks

The Decline of the American Male (coauthor)

Still the Most Exciting Country

The Man Who Could Grow Hair

THE
TWILIGHT
STRUGGLE

Tales of the Cold War

WILLIAM ATTWOOD

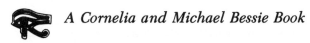 *A Cornelia and Michael Bessie Book*

HARPER & ROW, PUBLISHERS New York
Cambridge, Philadelphia, San Francisco, Washington
London, Mexico City, São Paulo, Singapore, Sydney

FIRST EDITION

Designer: Sidney Feinberg

Copy editor: Mary Jane Alexander

Indexer: Olive Holmes for Edindex

Library of Congress Cataloging-in-Publication Data

Attwood, William, 1919–
   The twilight struggle.

   "A Cornelia and Michael Bessie book."
   Includes index.
   1. United States—Foreign relations—1945–
2. World politics—1945–   ., I. Title.
E744.A82 1987   327′.09′04   86-46042
ISBN 0-06-039068-9

---

87 88 89 90 91 HC 10 9 8 7 6 5 4 3 2 1

Now the trumpet summons us again—not as a call to bear arms, though arms we need; not as a call to battle, though embattled we are; but a call to bear the burden of a long twilight struggle, year in and year out, 'rejoicing in hope, patient in tribulation,' a struggle against the common enemies of man: tyranny, poverty, disease and war itself.

—President John F. Kennedy
Inaugural Address, January 20, 1961

Contents

Foreword

The idea for this book came to me while sorting out the pile of crammed manila envelopes and file folders assembled by my father, who died in 1969, and bequeathed to me by my mother, who died thirteen years later. As I looked through them I discovered that my father had preserved every letter I'd written home since World War II, as well as every published article that carried my by-line in both newspapers and magazines. Rereading this collection, I found myself reliving long-gone times and remembering the details of events that normally languish in our memory banks, seldom if ever retrieved.

Digging deeper, I came across letters I had written my wife, Sim, in the forties and fifties and others she had written me. (People still wrote letters then; the phone was for emergencies.) And I found boxes full of old diaries and reporter's notebooks, squirreled away through the decades, God knows why. The diary of my world trip with Adlai Stevenson alone ran to more than 100,000 words, and the one with Sim across America to 70,000. I also kept a necessarily cryptic journal during my five years in the State Department, and that had survived too.

So I had a lot of raw material—primary, eyewitness stuff, not the product of secondary sources—and as I read it I felt an obligation as well as an impulse to shape it into a book of observed and experienced history—subjective to be sure, but also accurate within its scope. The ranks of those of us able to remember the sights, sounds and smells, as well as the words, of an era like these past forty years are thinning rapidly; and if *we* don't get the essentials down on paper, who ever will, or could?

And I remembered George F. Kennan's comment a few years ago on writing about recent history:

When my mind returns to the events in question, what comes to it is primarily the memories of individual experiences along the way. Some of them, it seems to me, speak for themselves; and I would rather recall them as they were, and let them tell their own story, than try to embroider them analytically.

So I made the decision to embark on this project, Kennan fashion, letting my accumulated memories speak for themselves. Eventually, of course, it became something more—part memoir, part history and part essay. The memoir chronicles my own involvement in the cold war, both as a journalist and a diplomat; the history (much of it culled from *World Almanacs*) adds a kind of background newsreel of what was happening globally during these years so as to keep the eyewitness stuff in context; and the essay, which I've tried to confine to the last chapter, gives me a chance to comment on this extraordinary era, now that I can view it in retrospect.

I talked to some thirty or thirty-five knowledgeable contemporaries and cold war scholars, none for more than an hour or so and primarily to verify some of my own hunches and recollections. There's no point in naming them. They know who they are and that I'm grateful for the time and help they gave me.

I must confess that it was both surprising and somehow reassuring to discover during some of these talks that their memory of the kaleidoscopic sequence of events we had all lived through was often as deficient as mine. What prompted the Berlin airlift? Who succeeded Stalin and when? Why did Ike send marines to Lebanon? Was that after Sputnik? Before the U-2 incident? These forty years remain, for most of us, a jumble of tenuously related happenings; and sorting them out has been a strangely satisfying exercise, like tidying up the random clutter in some long neglected attic or basement.

I also read or consulted several books for the same reason. The most useful was André Fontaine's *The History of the Cold War,* which covers the 1945–68 period. Raymond L. Garthoff's *Détente and Confrontation* leaves no stone (or rock) of the seventies unturned. For clarity, brevity and durability, Arthur Schlesinger's *Foreign Affairs* article "The Origins of the Cold War," published in 1967, is unsurpassed.

No one helped me with the manuscript or even read it except for my wife, Sim, and two friends. Their words of encouragement sustained me and their suggestions, I know, helped make it a better book.

THE TWILIGHT STRUGGLE

Chapter 1

Genesis

T HE COLD WAR STARTED for me on March 27, 1946, and has dominated most of my professional life ever since. Forty years is a long time
to be stuck with any assignment, especially one that engages so many
of your waking hours (and even invades your dreams), and I hope that
compiling this book of reminiscences may purge my memory banks of
cold war data and perhaps make room for more relaxing and even
frivolous concerns.

Why that particular March 27? The explanation requires some
backpedaling to December 11, 1945, when I was discharged from the
U.S. Army as a rather restless and impatient captain exactly four years
after enlisting as an enthusiastic private. Like a good many other veterans, I was in a hurry to make up for what seemed like four wasted years,
so we job-hunted all day and stayed up too late most nights, sometimes
drinking, sometimes fending off marriage-minded girls, sometimes
both. It was a time accurately chronicled in Merle Miller's novel *That
Winter.* Eventually we decompressed and disbanded.

In February I was lucky to land a job with the New York *Herald
Tribune* as a copy editor on the cable desk at $60 a week. Reading the
incoming stories of postwar political unrest from France, Germany and
the Balkans, I decided that Europe was where the action was and where
I wanted to go. Joe Barnes, the foreign editor, was sympathetic and
understanding. He had once been a foreign correspondent and told me,
"In no other job can you feel so much a part of the history of your own
time." The paper did need a replacement in the Paris bureau, and my
speaking French was a useful asset. But Joe suggested a stint in the
Washington bureau first to prove myself as a reporter.

And so in March I became the thirteenth man in a thirteen-man bureau with little to do but cover events that rated two-paragraph stories. One of these was a three-day meeting of the newly formed Federation of Atomic Scientists. I soon learned enough of their vocabulary—words like reactors, isotopes, denaturing, plutonium and the rest —that I became the bureau specialist on all things atomic. Consequently, when a special committee headed by then Under Secretary of State Dean Acheson issued what was to be an historic, seventy-eight-page report about the new atomic age on March 27, it became my assignment, and I wrote the following lead on my first bylined front-page story: "The blunt fact that mankind faces self-destruction unless the United Nations control atomic power was made very plain today by the State Department's committee on atomic energy."

In essence, the document, known as the Acheson-Lilienthal Report, proposed that the United States "progressively" share its atomic know-how with the other nations of the world while international control machinery was being set up. Thereafter, the U.N. would control all mining, denaturing and conversion of uranium and its issuance to licensed users for industrial purposes.

In the weeks that followed, the story stayed on the front page. Senator Brien McMahon proposed legislation placing the production of atomic energy under civilian control, while the military naturally wanted to play a role. The atomic scientists urged prompt international action to avert what they predicted would be a worldwide "state of nerves and suspicion unlike anything man has ever suffered before." Meanwhile, the navy said it was going ahead with plans for atomic bomb tests in the Pacific in July. So I had more than my share of by-line stories, and in mid-April was given the ultimate accolade by Bert Andrews, the bureau chief—an invitation to join the Washington staff on a permanent basis. When I turned him down, saying I'd rather go to Europe, everybody on the paper but Barnes put me down as an eccentric; Washington was considered the capital of the world and Washington correspondents the aristocracy of our trade.

What did my *Herald Tribune* stories that spring have to do with the cold war? Simply that the Acheson-Lilienthal Report was presented in the summer to the United Nations by Bernard Baruch (who put his own name on it), where it eventually expired from an overdose of that mutual distrust which has soured U.S.-Soviet relations ever since and led Baruch to coin the phrase "cold war" in a speech on April 1946. It gave the world a taste of things to come. In short, we wanted to keep our monopoly of the atomic bomb, our technological lead and our option to build more bombs and test them—at least until the U.N. control machinery was in place. The Russians, on the other hand, wanted all further production of bombs to stop (with verification to be conducted by each country on its own soil) and retention of the big-power veto on atomic questions arising in the Security Council of the United Nations. The Soviet bloc was then outnumbered in the General Assembly, ten to one, and Moscow was understandably opposed to a majority vote.

In retrospect, it seems naive of us to have believed that our existing supremacy, along with further testing, would frighten the Russians into accepting international controls as a preferable alternative to escalating U.S. superiority. Predictably, the result of our proposal was simply to goad them into redoubling their efforts to catch up. They chose the challenge of an atomic arms race because they didn't trust us; we sought to freeze the status quo while we were still ahead because we didn't trust them. And so the costly, ever-spiraling competition was on, fueled for the next forty years by the same persistent distrust that surfaced in 1946 over the Acheson-Lilienthal Report.

Actually, the race probably started at least a year earlier, on July 24, 1945, when President Truman informed Stalin at Potsdam that we had The Bomb and would soon be using it in Japan. Stalin, who knew much more about it than we suspected, took the news calmly but, according to the memoirs of Marshal G. K. Zhukov, told him later, "It looks like we are going to have to talk to Kurchatov and get him to speed things up." (I.V. Kurchatov was the physicist in charge of the Soviet atomic program.)

The atomic issue was a momentous one for mankind, but only the scientists most familiar with the subject seemed really alarmed. "The splitting of the atom," said Albert Einstein, "has changed everything save our mode of thinking, and thus we drift toward unparalleled catastrophe." But few of us were listening. In 1946, we were becoming aware that the Russians were no longer our gallant allies but exasperating antagonists. We resented the snide distortions of Europe's Communist press and the vicious cartoons in *Krokodil*. But we could not take the idea of another armed conflict seriously—not yet. And when we finally did, in the late forties, we thought of it in terms of conventional warfare. The alleged existence of 175 Soviet divisions in Eastern Europe was therefore deemed more important than the detonation of their first atomic bomb in August 1949.

As for our own test at Bikini Atoll in July 1946, its chief consequence in Paris—where I had gone in May—was to engender an anything-goes mood, and its most lasting impact was to provide a name for the world's most daring bathing suit. Let me explain.

When the U.S. Navy announced in June that another atomic "device" would be set off less than a year after two similar devices had obliterated Hiroshima and Nagasaki, rumors began circulating that this was going to be a new kind of superbomb very likely to get out of control and start a massive chain reaction that would blow up the whole world. This gave hostesses an excuse to toss "end of the world" parties and young men an additional argument to use with coy or reluctant girl friends. All things considered, Paris was not a bad place to be just then, in spite of the lousy coffee.

And the chic word became "Bikini" when the site of the test was made known. The parties became "Bikini" parties, and the promotion manager of the Piscine Molitor—a fashionable swimming club—quickly saw the value of unveiling a "Bikini" costume that would go as far as anybody in that pretopless era thought a bathing suit could go, even in Paris. (No one could foresee the advent of the monokini, let alone the nokini.)

And so a fashion show was held at the pool on July 5 to launch its first postwar season, and a model named Micheline Bernardini displayed the bikini for the first time in public. The event did not go uncovered. Tex O'Reilly, the *Trib*'s Paris bureau chief, sensed that history was in the making and assigned all hands, including some visiting reporters in town for the Peace Conference, to cover the happening from all angles—social, diplomatic, cultural, political and just plain visual. Our stories ran under a three-column headline in the next day's Paris edition, and as I look at the now yellowing copy of that paper, I find that the story which best stands the test of time also exemplifies the best reporting of the day, in terms of brevity, clarity and punch. It was turned in by—who else?—our fashion editor, Lucie Noel. She took one look at the bikini and batted out the only one of the news stories worth reprinting here in toto, forty years later:

"Wow!"

All right. Back now to the early chronology of the cold war—an essential backdrop to the stories and recollections that will follow.

Most historians of the period agree that suspicion of the West was deeply ingrained in Stalin's psyche and evident all through the war. He believed the Allies deliberately delayed opening a second front in Western Europe until the Soviet and Nazi armies had bled each other white.

He was ever alert to rumors that we were about to sign a separate peace with Germany. His own accommodation with Hitler in 1939 was never mentioned, although he did have the nerve to sound out American diplomats before the Yalta conference on whether we would accept the terms of the Nazi-Soviet pact giving the Russians a free hand in Iran and South Asia. And at Yalta, his insistence on a postwar world order based on spheres of influence betrayed his obsession with security—and clashed with our belief in peacekeeping through the universal application of the U.N. Charter.

On our side, the Red Army's connivance in the crushing of the Warsaw uprising in 1944 (which all but wiped out the non-Communist Polish resistance forces) also convinced many of our diplomats that Stalin meant to impose the Soviet system on Eastern Europe, whatever assurances he gave us about democracy and freedom of choice.

Thus the stage was set, well before the war ended, for an East-West confrontation. Among President Roosevelt's and President Truman's most hard-line advisers were Averell Harriman and George Kennan, who—paradoxically—became the leading advocates of accommodation with the Soviet Union in later years. But there was no inconsistency in the evolution of their thinking. Knowing the Russians, they understood that Stalin—once the Red Army had penetrated deep into Europe—would have to be discouraged from further expanding his empire by a policy of firmness and containment. They knew we would have to take on this risk, since our Western allies were prostrate. And in time they also understood the genuine need and desire of a new generation of Soviet leaders to relax tensions and lessen the crushing burden and mounting danger of a perpetual arms race.

Moreover, like most Americans who had lived in the Soviet Union in the thirties, they were aware of the latent hostility that had so long curdled relations between these two huge but curiously adolescent nations. The Russians have never forgotten (though we have) our military intervention in support of the White armies in 1919–20, nor our refusal to recognize the Soviet Union diplomatically until 1933. And we were conditioned early on by the Red scare of the early twenties and the cartoons of bearded Bolsheviks in tunics and boots holding big round bombs with lighted fuses. No, we never did look on the Russians as buddies, not even in the days of the czars.

There are scholars, like Professor Stephen Cohen of Princeton, who assert unequivocally that "the cold war began in 1917." A plausible case can be made for this view. Obviously, our relations with Moscow never reached the stage of military posturing, covert activity and overheated rhetoric that has been the norm for the past forty years, but it is hard to think of a period since the provisional Kerensky government was overthrown by the Bolsheviks in the October 1917 revolution when U.S.-Soviet relations were harmonious, let alone friendly. The Red scares of the early twenties fizzled out, but mention of the U.S.S.R. never failed to evoke images in the American mind of a brutal, primitive, atheistic, collectivist, not-to-be-trusted power, hostile to every democratic and capitalist virtue we professed to honor and, more often than not, did. Communism was simply a bad word in America, which was not the case in most of Europe, where Communist parties were regarded much like other political entities. The most votes the Communist Party (U.S.A.) was ever able to garner in a national election was 100,000 in 1932, in the slough of the depression. Whatever protest vote that year did not go to the Democrats went rather to the relatively moderate Socialist Party, which pulled 900,000.

The myth that cannot be dispelled too often—because it has been propagated for so many years in Communist circles—is that the cold war might have been avoided altogether had Franklin Roosevelt not died when he did. No one has promoted this myth more assiduously than Valentin Berezhkov, Stalin's wartime interpreter and author of *History in the Making.* He told me a year ago that had Roosevelt lived "maybe only six months more" and had we offered low-interest reconstruction loans to the U.S.S.R., "there would have been an entirely different attitude in our relations."

After his death, Roosevelt was virtually canonized by the Communists—the deceased being both silent and harmless—but there is no evidence to suggest that his policies would have been any different from Truman's. According to Kennan, Roosevelt's cables to Stalin in 1945 were increasingly sharp and tough. And Arthur Schlesinger, Jr., has quoted a revealing account by Anna Rosenberg Hoffman of a lunch with Roosevelt on March 24, 1945, the last day he spent in Washington. He was handed a cable. "He read it and became quite agitated," she reported. "He banged his fists on the arms of his wheelchair and said, 'Averell is right; we can't do business with Stalin. He has broken every one of the promises he made at Yalta.'"

Stalin's opinion of Roosevelt was no more flattering. He liked to tell people that "Churchill would pick your pocket for one miserable kopeck but Roosevelt would always go after more." In March, he even accused FDR of making a deal with Hitler, whose troops were surrendering to the Allies but fighting the Russians. Roosevelt replied, on April 4: "Frankly, I cannot avoid a feeling of bitter resentment towards your informers, whoever they are, for such vile misrepresentation of my actions or those of my trusted subordinates."

In May 1945, the European war over, we canceled lend-lease deliveries to the Soviet Union, ignored (partly through bureaucratic inefficiency) a Soviet loan request and opposed German reparations. All this nourished Stalin's already deep-rooted suspicions, and during the winter of 1945–46 a consensus developed in Washington that real collaboration between our two countries was not in the cards. Our differences were too profound, our interpretations of the Yalta accords too different and Stalin's paranoia too advanced.

We still believed in a long-range modus vivendi with the Russians, but they seemed not to look beyond a temporary accommodation while they recovered from the devastation of the war. Moreover, Leninist ideology concerning capitalism, imperialism and war, together with the probability that the Soviet dictatorship could not survive close collaboration with the West, made confrontation inevitable. The tragedy is that ordinary Russians would have welcomed close ties with the West, especially the United States. On V-E Day in Moscow, cheering throngs spontaneously converged on the American Embassy, where George Kennan addressed them from the balcony. But no one could reverse Stalin's conspirational and Byzantine policies except Stalin himself, and by the late forties, his madness seemed the equal of Hitler's.

The first direct and overt confrontation of the cold war, the first instance of brinkmanship, occurred in Iran in the spring of 1946. It had been agreed at a London meeting of foreign ministers in September 1945 that the British, American and Soviet troops in Iran would be evacuated by March 2 of the following year. That date passed, and the Soviet forces remained in northern Iran. But a stiff note from Washington, coupled with an appeal to the U.N. Security Council by Iran (with our encouragement), persuaded the Russians to back down and pull out by the end of the month. They had lost this first test of will and had succeeded only in confirming Truman's suspicions about the value of Stalin's assurances; but there would be many other tests in the years to come.

On March 5, 1946, Churchill told nearly forty thousand people at Fulton, Missouri, that "an iron curtain has descended across the continent" and that only military strength impressed the Russians—"our friends and allies during the war."

While Churchill spoke as a private citizen, he had Truman's tacit concurrence. But the U.S. and British governments officially disassociated themselves from the speech out of consideration for the wartime alliance. It was, after all, less than a year since Soviet and American soldiers were embracing at the Elbe. Stalin was nonetheless infuriated and charged Churchill with "slander, discourtesy and tactlessness." He also warned the Western powers that any attempt to organize an armed campaign against communism would fail "as it did twenty-six years ago."

The atomic minuet over our U.N. proposal described above occupied center stage from March until July. Then came the diplomatic sparring at the Paris Peace Conference, the start of the Indochina war, the resumption of the Greek civil war, the consolidation of Communist control in Eastern Europe and, on March 12, 1947, the announcement of the Truman Doctrine for Greece and Turkey. The Congress voted $400 million in aid to these two strategically important countries after hearing the president state that "it must be the policy of the United States to support free peoples who are resisting attempted subjugation by armed minorities or by outside pressures."

We were no longer mincing words by 1947, and the film of frost that already blanketed East-West relations a year earlier had by now frozen into thick and solid ice. The cold war was under way, and the point of no return finally reached on July 2, 1947, when the Soviet foreign minister, Vyacheslav Molotov, walked out of the Paris conference held to discuss the Marshall Plan and thereby ironically ensured its success. His refusal to participate was Moscow's biggest mistake in the cold war thus far; and there were more to come.

Looking back, it appears the cold war was inevitable, once the Red Army had moved into Central Europe, and there consolidated its power, though it might have been less frigid—that is, less acute and militaristic—had there been more mutual comprehension of each side's differing views of the postwar world order: on ours, containment of Soviet expansionism, should it occur, and maintaining a power balance in Europe now that Britain was no longer able to assume that responsibility; on theirs, a Soviet state secure against aggression, accepted as an equal and entitled to reach out beyond fortress Russia to promote the Communist gospel.

Unfortunately, each side was constantly and erroneously assumed by the other to be much more belligerent than it actually was. But given Stalin's obsession with security, his distrust of Roosevelt and Churchill and his fear of a resurgent Germany, there is no deal we could have struck with him while we were still allies short of giving him a totally free hand in Eastern Europe (along with a license for subversion in Western Europe), coupled with massive credits to rebuild the Soviet Union's war-shattered economy. (Most Americans are still unaware of how much more Russia suffered in the war than we did. For example, there is a cemetery outside Leningrad where 650,000 victims of that city's 900-day siege by the Nazis are buried; we lost only 400,000 soldiers in all of World War Two.)

And so, while we can describe the cold war, we can't explain it except in terms of a human tragedy grounded in ancient grievances that escalated into outright hostility as actions were taken by each side —whether in Berlin, Czechoslovakia, Egypt, Hungary, Greece, Korea, Cuba or China—that only reinforced and confirmed almost every dark suspicion harbored by the other.

It is true that for a brief period we sincerely sought an understanding with the Soviets and that Stalin was as much at fault as anyone for initiating the cold war. But he saw his policies in Eastern Europe as not only guaranteeing security at last for his country from German and other potential aggressors but also as protecting the new "people's democracies" against a return of prewar feudalism and fascism.

Consequently, both sides embraced the fallacy that you add to your own security by increasing the insecurity of your opponent, and by 1953, when Stalin died and the Korean War was ended, it was too late to return to a rational reappraisal of where we were headed. Our deeply ingrained anticommunism, fortified by seven years of Soviet duplicity, had become as rigid an ideology as communism itself. With Senator Joe McCarthy riding high, our own paranoia now made it difficult politically, even for President Eisenhower, to engage the post-Stalin leadership in any serious conciliatory talks, at least for several years.

Also, by then, both sides had grown used to the cold war and in fact needed it—the Russians to exact further sacrifices from a war-weary populace and to explain perennial austerity in terms of an "imperialist" threat; and the West to persuade its citizens to accept another military buildup and to support the Marshall Plan as a means of stopping communism by creating prosperity in Europe.

Contemplating these four decades of cold war, it is hard to understand what it has really been all about. Is our quarrel with the Soviet Union of such magnitude that it has justified placing the very survival of mankind at risk? Obviously not. The traditional causes of war are absent. We really do not covet their territory, their raw materials or their markets; nor they, ours. There is no central issue at the heart of our conflict. The postwar military buildup in Western Europe, culminating in NATO, was motivated by the still current assumption that the Russians are poised and eager to launch an armed assault across the iron curtain. But I have never met a serious student of Soviet policy who believes that even Stalin—let alone his successors—ever considered risking a third world war simply to maintain occupation forces in the hostile environment of Western Europe. If Western Communist parties managed to attain power, the Kremlin would no doubt be pleased, but only so long as the Red Army was not called upon to help.

So what we have been witnessing has been merely a long progression in the art of weaponry to the point that the weapons now being produced and planned are no longer usable, at least by rational beings. The atom bombs that ended the hot war came to dominate the cold one in ever more lethal forms.

As Thomas Powers, an author of books about nuclear weapons, wrote recently, "The fact of the matter is that the cold war is not about anything in the usual sense. It has a history, but the history describes rather than explains it."

And the tragedy of our time is dramatized by the fact that while we have no irreconcilable differences with the Russians, we do have a mutual interest in survival—an interest sometimes alluded to but usually drowned out by outbursts of now monotonous invective. Momentary lulls in our war of words have been regularly interrupted by emotionally charged crises—the Berlin airlift, the Korean War, the Cuban missile flap, Afghanistan, Nicaragua, whatever—that vindicate the Cassandras and perpetuate distrust.

While I have noted that Stalin was as much at fault as any one man for starting the cold war, it eventually acquired a momentum of it own, with both sides contributing to it. Fairly predictable events—repression in Eastern Europe, the downing of the U-2 in 1960 and KAL 007 twenty-three years later, our warming up to China—managed to turn promising thaws into renewed deep freezes. Constituencies to prolong the cold war developed among both the military and civilian bureaucracies in Washington and Moscow. And sometimes our policies have seemed to be based on the assumption that Stalin is still alive and well in the Kremlin.

Future historians, if any, will surely look back on the cold war as a needless distraction from the most urgent problems threatening our planet—such as overpopulation, environmental pollution, the depletion of natural resources and endemic poverty and hunger. Efforts to cope with these life-or-death challenges have taken a backseat to the accumulation of deadly nuclear arsenals and to a race to catch up with or to surpass those we perceive to be our mortal enemies. It has indeed been "a long twilight struggle," in John F. Kennedy's words, and ever more sophisticated technology has made the sky darker now than when he uttered them.

The chapters that follow are a memoir of a period in human history that I have learned to my surprise is less known and understood than more remote periods, such as the decades encompassing our Civil War. Perhaps the reason is that the start of the cold war is still too close to the present to be regarded as history by the old, and too far away to be remembered as a current event by the young. It is both part of history and part of the news; it has happened and yet it also goes on. It has produced a literature, but the literature seems strangely evanescent: books to be read or skimmed through, like magazine articles, and then discarded as their subject matter is overtaken by events, gone stale, forgotten.

"America is a country without memory," wrote Anthony Lewis in 1985. "That feeling in the society seems to me stronger now than ever. Those of us who are middle-aged or older have all had the experience of talking to people in their twenties about some central part of our experience and finding an utter lack of recognition. In college classes today even a reference to Vietnam is likely to produce blank looks."

A central part of my own experience has been the cold war. Perhaps two-thirds of the more than a million words I've written for publication relate to it. And so I feel an obligation, as a surviving eyewitness of this period, to tell it the way I saw it while still able to do so before my notes, diaries, letters and clippings are all faded beyond legibility or mislaid for good, and my memory becomes completely enshrouded in the mists of old age. Face it. We veterans of this long cold war are not so very numerous anymore, and not so very young.

Chapter 2

A Reporter in Paris

T HE YEAR 1946 was a time of transition from the afterglow of the hot war to the early frost of the cold one, and my first two stories filed from Paris illustrate the point.

I got off the boat train from Le Havre at the Gare St.-Lazare on May 10 and was assigned to cover the first celebration of V-E Day on May 12. It was a listless event, a military parade under overcast skies past sparse and indifferent onlookers and an uninspiring and now forgotten president, Félix Gouin. The euphoria of the liberation had evaporated long ago—sometime in the winter of 1944–45—when it dawned on the French that being free at last meant that they now had twenty-eight shrill, quarreling newspapers to choose from, but not much else to buy, nor money to spend. And their war record, compared to that of many other Europeans, was nothing to brag about nor even remember. Except for one armored division, a few romantic Gaullists and a commando network of disciplined Communists (after June 1941), the resistance movement was no big thing until it became obvious the Germans were losing the war. Most Frenchmen had been *attentistes* (wait-and-see-ers) or outright collaborators who often out-Nazied the Nazis, and this private knowledge preyed on the nation's collective conscience and explains much of the adulation lavished on de Gaulle. For he had resisted. And he had proclaimed himself to be, in effect, the incarnation of France. Therefore, to complete the syllogism, France had resisted. Yet V-E Day was really not their celebration: they knew in their hearts how little they had contributed to the victory.

It was a tough story to write, and I wondered, like so many reporters immobilized before their typewriters, whether I'd lost my touch.

My next by-line story was a speech by the Soviet Union's chief prosecutor, Andrei Vyshinsky, to a group of eminent French jurists at the Palace of Justice. His attempt to explain that the Soviet principle of justice was based on "democratic dictatorship" and that the Soviet penitentiary system was based on "the principle of work" left his audience visibly perplexed; his performance also elicited rustling and murmurs when he told a questioner that a prisoner who refused to embrace the principle of work would be "categorically exterminated." By the end of the evening the jurists were quite agitated.

I hitched a ride back to the office with three French Communists—a parliamentarian and two journalists. (In 1946, it was still permissible for them to be on friendly terms with Americans.)

"Your article about the speech will no doubt distort it," one of them said. I told him the speech was funny enough already without retouching. They let me pay for the cab.

I learned two things that summer: that the cold war was on and probably irreversible, and that the life of a foreign correspondent was much shorter on glamour and much longer on drudgery than my friends back home imagined. I'll comment on the second lesson first.

For an American, the Paris of the late forties was a far cry from the romanticized Paris of the roaring twenties. Jake Barnes, in *The Sun Also Rises,* never seemed to have much work to do; as I remember, he'd spend an occasional afternoon batting out feature stories in time for the next boat train and then wander around the bars and café terraces in search of friends who had even less work to do. But our four-man bureau filed about eight stories a day, which involved a good deal of attendance at press conferences, interviewing and checking out as well as developing sources. And we worked a six-day week, usually from about noon to 10 P.M. Readers had become accustomed during the war to seeing stories with overseas datelines, so we covered French politics almost as a hometown weekly covers school board meetings. And gradually, as cold war tensions mounted, we metamorphosed into war correspondents, dealing in conflict, writing of victories and defeats on the political and diplomatic fronts, rooting for our side against the sinister Soviet empire and its local puppets.

And the tensions did mount perceptibly that summer with the convening of the Paris conference of foreign ministers, whose task was to draw up peace treaties with the five European nations that had sided, however briefly, with Germany—Italy, Finland, Hungary, Romania and Bulgaria. My assignment was to keep in touch with these "enemy" delegations, while the more seasoned staffers—like Walter Kerr, John Metcalfe and Tex O'Reilly—covered the American, British, Soviet and other Allied contingents.

I liked my people, and they trusted me once they saw that what they told me was accurately reported the next day in the *Trib*'s Paris edition. Only one, a gentle and genial Hungarian named Ivan Boldizsar (doomed in the long run since he wasn't a Communist), came by to protest quietly that I kept misspelling his name and thus subjected him to ridicule. Apparently, putting the "s" before the "z" in the last syllable made it come out as "shit" in Hungarian. I have been scrupulous about this ever since.

They were naive, many of these Central Europeans who belonged to Social Democratic or Peasant parties. They really believed that Stalin would live up to the Yalta Declaration, which stated, "The establishment of order in Europe . . . must be achieved by a process which will enable the liberated peoples to . . . create democratic institutions of their own choice." And so, when the Smallholders' Party whipped the Communists in the November 1945 elections in Hungary, 59 to 17 percent, the winners thought they'd be running the country. But all the election accomplished was to hasten the day when the Russians, now alarmed, proceeded with the systematic liquidation of all opposition parties.

Still, we all made believe we'd meet again in Budapest and toasted freedom and democracy at picnics in the Bois de Boulogne between conference sessions.

I got a brief respite from the conference on July 14, when I celebrated my twenty-seventh birthday by covering a speech by Winston Churchill at Metz. After a parade down the avenue du Vingtième Corps Américain, we repaired to the City Hall for a seven-course banquet washed down by gallons of wine. Churchill finally fell asleep during the welcoming speeches, his head on the tablecloth. When his daughter Mary woke him, he looked around, bewildered, then spotted us British and American reporters just below the dais.

"Where am I?" he whispered. "And why?"

"Metz," said one of us. "Bastille Day."

That's all the cue he needed to launch into a Vive-la-France type of oration—in halting but fluent French—that delighted his audience. At times he leaned over to us reporters for help in handling an idiomatic phrase and, surprisingly, he struck a markedly different note from his "iron curtain" speech in Missouri in March. His theme was European unity, and his only reference to the Soviet Union was as "the heroic ally which has twice shed its blood in battles originating in Europe's quarrels."

We drove back to Paris in a haze of brandy and Allied good fellowship. I could understand how even a glimpse of Winnie could have buoyed Londoners during the darkest days of the Battle of Britain.

As the conference dragged on, it got progressively harder to find anything new to write. One day O'Reilly, our bureau chief, obtained the full text of the draft peace treaties from a friend at the French Foreign Ministry who got them out on a Sunday and had to have them back in the safe by Monday morning. I had Sunday duty, which was normally uneventful, so I sauntered into the office about 5 P.M. and found all hands typing stories.

"Where the hell have you been?" yelled O'Reilly.

"Having a swim at the Racing Club," I replied.

"Well, for that you get Trieste and the new Franco-Italian boundary, which nobody else understands." So I went to work. Trieste really was a conundrum; I don't think anyone ever did understand it. But our small scoop probably made the *New York Times* squirm a little.

My best source was Jan Masaryk, the foreign minister of Czechoslovakia and a big, jovial, warmhearted man. I would bring him letters from Marcia Davenport, the American novelist, our mutual friend and his (unannounced) fiancée. Masaryk's name—his father was Czechoslovakia's first president—and international prestige were his best protection against the Communists, who, backed by the Kremlin, exercised the real power in Prague despite a facade of democracy and civil liberties. One day he told me, "The Russians cannot make mistakes—by which I mean they cannot admit making a mistake. That's because they all suffer from a massive inferiority complex."

That is the kind of remark you don't forget because experience teaches you over the years to appreciate the truth of it. I remember how only a few years ago the Russians preferred to be regarded as trigger-happy outlaws after they shot down the Korean airliner than to admit they mistakenly identified it as a U.S. spy plane.

Eventually the petty but almost incessant haggling at the Paris conference grated on everyone's nerves. We weren't yet accustomed to the Soviet obsession with scoring propaganda points even when these slowed down the negotiating process. On August 15, Secretary of State James Byrnes finally upbraided Molotov in strong language and was backed up by the British. In my diary I noted, "It's a wonder he's restrained himself as long as this."

I was becoming a cold war correspondent, like most of my fellow reporters . . .

How did I spend my days in that first summer of the cold war? Well, I rose late, partly because I usually went to bed late and partly because the office didn't begin to stir until lunchtime, when it was only 7 A.M. in New York. Some mornings I'd get up and drive my tinny little 1946 Renault to the Racing Club. (French cars were just getting back into production and were available only to buyers with foreign currency.) There, I'd play tennis with friends from the office and watch the nubile but aloof young women around the pool, most of them the property of more opulent admirers and many the same who were being ogled two years before by German officers.

Lunch was at the bistro nearest the office, a place called Le Tangage, where chilled rosé wine would usually cure whatever headaches had been acquired overnight. A story conference of sorts would be conducted by O'Reilly, and by two o'clock we would be out bird-dogging our assignments, while Sydney Hodges, our gentlemanly and underpaid British office manager, would peruse the wire service copy. We moved around town faster than today because traffic was sparse and Americans generally made welcome—even in Communist Party headquarters.

By six or seven we'd be back at the *Trib* building on the rue de Berri to make a few phone calls and begin writing. We'd generally do one story before dinner, which normally included a stop at the Hotel California bar across the street for a mock martini concocted with a Saigon-made gin called Gordan's, and then do a second story later. At ten or so we either dispersed or, on occasion, coalesced into an expedition to Montmartre for no purpose other than to prolong conviviality. Walter Kerr, our chief diplomatic correspondent, would normally combine his pub crawling with work by inviting Chip Bohlen, Byrnes's deputy and later ambassador to Moscow, to join his group. The rest of us, the bachelors, anyway, would often end the evening with a house guest selected from the amiable, semipro young women—many of them war widows—who frequented the neighborhood bars and accepted money from acquaintances who weren't *copains,* or pals. Journalists, known to be undemanding and underpaid, were always treated as *copains.*

It was not a glamorous life; we seldom grazed the celebrity circuit. But it was not unpleasant once you learned about the perils of brandy and the importance of eight hours' sleep. None of us agonized about writing or not writing novels or painting pictures, as Hemingway's characters did. Even when we caroused, we mostly talked shop or politics or planned future stories. At revels' end, say 2 A.M., Paris in those days seemed like a great, peaceful village. The subways no longer rumbled underfoot—they stopped running at one. The buses and pre-war taxis were long since garaged. The streetlights were dim, and the streetwalkers had quit for the night. Walking up the Champs-Elysées by moonlight, through the Arch and down the tree-lined avenue Victor Hugo to my apartment, I could hear my own footsteps on the sidewalk. Now and then a barking dog or passing truck would break the silence. Otherwise the city basked in a haunting nocturnal serenity it would never know again.

No, we were not a lost generation and in fact felt like aliens whenever we ventured over to the left bank, to St.-Germain-des-Prés, where the young existentialists postured and brooded in smoky underground caverns like the Tabou, or cadged drinks from a few solvent poets and artists on the terraces of the Flore and the Deux Magots. I suppose we American reporters really didn't fit in anywhere, except with each other, in our own haunts, like the Tangage or the Big Ben. And most of the time we were too busy to socialize; there was always work to do, magazine pieces in the works, projects on the drawing board.

Now and then, when I happened to be alone in my studio apartment, looking out over the police department athletic field that was my backyard, I'd wonder what all this was leading to, and I'd conclude that it was probably marriage and a desk job eventually, after I'd made up for lost time and had explored some more of the world and felt totally secure in my profession and had appeased my inner restlessness. And of course marriage did come along in due course when the novelty of freedom wore off and the spells of loneliness set in. And I had the good luck to be able to go on satisfying the restless and inquisitive streak I was born with, as well as to continue tracking the never-ending trail of the cold war.

I say we talked shop even on our midnight excursions to now forgotten cabarets. We did, mostly about the cold war that loomed ahead. Many of our French companions, cynical by temperament, thought a Soviet-American war was inevitable. Oddly enough, even though France would probably again be a battleground, the prospect didn't seem to disturb them. Nor did the atomic bomb, whose fearful power hardly anyone yet comprehended.

The Americans were divided. For example, Walter Kerr believed we would avoid war; Joe Alsop was certain the Russians would move their 175 divisions "across the broad Danubian plains when the harvests are in." This became his perennial prediction even though there was clear evidence the 175 divisions were skeletonized units occupied chiefly in hauling factories away to the Soviet Union and keeping the screws on the restless and not yet wholly intimidated Eastern Europeans. The Soviets were in no shape, militarily or economically, to launch a war of conquest in Europe, even if they thought the prize worth the risk, but a surprising number of Americans and Western Europeans expected them to (and to this day, still do). I kept reassuring friends and family back home about my own safety "overseas." But by 1946, Ivan, G.I. Joe's gallant wartime buddy, was in American eyes rapidly turning into bad Boris, the lying, aggressive bully; and in the years to come, Boris would become ever more diabolical as the cold war hurtled on.

As I mentioned earlier, both the U.S. and the U.S.S.R. needed each other's enmity at this moment in history. With the war over, an undercurrent of isolationism was developing at home that could be checked most effectively by creating a new external threat to replace Germany and Japan; in the Soviet Union, the hard work and discipline that would be required to rebuild a devastated country would clearly be easier to demand if the people were convinced that a voracious American imperialism was now on a rampage to destroy their *rodina*—that Mother Russia they had suffered twenty million casualties to defend.

So the intensification of the hostility that occasionally flared up during that summer of 1946 was, in retrospect, unavoidable; especially since no leading politician on our side or theirs, Henry Wallace excepted, seemed to want to avoid it. As Berezhkov said of that summer, "Suspicions fed suspicions. And Byrnes *did* threaten Molotov . . ."

When the conference disbanded in the fall, I took a breather from the cold war's main event by driving to the Spanish border, then closed to all traffic from France. (General Franco, who had come to power with Hitler's and Mussolini's help, was now a pariah in Western Europe.) On the way, I stopped in Andorra, a tiny, medieval Pyrenees principality that was growing rich and corrupt as a transit point for illicit Franco-Spanish trade. I made the most of my two days in this smugglers' Shangri-La: three *Herald Tribune* stories, articles for *This Week, Holiday* and *The New Yorker* and a chapter in a book about postwar Europe. Then I walked across the Spanish border at Irun, took a cab to a plush San Sebastian hotel and was eventually visited by a young woman who gave me the name of a bar where I was to identify myself with a password she wrote on a piece of paper—normal precautions in a police state. And for the next four days, members of the Basque underground guided me around their homeland in northeast Spain, where, as I wrote later, "the term 'anti-Fascist' doesn't sound as old-fashioned as in the rest of the world."

This respite from the cold war was brief. Back in Paris, whose citizens were bracing for another austere winter and the threat of Communist-led strikes, I was suddenly ordered to Germany; our Frankfurt bureau chief, Ed Hartrich, was going on home leave for Christmas.

It was a two-day drive, so I broke the trip at Saarbrücken, where the French Army, having temporarily annexed the Saar to France, housed me in an elegant officer's billet. In the morning, when I crossed into Germany, the weather had turned chill and drizzly, as if to match the scenery—all but deserted roads, somber villages, occasional pedestrians trudging along the wet pavement carrying heavy bundles. Everything —the houses, the people, the land—looked dark brown or gray. Whenever I offered people a lift, they were surprised, then gruffly thankful, then—on discovering I was an American—obsequious and cringing. Whenever I lit a cigarette—mainly to overcome the odor of unwashed passengers—I'd pass the pack around, and everybody would take one and carefully place it in a wallet or handbag; cigarettes were precious currency in 1946 Germany.

In the towns, shop windows were all but empty, and dimly lit. I saw only one sign, a wall poster that read: "Cold rooms, no potatoes, vote Communist."

Theodore H. White, in his book *In Search of History,* describes his own first postwar crossing into Germany, in February 1949, as follows:

> I lost my way after crossing from the Saar into Germany. I was American. My car was French, with French license plates. I had nothing to fear—but I shook with fear. And I found I had strayed from the main road into the villages between the Saar and the Rhine. In most of these villages, electricity had not yet been restored, and where it had been, it furnished only a string of dim yellow lights along the main streets. Elsewhere there was no light. I hated and feared those villages. I did not want to be caught among them.

I felt no such fear in 1946, only fatigue and impatience. But I know what he meant. As I crossed from the French to the American Occupation Zone, near Wiesbaden, my headlights swept a knot of people clustered around two U.S. Army trucks—three or four naked girls surrounded by a dozen GIs. One of the girls screamed and waved her arms at me. I slowed down and two burly soldiers, thinking I was a German in my civilian car, edged toward me.

"Keep movin', ya fuckin' kraut!" one shouted.

I drove on, letting the occupation forces carry on, and finally reached Frankfurt am Main, where the press billet in the Park Hotel seemed like a warm, cozy igloo in the dark, forbidding tundra. In the bar, I found Ed Hartrich and his wife and some other correspondents, and I almost felt I was at home.

The cold war had not yet impinged on 1946 Frankfurt, though there were straws in the wind, sometimes blowing in different directions. For example, I reported on December 21 about Soviet and American inspectors together supervising the dismantling and shipment to Russia (as reparations) of part of the Kugel-Fischer ball-bearing plant in Schweinfurt after some Germans, faced with the loss of their jobs, were caught sabotaging the equipment; at the same time, while visiting a U.S. Counter Intelligence Corps unit in Bamberg a few days later, I learned that American agents had secretly raided the Soviet Occupation Zone to recover stolen jewels, and that the CIC was now spending much more time chasing Soviet spies than tracking down elusive Nazi war criminals.

And what about the Germans? Early on, I decided to spend more time with them than at U.S. Army headquarters, where many of the resident correspondents, who had not long ago been covering the war, were content to pick up and file the routine daily press releases. But the story here in 1946 was no longer about the U.S. Army but about Germans and their role in the burgeoning cold war. So I sought them out, and ended my five weeks' Frankfurt duty with an ed-page series that read in part:

> Bitter about his fate, cynical about a democracy he doesn't understand, today's German in the American Occupation Zone seems to be living in limbo. Actually he is beginning to watch with shrewd attention the jockeying for power going on between the allies who conquered his country.
>
> The fact is the typical German's initial postwar bewilderment, which quickly turned into self-pity, is now evolving into a hard core of nationalism. He is now beginning to find solace from physical and psy-

chological grief in the old idea that Germans are superior beings getting pushed around by a lot of unworthy Slavs and Anglo-Saxons.

Aware that the Fatherland is temporarily prostrate, he wonders which power bloc he should string along with. Unconvinced that American Occupation Forces are here for a long stay, he hesitates to do anything which might some day put him on a Soviet blacklist. . . .

Thanks to having my own car—most American reporters depended on the U.S. Army for transportation—I explored the area around Frankfurt. At Hanau, I found a displaced persons camp full of Balts and Poles resisting repatriation to their Soviet-occupied homelands. The Russian prisoners of war had already been sent back, many of them forcibly, with our cooperation, to almost certain imprisonment in Soviet labor camps. Now, fortunately, we were stalling about turning the Balts and Poles over to the Red Army.

Apart from these occasional chilly gusts that foretold the advent of the cold war, the stories I filed that winter from Frankfurt dealt mostly with the dingy landscape that lay beyond our hotel's parking lot. Across the square, the grimy, penumbral railroad station provided shelter of sorts for black marketeers, scroungers of cigarette butts, derelicts in faded German uniforms, family groups huddled around kerosene cooking stoves and young girls playing erotic games with GIs in the shadowy alcoves. Up the street was a German restaurant of sorts where I bought an ersatz meal for Mildred Gillars, better known as Axis Sally, after her release from confinement as a traitor for her pro-Nazi broadcasts from Berlin during the war. (She was unrepentant: "The longer the peace lasts, the more of Hitler's ideas we will adopt—especially concerning the Russians," she told me, more prophetically than I then imagined.)

And in Kassel, to the north, I found and interviewed a bright, sexy nineteen-year-old German girl starting a ten-year sentence at hard labor imposed by a U.S. tribunal for "impersonating an American intelligence agent." All she'd done was pretend she worked for the CIC so as to live the plush life in officers' clubs all over our occupation zone. Her real crime was that she'd embarrassed the army by getting away with the deception for so long. So they threw the book at her. My story was front-paged and may have got her paroled. I hope so.

Before leaving Germany in January 1947, I took a night train to Berlin, which involved, and still does, crossing 125 miles of what was then the Soviet Occupation Zone and is now the misnamed German

Democratic Republic. In every story I wrote from Berlin in the next three decades, I mentioned Berlin's isolated location; all during the 1948 airlift, people read of the flights that supplied the then virtually besieged city, yet sometimes I wonder if any Americans remember the news they read or know anything about geography. For as I write these words, I have before me a report dated March 28, 1985, from Berlin by a member of the prestigious Institute of Current World Affairs that starts: "Any map will show that Berlin lies in the eastern part of the German Democratic Republic (i.e., East Germany), almost 100 miles from the nearest point in West Germany, but I was nevertheless unprepared for the fact that one must really enter the G.D.R. when driving by car to West Berlin." Unprepared—by forty years of reporting!

When I wrote for the *Trib,* I always had a person in mind who fitted the demographic profile of our readership. He was my former college roommate, a banker who now commuted to New York from Rye. I thought of each story as a personal communication to him. Picturing him reading it on the train the next morning made it easier for me to write clearly, simply, colloquially yet intelligently—the way he'd want it. However, since then I've learned that in writing for a mass audience about foreign affairs it's best to assume total ignorance on the part of the end-users about what you are telling them.

I've seen Berlin probably a dozen times between 1947 and 1979, but that first visit remains the most memorable. There were no barriers of any kind dividing the sectors, so you could drive at will all over the snowy, desolate ruined city. On the eastern side, the sentries at the Soviet war memorial, an occasional truck or military vehicle or a cluster of people at a subway entrance across the frozen wastes of the Alexanderplatz were the only reminders that the city was still inhabited. At dusk you hurried back past the acres of burnt-out buildings to the warmth and camaraderie of the American Press Club in suburban Zehlendorf and wondered how this city would ever come to life again. But it did, very soon in the Western sectors, somewhat later in the more ravaged and looted Soviet part—where in later years I would be "detained" by the Communist *Volkspolizei* on four different occasions.

I came back from Berlin by air. My seatmate was a big, curly-haired lawyer named Joel Fisher, who told me of his arrival in Frankfurt in 1945, soon after the German surrender. He was Jewish, a U.S. Navy commander and spoke fluent German. When he walked into the Carlton Hotel, his assigned billet, he found the German staff surly, indifferent, not sure if they could find him a room with a bath.

"So I put my hands on my hips," he recalled, "and started barking out orders in German. I didn't ask them for anything, I just told them what to do. Within a few minutes I had the best suite in the place with the assistant manager, two maids, two bellhops and an elderly shoeshine man darting around, putting drinks and ice on the table, unpacking my bags, running a hot bath. I didn't tip anybody. I just said, 'Well done,' and ordered them out. But before they left they stood at attention in the hall and the assistant manager said, 'You understand us, Commander, you are firm and just.' And one of the maids added, bitterly, 'The Americans have taught us nothing!' "

This was the most depressing aspect of the occupation—that, with few exceptions, the American personnel in military government were incompetent, unfamiliar with the country and the language and easily manipulated by their German mistresses. No wonder many Germans felt Hitler was right about their being the master race. Fortunately, there were enough Germans untainted by Nazism to run the Federal Republic once we granted them self-government and gave them the incentive and resources to rebuild their country. Sulking and self-pity quickly dissipated as jobs became plentiful and work meaningful. And a new generation, still barely out of kindergarten in 1946, would soon be creating a new nation no longer haunted by the pagan obsessions of the past.

It was good to get back to Paris where politics percolated like fresh coffee and governments fell, arose and fell again as one precarious coalition followed another. The problem was that the Communists held about a quarter of the seats in the Assembly, benefiting from the votes of Frenchmen who cared nothing for Stalinism but saw no other way to protest high prices, low wages, social injustice and the housing shortage than to vote extremist. The Gaullists, at the other end of the political spectrum, figured the general, who had retired in February 1946, would be summoned once again to save France when things got bad enough. And the center parties, including the Socialists, didn't have the cohesion or popular appeal to govern effectively.

In the spring of 1947, Paul Ramadier, a tough little Socialist with a white goatee and an honorable war record, managed to form a government, at first with tacit Communist support. But when he announced a drastic economic program to check inflation by freezing wages and increasing production, the Communist-led trade unions balked. He reacted by ejecting all the Communist ministers from his cabinet and replacing them with Socialists and centrists. He had shattered the so-called Popular Front, and few thought he could get away with it in view of the residue of personal and nostalgic ties between members of the two "working-class" parties. But on May 4 he faced an emergency meeting of the Socialist National Council. A member named Pierre Guillet phoned me in the afternoon. "You'd better come," he said. "The vote tonight could determine which way France is going to go."

The meeting was taking place in a vast auditorium hazy with the fumes of acrid Gaulloise tobacco. The delegates had been debating heatedly for eleven hours. Along about midnight, after Ramadier's quiet but eloquent speech, Guillet nudged me. "We've won," he said. "I know, because he used a secret phrase understood only by Freemasons that means 'Come to my aid.' And there are enough Freemasons among the left-wingers who'll respond, regardless of their sympathies."

Sure enough, when the votes were counted, Ramadier's break with the Communists was approved, 2,520 to 2,125.

But France, like most of Europe, was a long way from sustained economic recovery. Emergency loans and stopgap wage and price freezes only bought a little time while the Communists, the biggest party in the Assembly, stoked the growing unrest.

In March, the Truman Doctrine made it plain the U.S. would take over Britain's traditional responsibility for keeping the eastern Mediterranean secure. In June, Secretary of State George Marshall outlined an ambitious plan to assure and maintain Europe's economic recovery. For it was clear by now that without a massive infusion of capital, and advice on how to use it, Europe would be in a state of permanent convalescence and increasingly susceptible to Communist blandishments and even insurrection.

Our invitation to participate in what quickly became known as the Marshall Plan was not limited to our Western friends. The Soviet Union was welcomed to the preliminary discussions, and Foreign Minister Molotov turned up in Paris in late June with a retinue of eighty-nine. But it was soon obvious that the Kremlin would not raise the iron curtain and open up its closed society to American technicians and plan administrators, much as the Russian people would have welcomed them.

On July 2, I was standing with a cluster of reporters at the foot of the grand staircase of the French Foreign Ministry on the Quai d'Orsay while the Big Three foreign ministers conferred upstairs. I still remember one of the jokes going the rounds while we waited—a joke as good as any to emerge from the cold war. Supposedly, as the three statesmen took a cigarette break, Georges Bidault, the Frenchman, passed his silver case around to the others, noting the inscription—"To Georges Bidault from his comrades in the Resistance." At the next pause, Ernest Bevin, the Briton, offered *his* case to his colleagues; its inscription read, "To Ernie Bevin, from the British Labour Party Executive." The next time they stopped for a smoke, it was obviously Molotov's turn. Reluctantly, he produced a lavish gold case inscribed, "To Count Esterhazy, from the Budapest Jockey Club." The best thing about the joke is that it just possibly could have been true.

Finally the doors on the upper landing swung open, and Bevin and Molotov came down silently, followed by Bidault. None acknowledged our questions, but as Bidault passed us, he winked and made a thumbs-down gesture.

He meant that the Russians were not going to participate in the Marshall Plan, and that it would therefore go forward. We all knew, even at this early stage of the cold war, that the U.S. Congress would balk at voting the funds had one of the recipients been the Soviet Union.

So the Russians missed their chance to hinder Europe's recovery; and the cold war, which had been drifting into the ice floes for a year or more, was now firmly locked into pack ice.

Why did Stalin fumble his chance? The explanation given me years later by Soviet historian Berezhkov is that he suspected Congress might approve it anyway, if only to introduce Americans into the Soviet Union and Eastern Europe and undermine the Communist system with corrupting capitalist ideas. "In retrospect," said Berezhkov, "we should have agreed. But Stalin feared a trick." One man's pride and suspicion blocked one last, slim chance to establish a good working relationship with the Russians—slim, because aid to Russia would have been a hard sell on Capitol Hill.

Eastern European countries, eager to take part, waited for the green light from Moscow. The Czechs even jumped the gun and announced they were coming to Paris but were quickly reined in; and when the Soviets walked out, all the states later called satellite fell in line. It was conclusive evidence of total Kremlin control behind the iron curtain.

How had the Russians taken over these once independent states so quickly and so completely? In May, I suggested to Joe Barnes that we assign a team of reporters to tour the countries which had either Red Army garrisons or a substantial Soviet bureaucratic presence, or both. These ranged from still democratic Scandinavian Finland in the north to Bulgaria, which was Slavic and Balkan, to the south; others included in the survey would be Poland, Czechoslovakia, Austria, Hungary, Romania and Yugoslavia. East Germany, then the Soviet Occupation Zone and not yet a country, would be omitted along with Albania, which barred all western newsmen.

In June, the project was approved, and four of us—Russ Hill, who had been in Berlin, Ned Russell from London, Walter Kerr from New York, and I—were assigned to write the series—naturally entitled "Behind the Iron Curtain"—under a quadruple by-line. So we spent July and August of 1947 in Eastern Europe. The story of those two months and what we learned will be covered in the next chapter.

Meanwhile, I'd accompanied President Vincent Auriol of France on a two-week tour of French West Africa, which was about twelve years away from independence. For some reason, not wholly irrational, French officialdom lumped the foreign and French Communist press together, so I found myself sharing the same billets in dusty desert outposts with Hank Wales of the Chicago *Tribune,* two Britons, a Swiss, a Swede and four French Communists. We generally were assigned the least desirable accommodations and flew in the most dilapidated DC-3 with the booziest flight crew. But most of us were young enough not to care, and a kind of camaraderie developed between us, even with the Communists, who always addressed me jovially as "Truman" or *"la bombe atomique."* They never filed any stories but used the junket to hold strategy meetings with local pro-independence organizers for the African Democratic Rally (RDA). The Communists had a better sense of how the wind was blowing in Africa than the earnest colonial administrators who saw the future in terms of a "francophone community" in "Eurafrica."

The fall of 1947 was a season of Communist-organized strikes—especially in France and Italy where the Party was strong—designed to paralyze the economy and topple governments before the Marshall Plan got under way. An invasion by the Red Army, which was regularly predicted by commentators who should have known better, was not in the cards; but subversion was. On October 5, Moscow announced the establishment of a new Communist international, with headquarters in Belgrade, called Cominform and grouping seven Eastern European states and the Communist parties of France and Italy. Its announced purpose was to combat the new American "imperialism" exemplified by the Marshall Plan.

About this time, the fledgling Central Intelligence Agency entered the contest with harmless enough operations such as a printing plant and a cultural magazine in Germany, a flotilla of hot air balloons to drop leaflets in Eastern Europe and some subsidies to non-Communist trade unions like the Socialist Force Ouvrière, as well as to an organization called Paix et Liberté, whose hard-hitting posters and pamphlets challenged Communist efforts to preempt the word "peace." In those days, it wasn't hard to be a fan of the CIA.

U.S. labor also joined the fray, especially the CIO, which had not yet merged with the AFL and was still a member of the Communist-dominated World Federation of Trade Unions. When I heard Jim Carey, the CIO's secretary-general, calmly and forcefully defending the Marshall Plan against slanderous Communist charges at a WFTU meeting in November, I felt a surge of pride about being an American at just that time and place. (The only sour note for us Americans was the refusal of the State Department to allow French Confédération Générale du Travail leaders to come to Chicago at the invitation of the CIO. The reason: they were Communists. The result: to make the U.S. look scared, silly and secretive.) After Carey's speech, even the Communists on the executive board who had tried to bar him from speaking talked to him with respect and even deference.

The powerful French CGT had already voted against the Marshall Plan, 857–125, but at least the lines were now clearly drawn and the bad guys were on the defensive. The CGT was irrevocably split, and the CIO soon after pulled out of the puppet WFTU.

The latter move caused me some personal problems since a *Trib* copy editor and I had rented a suburban house from Elmer Cope, the CIO representative in Paris, who assured us that, as a fraternal labor leader, he'd been promised ample coal by the Communist unions to get through the winter. But after the break with the WFTU, the French stopped delivering the coal, and we had to move into a dank and expensive Paris hotel.

By the end of 1947, the assumption that the Soviet Union was bent on aggression or at least expansionism was firmly established. The only real difference of opinion within the Truman Administration was between partisans of George Kennan, who believed it unwise for us to try to respond to every Communist thrust (such as China) as a threat to U.S. security; and partisans of Paul Nitze, who defined as vital *any* interest threatened by the Soviets and advocated the use of force to meet *any* aggression.

Events in the first six months of 1948 reinforced the position of our coldest warriors and paradoxically added up to one setback after another for the Kremlin. The rash of strikes fizzled out when union members began to realize that they were aimed not at improving working conditions but at Moscow's political interests. The brutal Communist coup in Czechoslovakia in February shocked the non-Communist left in Western Europe. The Berlin blockade turned into a dramatic triumph for the U.S. (and helped cement German-American relations). The first Marshall Plan credits were approved by the Congress. Stalin and Tito cut off aid to the faltering Greek Communist rebels, ending that threat. And in June, Tito pulled out of the Cominform and asserted his independence from Moscow.

In less than three years, almost all traces of our wartime alliance with the Soviet Union had been wiped out, and the groundwork laid for new military alliances—NATO and the Warsaw Pact—to confront each other across the iron curtain (now somewhat dented by Tito's defection). The cold war was under way, yet these face-offs in 1948 were only preliminary skirmishes.

As it turned out, our *Trib* team's journalistic venture behind the iron curtain was well timed. In the summer of 1947, it was still possible, if laborious, for Westerners to obtain the necessary visas and Soviet passes to visit Eastern Europe; a year later, we would have been turned down flat in all but three of the eight countries. For the iron curtain, by 1948, had been bolted shut.

Chapter 3

Behind the Iron Curtain

W HEN WINSTON CHURCHILL popularized the term "iron curtain" in his March 1946 speech, he created the impression that darkness and despair were everywhere the norm on the far side of this ideological boundary that now divided Europe from the Baltic to the Adriatic. The image of entire nations transformed into chain gangs lashed by brutal Soviet guards gradually took shape in the West. When we reporters played the cliché game, the accepted lead for any Eastern European story was: "Red terror gripped this city tonight as grim-faced, jack-booted tommy-gunners patrolled the rubble-strewn streets."

Yet the truth was that Eastern Europe, then as now, was a patch-work of culturally diverse countries enjoying varying degrees of inde-pendence, well-being and even freedom despite the pervasive tutelage of the Soviet Union. In 1947, of course, the process of Sovietizing many of these countries was still under way—almost complete in some, barely evident in others; while today, the process is completed though not fully stabilized—with five countries (Romania, Bulgaria, Hungary, East Germany and Czechoslovakia) relatively docile, two (Austria and Finland) neutral and Western-oriented, one (Poland) restless and still feisty and two (Yugoslavia and Albania) Communistic but no longer subservient to Moscow.

The purpose of our *Herald Tribune* survey in the summer of 1947 was to report on how this process of Sovietization was being carried out, how Moscow's policy differed in each of these supposedly "captive" states and how the prospects for piercing and eventually dismantling the iron curtain looked at this stage in the cold war.

So the four of us gathered in Paris in July to map out our itinerary

and draw up a list of basic questions to which we would seek answers
in each country we visited. Hill and I would take the four northern
countries that lay wholly or in part behind Churchill's demarcation line
—Finland and Czechoslovakia (both still free but at risk), Poland (being
absorbed) and Austria (divided and in limbo). Kerr and Russell would
go to the four southern countries—Romania and Bulgaria (almost
wholly Sovietized), Yugoslavia (apparently so) and Hungary (on the
way). We boned up on facts and figures and set out in mid-July after
making plans to reconvene in Paris in September to write up our
findings.

For Hill and me, the first lap of our journey was blurred by the fact
that John Steinbeck and Robert Capa, the photographer, who were en
route to Russia to do a picture book, suggested we fly as far as Helsinki
together. But their capacity for tossing off aquavit with beer chasers was
so much greater than ours that in Stockholm we dropped out of the
party and checked into a different hotel. We decided the Russians, who
probably gave them visas because they remembered Steinbeck as a
radical writer of the thirties and Capa as a chronicler of the Loyalist side
in the Spanish Civil War, would very likely regret their invitation, much
as they indulged in strong drink themselves.

In Helsinki, we checked into the Hotel Kämp, a venerable but
homey relic of czarist days whose bar was a meeting place for politicians
and journalists. We had some names and phone numbers of people
who'd be helpful—government officials, editors, diplomats—and Helsinki had a small-town ambience: everybody of any importance knew
all the others. So one source led to another. After all, the whole country,
which was twice as big as Florida, had a population of barely 4,000,000.

Finland became independent of Russia in 1918 after a bloody civil
war that was won by the "Whites," who outlawed the Communist
Party. Hardworking, hard-drinking, patriotic and proud of their impossible language and ancient legends, the Finns labored and prospered
and were admired in the United States as the only country in Europe
that paid up its debts to us in full.

Then, at the start of World War Two, the Russians decided to protect
their northern flank against their temporary Nazi allies by annexing
part of Finland, along with the Baltic republics. But the Finns chewed
up two Soviet divisions and held off repeated attacks for four months
before surrendering when they finally ran out of ammunition.

So gallant was their resistance against hopeless odds that even so
thoughtful a columnist as Walter Lippmann impulsively advocated our

giving them military support. He told me years later this was the silliest proposal he had ever made. (Had we done so, we might have found ourselves helping Hitler fight the Russians in 1941 while helping Britain fight Hitler.)

But when the Germans invaded Russia in June 1941, Finland joined in the attack with the limited objective of recovering the territory taken from them a year earlier. Even so, the British declared war on Finland as their enemy's ally.

Three years later, as the Germans were being driven back on the eastern front, the seven divisions they had stationed in Finland vented their fury on the Finns. Rovaniemi, the capital of Finnish Lapland, was burned to the ground as part of their scorched earth retreat. So the Finns ended the war by fighting Germans after starting out by fighting Russians.

The latter did not want to spare troops to occupy Finland after V-E Day, but merely stationed a Control Commission in Helsinki to supervise the delivery of more than $300 million in reparations they had levied on Finland, in addition to taking back the territory they had grabbed in 1940.

When Hill and I got to Helsinki, the Finns were celebrating the fact that deliveries were running slightly ahead of schedule, thanks in part to lines of credit from the U.S. and Sweden with which to purchase consumer goods, foodstuffs and equipment, chiefly to modernize the pulp industry. The output of their paper mills was then shipped to the U.S. and the proceeds used to buy machinery to help manufacture the products demanded by Russia. (No U.S. credits or goods were thus sent directly to Russia as reparations.) And the Finns had plenty of green gold—millions of acres of timber which earned them hard currency in the world's newsprint market. But in 1947, Finland was a country totally without frills or luxuries. And no one complained. They knew that their salvation and future freedom depended on at least five more years of unremitting hard work.

So we studied the charts and collected statistics and even made a stab at meeting the unobtrusive Russians on the Control Commission who occupied two large buildings in downtown Helsinki but generally kept to themselves. Phone calls didn't get through, so one day we simply walked past the barbed wire and on into one of the buildings, the twelve-story former Hotel Torni, nodded to the two guards, bade them a crisp *"dobroe utro"*—"good morning"—acknowledged their salute and proceeded to where another uniformed Russian was sitting at a desk. When he looked up, Hill snapped out another *"dobroe utro"* without breaking stride and we moved on, climbed some stairs and finally reached a cluster of Soviet officers on the third floor. In English, we identified ourselves as American reporters and said we wanted to see the boss, General Savorenko. A young officer, flanked by three burly plainclothesmen, promptly escorted us back to the entrance, asking en route which sentries we had passed. As for seeing the general, the officer simply waved his hand helplessly. "No, no, no," he stammered. "Impossible. He is not here. I do not know." He seemed somewhat dazed. Back on the street, I looked back. There must have been at least a dozen Russians standing in the doorway, staring at us. I was reminded of how a herd of cattle will stop grazing and watch you, with a kind of ponderous curiosity, until you have walked out of their pasture and are out of sight.

Our penetration of the Hotel Torni was a stunt, for we knew from experience that our chances of interviewing a Russian general were nil. In Paris, in 1946, Molotov had brought along his attractive, pigtailed, seventeen-year-old daughter, and O'Reilly decided a talk with a Russian teenager would make a nice feature story. So I went to see the Soviet Embassy press attaché, an unsmiling, squarely built young man named Vidiassov. I suggested that a chat with Miss Molotov would be an adornment for our women's pages in New York as well contributing to Soviet-American understanding.

"I do not see how the opinions of a young girl are of any importance whatsoever," he said solemnly.

"Perhaps they wouldn't solve the Danube question," I agreed, "but they would make good reading in America. It would be an amusing story."

"There is nothing amusing about Miss Molotov," said Vidiassov.

"Well," I persisted, "her clothes, her studies, her hobbies—such things would be of great interest to Americans."

"I do not feel that the clothing or the opinions of Miss Molotov would be of any interest or significance to readers of American newspapers," he said politely.

I nodded and stood up. "Well, perhaps you might arrange an interview for me some time with a member of the Soviet delegation."

He almost smiled. "I am at your disposal," he murmured as we shook hands. "We are always happy to facilitate the work of objective journalists."

I was never able to reach Vidiassov again. That's when I learned that the function of a Soviet press attaché in those days was not to cultivate newsmen but to avoid them.

The only other Russian installation in 1947 Finland was the naval base they were constructing at Porkkala, a peninsula west of Helsinki which they occupied in 1944. Not only was it off limits to everybody, including Finns, but when trains passed through the twenty-mile-wide Porkkala enclave, the Russians insisted the windows be covered so that passengers could not see the activity outside. While we were in Helsinki, the Finns delivered cars fitted with plywood shutters for inspection by the Russians, who rejected them, saying only iron blinds would do. So the Finns now had to make a three-hour detour to get to Turku, their most important port city.

But on the whole, Finland enjoyed far more freedom, given its geographical location, than we'd expected. Save for direct criticism of the Soviet Union, the press was free to print what it wanted. Just before we arrived, an anonymous letter appeared on the front page of the newspaper *Socialdemokratti* charging Yrjo Leino, the Communist minister of the interior and chief of the secret police, with being a crook and the agent of a foreign power. But Leino took no action other than to threaten a libel suit. Earlier, a cabinet minister was overheard reciting a violent anti-Russian poem to some friends. The prime minister, Mauno Pekkala, suggested he read the verse to the assembled cabinet before any action was taken. As the poem was being recited, another minister arrived late, took his seat and listened to the reading with growing amazement. Finally he whispered to his neighbor, "Am I crazy? Or is he crazy? Or has the whole government gone crazy?"

The Soviet Control Commissioner was reported to have been so amused by this story that he told Mr. Pekkala to forget the incident. The indiscreet minister was let off with a reprimand.

In short, it seemed to us, after a week in Finland, that its people were living in greater freedom than if their former Nazi allies had won the war. More than 85 percent of the economy was in the private sector, about the same as before the war, and while the Communists garnered about 25 percent of the vote, the ballot was secret and political activity unfettered. Refraining from jibes at their big Soviet neighbor did not seem too high a price to pay for what they had.

The year Finns looked forward to then was 1951, when they hoped to pay off the last of the reparations bill to the Soviets, ahead of schedule. So far they had discharged almost half of their obligation. Their one anxiety was that the U.S. might cut off their line of credit (and thus half their American imports) if it appeared to Washington that Soviet control was becoming too manifest. In that case, default on the reparations deliveries might invite Soviet pressure. What sort of pressure? "Perhaps by methods they have used in the Balkans," we were told by Lauri Kivinen, director of Soteva, the central planning agency for reparations.

Fortunately this didn't happen, and Finnish *sisu,* over the years, has made it one of Europe's most attractive and prosperous countries. (*Sisu* is an untranslatable word denoting tenacity, resourcefulness and guts; it was once described by Paavo Nurmi, the former track champion, as "the spirit that enables you to finish a race when you feel too exhausted to take one more step.")

We flew from Helsinki to Stockholm to catch the weekly Polish Airlines (LOT) flight to Warsaw via Gdansk. The DC-3 offered beltless canvas seats, a bare-legged, haggard stewardess and a box lunch consisting of a ham sandwich and an apple. In Warsaw, transportation from the airport was by a truck that weaved through rain-soaked, rubble-choked streets past carcasses of buildings to the Polonia Hotel, the only one with acceptable accommodations that was still intact. It was fully booked, so we dumped our gear in the lobby, found a table in the dim and smoky bar and wondered aloud what to do next. A British captain nearby berated us for not "laying on" a room in advance: "Warsaw's not Paris or London, you know. Filthy, primitive place."

Just then a blond young woman who had been talking to the barmaids approached us. "You will excuse me," she said in deliberate, guttural English. "When you wish a room, I am perhaps able to help you."

It seemed she knew of a pension, newly renovated and very comfortable. She would be glad to show it to us. In fact, she lived there.

While she and Hill chatted in German, the British captain nudged me and nodded toward the door. I followed him out and he introduced himself. "Tisdale," he said. "War Office. You chaps really must be more careful. That girl. Paid agent of the U.B.—the secret police. Obviously setting a trap for you. Always does with newcomers. I don't mean to alarm you, old boy, but you really shouldn't go to this place with her. Just a friendly warning. We chaps have to stick together here. Behind the iron curtain, you know. Really no joking matter."

He seemed genuinely distressed, so I thanked him and returned to the bar, where Hill had paid the check and was offering his arm to our benefactress.

"If you are ready, *gnädiges Fräulein,*" he said, "I shall summon a droshky."

We picked up our baggage and passed through the lobby, where Captain Tisdale glared at the girl and looked at me as though I were about to step off a cliff.

It was still raining, but fortunately there was a creaky victoria parked by the curb and it had a top. We wedged ourselves onto the narrow seat, the girl gave the coachman an address and we started off. She told us her name was Anna and that there was or had been a husband. She was skinny for a Pole, but her clothes were well cut, and the fact she wore lipstick set her apart from the few women we'd seen so far in Poland.

The pension turned out to be the patched-up fifth floor of a shabby-looking building flanked by two skeletonized, burnt-out ruins. We were let in by a rather pretty maid who showed us a newly plastered room containing two beds, a table, a chair and a plywood closet. Light was provided by a strong bulb suspended by a cord from the center of the ceiling.

Anna followed us in, sat on one of the beds and—so help me—inserted a cigarette into a long holder and crossed her legs.

The correct thing, of course, was to ask the maid for some vodka. When the three of us were alone, Anna waved her cigarette holder at our typewriter cases. "You are writers," she said without conviction, the implication being that our disguise was transparent.

"Reporters," said Hill.

"It must be very interesting work," she observed, sipping her vodka.

"Yes," I said in German, constructing my sentence carefully. "It is a profession in which one meets many important people." I felt that this was the proper remark to make, guarded but not unfriendly, and suggesting, ever so blandly, that we might possess valuable information. I didn't want to encourage her too much, but on the other hand I didn't want her to feel that she had wasted her time getting us a place to sleep.

And yet, even as she nodded and mashed out her cigarette, I knew I was missing the sense of high adventure I should have felt as a participant in a real-life spy drama on the wrong side of the iron curtain. Perhaps it was the sight of Hill yawning into his vodka, or the too bright light, or the chunks of plaster that had dropped off the wall the last time the door was slammed; or perhaps it was our secret agent's bare, mottled legs, or her bored expression, or her long sigh as she scratched one knee and finally rose to go.

We stood up and shook hands. *"Schlafen Sie wohl,"* said Anna. At the door she added, like a wan postscript, "My room is the next one down the hall."

We rarely saw Anna during the next two weeks except in the evenings at the Polonia. She usually came home after we did and was asleep when we left in the morning. I assume she was supposed to keep us under observation, and this she evidently did, after a fashion. At any rate, the maid met us in the vestibule one morning and told us she had seen Anna going through our papers and notebooks. For a girl who had been a slave laborer in Germany, the maid was quite sweet and shy. "I think that woman is from the police," she said at last. "I thought you ought to know, in case you find that something is missing."

We thanked her and promised not to say a word to Anna. As it turned out we never even had the chance. The next afternoon two security policemen came to the pension looking for her on a black market charge. The maid told us about it later. It seemed Anna had been doing illegal money changing on the side while patrolling the Polonia.

That evening, we ran into her near the hotel and tipped her off about the cops. *"Mein Gott!"* she exclaimed and clapped a hand over her mouth in dismay. She didn't even say good-by; the last we saw of her, she was hurrying down the Aleja Stalina, between the patched-up ruins and the clanging streetcars. Then she turned a corner and was out of sight.

After that there was a different girl chatting with the Polonia barmaids. Whatever Anna had found in our baggage must have made pretty dull reading back at headquarters, because the new girl never paid any attention to us, and the U.B. never sent anyone to replace Anna at the pension.

Our other Anna in Warsaw was more interesting. She was an attractive, spirited young woman who worked for the press department of the Foreign Ministry, and her current man friend was a British correspondent who had quit his job to help "build socialism" in Poland. I asked Anna why there were so many armed soldiers guarding government buildings and patrolling the streets with tommy guns.

"I don't know," she said, "nor do I care. The thrilling thing to me is that they are *Polish* soldiers and not Germans!"

Patriotism and hatred of the Germans were the dominant emotions in 1947 Poland. There was still a legal opposition—Stanislaw Mikolajczyk's Peasant Party (PSL)—but it was being systematically discredited and decimated, and except for some small Catholic weeklies there was no really critical press. When I heard that a PSL leader was being tried for treason in Cracow, along with a former colonel and the editor of *Piast,* a relatively outspoken newspaper, I flew down there to look around while Hill headed north to Gdansk. For a police state, Poland was still surprisingly relaxed about foreign journalists. No one seemed to be tracking our movements, and the copy we filed was never censored or held up. But before going to Cracow I got some officially stamped travel documents. I'd been told, and later learned from experience, that there's no safer place for an American than a Communist country—provided all your papers and permits are in order and you are careful about changing money and what you photograph; but also, that there is no place *less* safe if you don't take routine precautions. The authorities that protect the obedient visitor can be the scourge of the careless one.

The trial was due to last three weeks, too long for me to hang around even so picturesque a city as Cracow, which was barely scarred by the war. But it was plain that accusing (and almost surely convicting) the deputy general secretary of the PSL, Josef Mierzwa, of treason was part of an accelerated campaign to tarnish his party. A few days before, Sygmunt Augustinski, editor of the PSL organ, *Gazeta Ludowa,* got his —fifteen years in jail—for being in touch with an alleged underground movement.

So I drove out to Auschwitz, now Oswiecim, with two American free-lance writers, Roy and Myra Blumenthal, and visited the "museum" through which groups of children were being taken to see and hear how the Nazis had operated the greatest human slaughterhouse in the history of mankind. Six million died here, at least half of them Jews, and less than three years earlier, this murder factory had been going full blast. Today, scattered in the gravel paths, were fragments of human bones that had not been entirely consumed in the ovens.

The Polish authorities were making sure that the younger generation would never forget what the Germans did here, and I began to understand the passion I encountered among normally pro-Western Poles about our reported intention to help rebuild Germany. "I don't care if they live on a thousand calories a day forever," said a survivor of the Warsaw occupation. "They made us live on five hundred."

I decided to go on to Wrocław (pronounced Vrotslav) partly because it was not too far away, but mainly because, as Breslau, the city had been the capital of German Silesia, a region annexed to Poland after the war by the Russians in compensation for the Polish land they had seized in the east. In effect, Poland had simply been moved westward, as well as reduced in size, by the Red Army.

There was a night train from Cracow to Wrocław in which the top class, second, provided space for ten people per compartment on wooden benches. The light was on all night, and everyone smoked cigarettes. So I made notes for an ed-page piece and smiled mutely at a strikingly pretty blonde facing me. Finally she spoke to me, in French, and by the time we reached her destination, Katowice, at about 1 A.M., I almost got off the train with her. But I was too young and therefore too conscientious about my mission to Wrocław to follow an impulse. (I'd miss out today too since I can't imagine boarding a cramped Polish night coach no matter who might be sitting opposite me.)

Wrocław was about 90 percent destroyed, and at dawn, walking from the railroad station to a still usable hotel past leftover night people —some haggard streetwalkers and meandering drunks—I began to wonder why I was here. What was the story? Rubble? What else was new in Eastern Europe?

After a shower and a restless nap, I set out on foot and by streetcar to find the Communist Party headquarters. I had an official letter to the local party secretary and figured I might as well stay in the good graces of the power structure. While nobody in authority seemed to be at his or her desk, I did find some garrulous journalists who plied me with warm beer and questions about the U.S.; and also, the regional director of the Central Committee for Jews in Poland, a man named Jacob Egit, who told me that fifty thousand Jews who had survived the Nazi occupation were now pioneers in the colonization of Silesia, from which most Germans had by now been evacuated. Nearly four hundred Yiddish theaters, schools and cultural centers had already been established in the province of Silesia, and an American observer just back from a tour of the "recovered" territories reported that "most of the credit belongs to the Polish government," whose policies were actively combatting the latent anti-Semitism that had festered for generations in Poland. Random interviews I had with Jews during the day corroborated this view, so I had to conclude that, in some respects, not even a Communist government is all bad.

And this reflection impelled me, back at the hotel, to go over the notes I'd made since our arrival—which in turn led me to start a rough draft of a piece that would try to sum up the complexities and paradoxes of 1947 Poland. Writing it then would also be helpful when the time came to put together our joint iron curtain series in September.

It started out:

> The only really clear-cut facts about Poland today are that the country is being rebuilt with an energy and enthusiasm unmatched in postwar Europe; that a Communist-dominated government is in full charge of this mighty effort; and that the people, who are neither terrorized nor oppressed, are cooperating closely with the present regime even though most of them oppose it . . . But temporarily submerged beneath all this surface activity are a jumble of factors that could spell trouble for Poland and the world and whose complexity just now is likely to drive an honest reporter to drink . . .

I went on to cite the hatred of Germany, the distrust of Russia, the controlled press, the Catholic resistance, the opportunistic Communists, the terrorists egged on from abroad, and concluded:

> The possibility of war between Russia and the United States seems less likely the longer one stays behind the so-called iron curtain. Nevertheless, power politics are still in vogue throughout the world, and if only for this reason, any effort to retain the friendship of the more liberal, non-Communist Polish leaders makes sense. In any showdown between democracy and communism their support would be a valuable asset to the cause of freedom.

By the end of the afternoon, my article done, I felt like the honest reporter driven to drink, and after dining alone among uniformed Russians in the faded Teutonic elegance of a nearby restaurant, fell in with a group of young Poles celebrating somebody's engagement. I contributed a pint of whiskey and got a lot of affectionate backslapping and embracing and an earful of political talk in return. Almost everyone in Europe talked politics in those days. They said they were all socialists "but not Communists—that's the same as being a Russian." And since Americans were a rarity in Wrocław, they hammered me with questions about U.S. support of Germany. I did more listening than talking and broke away just before dawn, satisfied at least that the evening's talk had borne out much of what I'd written in the afternoon.

I flew back to Warsaw in the morning, not exactly in the pink of condition, on a plane with wooden benches, and found Hill, who had just interviewed several officials and diplomats, seated at our desk, piled high now with Polish government and U.S. Embassy documents. I was learning every day what few of my friends back home ever suspected —that being a foreign correspondent for a serious newspaper was mostly drudgery and fatigue, and that even an engagement party like the one in Wrocław usually turned into a work experience. A reporter on a long-range assignment, then and now, has to get used to never really being off duty—not if he or she is conscientious, and most are.

Did the precision and detail we strove for matter so much to our readers—for instance, to my old buddy on the commuter train from Rye to Manhattan? Wouldn't he have preferred a less complicated story that could have run under a headline such as POLES DEFY RED TYRANNY or RUSSIANS SMASH POLISH RESISTANCE? Probably, but it mattered enough to us, as artisans of a sort, and also perhaps to a handful of readers—editors, scholars, exiles—to make our efforts to be accurate worthwhile.

Prague, our next stop, was striking for its beauty, particularly of the old city, and depressing for the sense of impending doom that hovered over it. For Czechoslovakia, one of the few genuine prewar democracies of Central Europe, was now democratic by sufferance only. In free elections in May 1946, the Communists won 38 percent of the vote and 114 out of 300 seats in parliament. Unlike the Finns, whose democracy was also at risk, the Slavic people of this country felt no great animosity toward the Russians, whom many regarded as liberators. (In fact, the Red army "liberated" Prague in 1945 only because American troops, who had reached Pilsen, were ordered to advance no further.) So Communists held the premiership and the Interior Ministry, and a few days of interviewing convinced us that they hadn't made their power play only because it wasn't yet on the timetable. Czechoslovakia was to be the industrial base of the Soviet empire in Eastern Europe, while the others had been designated by the Kremlin as food producers (a decision that contributed to Yugoslavia's break with Moscow in 1948). So the best policy from the Kremlin's point of view was to let the Czechs alone while they built up their industrial plant. What's more, no Russian troops were stationed there, where they might be corrupted by seeing freedom in action and a relatively high standard of living.

But the end of Czech democracy was predictable: the Russians could not long tolerate one dog barking and wagging his tail among a cowed and silent pack.

We called Masaryk soon after arriving and met him at Marcia Davenport's apartment. We then drove out to his country house for lunch.

He told us he would stay in the government as foreign minister only so long as he thought he could stave off the probably inevitable takeover. He had a high regard for Stalin's intelligence but felt he was misinformed about the West by underlings. He spoke of the humiliation of having to withdraw Czechoslovakia's acceptance of the Marshall Plan invitation under Soviet pressure. But Masaryk was a patriot and hoped to use whatever prestige he had, as the son of his nation's first president, to prolong its independence. (He could not anticipate that his prestige was too great for the Communists even to let him go abroad when they finally made their move the following February.)

So Masaryk, who once worked in an American factory and married the boss's daughter, maintained a cheery, irreverent facade, knowing he had nothing to lose except—as it turned out—his life. One evening, at a starchy reception for Romania's boss at the Hradcany Palace, he spotted Hill and me across the room and called out, "Hey, boys, come on over and meet some big shots!" It was a conversation stopper, and heads turned to see who these mysterious Americans might be. And it was typical of Masaryk's irrepressible and un-Communist behavior. We shook hands stiffly with some Romanians and Russians and drifted away.

A few days later, after interviewing the leaders of all the political parties (the Communist by submitting written questions), I accepted an invitation from the acting American military attaché in Prague, a lieutenant colonel named Tom Foot, to accompany him to a remote Slovakian town where he was to be guest of honor, along with a Soviet general, at a ceremony organized by the Slovak Partisan Association. The community, a wartime center of resistance activity, was called Turcansky Svaty Martin, and the purpose of the affair was to confer honorary citizenship on Stalin and Roosevelt—in FDR's case, posthumously.

After an eight-hour drive, we reached the town's only hotel and found a U.S. Navy lieutenant from our Belgrade embassy asleep on one of three cots reserved for the U.S. delegation. When I woke in the morning, Foot and the U.S. naval officer had gone off to the ceremony, so I strolled around the town taking pictures of pretty girls in Slovak costumes and of Premier Klement Gottwald reviewing a military parade, as well as meeting a lot of people who had relatives in Pittsburgh. Late in the afternoon, I returned to the hotel, filed a story (mainly for the dateline) and waited on the town hall balcony to catch a glimpse of the Russian general when he arrived for the banquet.

Below, the sidewalks were jammed with people craning their necks as car after car pulled up and disgorged an assortment of local and regional dignitaries. Finally, two sleek Mercedes limousines swerved around the corner and braked to a stop before the entrance. Four tommy-gunners and a Russian officer scrambled out of the first car, shoved the crowd back and stood at attention as the portly general, wearing a cape and a chestful of medals on his uniform, stepped out of the second car. He surveyed the silent crowd for a moment and marched up the front steps, followed by his armed escort.

Then I caught sight of Tom Foot's 1940 Chevrolet coming down the street with its small American flag fluttering on the fender. He parked across the way, and he and the naval officer got out and sauntered over to the town hall. Someone in the crowd applauded, and Foot smiled and responded with a salute. At this, everyone seemed to start cheering and applauding and those in front reached out to shake hands.

I met them in the lobby. "Nice going," I said. "You put on a much better show than the Russians."

Foot grinned. "It's good publicity for our side. The Russians have to strut around because they think it wins them respect. But informality is what people like best."

But not the reclusive Russians, as I learned once again at the banquet, when I managed to slide into a vacated chair across the table from the general. He spoke fair English, and when I identified myself and suggested an informal interview, he raised his hand. "Of course," he said, "but first a toast." He filled two glasses with fiery slivovitz, held up his and intoned, "Roosevelt." We drank. This gave me an opening to ask whether he thought Roosevelt's death had adversely affected U.S.-Soviet relations. "You toast now," he replied impassively. "Stalin," I said. We drank. He refilled the glasses and said, "Vallace." I responded, "Molotov." We worked our way through Eisenhower, Zhukov, Tolstoy and Steinbeck. Then I realized, foggily, that I had been the victim of the old vodka dodge, equally effective with slivovitz, and gingerly groped my way to bed.

Anyway, thanks to Foot, our side did score some points in Slovakia that day, and maybe in Bratislava the next evening, where we fraternized with a friendly throng in the hotel cabaret who wanted to know why our troops hadn't taken over Czechoslovakia before the Russians. It was a question for which we had no answer.

But we weren't scoring many points overall in what was then called the war of ideas. As in Warsaw, the U.S. Information Service office in Prague was subsisting on starvation rations: the annual budget for Czechoslovakia was $31,000, a sum that included the salaries of two American and eight Czech employees. The far less affluent British were spending $240,000 a year to promote their point of view and culture, and the French, nearly as much. The Russians, of course, had the Communist Party doing most of their propaganda work, and much of it was effective.

Not only was America's voice almost unheard, but the State Department missed opportunities to confront the Communists at such gatherings as the World Federation of Democratic Youth in Prague a month earlier, when thirteen thousand young Europeans were subjected to extravagant and mendacious indoctrination by the Communist organizers. The only Americans at this festival were a few score dupes and fellow travelers, whose only message was to advertise alleged lynchings in the U.S. As Masaryk told us, "Why the hell didn't you put on a good show at this youth congress? I was hoping for a big American turnout, and then look at the delegation that turned up—seventy missionaries, seventy fellow travelers and a chiropodist! If you'd just sent over a swing band or a couple of good baseball teams, I'd have umpired the game myself and we'd have stolen the show from the Russians."

The only answer was that the State Department was squeamish about showing the flag at a Communist-organized gathering, and that Congress, which willingly voted millions to buy guns for the Greeks, could not, then as now, appreciate the importance of the so-called cultural front.

Austria, our fourth country, was an anticlimax. It was then divided, like Germany, into zones of occupation—and a permit to visit the Soviet zone was hard to get—while Vienna was carved up, like Berlin, into four sectors, plus an international sector in the center of the city. This area was patrolled by four-man, jeep-borne teams of military policemen from the four occupying powers. By 1947, these jeep patrols were one of the very few visible examples of cooperation between the Soviets and the Western Allies.

The international sector was also becoming a shadowy arena for intense intelligence activity, and the customers who frequented its proliferating nightclubs looked like members of the cast of the 1949 film classic *The Third Man.* The spy game was played by certain unwritten rules. For instance, there were murders, but not of legitimate adversary agents. And so this divided city, relatively unscarred by war, seemed deceptively easygoing, with a tranquillity amid its seedy grandeur that was missing in nervous, shell-shocked Berlin. There was also virtually no chance of a Communist takeover in Austria: the Communist share of the vote in municipal elections was barely 5 percent, and Western troops were present in sufficient numbers to prevent a coup.

I did have yet another Soviet "experience" in Vienna. At a British Press Club party, I met an affable young man who introduced himself as Alexander Novogrodsky, Vienna correspondent for Tass, the Soviet news agency. He assured me that Russian officials in Vienna were both friendly and gregarious. "If you are an objective journalist," he said, "they will be delighted to answer your questions."

"All right," I said. "I'm objective. So how do I get to see General Kurasov?" I pointed out that I had appointments with the three other Allied military governors in Austria and would like to include the Soviet point of view in my report.

"Why don't you write out your questions," he suggested, "and I will show them to the general tomorrow."

So I tore a page out of my notebook and jotted down some questions. "Will these do?"

He read them carefully, crossed out one and put the paper in his pocket. "They are quite satisfactory," he said. "After I see General Kurasov I will phone you at the press club. How long will you be in Vienna?"

"One week more."

"Only a week? Good."

That should have tipped me off. In one week, the general managed to be sick, then on an inspection trip and finally on holiday.

The day before I left, I went over to the Tass office to say good-by.

"What a pity you are leaving!" said Novogrodsky. "You surely would have seen the general on Monday." But, he added, he would mail me the answers to my office in Paris. "You will have them in a week. What do you say to that?"

I didn't say it. I just nodded. And we both smiled, both knowing that the scenario we were acting out did not call for my receiving any answers from General Kurasov.

After Vienna, Hill flew to Berlin to gather some statistics on Soviet troop strength, while I headed south, to Florence, for a few days of culture and dalliance. No cold war hobgoblins haunted Florence.

On September 20, the four of us met in the *Trib* office in Paris and roughed out some outlines of a series of eleven articles from more than 60,000 words of notes, not all of them legible. Kerr and Russell had had a harder time than Hill and I. Hungary and Bulgaria were accessible enough, but Yugoslavia barred Kerr for his "unfriendly" reporting during the Paris Peace Conference, and Russell could get no entry permit for Romania. Kerr couldn't either but bluffed his way in. Very few officials consented to see them in these two countries, but they were free to talk to other sources and in ten days you can see a lot of them.

Our method of collaborative writing was to assign three or four topics—political repression, say, or living standards—to each writer, exchange our notes and then pass the completed articles around to other team members for editing or rewriting. The result was workmanlike but not lyrical prose.

Two trends stood out: first, the rising influence of local Communist parties backed by the Red Army; and second, the growth of state-controlled economies tied to the Soviet Union. It was not hard to foresee an eventual "division of Europe into two separate worlds."

Yet we agreed these countries had not so far become a monolithic unit, nor were they necessarily headed for the same fate. Finland and Czechoslovakia resembled Western Europe and Yugoslavia the Soviet Union. Americans stationed in Belgrade had even composed a parody of a current hit song that went: "Everything's up to date in Yugoslavia / They've gone about as far as they can go / They've got a secret po-lice a hundred thousand strong / You may be out of jail, but not for very long . . ."

But people even then were willing to talk, and our movements were on the whole unrestricted—once we got past the frontiers. Most people we talked to would have liked more personal liberty, but we kept being reminded that only in Finland and Czechoslovakia were democratic freedoms the norm before the war. Arbitrary arrests by the secret police were nothing new in the Balkan countries, nor even Poland. We did find, to our surprise, that freedom of worship had not been restricted.

As for the Red Army, we learned that there were 600,000 to 700,000 troops stationed in Eastern Europe, including Germany, though none in Finland, Czechoslovakia or Yugoslavia. About the same number of indigenous forces (of dubious value) were also in place.

Thanks to their visits to Romania and Bulgaria, Kerr and Russell were able to delineate the Communist technique of takeover that would be, and indeed was, applied in several of the other countries at opportune moments.

It consisted of two stages—the legal and the combat. The legal stage required that seven conditions be met: Communists in charge of the

Interior, Justice and Defense ministries—which gave them control of the police, the courts and the army; a clear majority in the cabinet and in parliament brought about by fraudulent elections (as in Romania); press censorship (on security grounds); and finally intimidation of major opposition parties—such as Iuliu Maniu's majority Peasant Party in Romania and Nikola Petkov's strong Agrarian Union in Bulgaria, neither of which now dared hold public meetings.

When these seven conditions were met, Communist leaders moved to the combat stage. This was the scenario: Accuse the opposition of plotting civil war. Ban the opposition press by decree. Go ahead and make your arrests—no one will even notice. Ban the strongest opposition party but keep a couple of small, docile and ineffectual non-Communist parties around for show purposes. Finally stop and digest your gains. Hang the opposition chief (Petkov) or sentence him to life imprisonment (Maniu) and never mind their anti-Nazi credentials. Your work is done.

In Yugoslavia the work was done by Tito without the need of Russian coaching, a fact that made it easier for him to loosen the screws after 1948 without their interference.

But the threat of the takeover timetable loomed over all the other countries we visited, with the exception of Austria. In 1947, Communists could claim about 25 percent popular support in Finland, 15 percent in Poland, 20 percent in Hungary and 35 percent in Czechoslovakia. And the local Communist leaders were tough and Moscow-trained. In Prague, Premier Gottwald told us in an interview that a Communist majority in the May 1948 elections "is necessary in the interests of the Czechoslovak people and state, and is likely and possible." Public opinion polls in January 1948 showing a 10 percent drop in Communist support may well have speeded up the timetable and triggered the February coup.

Matyas Rakosi, Hungary's Communist boss, told Russell that "only people with guilty consciences feel terrorized today." But in a 1952 lecture, he was more candid about his tactics: "We did not discuss the problem before the people at the time," he said, "because even a theoretical discussion of a dictatorship of the proletariat as a final aim would have caused great alarm among our partners in coalition."

We found all but two of the countries (Finland and Austria) were undergoing economic revolutions transforming their way of life. And we found the U.S. underrepresented, our missions understaffed as well as poorly staffed, our news agencies relying generally on local stringers who wrote nothing that might get them in trouble, and a cultural effort everywhere outstripped by the Russians (in Romania, one USIS library to their 306) despite enormous sympathy for and curiosity about America. At the University of Cracow, I had met a young American professor who had five hundred applicants for his course in American literature, as against four who chose Russian lit. Obviously he couldn't cope with the demand. There was only Congress to blame for our stinginess; in Washington, the people "behind the iron curtain" had been prematurely written off.

So we concluded our series by saying there was such diversity, national pride and plain courage to be found in these captive and threatened nations that it would be unfair to their people as well as too soon to say that the iron curtain had been rung down for good.

(Interestingly, the curtain was moved back, not forward, in the next few years: in Austria, when the Peace Treaty, signed in 1955, led to the Red Army's evacuation; in Finland, when the Russians returned the Porkkala naval base to the Finns after the reparations were paid off; and of course in the Balkans, when Yugoslavia and later Albania withdrew from the Soviet fold.)

The series out of the way, we returned to our regular chores. Mine included doing a story on the establishment in Belgrade of the Cominform—an association of Communist states plus the French and Italian Communist parties, ostensibly to exchange information. (Yugoslavia was a member for just eight months, and the headquarters were then moved to Bucharest.) At the opening session, Andrei Zhdanov issued, on behalf of Stalin, a kind of official declaration of permanent cold war against the west.

In October, we were summoned home to appear at the annual *Herald Tribune* Forum and report on our trip orally. Edward Murrow was the moderator, and the Forum was televised, but no one I knew saw it because no one I knew in 1947 had a set.

In reply to one question from the audience, I said that, in terms of his reputation, it was safer for a Czech to criticize the Soviet Union in public than it was for an American to defend it. There was some applause, but the next night, when we appeared before five hundred people at the Yale Club and Kerr deplored the current Red-baiting going on in Hollywood, several of the members angrily asked Whitelaw Reid, one of the *Trib*'s owners, what he was going to do about the "Reds" on his staff.

The mood that Joe McCarthy was soon to exploit was already evident, not only in 1947 but more than a year earlier, when I was in the Washington bureau covering atomic matters. One of my friends in the State Department, a former army intelligence colonel named Alfred McCormack, was accused by the House Military Affairs Committee of bringing personnel "with strong pro-Soviet leanings" into the State Department's intelligence service.

McCormack, a Princeton graduate and corporation lawyer soon to return to private practice, didn't knuckle under as government officials too often did in later years. He just fired off a letter to the chairman, Andrew J. May, of Kentucky, saying the committee had "impugned" the character of his staff "by circulating charges made by rumormongers and malcontents whose grievances have no better basis than their own incompetence." Then he made the letter public.

May called off his intended investigation of McCormack's unit on the grounds the committee "lacked jurisdiction"; but he did not retract his allegations.

And so this cold war by-product that soured relations between Americans and tarnished the good name of many a patriotic public servant was not long in getting under way. In the years after 1948 it would get much worse. In fact, the domestic Red scare that we could recognize for what it was abroad, and even joke about, was no laughing matter at home. For people were now allowing fear to erode their traditional self-confidence and even beginning to doubt the power, the relevance and the attraction of American ideals in an emerging revolutionary world.

Chapter 4

Winter and Spring 1948

IT WAS BITTER COLD all over Europe during that winter of 1947–48, and it seemed to get dark sooner than usual in the afternoons. Even in Rome, where I was on temporary assignment for the New York *Herald Tribune,* just driving around town in the office jeep could be a bone-chilling experience; but cabs were hard to find then, and buses were jammed. On this particular day, at dusk, Igor Gordevitch and I swung into the Corso Umberto, in a hurry to get back to the office with its kerosene stove, when we saw the flashing lights and heard the sirens and the muffled roar that told us there was trouble up ahead. We parked next to the colonnade and just then the police lines broke and a crowd of demonstrators surged around us while Igor yelled, *"Stampa! Stampa!"* so they would know we were the press and thus neutral. They moved on by, giving us the clenched fist salute, glad of the publicity. And then suddenly, a fleet of riot police jeeps marked REPARTO CELERE charged out of the side streets, disgorging truncheon-swinging helmeted cops, and bounded onto the sidewalks, tires squealing, while demonstrators ducked into doorways or pressed against the columns of the arcade. Igor shouted *"Stampa!"* to a burly police officer, who came over and checked our papers.

I asked him what the commotion was all about.

"The Communists again. The general strike fizzled out today so they're raising a little hell. Most will be dispersed in two minutes. We have ambulances for the others."

So we made our way back to the parking lot in the piazza next to the Via della Mercede and used the creaking elevator up to the *Trib* office, where I took off my gloves but not my overcoat, and typed about

500 words reporting that the CGIL (Italy's powerful, Communist-dominated trade union) had been no match for a few jeeploads of quick-acting riot police. Igor, who was my multilingual young assistant, looked over the Italian newspapers and wrote a couple of shorts. Then, after arguing with the long-distance telephone operator, as we did every evening, we managed to place an *urgentissimo* call to Paris and read our copy to a machine whose operator would transcribe it and somehow or other get it off to New York in time to make the next day's paper.

Now ready for something to eat, we walked through the maze of cobbled side streets below the Spanish Steps to the Re degli Amici—a noisy, smoke-filled gathering place for politicians, journalists, artists, musicians and other eccentrics. Palmiro Togliatti, Italy's Communist leader, occasionally ate there, and he was at his usual table tonight. He knew who we were.

"Not much of a demonstration," said Igor in Italian.

"There was a demonstration?" said Togliatti.

Smiles all around, and we moved on to a vacant table.

Giuseppe, the owner, was busy changing the paper tablecloths at the artists' table. They had been doodling, and it was Giuseppe's practice to get them to sign their names (some, like Giorgio de Chirico, were well-known); he then sold the authentic signed doodles for more than he charged the artists for meals.

He came to take our order. Igor had been listening to an animated group talking German nearby.

"Who are they?" he asked.

"German film actors. Roberto Rossellini brought them here from Berlin, where he was making a picture. Tonight's their last supper. They've gained so much weight in Rome he's putting them on starvation rations for a week so they'll look like they did in Germany."

We sniffed a story and before long were sitting at their table. I found myself next to a beguiling and vivacious blonde who said she played the prostitute in the movie, which was called *Germany Year Zero*. My German was as rusty as her English, but I managed to persuade her to ignore her diet one more day and dine with me the next evening. I took her to a rustic suburban taverna—now probably obliterated by high rises. We were the only customers. While a violinist played and sang romantic ballads, Liselotte (Lilo for short) told me she lived in Berlin, was divorced and had a daughter. Her father, a lifelong Social Democrat, had joined the SED—the Socialist Unity Party that the East German Communists had created to entice and then cannibalize their Socialist opponents, as they had all over Eastern Europe. But Lilo could not believe this would happen in Berlin. There had been so few anti-Nazi Germans that she trusted them all.

I encouraged her to talk about her father, who had been sent to a concentration camp as a security risk early in the war. Released in 1944, he opened a stationery store and kept quiet, waiting for the war to end. On the day the Russians entered Berlin, Lilo said they got their bicycles and pedaled down through the flaming center of the city and thunder of gunfire to his shop, just off the Kurfürstendamm. There, using her lipstick, he wrote the words "Hauptquartier, Sozial Demokratische Partei Berlin" on a square of white cardboard and placed it in the shop window. Then he stood outside, looking at it with eyes blurred by tears. He had waited twelve years for this moment.

Well, I said, perhaps too harshly, he was now unwittingly serving a new tyranny, obedient to Moscow. (In 1949, he finally fled to West Germany, where his former Socialist associates rejected him as a latecomer.)

Lilo, like many artists and actors in postwar Berlin, was politically naive and, at least until her father's defection, accepted without question the Communist slogans proclaiming their devotion to peace and freedom. One evening at a party she even got angry when some of us started singing a Soviet Air Force song written during the time of the 1939 Nazi-Soviet pact. So we argued now and then, but not for long. I invited her to go to Capri for a few days while Rossellini was rewriting his script, and she accepted.

First, Igor and I and Claire Sterling (then Neikind) and a French reporter drove to Taranto, a port in the south that our Mediterranean fleet had just started using as a regular anchorage. We found the teenage sailors, too young to have experienced World War Two, impatient for the shooting to start so they could "see some action." The older combat veterans were not so eager. The gaudy delights of the local Snake Pit Club and a hundred dives like it along the shores of this ancient sea provided all the action they craved.

Farther on, at Bitonto, an impoverished town near the heel of Italy, we stopped to get a glimpse of a part of the country of which the crowds on Rome's fashionable Via Veneto were scarcely aware—the wretched rural south, the *mezzogiorno,* where poverty was chronic. In one house without electricity, running water, floors or even a door, we found a family of twelve subsisting on one meatless meal a day. None held a job.

Two sons were crippled by wartime bombing; the father was going blind; only one member of the family, a daughter, could read. They had nothing to look forward to. On Sundays, they went to mass and prayed. Did they vote? Yes. For what party? "Communist," said one of the sons. "Wouldn't you vote Communist if you lived in Bitonto?" I said I honestly didn't know. But how else could you get anybody to pay attention?

We found a formerly four-star hotel in nearby Bari—the delle Nazione—where we were the only guests in the vast and ornate dining room save for a lone middle-aged Italian, probably a traveling salesman, a few tables away. He could not take his eyes off Claire, who was striking in a robust, raven-haired Mediterranean way, and finally the expected note arrived inviting her to join him for an after-dinner liqueur. She politely declined, explaining we all had stories to write up in our rooms.

When we gathered upstairs for *our* after-dinner shot of bourbon, a second note arrived via bellhop. It read, in Italian, "Your courteous refusal in no way diminishes the lively admiration which the sight of your beautiful figure has aroused in my heart." Only in Italy . . .

Lilo and I took a bus to Naples en route to Capri. There was a luncheon stop at Formia. The proprietor of the trattoria greeted me in English (in 1948 no one in Europe ever mistook an American for anything else) and offered the menu to Lilo. I told him she was German.

"La signorina è una tedesca?" he cried. "Ah, it was so wonderful when the Germans were here! I will give you one of my old German menus, *fräulein."* Then he smiled at me. "And of course, sir, it was also wonderful when the Americans were here!"

The proprietor reinforced my impression, after two months in this country, that what most distinguished Italians from other Europeans was that they sincerely wanted everybody to feel happy, or at least pleased to be here. In France, where I preferred to live, people generally didn't much care how you felt, which I found more natural and more relaxing.

When we left, the boss presented Lilo with a bouquet for being the gracious advance party of what he hoped would soon be a deluge of German tourists.

He would not have long to wait. Germans have always had an affinity for Italy. Lilo remembered Goethe's lines, "Know'st thou the land where the lemon trees bloom . . . where wind ever soft from the blue heaven blows," and was delighted when I quoted them in German. Like so many German children, she had grown up with a tinted photograph of Vesuvius in her bedroom, and so when we reached Naples and

I told the desk clerk at the Excelsior that we wanted a room with a view, and the window opened onto the shimmering bay with the great and familiar volcano silhouetted in the background—at that moment, whatever hesitations she might have harbored about this escapade with me melted in the moonlight.

We took the ferry to Capri in the morning, unaware that Stalin had just invited a Finnish delegation to Moscow to negotiate a "defense" alliance. Two days later, on February 25, while we were exploring the island—first on donkey back to Tiberias' villa, then by rowboat to the blue grotto—the Communists snuffed out democracy in Czechoslovakia in a "constitutional" coup prepared and engineered by the Communist Party leader, Klement Gottwald. President Eduard Beneš had no choice but to go along or resign—which he did, in July. But there were no papers on Capri and our modest *pensione* had a spectacular view but no radio.

So I was in the right place to escape from the cold war that I had been living with, more or less on a daily basis, for nearly two years. I worked part of every afternoon on an ed-page piece I was writing about Church-state relations in Italy (where divorce was illegal but where Catholics with means could buy annulments), and then, my compulsion to write something every day satisfied, I would take Lilo out to dinner, usually at the nearly empty Quisisana Hotel. The only other regulars were a well-dressed couple in their twenties. The bartender explained, sotto voce, that one was a German woman left behind by the retreating Wehrmacht and now posing as a Swedish countess, and the other a British army deserter posing as a wealthy, aristocratic remittance man. "They believe each other's stories so far," he said, "but when they discover they are both playing the same game, there will be a lively scene. I hope you stay to see it."

But on the morning of the twenty-ninth there was a telegram from Igor saying the office wanted me back in Paris right away—from where I would be flying to Helsinki to cover the imminent Soviet takeover of Finland. The Czech coup, following by two days Stalin's summons to the Finns, had focused attention on democratic Finland up on the Soviet Union's northern border as another likely victim of Stalin's paranoia.

We packed hurriedly and just made the the noon ferry to Naples and then the express train to Rome. Repairs on a bridge diverted us to a detouring freight train, where we sat on straw, legs dangling out the door, watching the sunset while our Italian fellow passengers passed around the Chianti and sang operatic arias.

I felt good. Most of the time that I'd been a cold war reporter since my discharge from the army in 1945, I'd been inwardly tense, even anxious, no doubt working too hard to make up for the four years I'd lost—or felt I'd lost—in the traumatic, Catch-22 global labyrinth of the U.S. military establishment. But this evening, soothed by an unexpected idyll in the land of lemon trees, I was loose and high and I reveled at the thought of being only twenty-eight and in good health and secure in my profession and on my way now to witness and write about some more history in the making. I sensed, too, that I wouldn't forget this brief interlude. Some day I'd be married, probably not to Lilo, but some day was not in the near future; marriage just now seemed like an encumbrance while I yet had things to do and learn and could travel light—with little more than a suitcase, a typewriter, a press card and some traveler's checks. I guess I felt good because I felt free. I took Lilo's hand.

"Bist du froh?"

She smiled. *"Ja, natürlich."*

"Ich bin auch froh."

My German had improved on Capri.

Igor was waiting at the Rome station and led us to the Paris train, which was leaving in ten minutes. He had an armful of newspapers so that I could catch up on the developing crisis. The Finns hadn't replied to the Soviet summons, and Stalin was reported to be annoyed.

The whistle blew.

"Come to Paris, Lilo!"

"Du bist verrückt! Aber ich liebe dich."

"I'll arrange it somehow. Take care of her, Igor."

"My pleasure. Be careful of the Russians. They're really bastards."

Igor was Lithuanian-born.

Then came the wonderful and today all-but-forgotten chuffing sound of the steam engine getting under way, and we all waved good-by.

In the morning, during a one-hour stopover in Milan, I went out and bought some more papers. In five days, Czechoslovakia had been all but digested by the Soviet imperial system. Most of the pundits agreed Finland was next in line. The walls around the Milan station were daubed with hammer-and-sickle and "Yankee Go Home" signs. The Communist labor unions were strong and very busy in this industrial city, and the Party had hopes of winning the national elections in June. I got back on the train and read all the way to Paris.

Then came the usual frustrating delays while I got my Finnish visa, repacked and booked space on a plane that was then canceled. There weren't all that many flights out of Orly, the main airport, which was then a small cluster of buildings with one waiting room no bigger than a tennis court. Finally, on March 6, I lugged my bag to the Invalides airline terminal at 6 A.M. (there were no taxis at that hour), boarded a Norwegian DC-4 that put down at Brussels and Amsterdam, switched to a KLM flight to Stockholm and checked into the Grand Hotel around dinnertime. The Finns still hadn't replied to Stalin.

The next day, our embassy people told me they were sure the Russians had designs on Scandinavia; so did a Swedish editor I talked to before flying to Helsinki on March 8. There, the hotels were full but I found Spartan accommodations at a *hospiz*—a cross between a YMCA and a youth hostel—and headed for the Associated Press office, where the Stockholm bureau chief was now installed. He handed me a terse communiqué from the Foreign Office: the Finns had finally agreed to send a delegation to Moscow to negotiate a "friendship and defense" pact with the Soviet Union. I made one call to a friend in the Foreign Office, another to an editor I knew and wrote a 700-word story that was sure to be front-paged. Then we went out into the dark—in March, Helsinki's daylight starts at 10 A.M. and ends at 4 P.M.—and found a place to eat. I was following the traditional foreign correspondent's routine on arriving in a new locale: line up a bedroom, call a source or two, knock out a story, track down some food and drink. If you could do all four in an hour or less, you qualified as a pro.

In the morning, I hired a woman from the Foreign Office press department to read the Finnish papers for me and I moved into a hotel. As at the *hospiz*, there were paper sheets on the beds and no lampshades, but the hot water tap worked. The day's main story was that the seven-man delegation chosen by President Juho Paasikivi to go to Moscow included three Communists (who called themselves Popular Democrats) and one Communist sympathizer. The other parties and most of the press protested that the delegation didn't reflect public opinion, which was mostly opposed to any pact with the Soviet Union.

The next day—March 10—brought news of Foreign Minister Jan Masaryk's "suicide" in Prague. The Communists, who had just taken over Czechoslovakia, said that nervous exhaustion had caused him to jump or fall from the window of his office. Knowing of Masaryk's intention to join Marcia Davenport in England if Czechoslovakia ever became a Soviet satellite, I also knew that Jan Masaryk didn't jump or fall from that window; he was pushed.

Dave Nichol of the Chicago *Daily News* arrived in town, and we agreed the Russians were flexing muscle and the Finns would have to be very firm and calm in the days ahead to keep their freedom. In my weekender, I wrote: "There is an outside chance that the Soviet bulldozer can be stopped in its tracks up here on its northern flank. This chance depends on the Finns' courage and awareness of the peril. The latter has been greatly sharpened by events in Czechoslovakia. Courage is not lacking but can be immeasurably strengthened by the feeling that the United States is backing them up."

We all marked time, waiting for the Finnish delegation to leave for Moscow, while I nursed a fever. On March 16, feeling better, I had dinner at the residence of the American minister, Alva Warren. While we were playing bridge, the front door was flung open, and a disheveled, excited U.S. naval officer strode into the room. "No good, sir," he told Warren. "I couldn't persuade the old man to stay. He's convinced the Russians will move in and that he must set up a government-in-exile in Sweden."

My ears were twitching like a rabbit's, so Warren said that since I'd heard this much I might as well know the whole story. It seems our naval attaché had been dispatched to the port of Turku to try to dissuade Marshal Karl Gustav Mannerheim from boarding a ship to Stockholm. We felt this was a time for the Finns to hang tough, and that their grand old man, hero of the Winter War and former president, should set an example. But our mission had failed.

Could I write the story? Warren agreed, if he could read it before I phoned it in and if I promised not to reveal the source. Within an hour I'd dictated the copy to Paris on the legation phone and went back to my monkish quarters at the Hotel Helsinki.

Next morning the Foreign Office called a press conference to deny my "sensational" and "irresponsible" story. My Finnish friends were shocked: "What were you drinking? We thought you were a serious reporter!"

To make things worse, I could not divulge my unimpeachable source, and Mannerheim, on arriving in Stockholm, told the press that he'd only come to consult his doctor. Feeling like a pariah, I went over to the legation, where Warren said he'd called the *Trib* in New York and told management that my story was accurate. My AP colleague, to whom I'd confided my problem, said he'd write a few hints into his story about Mannerheim's well-known distrust of the Russians that would make a gesture like this plausible.

So I felt better and was further cheered by listening to a speech by President Truman on the legation's shortwave radio. It was a veiled but unmistakable warning to Moscow not to meddle in Scandinavia and a pledge that the United States was prepared to defend the independence of "free democratic nations."

The speech was prominently featured in all local papers, but without comment. None was really necessary, and as one official told me, "The wisest Finnish reaction just now is not to react." While it was bound to stiffen parliamentary opposition to a military pact with the Soviet Union, this was no time for Finland to appear provocative or ready to align itself with the West. They knew the Russians from long and bitter experience and understood that a policy of strict neutrality was their best insurance against Soviet aggression.

My own reaction was mixed—an immediate glow of pride in my president and my country followed by a momentary chill at the thought that Stalin might just strike back in anger at this American intrusion into what he regarded as his sphere of influence.

Helsinki in March—chill, somber and damp—was getting me down, along with chronic indigestion and recurring fever, so I was glad when the delegation, now less weighted with pro-Communists, left for Moscow on March 20. A large, silent throng that filled the railroad station spontaneously began singing "Our Country," the national anthem, as the train was about to pull out. The message, all the more eloquent for being unstated, was clear: Stand fast.

I had arranged an interview with President Paasikivi for March 22 but felt almost too sick to go through with it. As soon as we sat down he pointed to my eyes and said something to the interpreter. "The president says your eyes are yellow—you probably have hepatitis." Some more Finnish was spoken, and he added, "He will send you to a doctor, then you must go straight to Stockholm, where they can take better care of you."

The doctor confirmed the president's diagnosis, and the next day I was a patient in Stockholm's Serafim Hospital, and glad to be there. The U.S. Embassy sent me books and magazines, and three Swedish interns and a nurse who were studying English visited me every day to brush up on their conversation. "Good afternoon, Mr. Attwood," they would say, in their formal, singsong Swedish accents; and then, invariably,

"You are looking less yellow today." Hepatitis does not make the victim very sociable, so my responses were usually curt. But they persisted, even suggesting one day that, since I would be here at least a couple of weeks, I might as well have an appendectomy. "It will cost you but ten dollars," said one, "due to what you call our socialized medicine." I declined the offer.

By the time I left the hospital, the crisis that had brought me to Scandinavia was over. On April 6, Finland and the Soviet Union signed an innocuous friendship and mutual assistance treaty that committed the Finns only to help repel any attack on Russia through Finland. There were several reasons why the Finns escaped the fate of the Czechs: first, the local Communists were isolated and outnumbered. When Yrjo Leino, the Communist minister of the interior, was found in May to be implicated in a plot, he refused to resign and called instead for a general strike. But in Finland, unlike Czechoslovakia, the socialists would not go along. Leino was removed from office by parliament, and the Social Democrats and their allies crushed the Communists in the July 1 elections.

Second, Stalin remembered the resolute Finnish resistance in the 1939–40 winter war, when they held out until they were down to fewer than ten rounds of ammunition per man. He did not relish the prospect of fighting them again, especially now that Truman had promised American support.

Third, Stalin may have concluded that an independent democracy on his border, especially one that posed no possible threat to the Soviet Union, had a certain propaganda value in showing that the fearsome Russian bear could also be an inoffensive neighbor, and Sweden would consequently not be frightened into joining a Western military alliance.

Finally, the Russians like cheap and easy victories. Seizing Finland could be costly. As Molotov once told George Kennan, "The Finns have oak heads." But he smiled as he said it. The Russians respect stubbornness.

And so Mannerheim never had a pretext to set up his government-in-exile, and I returned to Paris in April, hitching a ride on the U.S. Embassy plane.

I checked into the office, found a note from Lilo saying she was in town and went to my apartment, feeling shaky. She came over and said she'd wangled a two-week transit permit—thanks to an accommodating official of the French Ministry of the Interior with whom I'd arranged an appointment for her. He had bought her a drink and after some amiable small talk, exclaimed, "If the Germans had all been like you, madame, we would have welcomed the occupation!" Attractive women seldom have problems dealing with the French bureaucracy.

To speed my recovery and enliven it with some relatively effortless work, we decided to drive around the verdant French countryside, stopping at a small town in Normandy where I'd found widespread bitterness, cynicism and a thriving Communist Party early in January, along with a feeling that "we were better off during the German occupation." Today there was still some skepticism but no more cynicism. Prices had fallen, food and consumer goods—many of them American —were more abundant, the local factory now had plenty of fuel oil, from the U.S., and people were no longer shrugging off the Marshall Plan as a hollow political gesture at best and an imperialist maneuver at worst. (The U.S. Congress had just approved $5.3 billion for European recovery, and not only the French were impressed.)

I tried to capture the French mood that April in the first paragraph of a book about postwar Europe I wrote later in the year:

Another spring had come to Paris, and once again the streets were thronged with leisurely people rediscovering its beauty in the pleasant sunshine. Along the Champs-Elysées, where the trees were hazy green with fresh foliage, you could almost feel the city thawing out after the long chill winter. People were no longer walking as though they had to get somewhere: young couples kept pausing for kisses, and the elderly ones slowed their pace to that of their numerous dogs. At the Select, the wicker chairs and marble-topped tables were already deployed along the sidewalk, and those of us who were overcome by spring fever could just sit quietly and observe the gentle transformation wrought by the month of April.

And yet the darkest and grimmest years of the cold war still lay ahead; indeed, it was just then going on, unabated, for those of us reporting the news. On March 31, the Russians had started interfering with rail traffic moving between West Germany and Berlin, 125 miles inside the Soviet Zone of Occupation. Pressure was turned on and off, whimsically it seemed, but in fact sending unmistakable signals to the Allies that they were in Berlin at Soviet sufferance.

And so, with my liver back to normal and our Berlin correspondent, Marguerite Higgins, away on leave, I was told in early May to take charge of the Berlin bureau for a couple of weeks—just in case the squeeze developed into a crunch.

I was glad to go. I liked Berlin. As a cold war correspondent (which most American reporters in Europe were in those days), going behind the iron curtain was like going behind enemy lines in a hot war. Now, in Berlin, there was tension and excitement in the air. How far would the Russians go? Already, Allied military personnel and supplies were being airlifted into the city. The Russians often buzzed the planes as they flew across the Soviet zone. As General Lucius Clay, the American representative on the Allied Control Council, said in early May, "Berlin is no place for a nervous person."

I landed at Tempelhof Airport in the U.S. sector on May 7—without being buzzed. Lilo was waiting outside the airport perimeter (Germans were not yet allowed inside the gates) and we took a cab to Zehlendorf, one of the few undamaged parts of the city, where the *Herald Tribune* house and hers were both located.

The Berlin crisis was slowly simmering, and my daily stories reflected the mounting pressure. But there was little sense of danger. As I wrote my parents on May 15:

> The atmosphere here is far less tense than American newspaper readers must suppose. It seems evident that the Russians want to get us out of Berlin. When and if we set up a West German state, they probably will have an excuse, and proceed to cut off the food supply for the city. Then we will have to leave or risk starting a war. . . . While the blame for the present frightful situation belongs to the Russians, we are by no means completely innocent. . . . But things have come to the point where, right or partly wrong, we have got to stand up (very calmly) and say we aren't budging.

In effect, this is what we ultimately did, when the Russians stopped all surface traffic in and out of Berlin on June 24 in response to the issuance of a new currency in the three Western zones of Germany on June 18. General Clay suggested sending an armed convoy through. But Truman wisely decided to provision the city by air, pending a diplomatic solution. (A convoy could more easily have triggered an armed clash.) On June 28, 150 planes landed at Tempelhof with 400 tons of supplies. The Russians, who didn't think the airlift could succeed, told the Western commanders on July 9 that the "technical difficulties" blocking traffic would continue until the West abandoned its plans to create a West German government.

But the airlift did succeed. By July 20, 2,400 tons of supplies were reaching Berlin daily, and soon after, 4,500. Two groups of B-29s, capable of carrying atomic bombs, were sent to England in July to help out—as well as to impress Moscow. So the Soviet blockade, which the Kremlin figured would either drive us out of Berlin or at least block the emergence of a West German state, succeeded only in bringing the Germans and the Western Allies closer together in a dramatic undertaking that involved 280,000 flights, made worldwide headlines and cast the Russians in the role of bullies—and unsuccessful ones at that. They finally backed down the following spring and lifted the blockade, which in the end turned out to be their first major cold war defeat.

I missed the start of the airlift, as I had to return to my Paris base at the end of May after Marguerite's return. But thanks to Lilo's Communist connections, I had some interesting if sometimes acrimonious discussions in East Berlin during my stay. There were still no barriers between the sectors then, no wall or checkpoints, so we often met in the Soviet Intourist restaurants where the caviar and shashlik were a bargain in dollars. Driving back, past the dreary rows of ornate Stalinist buildings rising from the rubble along the former Unter den Linden, we'd pass through the Brandenburg Gate, where a solitary East German policeman waved us by, and be home in ten minutes, glad as always to be back on the Western side of the line that would some day become a wall.

One afternoon I went to the headquarters of the Soviet Berlin Command, where Lilo introduced me to the press spokesman, a slight, nervous chain-smoker named Greenberg, who spoke fair English. He was surprised to see me but pleased that he could deny a spate of stories that were being played up in the West Berlin papers. Most of these concerned purges and dismissals of Soviet officials, including General G. S. Lukianchenko, the Red Army chief of staff in Berlin.

"I know how these stories get started," he said. "Some American reporter invents something that will make a headline. Then the others add to it. And of course no one bothers to check it with us."

Greenberg also denied that a General Scharnov was in town directing the shake-up and that a Russian officer had killed himself and his family rather than return to Moscow. "This sort of thing is so fantastic that I am embarrassed even to have to deny it," he said.

And he scotched a French-inspired rumor that two daily trains from East Berlin to the Western zones would soon be put into service, with fares to be paid in dollars.

As we parted, he promised to get me an interview with Marshal

Vassily Sokolovsky, the Kremlin's top man in Germany, and I knew he knew that I knew he wouldn't. But anyway, I had something to write that day, and Lilo was delighted, in her peace-loving way, that Greenberg and I had gotten along so well.

"Aren't you glad you came?" she said. "When you get to know them, you'll find the Russians are very warm, very human. And now you will get an interview with Sokolovsky himself!"

"And we will talk of ships and shoes and sealing wax, and cabbages and kings," I replied. "Don't hold your breath, *liebchen.*"

"*Ach!*" she said, smiling. "*Du bist verrückt, ganz verrückt!*"

"If I'm crazy," I said, "blame it on taking too many Russian promises seriously."

And of course, I never got the interview.

The story I best liked covering before leaving Berlin at the end of May was the celebration of Israel's independence at the city's displaced persons camp. The United Nations, which administered these camps, had provided trucks that on this memorable day carried hundreds of cheering Jews waving makeshift Israeli flags through the streets of West Berlin. The convoy, escorted by German motorcycle policemen, turned into the Kurfürstendamm, where I watched it from the sidewalk, and the reaction of Berliners was fascinating. None had ever seen the Star of David proudly brandished on a flag; they could remember it only as a symbol of shame that Jews were forced to wear under Nazism. So they watched this clamorous convoy at first incredulously, then with smiles and finally with applause and cheers. It was one of those rare emotional moments that you know at the time will endure long after other memories have faded away.

By mid-June I was back in New York, having spent more than two years in postwar Europe watching the cold war gather momentum. So I missed not only the start of the Berlin airlift that month but also an even more momentous event: the expulsion of Yugoslavia from the Cominform after several months of Soviet bullying—over the issue of industrialization—and unexpected Yugoslav defiance. In Italy, meanwhile, the Communists, who had high hopes of winning a majority of seats in the June parliamentary elections, were decisively defeated by a coalition of Christian Democrats and center parties. So this was not a good month for what came to be known as "the other side."

The day before I left Paris for a year's stint in New York on the night city desk and at the *Trib*'s United Nations bureau, I walked into the Hotel California bar, which had become the favorite watering hole for both resident and transient American reporters. Joe Alsop, the syndicated columnist, was regaling a table of AP staffers with stories of his recent adventures in Vienna, another divided city technically behind the iron curtain.

Joe had been interviewing the usual top officials, both Austrian and American, in his usual fashion—which was to outline a scenario of coming events, nearly always involving Soviet perfidy or probable aggression, and then to ask the high official whether or not he agreed. If he seemed to, and then a few others seemed to, Joe would soon have a ready-made, normally alarming column attributable to "most senior officials in a position to know."

His last interview in Vienna, he told us, was with a Regular Army U.S. general, no doubt a competent soldier but out of his element in Joe's arcane and conspirational world of big power diplomacy. After listening to the elaborate question, the general paused, frowning, for at least half a minute—as Joe told it—and then replied, "Well, Mr. Alsop, it sure is a cold war, and the Russians ain't our buddies!"

Which was a pretty good summary of the way things were in June of 1948, and have been, off and on, ever since.

Chapter 5

The Deep Freeze

As it turned out, the action for us cold warriors didn't seem to be in New York—at least not at the *Trib*'s night rewrite desk where I worked a four-to-midnight shift, or later at the U.N. out at Lake Success, where the Arabs and Israelis were already at it, tooth and claw. Off duty, I met girls at Pyramid Club parties (there were no singles bars) and became enmeshed in a couple of desultory but complicated love affairs. Between these, I wrote a book about the lighter side of Europe because, as I said in the Foreword, "I am tired of arguing with my fellow-citizens who think that Europe is just a grim shambles where everybody is either a Communist, a black-marketeer or a starving D.P.—and where nobody has any fun. . . . Europeans have had a hard time and they live in a terrible shadow, but they have guts and resiliency and they know how to laugh."

By the spring of 1949, I'd had enough and decided to go back. Dave Perlman, the former city editor of the Paris *Trib*, and Sy Freidin, who'd been brought home from Vienna, felt the same way, so we joined forces as a free-lance writing team. In July, we had enough assignments from *Life, Collier's, Look, This Week* and the New York *Post* to carry us through at least a year. Only Dave was married, with kids, and all of us were ready to roam again.

When we reached Paris—which would be our base—in August, the cold war was more than ever the big story, worldwide. Not only was the Marshall Plan well under way (and under savage attack by the Communists) but its military counterpart, the North Atlantic Treaty Organization, had been approved on July 21 by the U.S. Senate, 83–13. In the Far East, the Chinese Communists, then regarded as Moscow's surrogates, were chasing Chiang Kai-shek's forces off the mainland. And August was the month the Russians detonated their first atomic bomb, while occupied Germany was finally sundered with the creation of an independent West German government.

Except for our first *Collier's* assignment, a story from the Vatican about the forthcoming Holy Year, and a profile of King Farouk of Egypt for *Life,* every magazine piece we worked on for the next two years reflected America's preoccupation with the cold war, as well as our own. Consider the titles of our *Collier's* stories alone: "Vienna's Crimson Shadows," "Our Fightingest Allies," "Why Stalin Must Be Tried for Murder," "Showdown in the Middle East," "Next Targets for Stalin," "Don't Count on Germany to Fight," "Russia's Most Mysterious Colony," "The Nazis March Again—This Time for Stalin," "28,000 Children Missing—Pawns in the Communist Game of Conquest" and "General Ike's Miracle Man."

Juicy titles all, with Stalin's name always printed in red; but for all-out razzmatazz, none could top a 1952 *Look* roundup entitled, "Stalin's Assassins: Red Gestapo Bosses Rule by Terror."

My first trip was to newly sovereign West Germany to do a series for the *Post.* In Frankfurt, I met my former girl friend, Lilo, and her father, Erich Gniffke, who a year earlier had fled from Berlin, where he had been a top official in the Communist-directed Socialist Unity Party (SED).

"As a Social Democrat," he told me, "I stayed just so long as I felt there was still a chance for democracy in eastern Germany."

But after Tito's defection in June 1948, the SED was informed by Moscow that henceforth its policy would be guided solely by Cominform directives.

Gniffke then decided to quit. U.S. authorities, who saw him as a valuable intelligence source, agreed to fly him out of Berlin. On October 20 he entered the American sector and phoned two associates in the Party. Unable to dissuade him, they suggested he fetch his personal belongings from his house in the Soviet zone. They would guarantee his safety. He sent his son, Gert, who was promptly seized by Soviet MVD agents waiting at the house. That night, Gniffke, escorted by American officers, left Tempelhof Airport.

The next morning, Lilo, who worked in a film studio in the Soviet sector, got a phone call from her director warning her to stay home. The MVD was already at the studio. She managed to get to West Germany, too, but the director, Ilya Trauberg, soon afterward was reported in the

Soviet-licensed press to have died of a sudden heart attack. Gert was released a few months later by the Russians, who had vainly tried to get him to denounce his family.

Gniffke was now writing a book that he hoped would help other naive socialists see the light and also get him back in the good graces of Dr. Kurt Schumacher, the tough West German socialist leader. "The lesson I learned the hard way," he said, "is that you either become a puppet or a pariah."

From Frankfurt I drove to Berlin, a new experience, since I'd previously gone only by plane or train. Cold war conditioning caused me to tense up involuntarily when a Soviet soldier stopped me at the Helmstedt checkpoint and demanded my passport. And the tension persisted, quite unreasonably, all along the hundred-mile drive to Berlin. The only risk, and it was a slight one, was that a Soviet patrol might hurry me along if I went too slowly or stopped for any other reason than motor trouble or a flat tire. (This happened to me once, and I changed the tire alone in the waning daylight while a truckload of Soviet soldiers watched me impassively and a rising wind swept the empty plain. It was an eerie scene. Finally the job was done. I turned to the Russians. *"Do-svidánya,"* I said before driving off. The officer in charge, who was leaning against the truck, hesitated and then replied, "Good-by.")

The other problem for American motorists was that if you exceeded the speed limit, the American military police, who checked your departure time at Helmstedt, would sock you with a speeding ticket if you got to the Berlin checkpoint too soon. And so you drove at a monotonous 55 mph for nearly two monotonous hours under the watchful eyes of both superpowers. The Helmstedt-Berlin autobahn has never been a road to high adventure.

Wherever our assignments took us, we sniffed out the cold war angles, like trained bird dogs. Covering the British elections for the *Post* early in 1950, I spent a cold and drizzly evening among the drab row houses of Mile End in east London simply because the district's incumbent MP, Phil Piratin, was Parliament's lone Communist. Could Labour's Wally Edwards, the only other candidate, unseat him? "I rode a Labour Party sound truck through London's toughest Red wards last night," said the lead on my story predicting a Communist defeat. The outcome was of small importance to Britain, but to our readers the word "Red" in the lead was a teaser.

The best thing about the Piratin story was that I came back to the hotel with a sore throat and incipient cold that helped propel me into making a decision I never regretted. Waiting there with aspirin, rum grog and tender care was my companion on this trip, a brown-eyed blonde named Simone Cadgène. We had met during the war at a wedding in Riverdale, New York, and had seen each other off and on ever since. Marriage had been in the back of our minds, but the time never seemed to be propitious. Now she'd recently broken off an engagement, and we were both ready for what I guess had always been inevitable. Anyway, after three hot rum drinks and some pillow talk, I impulsively phoned her mother in Florida to say we thought the time was getting very propitious. She sounded pleased. And so we were married on a bright June morning in Paris, four months later, and we still are, thirty-six eventful years later. It sometimes takes a London fog and a sore throat to blast a thirty-year-old bachelor out of a rut.

An article that didn't mention communism in those days was almost inconceivable. In Finland, not long after the British elections, I was researching a big one for *Life* on how the Finns had kept their freedom when I heard that two Polish diplomats had defected from their Helsinki embassy and escaped to Sweden. I got on a plane to Kemi, hired a car and found them just across the border in a crude clapboard village called Haparanda. The diplomats, who were not Party members, had left Finland with their families upon learning they were being recalled to Warsaw for sudden "consultations."

STALIN'S SATELLITES PURGING ENVOYS TO HALT RISING WAVE OF DEFECTIONS was the banner headline on my *Post* story based on interviews with the Poles.

That summer, in Istanbul, I'd found a Romanian who had jumped off a freighter in the Bosporus and swum ashore to "freedom." He gave me a grim but plausible account of life in Romania under Soviet rule, and the headline on *that* story read: PLAIN ORDINARY JOES IN BALKANS CAN'T TAKE RED TERROR ANYMORE.

These secondhand glimpses of life behind the now all but impenetrable iron curtain were tantalizing. Having read George Orwell's new novel, *1984,* we cold war correspondents yearned to see for ourselves whether the Soviet Union Josef Stalin had in mind was destined to resemble the nightmare world of Ingsoc and Big Brother. We applied routinely for visas but to no avail. We prowled the periphery of the iron curtain and peered into forbidden territory: In Finland, I stood with a farmer in one of his fields now bisected by the barbed wire that marked the iron curtain; in Turkey, I took a picture of a border guard striking a heroic pose while the Bulgarians a few yards down the now untraveled highway watched us through binoculars; at Travemünde, on the Baltic, Sim and I walked down the beach as far as the fencing that extended into the sea while East German *Grenzpolizei* snapped pictures from a watchtower; in Berlin, while doing a story on General Maxwell Taylor for *This Week* ("Sitting on Berlin's Lid"), I drove down a side street in the Soviet sector and ran smack into the zonal border where a ditch and barrier bisected the street. Soviet soldiers on the far side raised their guns at my unexpected appearance, so I waved at them amiably and made a hasty U-turn.

The only non-Communist Paris-based reporter to get a Soviet visa in 1950 was Michel Gordey, a good friend who had worked for the U.S. Office of War Information and was married to an American. Fluent in Russian, he was chief foreign correspondent of the nation's largest daily paper, *France-Soir.* He apparently got the visa in return for having befriended Yuri Zhukov, the Paris correspondent for *Pravda,* and introduced him around town. Zhukov told Gordey he was to be a kind of test case: if his reports were "objective," other Westerners might be granted visas.

Michel toured the Soviet Union for nearly two months—from Moscow to Leningrad and on to Rostov, Stalingrad and Tiflis. Sometimes he had an escort, sometimes not. It made little difference, since he was unable to communicate with any nonofficial Russians—with one strange exception—despite his command of the language. People from whom he asked directions simply walked away; if he joined a table of Russians in a crowded restaurant, they would all get up and leave; in Gorky Park, parents collected their children and moved off as he approached. Why? Partly fear: in 1950, merely to be seen talking to a foreigner—and his clothes identified him as such—was to risk imprisonment. Also, he decided, it was partly patriotism; most Russians were by then convinced that all foreigners were spies.

The one exception occurred in a compartment of the Leningrad-Moscow night train. Normally, Gordey was assigned a compartment to himself. But once, to his surprise, a well-dressed man who was saying good-by to his wife in the corridor, came in and put his bag on the rack. Then he looked at Michel, and his eyes widened with surprise. He murmured that there must be some mistake and said he would sleep outside. He reached for his bag but Michel stopped him.

"Stay here," he said. "I won't speak to you and you don't have to speak to me. There'll be no problem. And you'll get some rest."

The man agreed. Silently they undressed and got in their berths.

Then, in the dark, Gordey heard him whisper, "Where are you from?"

"France."

"Tell me about it. What is life like there?"

Later, the Russian said he was an engineer and lived with his wife and children in Leningrad. He had lost four members of his family in the war. Then he asked, "Have you ever been to America?"

"Yes, many times."

"Why do they want to make war on us?"

Gordey told him he had never met an American who wanted a war, but that many of them feared the Russians did.

His companion became quite agitated. "But this is insane! If no one wants this war, why are we so afraid of each other? It's unbelievable!"

They talked in low voices far into the night—about living conditions in America, about politics, about everything but what Gordey had found so chilling in Russia: the extent to which the rulers had distorted the thinking of their people, and the extent to which the rulers were themselves victims of their own propaganda—and Stalin's paranoia. Every official he had talked to took it for granted America's intentions were aggressive.

In the morning, he took leave of his traveling companion with a silent handshake. Was the man a KGB agent? Gordey didn't think so. His curiosity was too intense, his shock too genuine. Putting them in the same compartment had simply been a bureaucratic slip.

Gordey's articles, written in Paris, were violently but not very effectively attacked in the French Communist press. It was hard to challenge the testimony of a reporter who had been there and also spoke Russian and wrote more in sorrow than in anger.

For the rest of us, the only legitimate access to the Soviet empire in 1950 was the international fair held in March in Leipzig, East Germany. When it was announced that permits would be issued to some Western journalists, four of us applied—Don Cook, the *Trib*'s Bonn bureau chief; Joe Alsop, the columnist; Rudy Hafter, a Swiss reporter for the *Neue Zürcher Zeitung;* and I, using my New York *Post* identity. Within a few weeks, the necessary documents arrived in the mail, and we convened by prearrangement for lunch at the Frankfurt Press Club. The steak tartare was delicious and the wine so plentiful that we got a late afternoon start, crossing at dusk into East Germany (now, officially, the D.D.R., or German Democratic Republic). The autobahn on the other side was dark and deserted, and with two hours or more of driving ahead, Joe spotted an exit marked WEIMAR and decided we should honor Goethe by breaking our journey in the city where the great author was born.

"Turn off to Weimar!" he ordered Cook's German driver.

"No, no! *Verboten!* Many Russian soldiers in Weimar!"

He explained that Weimar had become a Red Army garrison town after the province of Thuringia had been evacuated by the Americans, who captured it in 1945, in exchange for establishing a presence in Berlin. (In retrospect, a poor swap that only enlarged the Soviet area of Germany.)

But Joe was adamant. We swung off the autobahn and into the deeper gloom of Weimar, where we found the town's only civilian hotel on an empty cobblestoned square. Our arrival in Don's gleaming Chevrolet provoked delighted consternation among the staff and clientele, who had not seen Americans in five years. Joe ignored the meager menu and ordered up the kind of food and wine that must have been hidden away in some secret vault. The headwaiter, in his frayed tailcoat, was ecstatic. For him, Weimar had momentarily come back to life. But he was stumped by Joe's question as the brandy was being poured.

"Herr Ober, where is the night life in Weimar these days?"

"Well," he replied after a long pause, "there is the Soviet Officers' Club across the square."

"Splendid!"

Emboldened by the brandy, Joe, Don and I walked over, armed only with a fifth of Scotch. (Rudy had prudently slipped off to bed.) No one challenged us at the door, so we took a table in an enormous, brightly lit room where an orchestra was playing 1930s jazz. We were quickly joined by inquisitive female guests.

"Well!" boomed Joe. "The whores are leaving the Russians like fleas off a dog!"

Next came a mousy East German bureaucrat named Dittmar who confessed to a liking for whiskey and English conversation. After two minutes of listening to his defense of German communism, Joe declared, "Herr Dittmar, everything you've said so far is utter shit! Excuse me while I find the men's room, if there is one."

Two uniformed Russians with the blue headbands of the MVD on their caps suddenly barred his way. "Is possible," said one, "you go too far."

"You may be right," said Joe briskly. "It's long past our bedtime anyway."

We made our way back to the hotel and waited in Joe's room for the expected knock on the door by the Soviet military police. Finally the knock came.

It was Dittmar, wondering if he might have a nightcap.

We left in the morning, gaped at by pedestrians but unmolested by the Red Army, no doubt because Joe's bouncy self-assurance convinced the Russians that we must have had high-level permission to be in Weimar at all.

In Leipzig, we were sent to a suburban district to be billeted with a family in a third-floor walk-up. There was coal enough to heat only one room per house, and the air had a dank, stale smell. Everything connoted *1984:* the chemical soap that left a stench on your hands, the cracked toilet bowl, the single cold water tap, even the "victory gin" —oily, German-made vodka.

Neighbors came by to stare and listen to us, especially Alsop, who delighted our hostess by asking to have his pants pressed and his shoes shined. He claimed to have enjoyed this service in a Japanese prison camp, so why not here?

For three days we wandered through the drab, war-scarred city, talking to people who pressed against our car, stroking it almost reverently. "I would gladly hide in your trunk," said one boy despondently, "but then my mother would be arrested." He was wearing the uniform of the wholly misnamed Free German Youth.

We even visited the fair, where we found the Soviet Exhibition Hall dominated by a gigantic statue of Stalin benignly gazing over the heads of the silent, subdued, shuffling crowds.

"I say!" exclaimed Alsop. "This *is* appropriate. The principal export of the Soviet Union—statues of Stalin!"

Not far away, one of the ubiquitous, stony-faced police operatives in long black raincoats made some notes but left us alone.

One evening we found ourselves literally trapped in a packed underground cabaret where the too bright lights, the too loud swing music and the dense odor of unwashed bodies and cheap tobacco smoke compelled us to shove and elbow our way toward an exit. Some disheveled women groped at us drunkenly. One clung to me, grinding her body into mine, mumbling, *"Amerikaner, gut, gut . . ."* Her husband grinned at us blearily from a table. Finally we disengaged ourselves and emerged into the fog and drizzle of the ruined city.

Living standards behind the iron curtain appeared to be even worse than what we had seen in 1947. (The current joke was that economic conditions were certainly worse than last year—but much better than next year.) In a story for the *Post,* I wrote that going to Leipzig seemed like traveling backward in time—to the destitution of 1945, and also forward—to the fictional world of *1984.*

We returned to Leipzig a year later, with Joe Wechsberg, the writer and musician, replacing Hafter. This time we set out from Berlin, and Alsop arrived at our rendezvous followed by two sturdy porters carrying some large suitcases, a box filled with candy bars and cigarettes, a case of beer and another box full of sandwiches. Tucked under his arm was a copy of Xenophon's *Anabasis.* "This time," he said, "I am going to Leipzig as a student of history."

We'd been warned to stay on the autobahn, but as we approached Dessau, Joe got the old Weimar fever and decided he wanted to see the Junkers Werke, one of Germany's major wartime aircraft factories.

"If the Vopos catch us, there'll be trouble," I said. Every member of the *Volkspolizei*—the "peoples' police"—I'd seen had the look of a Nazi SS trooper.

"We'll remain inconspicuous," said Joe.

Don's Chevy was as inconspicuous in Dessau as a flying saucer on Pennsylvania Avenue, especially when Joe began handing out candy bars and cigarettes, so when three armed Vopos came up to us and started asking questions, Joe quickly pressed cans of beer into their hands while we got back in the car and drove off.

In Leipzig, we had the same billet and our hostess was waiting for us at the top of the stairs. To her delight, "Herr Aslop" began issuing precise instructions—a hot bath at 8 A.M. sharp, four-minute eggs for breakfast, clothes pressed daily. She happily mobilized other housewives to cater to his needs. Joe's magic was that he radiated style and panache and a sense of fun—qualities not often encountered in postwar Leipzig.

At the ancient Auerbach's Keller, the setting for a memorable scene in Goethe's *Faust,* we chose the section reserved for Germans who paid in local currency and ate second-rate food simply because Joe decided we should "mingle with the population." But he took the precaution of pressing some dollar bills into the headwaiter's hand, so we got caviar and good Polish vodka. Two professional police informers at the next table were stunned when he asked them to join us "to facilitate matters." They accepted, awkwardly, but left after a quick vodka.

And we made our ritualistic visit to the fair to have our papers stamped. It had not changed much in a year—statistics and photographs still took the place of machinery and products. There were Czech Tatra automobiles (not for sale), clumps of soil representing the agricultural capacity of Albania, a few kernels of rice under glass sent by "our glorious North Korean allies"—and, of course, busts of Stalin galore. But there did seem to be more new housing and more consumer goods in the shops.

On our last day, we parked near the old Thomas Church, where Johann Sebastian Bach lies buried. We paid our respects to the composer, and I took some pictures of a nearby *Freie Deutsche Jugend* band while Joe sat in the car reading his Greek history. When we returned, I said, "We've had a very interesting half hour—"

Joe gave me a look. "I dare say, dear boy, you will find the next half hour vastly more interesting."

That's when I noticed the man wearing the usual black raincoat in the front seat. He held a pistol pointed at Joe's chest. It swung around to mine. *"Ausweis,"* he demanded. "Passport."

So we were taken to *Volkspolizei* headquarters after being joined by a Russian, and marched up five flights of stairs. There, a German officer, flanked by a Russian, said we were being held "on suspicion of espionage" while they developed my film. I protested that it was my private property. The Russian laughed. "Don't worry," he said in English, "there'll be no charge for developing."

While we waited, another Vopo interrogated us about our jobs, families, schooling and whether we had relatives in Germany. Then he said, "You pretended to come here to see the fair. You spent exactly twenty-three minutes at the fair. At two shops you provoked peaceful citizens of our People's Democracy. You made derogatory remarks about Comrade Stalin's picture near the Potsdam Bridge when you left Berlin. In Dessau you gave beer to the People's Police in an effort to bribe them. At Auerbach's Keller—"

Alsop, who was seated beneath a huge portrait of Stalin, finally broke in: "I hate discussing politics with policemen."

Just then a splendid military figure appeared, his shoulders covered with insignia. Everyone sprang to attention except for us prisoners. He asked who we were, so we asked about his rank and insignia.

"Dummköpfe!" he snapped, and stalked out. He was the chief of Leipzig's People's Police and he clearly didn't care for us.

"Now everything is lost," said Alsop matter-of-factly, and lit a cigarette.

But it wasn't. Suddenly we were told we were free to leave. Apparently there had been nothing incriminating on my film. Or perhaps, as one of our captors told us afterward over vodka at a nearby black-market bar, *"Ach, Sie sind nur kleine Fische."*

When Wechsberg duly translated to Alsop that he had just been called a little fish, Joe replied, "Tell him that's not very flattering. Just for that, he can pay for the drinks."

He did, and we were invited to return to headquarters to collect my film, but Joe mumbled something about "putting our heads back into the lion's mouth," and we climbed into the car.

"Don't get into trouble again," said our now mellow Vopo. "Stay on the autobahn and don't stop until you reach Berlin."

And we didn't.

East Berlin was also an easy place to get "detained" as an American, although there was still enough lip service paid to the four-power administration of the city that you didn't feel quite as isolated as in the D.D.R., where we had no diplomatic or military missions to call on for help in an emergency.

One illustrative incident, in May 1950, involved me and three other American reporters—my partner Dave Perlman, Allen Dreyfus of Reuter's and Bob Kleiman of *U.S. News and World Report.* We had been prowling around some kind of Communist festival in the Soviet sector and wandered into a hall where Walter Ulbricht, the bearded East German boss, was making a speech. We wore tags issued by the festival press office and were directed to seats in the balcony. At the end of Ulbricht's oration, the audience rose as one and began chanting, "Heil Ulbricht!" and clapping in unison, Nazi-style. We neither rose, chanted nor clapped, which caused some heads to turn. Within minutes, two black raincoats appeared and led us downstairs to a basement office where a Vopo captain sat behind a desk, his face scarred, his eyes cold. He held out his hand for our "documents." We had laminated Department of Defense cards accrediting us to the U.S. Army in Germany. His expression brightened. Then, as he read our names aloud, he burst out laughing. *"Wunderbar!"* he exclaimed. *"Vier Amerikaner und drei Juden!"* Four Americans, three of them Jewish—a good catch for an SS veteran, which he almost certainly was since the Vopos recruited most of their officers from Nazi veterans of the same trade.

He accused us of sneaking into this closed Party gathering for espionage purposes and then barked an order to his underlings: *"Draussen!"* And added, in German, "If they move, shoot!"

It was raining hard, so we got permission to sit in our taxi with our terrified West Berlin driver, who'd been subjected to intensive interrogation. Six Vopos surrounded the cab, guns pointed at us. The situation was not promising until I spotted Marion Podkawinski, a Polish correspondent who liked to hang around the American Press Club. I coughed loudly, and he turned around, sized up the situation immediately and trotted off.

In a few minutes we were summoned back inside. This time, Marion and a Soviet colonel were facing the German, now obviously chastened. The Russian had clearly been giving him hell for exceeding his authority. For one brief moment, a very opportune one, we and the Russians were allies again. We thanked the colonel, who I think enjoyed berating the ex-Nazi.

"Now," said Marion, "get on back to the Press Club."

"And the drinks will be on us," said Perlman.

There were always rallies and parades going on in East Berlin in the early fifties, and most of them could be attended by Westerners. In fact, wherever we parked our car, groups of Free German Youth, wearing blue shirts and short pants and red scarves, and usually accompanied by a squad leader about forty, would gather around to welcome us as American delegates to whatever was going on, and ask for autographs. Russians watched this activity benevolently and would sometimes come up to assure us they "knew there were two Americas" and felt only friendship for us, "the peace-loving, progressive Americans." After a few minutes' discussion about Korea and related matters, the smiles faded and we were left alone.

The most effective argument with East German youngsters—who mostly believed what they'd been told but were still prepared to disbelieve it—was just to listen very quietly to their memorized propaganda. Then, if invited to say something, we'd simply tell them they were dead wrong and caution them to be very careful about slandering America, reminding them of the last time German kids their age had been given uniforms (the shirts were brown then) and slogans to shout, and what happened to Germany as a result. We'd suggest, without sounding threatening, that we wouldn't put up with Red-hued fascism any more than the Hitler brand and that America, not Russia, was the number one power in the world. We'd warn them gently of the risks in provoking Americans, peace-loving as we were, and remind them of the airlift, when 380 planes, flying 200,000 trips, brought 1.5 billion tons of provisions into the western sectors of the city. "Tell your Russian friends not to provoke us again," we'd say. "It could be very dangerous for you Germans."

And then, if they shouted questions at us at the urging of their squad leader, we'd smile, reply, *"Freundschaft und Friede"* (friendship and peace), and walk away.

In the summer of 1951, the Russians staged one of their periodic World Youth Festivals in East Berlin, and I brought Sim along. Our new baby son was in good hands at her mother's summer home near Lyon and she needed a holiday. We got into the usual discussions with "progressive" youth and wandered into a campsite where an earnest, bespectacled young man who spoke English guided us around the East German and Hungarian compounds. He was a true believer but very courteous, so we sent him a large bar of Nestlé's chocolate from Paris for his children.

One month later, back came the chocolate, damaged but uneaten, with the following note:

Dear Friends:

I found today an excellent and thoroughly documented broschüre on the subject of Korea, which represents our view of the situation. I hope you will read it slowly and seriously and since I am keeping a copy of it too I will be glad to get your criticism on specific points. (With page no. please.)

For your little child I send a little book by the great Russian poet Mayakovsky and I hope he and you will enjoy it.

I read in the american Press yesterday that one can tell of the hardschips in our country by how eagerly children accept candy etc. Since the american press stoops to such lies in order to make propaganda against us I feel it is better to send back your Chokolat and I bought one for the children at the HO, which I will give them with your greetings, but you will understand that I would never like to inadvertently become a part of such kind of stories.

The truthful reporting that I know you will do about what you have seen here, without misterious implications etc. will do much to create a lasting peaceful relationship among our and all other people.

Yours Sincerely,

M. Eleigmann

My guess is that Comrade Eleigmann's letter earned him a gold star and that his future in the Party was assured. I did not bother to comment on his Korean pamphlet as the only honest criticism I could have made might have offended his sensibilities.

As usual, there was only a mock American delegation at this congress. It was not until the Vienna Youth Congress, in 1959, that the National Student Association, financed in part by the CIA, assembled an articulate and knowledgeable group of young Americans to speak up effectively for our side. Among them was Gloria Steinem, the feminist writer and publisher, who told me later she was not ashamed of her role as a CIA "operative" even though criticized by some of her more radical friends.

But one foolhardy anti-Communist American did manage to penetrate the 1951 congress as a member of the U.S. contingent. He was Jerry Goodman, who later used the pen name "Adam Smith" to write best-sellers and host a television show called "Adam Smith's Money World."

In 1951, he was a Harvard junior who decided it might be a lark to cover the youth congress for the Harvard *Crimson*. He informed U.S. authorities of his plan but got no encouragement. So he took the subway —the S-Bahn—to the congress headquarters in the Soviet sector and was directed to a billet occupied by a dozen or so scruffy and anonymous Americans who'd been living in Eastern Europe. They used only first names, took no photographs and accepted him, unenthusiastically, after some searching questions about his political beliefs. For two days he marched, fraternized and got himself photographed with Russians. At night, he went down to the billet's laundry room and copied the names of his fellow delegates off the tags on their laundry bags.

Then one evening the group leader, an older man, suggested to him they go to congress headquarters in the morning for a chat. Goodman decided he had worn out his welcome, and shortly after midnight made his way out of the building and to the nearest S-Bahn station. He boarded one of the last trains of the night going to West Berlin and then saw two Vopos entering the car to check identification papers. He had left his at the billet so as not to arouse suspicion and knew he'd be arrested if they reached him. The first station in the Western sectors, where he'd be safe, was still three stops away. Luckily the S-Bahn was crowded, and somehow he managed to worm his way through the crowd as inconspicuously as possible. Passengers who suspected his predicament helped slow the Vopos' progress by fumbling for their papers and getting in their way.

Goodman made it across the sector boundary just in time and came to the *Herald Tribune* house on Limastrasse, where Sim and I were guests at lunch the next day. When I heard his story, and also that the

Saturday Evening Post's man in Berlin had just offered him $2,500 for it, I phoned *Collier's* editor, Louis Ruppel, in New York.

"What's the title?" he asked after I outlined Goodman's adventure.

I paused a moment. "How about 'I Crashed Stalin's Party'?"

"I like it," said Ruppel. "Offer him three grand."

Since we old pros never got more than $2,000 or maybe $2,500 plus expenses for our stories, this was big money indeed for a Harvard junior. And so after he turned his laundry list of names over to the local CIA man and was debriefed, he joined Sim and me at the Hotel am Zoo, and for three days I helped him produce a real-life thriller about Stalin's "party."

Jerry figured his exploit would stand him in good stead a couple of years later when he was a Rhodes Scholar at Oxford and met a CIA recruiter. With the Korean War on and a draft notice due in the mail, he decided a stint with the spooks would be preferable to one with the grunts in the infantry. But he was turned down. The recruiter explained that his Berlin stunt was a negative: "We consider you to be too independent."

Year by year, Berlin changed ever so gradually. By the summer of 1952, when I went up for one of my periodic visits, East Berlin was being rebuilt, albeit in tasteless, wedding-cake Stalinist style; and West Berlin, after a period of economic stagnation, was prospering. Fears of a Soviet takeover had dwindled with the success of the airlift, and after four years of cold war alarms, Berliners no longer believed the Russians would risk war just for half a city; also, they'd been impressed by our quick reaction to aggression in Korea. In 1952, I found New Yorkers more concerned about a Soviet coup in Berlin, 3,500 miles away, than Berliners, who were used to having the Russians just a few blocks away.

Phone service was cut between East and West Berlin in June 1952, a first step in the bisection of the city. One day I lunched in the Soviet sector with John Peet, a British correspondent who had defected to East Germany and who predicted that "we'll make your free enterprise look sick." We were sitting in the restored and once fashionable Hotel Adlon, close by the sector boundary marked by the Brandenburg Gate, and he also predicted that the city would eventually have to be divided by a wall. And no wonder: East Germany was becoming depopulated; in the last six months of 1952, 128,000 people fled the D.D.R., 90,000 of them from Berlin. Many were skilled professionals, hard to replace; 1,716 were deserters from the newly formed and supposedly loyal East German army.

I saw other East German officials, all of whom spoke in guarded tones, but only my lunch with Peet caused repercussions. When the FBI was checking me out for a diplomatic assignment in 1961, an embarrassed agent came to Bill Arthur, then managing editor of *Look,* to ask about a letter I'd written Peet inviting him to that lunch nine years earlier. They had then been intercepting his mail and wanted to know why I had made contact with him. Bill was delighted to show the agent the story I'd been working on, and for which I needed to see Peet, the one called "Stalin's Assassins: Europe's Red Gestapo Bosses Rule by Terror." The FBI man sighed with relief. "Beautiful," he said. "Now I can close the case."

By 1952, the mood in Berlin and indeed in most of Western Europe was far less apprehensive than it had been two years before. When we came back to start our free-lance writing project in 1949, tension was the norm. But 1950 was an epochal year in the history of the cold war. The reason was Korea. For the Communist invasion, which started on June 25, climaxed several months of disarray and even defeatism in the West.

I was in Italy when the year began and went on to England in February to cover the elections (and propose to Sim). In March, after my first excursion to Leipzig, she and I joined Alsop in Germany to drive to Vienna, where I was to meet Freidin and Perlman to work on a *Collier's* story. Joe hugely enjoyed his role as self-appointed chaperon to a betrothed couple (he was fortunately negligent), and of course we broke the rules in the Soviet zone of Austria by stopping in a village to buy sausage, bread and wine and again by having a roadside picnic. But Joe's gaiety was only skin-deep. "I would say the odds are now four to one that we're doomed," he said during our lunch. He was convinced that in the next three years the Russians would seize Berlin, Vienna and Belgrade, in that order, and we would be unable to stop them. (His assumption that war was imminent was then widely shared by Americans, to the point that a contrary opinion was actually newsworthy. Early in 1951, Robert Yoakum, of the *Trib*'s Paris staff, interviewed five U.S. ambassadors to iron curtain countries, and his two-page story stating they believed that "Soviet satellite nations are not planning an immediate war" got heavy play on the editorial page.)

In Vienna, Alsop could find no officials, Austrian, British or American, who agreed with his timetable or sequence of aggression, and I think he was vaguely disappointed not to find the city in a state of nerves. (In May, the small but militant Austrian Communist Party did challenge the government with a major strike and mass demonstrations that almost overwhelmed the police.)

I didn't agree with Joe's doomsday scenario either because I didn't believe, even then, that the Soviet threat was essentially military, but our side did seem to be on the defensive psychologically. Only the Marshall Plan seemed to be functioning as planned. Soviet propagandists, who had appropriated the word "peace," were playing on the fears of German rearmament within NATO, with some success; and in the East they were promising economic security in exchange for a political freedom that only the Czechs had really known. Youth was pampered, relatively speaking, for, as banners in East Berlin proclaimed, *"Die Kinder Sind Unsere Zukunft"*—"The Children Are Our Future." And they seemed at the time to be making converts.

I came back from a *Life* assignment in Finland in June, and Sim and I were married and left for a honeymoon in Brittany on the twenty-second. A few days later, our secretary in Paris called to say the *Post* wanted a "reaction" story on the invasion of South Korea, and that was the end of the honeymoon.

It was generally assumed the Russians had masterminded the Korean strike. Today, all of the Sovietologists I've talked to agree the invasion was conceived and organized by Kim Il-Sung, the North Korean leader, who wanted to unite the country under his rule, and that the Russians raised no objection. It looked like a cheap and easy victory: the U.S. occupation forces had been withdrawn, and the South Korean army was a likely pushover for an Oriental blitzkrieg. Besides, had they objected, the Russians figured that Kim would probably turn to the Chinese for support.

Even more important in Soviet calculations was an unfortunate statement by Secretary of State Dean Acheson on January 12 which probably convinced Stalin the operation was virtually risk-free. After declaring that the U.S. defensive perimeter (as drawn by the Joint Chiefs of Staff) extended from the Aleutians to Japan and then to the Philippines—thus excluding Korea—Acheson added that "so far as the military security of other areas in the Pacific is concerned, it must be clear that no person can guarantee these areas against military attack."

Truman's decision to commit American troops to Korea without consulting the Congress (and against the advice of the Joint Chiefs of Staff) therefore took the Russians by surprise. Had they anticipated our response, they would at least have been present at the United Nations Security Council meeting that condemned the invasion and would have used their veto to prevent the war from being portrayed as a U.N. "police action" against aggression. As a result, British, French, Dutch, Belgian, Turkish, Philippine, Thai, Canadian, Australian, New Zealand and even Indian contingents joined us and the South Koreans.

In retrospect, it's clear that giving the green light to the North Koreans was yet another Soviet blunder of the cold war, as well as being costly to both sides. (Two million people died—four-fifths of them civilians—and there were 54,000 U.S. casualties.)

Consider these consequences of the North Korean lunge across the 38th parallel:

1. It lent credence to the argument of hard-line cold warriors that the Kremlin was indeed bent on world conquest and that we must quickly prepare for a hot war if only to avert one.

2. It impelled Truman to order production of the hydrogen bomb, dispatch military advisers to Vietnam and open the funnel of military aid to the French, whose hopeless colonial war had suddenly been transformed into a gallant crusade in defense of the free world.

3. Coming soon after the Communist victory in the Chinese civil war and the explosion of the first Soviet atomic bomb, it ratcheted the cold war up several notches. Gromyko cranked it up a few more in the summer of 1950 when he said in Berlin that a "Korea" could happen in other divided countries. He meant that East Germany might be attacked from the West, but we took it to mean West Germany was about to be attacked from the East.

4. It clinched the adoption of the top secret interagency blueprint labeled NSC-68, which had been delivered to President Truman on April 7, 1950, and which concluded that the Soviet threat was essentially military and should be countered by a massive U.S. arms buildup. This set the stage for the escalation of the cold war and the domination of American foreign policy by a rigid military strategy.

5. On the plus side, from our point of view, it discredited Communist propaganda in the West: even fellow travelers could not swallow the Soviet charge that the totally unprepared South Koreans had actually started the war.

6. It also brought neutralists and fence sitters over to our side; as an editor of the radical French daily, *Franc-Tireur*, told me, "Now at least everybody knows who the aggressors are."

How did I feel? Exhilarated, in a way, as I had been in Finland when I heard Truman's blunt warning to the Russians on the radio; but alarmed, too, at the surge of war fever back home induced by what was essentially a civil war in a then third-rate Asiatic country. (A Hollywood producer, to whom Perlman and I had sent a motion picture treatment, wrote us in July that studios were now hesitant about making pictures in Europe for fear the Russians would soon be taking over the continent.)

And so in my first "reaction" piece for the *Post*, I wrote about the widespread anxiety among Europeans who had suffered war's ravages so recently and so directly. And I wrote of what I had seen of war, which was not as much as some Americans but more than most. And I emphasized that "the cry for peace is the loudest and clearest sound in the world today."

What we "liberal" cold warriors wanted was aggressive competition with the Soviet system—a competition we were bound to win in the long run if we didn't shoot ourselves in the foot too often—but not a military confrontation in which we could both be losers. Yet hardly anyone in those days considered the consequences of war in the atomic age. Since the fighting in Korea seemed to be the same as in World War Two, why should World War Three be any different?

While I argued in my reporting for coolness and restraint, I could also get hot under the collar at what was being printed in the French Communist press. Papers that had gushed over the "heroic GIs" for chasing the Nazis out of France five years before were now accusing Americans of rape, torture, even cannibalism in Korea, while every North Korean advance was hailed as a victory over the U.S. "fascists." I think that even the Communist readers of this garbage found it hard to take.

If Moscow's error was in permitting the North Koreans to launch an attack that was sure to galvanize the West, ours was in prolonging the war nearly three years instead of stopping it when our forces shoved the aggressors back across the 38th parallel on September 24. But General MacArthur chose to press on to the Yalu River, despite warnings from the Indian government that the Chinese might react violently to having U.S. troops on their border. The Americans reached the Yalu on November 20 and four days later were driven all the way back to South Korea by a massive Chinese attack. Not until 1953, many thousands of casualties later, did the war finally end where it started.

In effect, there were two wars in Korea. The first, against the North Koreans, we won: our objective, to push them back across the 38th parallel, was achieved. The second war, against the Chinese, we lost:

MacArthur's objective, to unite the divided country under South Korean rule, was not achieved.

In 1951, wanting more latitude in our reporting, we started a newspaper column called "Dateline: Your World." Bob Shaplen, a veteran Far East correspondent, replaced Perlman, who went home to San Francisco, and we could thus offer clients more extensive coverage than just Europe and the Near East. The column also gave us a chance to choose our own topics without waiting to get a story idea assigned by or approved in New York. (We got a taste of the near panic about the "Reds" sweeping the U.S. when Joe McCarthy's two callow young henchmen, Roy Cohn and David Schine, barnstormed around American embassies in 1953 leaving demoralization and damaged careers in their wake. Some of their targets I knew, like Ted Kaghan and Bob Joyce, who had the guts to express his outrage to John Foster Dulles, then secretary of state. Both were patriots, both are now dead. I wonder if Cohn ever gave them a thought.)

We wrote a minimum of three columns a week for a dozen or more major papers like the San Francisco *Chronicle,* the St. Louis *Post-Dispatch* and the Milwaukee *Journal.* Many we did as by-products of *Collier's* assignments, where the accent was on the cold war. Of 172 columns we wrote that year, all but 32 consequently dealt with some aspect of the Communist challenge and how the West was responding to it. But their tone was generally less grim than our *Collier's* output.

Since our columns were the result of on-the-scene observation and interviewing, we logged thousands of miles in order to write as reporters rather than armchair pundits. But the format did permit us to express a point of view which I have already described as cold war/liberal. We favored imaginative competition with communism and a conventional arms buildup as a deterrent to adventurism by the Soviet Union. We liked the Marshall Plan, NATO and Ike. We considered Tito to be a tough and reliable ally and Franco an unreliable one who would eventually be replaced by a constitutional monarchy. We regarded Chiang Kai-shek as a loser not worth the billions lavished on Taiwan, and we were against getting involved in France's last hurrah in Indochina. We believed the Arabs and Israelis could and should settle their differences peacefully and that U.S. and Israeli interests were not automatically identical. We considered socialists more effective opponents of communism than right-wingers, in part because they knew and understood the Party's tactics and its ideological appeal. And by the end of 1951, we agreed with the Sixth Fleet admiral who told us the danger of war had receded during the year.

Not surprisingly, our non–cold war columns drew the most mail. People feel obliged to read for information but would much rather read for fun. Some of mine that all our papers used included a course-by-course description of a two-hour lunch at the Hotel des Pyramides, one of France's half dozen three-star restaurants, an evening of canasta with Perle Mesta and her military attaché when she was Minister to Luxembourg; and an afternoon on Gibraltar's rock with the pack of apes that were and still are wards of the British government.

I visited the apes on the way back from Morocco, where the U.S. was building air bases without much cooperation from the French, who seemed to resent our intrusion on what they still considered to be their turf. I stayed in Rabat at the home of Bob McBride, the American consul and an old Princeton friend, who was distrusted by the French authorities for associating with leaders of the nationalist Istiqlal Party. I called on them, too, and was shown the latest issue of their heavily censored newspaper—all but two columns on the front page were blank. When I went to see General Alphonse Juin, the French High Commissioner, he denied there was any censorship until I produced the newspaper. He then warned me about listening to "those Communists." And he added, "Your consul here, Mr. McBride, is also a Communist. Fortunately, the State Department has found out and is recalling him to Washington."

I didn't tell him that Bob was being promoted and would soon be the desk officer in charge of French affairs at the Department.

We discovered during those free-lancing years that magazine articles and some newspaper columns differed from newspaper reporting in two major respects. First, you weren't recounting events of the past twenty-four hours; you were dealing with a subject, and step one was deciding what the story was. For example, my profile of King Farouk became an inquiry into why a promising and popular young monarch slid so quickly into dissolution; my Frederica profile, also for *Life*, focused on how a German-born queen managed to overcome the hatred of the Greek people and even win their admiration during the civil war; my article on Clare Boothe Luce tried to answer the question of whether she had been a sensation or a disaster as a diplomat in Italy (the answer was neither).

Magazine articles also differed from news stories because of the effort required to concoct irresistible opening paragraphs. Leads are important in news stories, too, but while readers don't have to be cajoled into perusing the details of a hurricane, they do have to be enticed into tackling a 3,500-word magazine piece by a lead that, in effect, puts a hook in their mouths.

One of my two favorites of the early 1950s is from my Luce story for *Look:*

> Take a celebrated, middle-aged but still beautiful woman. Invest her with all the power and prestige of a U.S. ambassador in a top post. Send her to a country where the communists are riding high and hoping to ride higher. You have the makings of a story—lots of stories. In Rome this spring you hear them all.

The other I like opened our 1950 *Collier's* story "Vienna's Crimson Shadows":

> Austrian police found nine bodies floating in the beautiful blue Danube the first week we were in Vienna. They weren't swimmers sucked under by the swirling current. These bodies were corpses before they ever hit the water.

The fifties were the heyday of the big general magazines, and their editors and writers had a good deal more clout than representatives of the fledgling television networks, which were considered entertainment rather than news or information media. For example, after General Eisenhower took command of SHAPE, NATO's command center near Paris, I had no great difficulty, as *Collier's* correspondent, in getting in to see him. CBS might have had a harder time.

Ike never had much to say. He was likely to ramble on about the haves and the have-nots and our obligation to pay attention to the revolutionary forces in the world. And while he always disclaimed any intention of campaigning for the 1952 Republican nomination, he did admit on one occasion to being "interested" in the presidency, off the record. He was a genial, easygoing man, but even then he didn't seem to be on top of the job. When we asked him one day at a press conference how many divisions he had under his command, he flashed his famous grin and said, "I don't keep track of the details. You'll have to ask Al Gruenther about things like that." (General Gruenther, his chief of staff, was the man who ran SHAPE.)

The four big magazines didn't always agree, but they generally hewed to the same line on the cold war and equivocated about McCarthy until his downfall in 1954. Once, in 1951, I disagreed sharply enough with a *Life* article by their Paris bureau chief, André LaGuerre, that I wrote the editors a letter (which they printed) and suggested to *Collier's* that we rebut him. The article claimed that "the Reds are winning in France, not losing"—a statement I said in my letter was nonsense, adding: "Talk to the plain people of France, to the factory workers and the farmers and the hard-pressed office employees, as I have been doing, and you will realize what an injustice you have done this country and the cause of international understanding."

LaGuerre knew better, of course, but he was an ardent Gaullist who wanted the general to return to power to save France from the Communists; more important, he was catering to Henry Luce's whims. I had met Luce in Berlin a few months before, and he had told me that Chiang Kai-shek was worth the lot of our Western European allies, whom he considered craven, defeatist and riddled with subversion. So LaGuerre knew what line he had to take.

There was another, less political reason, as I gathered from *Collier's'* response to my rebuttal suggestion. I had recently spent time in grimy, industrial St.-Etienne, in south central France, where I found that factory workers had become fed up with Communist-led political strikes, and I suggested using this evidence (collected during long evenings drinking cheap red wine in dingy apartments) as a kick-off to my story about Communist erosion—which started then and has continued ever since. But the editors thought it "seemed thin," St.-Etienne being just one community; besides, they were reluctant to contradict *Life* directly and, face it, "the Reds are winning" was a punchier story than "the Reds are losing."

Our problem with *Collier's* editors wasn't Luce-like dictation but rather a massive ignorance on their part about Europe beyond its role as an arena for cold war jousting. Once we got a cable that read PROCEED SOONEST ALBANIA FOR FULLEST TAKEOUT MYSTERY SATELLITE PLUS PIX SOVIET SUB BASE. (They loved communicating in cablese.) Albania had of course been off limits to all Western journalists for years, but Freidin and I managed to produce an acceptable story with a title —"Russia's Most Mysterious Colony"—guaranteed to please if only because it contained a superlative. We did it by researching files and by getting as close as possible to our subject. I interviewed Italian fishermen along the Adriatic who had been to Albanian ports, and Italian and French diplomats recently stationed in Tirana, the capital. I even walked in and was quickly ushered out of the Albanian Embassy in Rome, which entitled me to write, "Standing on Albanian soil is a strange experience for an American."

Meanwhile, Freidin prowled around the mountainous Yugoslav-Albanian border, interviewing smugglers and Albanian exiles in Tito-grad who were accustomed to slipping back and forth. And he was thus able to write, "As I gazed out over the parched Albanian landscape . . ." So we stretched it a little, but we did piece together an accurate picture of conditions in what is still the most isolated country in Europe.

Some of the queries and story suggestions we got from New York made no sense at all, such as: "Is Dr. Schumacher, by any chance, 'The Most Dangerous Man Outside the Iron Curtain,' or something?" And the reaction to one of our stories, on the Baltic states, was all too typical of the anti-Soviet fervor that then pervaded the media: "This will be a piece that can be used to bang the Russian noggin at the U.N." So was a December 1950 editorial calling attention to a Soviet speaker at a recent Moscow Peace Partisans Conference who named a *Collier's* writer as a "warmonger." The editorial observed, "We were right happy to see our publication qualify under the Russian definition of warmongering," but regretted that more of the magazine's editors and writers, including Freidin and me, had not been mentioned too.

In fairness, I must say there were no taboo subjects, with perhaps one exception, so far as the publications we wrote for were concerned. The exception was any attempt to probe into the circumstances of CBS correspondent George Polk's death in Greece in 1948. His body was found in Salonika harbor, and evidence was quickly produced by the Greeks, and accepted by the Americans, that he was murdered by leftist terrorists. But in fact he was on his way to interview the commander of Greece's Communist rebels and had received threats from right-wing death squads. In 1985, a book by Grigoris Staktopoulos, the man who spent twelve years in jail for Polk's murder, revealed how he was framed and tortured into confessing—and how the trial was rigged. But in the fifties, nobody wanted to dig into a story that might prove embarrassing to our Greek partners in NATO.

By the end of 1951, after a year of almost constant travel, I decided to stop writing columns and free-lancing in order to go on *Look*'s payroll as European editor. The salary—$10,000—was less than I had been making, but the security of a regular paycheck and company benefits compensated for the lower income, especially now that I had a family, with another child on the way.

Ironically, I got some credit in our profession for breaking away from *Collier's* when I did, which was the same week the magazine unveiled a special issue conceived by Cornelius Ryan and so secret it had a code name (Eggnog) and was put out by a restricted group of editors and writers. Its title, "A Preview of the War We Do Not Want," was a shocking description of an imaginary war a lot of people did want—with illustrations of victorious GIs being cheered by ragged Russians in the bomb-blasted streets of Moscow. (The atomic weapons had apparently caused minimal radiation.) The idea of Russians welcoming *any* foreign invaders to their capital was preposterous but nevertheless plausible to Americans conditioned to believe that Soviet citizens were actually members of a "slave society" yearning for liberation. The wonder is that so many Americans who should have known better—like Edward R. Murrow and Robert Sherwood—wrote articles for this embarrassing project.

Anyway, Eggnog boosted *Collier's* circulation by more than half a million—all of it lost again within two weeks. Sensationalism, like heroin, can produce a quick high and lead to a slow death. *Collier's* died in 1956. And people praised my integrity for cutting my ties with *Collier's* over Eggnog, although I insisted in vain that I didn't even know about the thing.

Another reason the change pleased me was that *Look,* despite its barbershop reputation, had more class, in the best sense of that word. I knew the editors. They weren't like Louis Ruppel, a loud, brash alumnus of the rough-and-tumble Chicago circulation wars. Ruppel liked playing games with his staff. When he decided to get rid of his managing editor, John Denson, he sent him on a trip around the world. In Singapore, John picked up a copy of *Collier's* and saw he had been demoted to foreign editor on the masthead. When he reached Paris, he grabbed the latest issue in our office and found his name down among the associate editors. There was also a cable for him from Ruppel telling him not to come back to New York without an intimate profile of Mamie Eisenhower with lots of quotes and pictures. This was like asking poor John to swim the Hellespont in a thick fog: Mamie Eisenhower, who everyone knew had a drinking problem, was kept under wraps; no one ever interviewed her.

But Freidin and I went to bat for Denson and persuaded General Gruenther to give him some personal anecdotes about her and to arrange for a very brief visit to the Eisenhower residence: a handshake and a photograph in the flower garden. ("As Mrs. Eisenhower and I strolled among her lovely flowers, she confided to me that . . .") So John was able to go home and hand in his resignation, standing tall.

The cold war leitmotiv was present but more muted in *Look.* Early in 1952, I did the "Stalin's Assassins" spine-chiller in Berlin, along with

"Red Germ War Propaganda" and "Berlin Rides Out Its Pinprick War." But it was subsiding: in March I was doing a seven-page picture story in Rome about Ingrid Bergman, then a pariah in America for living with Rossellini out of wedlock. There was also an amusing story in Cannes, where Picasso had impulsively decorated the walls of a young couple's apartment, thereby adding millions to its value. The couple, who happened to be Communists, claimed the now priceless plaster was theirs, while the landlady, a Gaullist, insisted the walls were hers and wanted to evict the young people. "We'll scrub the walls clean if you throw us out!" they replied, and for all I know the battle may still be raging.

Before winding up this account of an ominous period of the cold war, I have to confess that I was yet again conned into believing I'd get into the Soviet Union when the Soviet press attaché in Paris told me early in 1952 that it was "quite probable" Sim and I would get visas to cover the Moscow Economic Conference on April 3. I even wrote Edward Crankshaw, the British Sovietologist and author of *Cracks in the Kremlin Wall,* to ask if he had friends he'd like me to call in Moscow. He sent back a four-page letter, with names and phone numbers, of which two paragraphs are worth quoting here:

> You might get some interesting sidelights out of Ralph Parker, one-time correspondent of *The Times,* now renegaded to the *Daily Worker.* He is married to a remarkable and highly intelligent bitch called Valentina Mikhailovna. Give her my regards and see what happens. . . . You may tell Ralph that he has no monopoly of affection for the Russians. And if he starts getting rough tell him that everything I have written about Russia since 1946 has been designed to show that the war-scare over here has been greatly exaggerated, if only because his precious masters (Stalin and Co.) were in no position to fight one, even if they wanted to. . . .

> It might be a good idea to sound your office fairly soon to see whether they could do with a piece angled provisionally on the danger we spoke of—the danger of our failure to recognize a change of policy when it comes—without waiting for much more in the way of straws in the wind. What do you think?

Crankshaw was correctly anticipating Stalin's imminent death and the changes that would ensue.

Well, as usual the visa didn't come through, and I never got a chance to call any of his intriguing list of Russian friends. Nor was I granted a visa in 1954. (Maybe the Russians had been reading my stuff in *Collier's.*)

Sim and I listened to the 1952 election returns at the home of John Carter Vincent, our minister in Tangier—and a favorite target of Louis Budenz and his ex-Communist ilk on the mud-slinging right. "Maybe the hysteria will calm down with Eisenhower in the White House," he said when the returns were in. I wasn't sure. I'd liked what I read of Adlai Stevenson. He seemed to be more in tune with the changing times.

But I didn't suspect then that four months later, when Stalin died and the cold war entered a new phase, I'd be on a plane bound for Hawaii to join Stevenson for a grueling trip around the world.

Chapter 6

Seeing the World with Adlai

I SAW, HEARD AND WROTE so much in the five months I traveled around the world with Adlai Stevenson in 1953—visiting twenty-nine countries and sleeping (or trying to) in sixty-eight different beds—that it's hard to decide where to start the story of an expedition still as vivid to me as anything that happened a month ago.

I could begin with an example of his engaging spontaneity, such as the time in Kyoto, Japan, where we were invited to tea with some Buddhist priests, and the abbot presented Stevenson with a gift—a curious, lacquered, oblong object. He turned to us. "Boys," he whispered, "what the hell do you suppose this is?" We shrugged. So he went over to the abbot and pumped his hand warmly. "Sir," he said, "I haven't the faintest idea what you've given me, but never in my life have I been so deeply touched!" The abbot was delighted.

Or I could even start at journey's end, in London, and work backwards, for it was in London that he faced a television panel of British editors and managed to surprise me, even after five months of companionship and collaboration. He was groggy with fatigue and fielded question after question, many of them booby-trapped, with grace and confidence. He answered the final one with a tribute to "the might, the majesty and the simple dignity of the American people" that caused the normally reserved studio audience to burst into applause. Later he told me he felt so tired he hardly remembered what he'd said: "Was it really all right?"

When we parted, I wrote in *Harper's:* "The trouble with traveling with Stevenson was that he set the pace. And he had one incurable defect: he suffered from chronic stamina."

Probably the best place to start is where most good stories do—at the beginning, with me flying off to Hawaii to join Stevenson and the rest of our party: Bill Blair, his law partner and executive assistant; Barry Bingham, president of the Louisville *Courier-Journal* and longtime friend; and Professor Walter Johnson, chairman of the History Department at the University of Chicago. (Bingham left us at Karachi and Johnson at Belgrade; Blair and I stayed the distance.)

My role on this safari was to see to it that Stevenson produced about 3,000 hard-hitting words every two weeks for *Look,* which was footing the expenses for everybody but Bingham. In addition to doing research and getting the copy edited and filed on time, wherever we happened to be, I was also expected to take or arrange for pictures, pay hotel bills, make plane reservations, set up press conferences and, on occasion, act as interpreter.

My duties were outlined by Gardner Cowles, *Look's* owner and editor, in January, as we walked up Madison Avenue to meet Stevenson at his New York law firm. Cowles didn't trust Stevenson—with good reason, as I found out—to meet the magazine's immutable deadlines with suitable copy. So my job was essentially to provide insurance for his investment in this project.

Together with Stevenson, we agreed on the number (eight) and length of the articles, and I guess he approved of me because he wrote Johnson a week later that although Cowles "insisted" I go along, "Attwood, early thirties, Princeton . . . has lived much abroad and seems a likely companion."

Two of the most important events during that first half of 1953 were the inauguration of a new U.S. president, Dwight D. Eisenhower, in January and the naming of a new Soviet prime minister, Georgi Malenkov, on March 6. As Eisenhower told the American Society of Newspaper Editors on April 16, "An era ended with the death of Josef Stalin," and he urged the new Soviet leadership to support efforts to ease tensions and reduce the arms burden so that there might be "at least a start toward the birth of mutual trust founded on cooperative effort."

The response from Moscow was guarded, yet several important initiatives were taken by Stalin's pudgy successor: priority was given to producing more consumer goods and lowering their prices, police and security forces were purged, diplomatic relations with Israel, Greece and Yugoslavia were reestablished, territorial claims on Turkey were dropped, prisoners condemned to less than five years in jail were amnestied and an agreement was reached in Korea in March to exchange sick and wounded prisoners of war—the first in a series of steps that eventually led to an armistice in July. Dag Hammarskjöld was accepted by Moscow as U.N. secretary-general, and in 1955 an Austrian peace treaty was at last successfully negotiated.

The Soviets maintained their iron grip on Eastern Europe and retained a paranoid view of the world. But Malenkov did state that nuclear war "probably" would mean the end of civilization—a view considered defeatist by Stalin—and Churchill was so impressed by the new sounds coming out of the Kremlin that he urged Eisenhower to propose an early summit meeting with this new team. Secretary of State John Foster Dulles argued against it, and the meeting was delayed until 1955, by which time Malenkov had been replaced by a less accommodative leadership.

Another major cold war event made headlines while we were on our world tour. On June 17 a proletarian uprising in East Germany shook the Communist world. Pictures of young construction workers hurling rocks at Soviet tanks in Berlin and other cities revealed the depth of disaffection in Russia's Europe. Lavrenti Beria, Stalin's despised security chief who had hurriedly allied himself with Malenkov, was made the scapegoat for the East German insurrection as well as for various other offenses attributable (but not publicly) to his former master. He was arrested in July and executed.

What else? In Indochina Ho Chi Minh invaded Laos, which lent credence to the domino theory and impetus to our military aid program for the French. And back home, Joe McCarthy kept "stamping around" (in Stevenson's words), fanning the Red scare and demoralizing our public servants. In February, Dulles went along to the point of issuing a directive to USIA that "no material by any Communists, fellow travelers, et cetera, will be used under any circumstances"; and in March ordered the removal of any magazine containing "material detrimental to U.S. objectives." Books and periodicals were tossed out of many of our libraries and even burned, a sight the Germans, among others, had not seen since Hitler was alive. And no one ever explained what an "et cetera" was.

All these events would influence what Stevenson said and wrote during the trip—and what he would be asked at press conferences.

In the Pan Am Clipper just before midnight on March 8, after two days of nonstop public appearances, Stevenson peeled off at least a dozen leis, sank back in his seat and sighed. "Well," he said, "that's that." What he meant was: no more receptions, flashbulbs, speeches or handshaking. But it didn't turn out that way. Two months later, Bill Blair was saying the trip reminded him of the 1952 campaign "except that out here we don't have any opposition."

My first impression of a man I'd known only through his campaign speeches was that he was more conservative and conventional in his cold war opinions than people suspected. He shared the prevailing view that the Soviets were bent on aggression and must be stopped everywhere by a policy of "resistance and assistance." But he was also openminded. When I gave him a memo in Tokyo from an American professor with the remark that some of its conclusions sounded pretty heretical, he replied, "What's the matter with heresy? We need it." He asked me to set up an appointment with the professor. And finally, behind his buoyancy, quick wit and easy charm, he fretted a lot about getting things right, be they facts in a briefing paper or words in a sentence.

We refueled at dawn on Wake Island. Later, in his first *Look* article, Stevenson recalled his thoughts that first night as he began "this journey of exploration . . . to lands in which dwell a billion of our neighbors":

> What are they doing and thinking about the Red Shadow? Can we avoid the lunacy of atomic war? What about Korea? Has Stalin's death really changed Soviet strategy? What mistakes are we making? Are we winning or losing the global struggle for men's minds and hearts? And what more can we do—or should we do?—These and many more questions kept me awake in the Clipper. . . . My thoughts ranged back to the night ten years ago when I took off from Pearl Harbor in a huge, noisy Navy seaplane for our outpost on Midway Island. Japan was our enemy then; Russia our ally. Now my companions and I were flying to a friendly Japan and Russia was the free world's foe.

Landing in Tokyo, our party became what the Tokyo *Evening News* flamboyantly described as "the vortex of a shoving, jabbing, prodding maelstrom of animate flesh." Late in a busy day that ended with a formal banquet, Stevenson held a press conference (at which he asked most of the questions) where he made his first public statement about Stalin's death the week before. He carefully said it would be unwise to assume that it would mean any alteration in Russian foreign policy.

In Japan our group learned to work as a reporting team. Whenever Stevenson was hemmed in by official obligations, the rest of us fanned out and interviewed knowledgeable people likely to talk more frankly to us than to him. Then we'd give him memos.

One night he escaped early enough from a dreary dinner party ("I learned nothing") to join Bingham and me at a "family" (no sex) geisha house. The girls poured sake, played the samisen and involved us in ritualistic dances and tiddledywinks games. An AP photographer who was with us reached for his camera when he saw Stevenson happily sitting on the floor playing patty-cake with a doll-like geisha; but to his dismay, he had run out of flashbulbs. And by the time he raced to his office and back, we had hustled our leader back to the hotel.

I learned on this first leg of our trip that Stevenson could be blunt as well as gracious. In Kyoto we breakfasted with a group of university students, all of whom wore fixed smiles as they told him 80 percent of the student body here were Marxist-inclined and watched with interest the "progressive reforms" being carried out in China. After listening with growing impatience to their litany of old leftist clichés about imperialism, Stevenson reminded them sharply of what we had done to help Japan since the war (the students went on smiling), wondered if they were aware of the tyranny that prevailed in Communist states (they weren't) and told them the trouble with intellectuals (which is what they called themselves) was that they see so much they do not always see things very clearly and, as a result, the intellectual is apt to be a little wobbly.

And this from Mr. Egghead himself . . .

Before leaving Japan, Stevenson met with some of the younger members of the U.S. Embassy staff who told him he'd get a warm welcome in Southeast Asia, where there was apprehension about Eisenhower and Dulles and where he was regarded as a symbol of a temperate, nonaggressive policy emphasizing economic assistance more than military might. Stevenson seemed embarrassed and pointed out the times were so critical it was more important to help Eisenhower than to attack him unless his policies were clearly against the national interest.

Stevenson was to reiterate this theme so frequently during the trip that when we got home I was impelled to write, in *Harper's:*

Stevenson traveled as an American first and a Democrat second. He calmed worldwide apprehension about the new administration by stressing the policies most Democrats and Republicans have *in com-*

mon: resistance to aggression, support of the United Nations, assistance to our friends, peace without appeasement. He spoke in calm, confident, eloquent tones about his country and his faith in the good sense of the American people. He never concealed his contempt for McCarthy and his methods—but he cautioned our global neighbors not to exaggerate one man's influence nor to confuse Senator Joe with Uncle Sam.

On the flight to Korea, Stevenson carefully studied a memorandum prepared by Donald Kingsley, director of the U.N. Korean Rehabilitation Agency, which succinctly summed up many things we'd already heard (and which remain pertinent to this day). Kingsley agreed we had to continue the military pressure in Korea and elsewhere on the Soviet periphery, but only until we had recaptured the ideological initiative. "For ideas, when related to the legitimate aspirations of men," he wrote, "have never been defeated militarily." He pointed out that in Asia, the Communists promised three basic things—land reform, national and cultural independence and peace. The United States could not counter these promises "by lectures on freedom of speech, constitutional rights, the American standard of living, television or free elections. None of these has any meaning out here. . . . What we *can* do is defeat the Communists in the area where they are weakest—namely, in that of performance. It is the problem of assisting these people to improve their own living standards, while assuring them of their independence. In the simplest terms, what they want is respect and rice. If we can solve this problem, we can stop Communism."

Thereafter, Stevenson was to use the "respect and rice" phrase frequently—along with the now familiar "revolution of rising expectations." But the militarization of the cold war was too far advanced for Kingsley's more subtle concepts to get much attention.

Pusan, Korea, teemed with 1,200,000 people, most of them living in makeshift shacks made of cardboard and wooden slats. But cheering schoolchildren lined the road from the airport, and there seemed to be more gaiety among the crowds than in Japan. As we drove to the U.S. Embassy, Stevenson mentioned wryly that he'd planned last August to come here (and Japan and Taiwan, too) if elected, but did not want to use this in the campaign; Eisenhower felt no such reticence, and his "I shall go to Korea" speech won him millions of votes.

At a U.N. military cemetery, Stevenson was escorted by an American colonel from Graves Registration who seemed deeply absorbed in

his job. "Would you like to see how we process them?" he asked. Stevenson demurred. When they passed a corner of the cemetery where the
Belgium-Luxembourg plot was located, the colonel remarked, "It
would look more symmetrical if we had a few more in there." Estheti-
cally, he was the right man for the job.

Wherever we went—to Air Force headquarters and Korean army
schools, or to call on President Syngman Rhee—Stevenson was invariably brisk, alert, seemingly interested in every detail of what was told
him and always ready with a smile and a greeting for anyone who came
up to say hello. At one airstrip I overheard three officers saying they
never would have voted for Ike if they'd been able to see Stevenson
before the election.

Even at Rhee's dinner party, which capped a long day and apparently consisted of his dour Austrian wife's specialties—soggy oysters,
clear soup filled with snaky objects, bony fish flanked with ferns and
seaweed, tough chicken served with a sour lumpy Korean vegetable,
and persimmons in syrup—even after such a dinner, unrelieved by any
wine or liquor, Stevenson managed to say, "Another meal like that and
I would be undone!" and make it sound like a compliment.

The front, north of Seoul, was static, a replay of World War I. We
donned helmets and armored vests and climbed up a ridge where the
Second Infantry Division had been dug in since November 1951 in
bunkers connected by eight-foot trenches. Chinese positions were
about a half mile away, and occasional artillery shells rustled overhead
while air strikes thudded on neighboring ridges. General Maxwell Taylor, our escort, sent us back to division headquarters when enemy mor-
tars started bursting 200 yards away. Unlike the airmen, who were
gung-ho for going back up to the Yalu and beyond, the ground troops
were satisfied to put in their time and wait for rotation as a substitute
for victory. I asked Taylor how long the war would last if all foreign
troops, including the Chinese and ours, pulled out. He guessed the
North Koreans, now reduced to two divisions on the line, would
promptly surrender.

That night we dined with Taylor and a retinue of generals, and later
I followed Stevenson into the war room where he had a private talk
with Taylor. Stevenson spoke of the mounting frustration at home and
reported that neither Eisenhower nor Dulles had any solution in mind.

Taylor explained there was no hope of achieving "victory" over the
Chinese short of all-out war—which would be extremely costly, bloody
and probably unacceptable to most Americans. He also had a low opin-

ion of Chiang Kai-shek's ability to be of much help. But he said he wanted to leave Stevenson with at least one optimistic thought. He recalled how the Russians had suddenly lifted the Berlin blockade when they realized we wouldn't yield. Here, the Chinese were hurting more than we were (our casualties averaged fewer than ten a day) and they might soon decide Korea was an unprofitable dead end. In short, a little more patience on our side could produce results. Of course, a split between Mao and the new Kremlin leadership would hasten a Chinese pullout, and we should be trying to drive a wedge between them.

Taylor spoke articulately and convincingly, and Stevenson was impressed. Later, he remarked with a slight chuckle that patience is just what he'd advocated in the campaign, while the Republicans implied there was a quick solution to the war—which is what the voters wanted to hear.

The next day, our last in Korea, we visited an orphanage and learned how many of these children were cared for by our troops (the 1st Marine Division alone had donated $74,000 to orphanages the winter before). I thought of the cartoons in Europe's Communist press showing GIs gouging out the eyes of Korean babies and of the Paris intellectuals denouncing the barbarism of Americans in Korea—and I felt my cold war anger heating up.

In his *Look* piece on Korea, Stevenson summed up the alternatives: 1. Withdraw (unthinkable). 2. Negotiate a settlement (possible). 3. Attack (and pay a heavy price). 4. Stalemate (what we are stuck with). And he added: "After four days in Korea, I have but one conviction. There is no easy way out of this war until Moscow and Peking have had enough. I am glad I said that during the campaign. . . . Perhaps patience is the price of world power . . ."

Patience did work. Armistice talks began on April 27 and were concluded three months later.

They made a big fuss over Stevenson in Taiwan. While Chiang Kai-shek figured he had the Republicans in his pocket, he wasn't so sure about the Democrats. So he saw Stevenson three times—twice privately and once at a stag banquet for our party. He was a spare, intense man with piercing eyes, a fixed smile, jutting false teeth and a tendency to bark "haw, haw" (good, good) every few moments.

Everything he said during these meetings was a repetition or variation of one of his answers in the transcript of his first talk with Stevenson: "Elimination of the Chinese Communists on the mainland is a prerequisite to a final solution of the Korean War. Minus this, Russia will become a strong power and the war will go on. So the recovery of the Chinese mainland is an imperative necessity."

This was his understandable obsession and he managed to convince many Americans of its validity, with the help of his wife's charm and the well-heeled China lobby headed by Alfred Kohlberg. So the word went out that Chiang's forces, variously reported to number from 400,-000 to 700,000 men, were waiting to be "unleashed" against the mainland.

But in fact, as we found out soon enough, his army totaled no more than 150,000 aging combat troops (the average private was twenty-nine) not at all gung-ho to leave the relative comfort and safety of Taiwan. The crack units who performed for us certainly seemed slack and inattentive compared to the Koreans. One colonel at the exercise told me the inflated figures of troop strength were the result of individual commanders' padding payrolls for their own profit.

One day, coming back from a lunch at the residence of our ambassador, Karl Rankin, I shared a car with General Sun Li-jen, the army's commander in chief. He told me frankly there was too much political indoctrination in the army—which was a slap at Chiang's son, Chiang Ching-kuo, who had a Russian wife and no great respect for democracy.

The general turned up at our guest house, unannounced and fidgety, late in the evening on our last day in Taiwan, and talked to Stevenson alone for an hour in a low voice—not knowing where the microphones were hidden. He told him this government was "built on sand" and dominated by the same people who lost the mainland. Personal power, buttressed by the secret police, was all that counted in the Nationalist regime, and he said the United States would have to mobilize its own army to recover China.

In his report on Taiwan, Stevenson was concise in his conclusions: "1. The Chinese are creating an impressive demonstration of good administration here. 2. There is dissatisfaction at many levels with police-state methods. 3. The Nationalist army is not as strong as people think."

The last two points were considered practically heretical in 1953 America, where candor was becoming a casualty of the cold war. But the futility of Chiang's stubborn dream of returning to the mainland was reemphasized for us in Hong Kong, where Western China-watchers congregated. Everyone we talked to—British, American, French or Chinese—agreed the Communists were consolidating their power and that even though at least a million "enemies of the people" had been liquidated, the masses were grateful that China now had a government that had restored order and an army that was not a pillaging rabble. As for friction between China and Russia, all thought it was inevitable—some day.

Hong Kong was still a beautiful city, unmarred by high rises, and Stevenson indulged his passion for tramping around back alleys and open-air markets. "Now we're really *seeing* something!" he exclaimed at one point. "I'm getting more out of this than interviewing Chiang!"

And of course he made the ritualistic journey to the Chinese border to peer at the Forbidden Country through binoculars.

Back at Repulse Bay, in the villa that had been lent us (along with fourteen servants), he started writing the first article of his *Look* series at a desk piled high with his own, Johnson's and my notes, plus my suggested outline and handouts and pamphlets galore. Looking at all this material, he sighed and remarked that the longer he was out here the mushier all the issues seemed. I told him that's what happens to good reporters who try to delve into their subject. "The neatest stories with the pattest conclusions," I said, "are written by reporters who stay no more than one day and never leave their hotels."

Manila was stifling, its streets jammed and its politics riddled with graft and corruption. The Hukbalahap Communist guerrillas, maybe four thousand strong, were raiding villages, as their successors are today. Ramon Magsaysay, the hero of the reformists, came to see Stevenson at the embassy residence with two gun-toting bodyguards. He appeared sincere but disorganized. In this respect he was like many Filipinos we met. They seemed to lack the animation of the Koreans and Japanese. Was it because they also lacked an indigenous cultural inheritance?

We visited Baguio, where I doubled as photographer, talked to all the usual disgruntled sources, labored long into the tropical night over the final draft of the *Look* article and finally sent it on its way. Stevenson kept muttering he should never have agreed to write these pieces while en route; but I learned, as we went along, that his moods, which varied from jauntiness to distraction, never exhibited the irritability which so often accompanies fatigue. In this respect, he was unique among the public figures I've known.

I have never returned to Manila, nor cared to, but I figure it hasn't changed much except that the buildings must be taller and the smog and the traffic far worse.

We reached Saigon after an overnight stop in Singapore amid the high ceilings, giant fans, louvered doors and barefoot houseboys of Raffles' Hotel. (Today it's most likely a replica of every other homogenized chain hotel.) I drifted into fitful slumber listening to local newsmen tell Johnson that the U.S. was losing the goodwill of Southeast Asia by supporting Japanese rearmament, Chiang's pipe dreams and French "colonialism" in Indochina.

In Saigon, both French and Vietnamese officials were at the airport to greet us, but the way the former elbowed the latter out of the way left no doubt that the French, for all their talk of transforming Vietnam into an independent "associated" state, were still playing at being *les patrons* in this distant remnant of their former empire.

Our days and nights were crowded, as usual, and perhaps the best way to recall this segment of our trip is to quote a piece I did for *Newsday,* twenty years later, based on my 1953 diary:

> One of the things I'd recorded was the arrival of the 100th American shipload of military equipment to the French army. That's right—*100th;* way back then—before Nixon, before Johnson, before Kennedy and before even Eisenhower was President—we were already spending about a million dollars a day to supply the French with what they needed to win their colonial war in Indochina. . . .
>
> Anyway, the captain of this particular ship had bought a Vietnamese flag in Manila to fly as he steamed up the river to Saigon for the welcoming ceremonies. But the flag he got was Ho Chi Minh's Communist banner—and the French shore batteries nearly shot him out of the water.
>
> "What the hell," he was quoted later as saying, "how did I know what the right flag looks like? I can't even pronounce the name of the place."
>
> Vietnam. Some of us got to speculating later about how many Americans could identify—let alone pronounce—the word if they saw it. We decided one in 10,000 would be a reasonable estimate. Maybe even fewer.
>
> Well, that's certainly one thing that's changed in the intervening years. No one can deny that our knowledge of Southeast Asian geography has improved dramatically since 1953.

Reading over my diary, I noted other significant changes wrought by the passage of time.

For one, the French had more motivation for fighting in Vietnam than we ever did. There was pride: After being humiliated in World War II, they wanted to hang on to their colonies if only to prove France was still a world power. And there was honest greed involved, too: I don't mean just the big rubber plantations, but less visible assets; for example, the Vietnamese piastre was artificially pegged to the French franc so that people dealing with the Banque de l'Indochine could get seventeen piastres for a franc and then change them back at eight to one. Obviously, plenty of influential Frenchmen had a vested interest, profiteering aside, in keeping the war going indefinitely.

Also, there weren't all that many Frenchmen doing the actual fighting. Out of 280,000 "French Union" forces, less than a quarter were French; the rest were largely Senegalese, Moroccans, Foreign Legionnaires (German for the most part) and some newly formed Vietnamese units . . .

Driving out of Hanoi one morning in a French army jeep, I noticed that the peasants in their conical straw hats working the rice paddies barely paid attention to the occasional clatter of a machine gun or the crackle of rifle fire. Here and there, gray ghostly cathedrals towered in the mist over clustered villages of thatched huts. It would be years yet before these peasants would experience the thundering fury of B-52 raids. This was still a relatively quiet war of small arms and tolerable firepower. The landscape was not yet cratered, the trees not yet defoliated, the cathedrals still intact. The big bombs, and napalm, too, were yet to come.

Hanoi, for a city besieged by the Viet Minh (that's what Ho's forces were called), was surprisingly lively and relaxed. There was a "front" of sorts two miles out of town, but the Viet Minh would drift in and out in civilian clothes to shop or see a doctor or even attend university classes. Of course the city had never quite recovered its former luster since its "liberation" in 1945 by the Chinese Nationalists, who liberated just about everything they could carry away, including several thousand young girls. But the Ritz Dance Hall was a merry gathering place at night for the French officers, and the only hostess off limits to all was General de Linares' special girl friend. It was not really a Westmoreland kind of war.

Out in the field, the French military did sound much like our brass many years later. "Vietnamization" and "pacification" were already part of their vocabulary. In the Red River delta, they claimed control of 1,000 villages, with 2,000 under Vietminh control and 3,000 more "ours by day and theirs by night." And they spoke optimistically of driving the Vietminh into the hills, where food was scarce, even while admitting the enemy could be "as elusive as quicksilver." A year later, overwhelmed at Dien Bien Phu, the French would call it quits, but in 1953 they were still talking like our statesmen and generals of the '60s.

Saigon, 600 miles to the south over Communist-controlled territory, was a lush, lazy city in those days. The Hondas had not arrived, and the nights were quiet. Rubber-tired trishaws and tinkling bicycles glided in the moonlight through the shadows of giant flame trees. By day, along the Rue Catinat, French soldiers lounged on cafe terraces ogling the passing parade of Vietnamese girls—haughty, delicate and sedate. Saigon hadn't yet turned into the raucous, smoggy, rundown honky-tonk that I visited 14 years later.

But if the Vietnam of my 1953 diary now seems remote in some ways, it's depressingly familiar in others. I remember the listless, war-weary peasants of Dong Quan clutching limp flags while French and Vietnamese officials harangued them about the advantages of "resettlement"; the French troops being airlifted to Laos to check a sudden enemy thrust into the Plain of Jars; the American ambassador to Saigon, Donald Heath, predicting confidently that "a military solution is possible"; the 45-man U.S. military mission trying vainly to keep track of what happened to the hardware we were unloading at Haiphong; the Vietnamese intellectuals complaining of corruption in the Tam government and the success of the Viet Minh in convincing the people it was the one true nationalist movement.

And up in his mountain retreat at Dalat, the plump young emperor, Bao Dai, hunted and sulked in secluded splendor; soon he would be back in France with his wife and children.

Nearly 20 years. We had dipped our toe in the Vietnam swamp but had yet to wade in all the way; that process would start in 1954, after the French made *their* face-saving deal with Ho and got out after a mere eight years of fighting. Dollars by the scores of billions were yet to be spent; young Americans and Vietnamese of all ages by the hundreds of thousands were yet to die or be cruelly maimed; a land the size of Oklahoma was yet to be devastated; legions of actors in the continuing drama like Premier Diem and Madame Nhu and General Harkins and Ambassador Nolting and Lieutenant Calley were yet to strut and fret their hour upon the stage and then be heard no more.

In 1953, we were not yet prisoners of our grand illusion; we had not yet deluded ourselves into thinking that with a little effort (or a little *more* effort) U.S. military might could give the Vietnamese a (non-Communist) government of their own choosing and stop the Russians and Chinese from overrunning Southeast Asia.

Now we know better. Now we know that all most Vietnamese ever wanted was to be left in peace and be rid of foreigners; and that the Russians and Chinese are too occupied with their own problems and with each other to contemplate rash military adventures.

As for ideology, I remember walking along the riverfront in Saigon one evening with Adlai Stevenson. It was soon after we arrived and we had finished a sumptuous French meal at the Hotel Majestic; so we decided to stroll it off before going to bed. But everywhere we turned there were people in rags lying on the ground—whole families huddled together under cardboard shelters on the muddy bank, the children thin and naked, their mothers clutching at us, begging for food. Here, a few blocks from the roof garden at the Majestic, were the wretched of the earth.

Finally, as we turned back toward the hotel, Stevenson murmured, "How can we even talk about these people fighting to defend freedom and democracy? What do words like that mean to them?"

It was a good question then; and still is.

From Hanoi, we had flown to Cambodia to see the spectacular temple of Angkor Wat—where a pioneer American lady tourist with a camera shouted, "Ad-lie! Stop right there! I was saving this last exposure for a water buffalo, but I'm going to use it on you instead!" And then on to the royal palace in Phnom Penh, where the regent, in the absence of then King Sihanouk, entertained us at a banquet followed by some thousand-year-old dances by the court ballet: one depicted the hopeless wooing of the queen of the fish by the king of the monkeys, while another portrayed—to the accompaniment of flutes and bells—the legend of a prince who turns into a bird, is taken to the princess's bed and then, in the words of the program, "reverts to his primitive shape while she sleeps, and after a short while, succeeds to seduce her." Cambodia was a tranquil, fragrant, tinkling place in those days; the war in Vietnam seemed far away, and creatures like Pol Pot unimaginable.

Back in Saigon, we had our final meal with Larry Allen of the AP and some French correspondents. All agreed the South Vietnamese would never fight like the South Koreans until they were truly independent.

Now, in Asia, they felt like the only kid in the park with a governess. So the reporters predicted that in a year the French would be beaten. (The fall of Dien Bien Phu was actually thirteen months away.) The U.S. was paying a third of the cost of this war, but our mission here had no say in how it was spent. The people were probably less anti-American than anti-French, but only because "it's better to be the servant of a rich man than a poor one." When we were asked if Americans knew what was going on out here, we replied that most Americans didn't even know where "out here" was.

In the end, Stevenson's conclusions in his Vietnam article were excessively mild—he was too easily charmed by the French and too prone to accept Eisenhower's domino theory. So he simply urged unequivocal independence for Vietnam, a buildup of the indigenous forces, free elections, land reform and U.S. participation in policymaking. "The symbols of colonialism should be removed and the symbols of nationalism sharpened," he wrote. This would have been sound advice in 1945. But history, for once on this trip, had passed Stevenson by. Nothing short of a cease-fire and a French military evacuation would work anymore.

I remember Indonesia mostly for its heat and its Hotel des Indes— the best in town but the worst first-class hotel I've encountered outside of Bulgaria. Stevenson and I wound up staying at the vacant embassy residence, where there was a power outage but no dearth of servants bearing buckets of water and warm orange pop. There, we worked on his second article—often at night or between the usual appointments, receptions, side trips and press conferences, while the others bunked in an elegant Esso guest house.

Chester Bowles was in town, on his way home from New Delhi— where he'd been Truman's very successful ambassador—and he insisted on briefing Stevenson about the subcontinent. Bowles, a man ahead of his time in many ways, could be a nonstop talker; he reminded me of another great contemporary American, Hubert Humphrey, of whom it was said he had more answers than there were questions. But this was typical of our journey so far: here was Stevenson in Jakarta, which we'd be writing about in two weeks, working on a piece about the Philippines, where we'd been two weeks before (while fretting over a Korean article), and talking to Bowles about a country we'd be visiting three weeks and two articles hence.

Bowles was concerned that Foreign Service officers were now reluctant to show any initiative because of McCarthy and their feeling that the State Department wouldn't protect them if they dared express views deemed "liberal."

At a press conference, Stevenson was also pressed on the more conciliatory tone of statements now emanating from Moscow. His response reflected his deep-seated suspicion of the Russians: "I hope that they're sincere. I can hope and pray that we may find the means of coexistence with communism. But I think that there is no evidence of it whatsoever at this point."

Wasn't war the alternative to coexistence, the reporters wanted to know. It was a valid point.

"As far as we're concerned, coexistence is possible. . . . I don't know, we have to find out."

This was not Stevenson at his best, certainly not from the perspective of the present. Blame it on the heat, or the sleepless nights. But in the piece he later wrote about Indonesia, he regained the high ground that set him apart from the with-us-or-against-us gladiators, like Dulles:

> In our impatience for all the free nations to see the peril in time, we should remember that neutrality long was the historical American position and that Indonesia's present policy is not harmful to us . . . Our best policy in Indonesia is one of benevolent detachment.

One of our more informal and enlightening visits in Jakarta was at the home of B. M. Diah, who with his wife published a daily paper and a Sunday magazine, both called *Merdeka*. They reminded us that only about one million of Indonesia's 80,000,000 people were "politically literate" and of these, ten thousand actively ran things, though there were nineteen parties and 121 newspapers. Two *Merdeka* editors who were present told us that communism posed no real problem since Indonesia was uncommitted and had little to lose. Anyway, they said, the U.S. would be around to help them.

I could see Stevenson bristling before he launched into an impromptu lecture on our self-reliance as a young pioneer nation and our reluctance today to help those who don't help themselves. "Ignorance about the United States," he added, "is one of the most disturbing things I have noticed on the trip."

This was the right note: tell them we would help them preserve their independence but only if they wanted us to. As I was to find out later, in Africa, a little indifference can be more persuasive in what we now call the Third World than cajolery or largesse.

Johnson and I went on to dinner with the Diahs at the Yacht Club and saw the faded square at the entrance where the "No dogs or natives" sign had been posted not so long ago. Today, the Dutch headwaiter was almost deferential. "Now that we are independent," said Diah, "we get along better with the Dutch who stayed on."

There was fighting in Malaya. About five thousand Communist-led guerrillas, mostly Chinese, were lurking in the vast jungle, and British troops were laboriously flushing them out. So independence had to be postponed until security was assured.

As usual, Stevenson was received with much ceremony and many flashbulbs. "Don't they realize I *lost* the election?" he protested plaintively after our third press conference in Singapore. The *Malay Mail* answered the question:

> Stevenson's visit is in many ways a unique one. Officially he has no standing whatever, and is only known to the mass of the people here as the man who failed to win a particularly important election. And, generally speaking, people are not very interested in failures, however distinguished. But Mr. Stevenson is in a very different category. He is still a power to be reckoned with in the United States and world politics, and many forecast with confidence that he will be the next occupant of the White House.

We scattered through the city to interview a variety of sources. Stevenson found Malcolm MacDonald, the U.K. commissioner general for Southeast Asia, optimistic about the outcome here, where the Malayans, unlike the Vietnamese, fully supported the security forces against the Chinese rebels. He foresaw an independent Malayan Federation in a few years.

General Sir Gerald Templer, the high commissioner for Malaya, was a first-rate soldier but also a character only the British system produces and promotes. At his residence, we entered the dining room in pairs, as in some kind of quadrille; Blair and I were partners. At the door, Lady Templer, who looked like a wicked and faintly eccentric bird of paradise, greeted us in the company of her daughter, the kind of big gangling teenager who ends up marrying a Guards officer. Templer brilliantly dominated the conversation right through the fruit pudding, cheese savory and port. In the drawing room, he had a way of sidling up, nudging you ferociously and cracking a joke, or an oath. He startled Bingham that way by whispering loudly, "Do you want to pee?" Later, he took me to see the portraits of his predecessors, adding a caustic comment to each. One, whom he described as a "pompous ass," had a large spot on his nose. "That's where a pigeon shat on him," cackled Templer, "and I won't have it removed."

We were put on a tight schedule. On just one day, April 15, we visited a satellite town (to replace slums), a tin dredge, a rubber estate, a resettled Chinese village, a leper hospital and an aborigine kampong in the jungle (where Stevenson greeted the half-naked chief, who handed him a blowgun, with a cheery, "Hiya, boss, how's the precinct?").

The day ended in a drenching rain which didn't deter Stevenson from getting out of his jeep and thanking every member of our British military escort individually. "Now what do you suppose he does that for?" a British officer asked me. "Our chaps will never be able to vote for him." It was his nature, especially when he felt ebullient after a day, as he put it, "really *seeing* things."

Our second foray into the jungle, by helicopter, almost ended in tragedy. Going over the rain forest, where the 200-foot trees provided good cover for guerrillas, Blair and I looked over at Stevenson's craft and noticed it was rapidly losing altitude as the rotor slowed down. A crash seemed inevitable, until a rice paddy appeared just in time for the pilot to clear the treetops and set down in the mud. We flew on to a British army encampment five miles away and made our way back by jeep while our chopper returned to pick up Stevenson, Johnson, Bingham and the pilot, the only one who was armed.

When we got back to Kuala Lumpur, Templer was waiting at the landing strip. "Well, Governor," he said, "I hope you don't think I laid that one on." Stevenson laughed it off, saying he wished he'd had a parang and gone after a bandit; and added, diplomatically, "I'm glad nobody reminded me it was an American helicopter with an American engine."

Back in Singapore, we learned the State Department wanted us to drop Iran from our itinerary: there was unrest there (which would culminate later in the year with the CIA's overthrow of Premier Mossadegh, a fiery nationalist who wore pajamas most of the time and was regarded as a "loose cannon"). I thought we should go where we damn well pleased but was overruled and assigned to do the first draft of the Malaya article, which Stevenson's schedule here didn't allow time for.

We took off for Bangkok after one last airport press conference, where Stevenson was asked for comment on Eisenhower's April 16 speech calling on the Russians to join us in "reducing the burden of armaments now weighing upon the world." Stevenson replied, "It was an admirable statement."

By the time we reached Thailand, halfway around the world, our spirits were sagging while the temperature kept soaring. In Bangkok we were lodged against our will in a government guest house next to the railroad track and devoid of blinds and screens—not to mention air conditioning, a rarity everywhere. There was one toilet down the hall. If we were honored guests, I couldn't help but wonder where ordinary guests were put up. Anyway, I vowed to move to the Orient Palace Hotel in the morning, even if a diplomatic crisis ensued.

Meanwhile, we were corralled into a suffocating U.S. Embassy dinner party and got "home" about midnight in time to hear the trains rumbling around while a thousand dogs barked out in the humid darkness, mosquitoes found the holes in the netting, lizards and myna birds came to call and the one fan stopped rotating. Stevenson, in shorts, was working on his Indonesia article when two Tuinal capsules knocked me out at 3 A.M. He was still at it when I woke, scratching furiously, at five thirty and headed blearily for the hotel to type up Malaya notes.

Lunch, a seven-course ordeal, was at the residence of Premier Phibul Songgram, and the two Siamese who flanked me insisted on asking questions in unintelligible English. At later meetings we learned that about a thousand people ran this 70 percent illiterate country, that it would yield to any invader—as it had to the Japanese—and that its rice and minerals made it a rich prize for the bad guys.

Next morning, while Stevenson explored the floating markets on the river, I talked with the brightest American in town, a black economist named Flurinoy Coles. Among other things, he explained the multitude of Coke and Pepsi signs. General Phao, the police chief, was the Pepsi distributor, and the premier had the Coke concession; so competition was fierce.

We left at last for Burma by BOAC Comet, then the only commercial jet in service. At the airport, Stevenson just had time to tell reporters that he saw "no evidence of sincerity or peaceful intentions in the Communists' activities in Southeast Asia" and feared that Thailand was the ultimate objective of the recent invasion of Laos by the Viet Minh.

It was 390 miles to Rangoon, and our actual cruising time was a mere eighteen minutes. Best of all, we didn't explode in the air, as a couple of Comets did before they were all grounded a few months later. My one regret was not buying a few $2 Comet souvenir banners on board; they should fetch a nice price in today's collectibles market.

We landed all too soon in the scabrous, dilapidated capital of newly independent Burma. But the very fact that it was independent made it relaxing. The night people sleeping on the cracked sidewalks, the run-down and poorly stocked shops, the squatters' shacks, the child beggars—all of this was *theirs*—Burma's. Unlike Indochina, white-ruled in fact, there was no animosity toward us here. As I was to find out in Africa, once a country is independent, no matter how poor, the whites are absolved of responsibility. Now present as guests, not masters, they are made welcome.

The Strand Hotel, shabby by today's standards, was the oasis to which I repaired for fitful naps between such challenging feats as finding a stenographer to type up 800 words in cablese and then, by pedicab, locating the Cable and Wireless office and persuading the suspicious Burmese clerk (who fortunately liked Kents) that the words had to be sent at press rates to New York via London in time to reach *Look* by the following noon in decipherable shape.

Stevenson and Blair stayed at the former governor's palace, which had two grass tennis courts, twenty servants and flocks of blackbirds in the halls. They also visited Mandalay while the rest of us checked out Rangoon. Burma was rigidly neutralist, generally friendly to the West and beset by a plethora of insurrections: at the moment the army was busy fighting the KMTs (Chinese Nationalists), Red Flag Communists, White Flag Communists, Karens, Anarchists, Mons tribesmen and something called the People's Volunteer Organization. The governing party—the Anti-Fascist People's League—described itself as Marxist but not Communist. Suspicion flourished. When the bodies of three white men were found in a jungle raid and they did not turn out to be Russians, it was announced they were American agents. What else? (They were finally identified as German deserters from the French Foreign Legion.)

The U.S. Embassy had a smart political officer. (We were discovering that every U.S. mission usually had one diplomat who knew and understood more than the rest of the staff combined.) He said our initial support of the KMT irregulars had been a blunder because the Burmese knew all about it. Candor was the most effective form of diplomacy out here, he said, because the Burmese were so much wilier than we were.

While Stevenson scribbled away among the blackbirds at the palace, I met with five young politicians, two of them Communists, three more or less progovernment. The Communists used the identical phrases I'd heard from their comrades in Europe. I couldn't disagree with some of their points—that the U.S. was too busy being anti-Communist to be pro-anything; that Chiang Kai-shek was finished and we should recognize Red China; and that a peace settlement ought to be reached in Korea as soon as possible. But when they called the Chinese revolution the start of the "liberation of Asia," I told them a few blunt truths about life in Eastern Europe, where the people didn't feel "liberated" by communism—quite the contrary.

"What you say is most interesting," said one of the Communists, "but I have many friends who have been in Russia and Eastern Europe, and they paint quite a different picture from yours. Whom should I believe —my friends I have known all my life or you, whom I have known for less than an hour?" All the others nodded agreement. There was nothing more for me to say.

In the plane to Calcutta, crowding a *Look* deadline, Stevenson rewrote part of my rewrite of his first rewrite of my original version of the Indonesia-Malaya article. At the Calcutta airport, I snatched it from him, retyped it at the Great Eastern Hotel and delivered it to the telegraph office, where I got the thing accepted and moving by paying cash. Frazzled, I headed back to my blessedly air-conditioned room but was sidetracked by Stevenson and Bingham on their way out to tour this miserable, swarming city. We stopped at the railway station, of which Bingham later wrote:

> The whole station is occupied by refugees, half-naked and living like animals on the floor of a vast smoky shed. Here we saw dying men, already rigid as corpses, stretched on the bare stones while women fanned the fetid air around them.
>
> In one corner cowered a dog, a symbol of all the human misery around him. One leg had been severed by a train, and the raw stump ran with blood. With a terrible dumb patience the dog stood waiting for death. No Hindu would destroy him to end his pain, for their religion forbids their taking of any animal's life.

Stevenson told us the next day he hadn't slept; he could not get the scene out of his mind.

While the others went off to Benares and Agra, to see the Taj Mahal, I flew to New Delhi in case there was a message from New York about the latest article. Bill Manchester of the Baltimore *Sun* was with me and said Indian National Airways had the worst accident record of any airline in the world because of nonchalant maintenance. (Our five-hour flight was uneventful but another crashed a few days later.) He also mentioned visiting a Calcutta bookstore with Stevenson the day before. The clerk tried to interest him in a pamphlet entitled "Why the U.S. Is Prolonging the War in Korea." Stevenson recoiled as though he were being handed a cobra. "Shocking!" he muttered and stalked out, leaving the clerk utterly baffled.

On the way I read up on India and learned that more than two hundred languages were spoken, twelve of them classed as major. Some were decidedly minor. A prewar survey revealed that one, Arunda, was spoken by only two persons, and another, Nora, by one. I wondered how the Nora-speaker could prove that what he was talking was a language.

We landed in 110-degree heat and I found my room at the Imperial Hotel equipped with a whirring, clattering device called a desert cooler, which consisted of a fan blowing against a block of ice. So I had two choices: insomnia from the heat or insomnia from the noise.

Ambassador George Allen, who met Stevenson at the airport the next day, seemed like a good choice to replace Bowles in nonaligned India. He'd been in Yugoslavia and was wise enough to appreciate that a nation was not an enemy just because it wasn't rabidly anti-Communist.

We took a three-day break from the heat in the high, cool vales of Kashmir. It helped some. The embassy doctor had diagnosed my fever, indigestion, rash, insomnia and sporadic dysentery as symptoms of extreme fatigue—which was nice to know but hardly elating with two months of travel yet ahead. So I tried in vain to phone Sim in Paris and finally wrote her suggesting she join us in Cairo. The way I felt, only she could get me to the finish line. How Stevenson, who at fifty-two was nineteen years older than I, stood the pace I can only explain by my theory that politicians are born with a different kind of body chemistry from ordinary folk. They can go without sleep and be refreshed and invigorated by large noisy crowds; they complain a lot but they don't really mean it.

And I knew, from watching the scores of postcards that Stevenson was dispatching to Democrats back home, that he was already thinking about another race for the White House in 1956. In fact, early in 1954, after meeting with him in Chicago, I wrote a piece for *Look* called "Stevenson's Running Again." He didn't tell me he was in so many words but he didn't have to.

Back from Kashmir and the limpid waters of Shalimar, we called on Jawaharlal Nehru, the one man, after Gandhi, with sufficient prestige —magic really—to have held this vast, diverse, squabbling nation together. The fifties were dominated by commanding leaders, whether you agreed with them or not. Nehru was one of that company of men whose names were known worldwide—de Gaulle, Adenauer, Tito, Nasser, Ben-Gurion, Mao Tse-tung, Khrushchev, Sukarno, Ho Chi Minh, Syngman Rhee, Chiang Kai-shek, Franco, Eisenhower. Today all are dead, and is there anyone who could name all their successors?

Nehru, wearing his usual white garment with a rose in one buttonhole, was soft-spoken and seemed almost shy. He gave an impression of inner strength and outer detachment, attentive but not animated. He had just returned from a long swing through the country, speaking extemporaneously to crowds of 200,000 or more, trying, as he said, "to teach them the principles of democracy." As we left, he held Stevenson's hand and, with a sudden flash of feeling, said, "I have looked forward to meeting you for a long, long time."

They dined together the same night, and Nehru explained that his foreign policy, which Dulles was to decry as neutralism, was in fact designed to maintain a stance that would enable India to be an "acceptable broker" to both sides in the cold war when mediation was called for. He considered this a useful "role" and Stevenson didn't disagree.

Nehru also foresaw the eventual break between Russia and China. "It is inconceivable to me," he said, "that Mao will accept the position of being a satellite." Nor did he think China had sinister ambitions in Southeast Asia—correctly as it turned out, but contrary to the view that prevailed in the West for years to come and which helped propel us into Vietnam.

India's own Communist movement was negligible: twenty-thousand hard-core party members in a population of 360,000,000 (of whom, admittedly, only three million were "politically aware").

Ambassador Allen, who was present, told Johnson that, after dinner, Nehru read a quotation to Stevenson and some cabinet ministers from the *New Statesman and Nation* of London, his favorite magazine. It was an eloquent plea for peace and for diverting arms spending to social purposes. He said this article illustrated Winston Churchill's supreme mastery of the English language.

While Nehru turned to Stevenson, Allen picked up the magazine and noticed a footnote stating the quote was from President Eisenhower's Inaugural Address, delivered on January 20. Knowing Nehru was prejudiced against Eisenhower as a military man (though he had never met him), Allen later handed him the magazine, pointing to the footnote. After careful scanning, Nehru tossed it aside and said with obvious annoyance, "Well, I'm dashed! I took it for granted it was Churchill!"

The next day, while I stayed with my desert cooler and wrote a *Look* piece under my own by-line about the trip so far, the others did penance by visiting a Community Development Project in the broiling sun, where Stevenson was smothered with floral garlands like leis. (He'd been briefed before to take them off and hand them back; this ritual meant that you were unworthy of such an honor, the garlands being reserved for maharajas.)

With the mercury nearing 115, Johnson and I tottered over to see a Dr. Mookerji, leader of the right-wing Jan Singh Party, who had some sensible suggestions for American policy in Asia, such as: stop supporting Chiang's bankrupt regime; show some humility, quoting Gandhi's remark about the late Lord Curzon ("He would be a greater man if he occasionally forgot he was superior"); don't assume our civilization is the best possible one; don't become identified with colonialism, as in Indochina; guarantee the security of India's northern borders to deter Soviet and Chinese adventurism.

I found it interesting that this right-wing politician talked about Taiwan and Indochina exactly like the Burmese Communists I met. This indicated that the spectrum of agreement on these issues in Asia was a broad one. Yet our policymakers paid scant attention to it and harbored the illusion that Asians would regard America as "a pitiful helpless giant" (in Richard Nixon's words) if we didn't keep on killing Reds.

Finally we left for Pakistan, convinced that India was the key to Asia and that the next ten years would tell if democracy's roots, so recently planted, would be strong enough for the inevitable crises ahead. The local Communist press was out of sync: *Blitz* said Stevenson the liberal had been "gagged" by the U.S. Embassy in India, while *Crossroads* said his trip was a "sinister assignment undertaken for Wall Street."

At his final airport conference, Stevenson said he favored Churchill's May 11 proposal for a four-power summit conference—which hit a snag when the Russians countered by supporting a five-power meeting that would include China.

And in the conclusion of the article he later wrote about India (in keeping with the fifties tone of magazine story titles, it was called "Will

India Turn Communist?"), he offered perceptive advice: "The more America presses India to join the anti-Communist front, the more I suspect that Nehru and, for that matter, most Indian leaders will balk." It was not advice likely to appeal to Dulles, the Christian crusader who so pervasively influenced Eisenhower's foreign policy.

I can't recall anything I liked about our ten days in Pakistan, starting with the cheerless Metropole Hotel in Karachi, a dusty, sweltering city swollen fourfold (to 1,200,000) by Muslim refugees from India. The Metropole's bellboys were all midgets with huge mustaches, and the one who ran the elevator needed a pole to reach the buttons; the lobby was swarming with earnest, scrubbed, bespectacled young American delegates to a Moral Rearmament convention who spoke only to each other. When I wasn't typing notes for Stevenson, I was getting vitamins and salt tablets from the Seventh Day Adventist Hospital or sharing spicy curried meals with hot-eyed Pakistani sources sputtering about perfidious India (which they called Bharat). While Stevenson visited Lahore and the Khyber Pass, I accompanied a nice and competent U.S. Embassy stenographer to Rawalpindi, where three solicitous Pakistani officials tried in vain to lodge us in a double room at Flashman's Hotel and then insisted I sign a requisition for six bottles of Scotch (I'd been off liquor since Honolulu) because this was the only way *they* could get booze in their dry Muslim country. I did swallow some Scotch, medicinally, the next day when the car that Blair, the typist and I were in almost skidded off a muddy road 9,000 feet up in the cold, dark, wet foothills of the Himalayas en route to isolated Nathia Gali. Stevenson, shivering in his seersucker suit, came scrambling down from the car ahead to help heave ours back from cliff's edge. And then for three days we wrote and edited copy in the former British governor's summer residence, ate mounds of curried food, strolled among the towering pines—past silent sentries who slammed their heels together and presented arms at our approach—and nursed our altitude headaches in the night, listening to the Pakistani officials in residence have their three noisy meals between sunset and sunrise (this being the month of Ramadan).

Finally, we drove back down the slippery road to Rawalpindi and flew on to Karachi, where Stevenson held an airport press conference ("I would like to see evidence of a Communist change of heart") and assured the embassy staffers present that McCarthyism would soon pass. Six hours later, he deplaned with Blair and Johnson at Dharan, Saudi

Arabia (Bingham had gone home to Kentucky), and ten hours after that I tottered off another plane at Cairo, via Basra, about 2 A.M. and was met by an Egyptian Foreign Ministry official with whom I'd be preparing Stevenson's schedule. The police stopped us: I was on their blacklist— a puzzling discovery since I was also listed as a member of Stevenson's party and therefore a guest of the government. Two phone calls located the problem: they were still using King Farouk's 1952 blacklist almost a year after he was deposed. The officer in charge grinned happily and welcomed us to "revolutionary" Egypt. "Farouk throws you out!" he cried. "And Neguib brings you back!"

Asia was over. The Near East and Europe lay ahead. And so to bed, as Samuel Pepys used to say, one hell of a long day's journey from Nathia Gali.

Notice my use of the British term "Near East." Our "Middle East" is a misnomer: If Japan and China are the Far East, then the Indian subcontinent is logically the Middle East (or South Asia), and the nations bordering the Mediterranean "near," at least in relation to the Western world. Hence my British usage.

The one overriding issue in 1953 Egypt was the occupation of the Suez Canal zone by the British, who didn't believe the Egyptians were competent enough to operate it, especially if war came. The Egyptians, who remembered that the British had promised sixty-six times since 1882 to leave their country (and never had), were unanimous in wanting to be sovereign on their own soil. Economic woes—poverty, irrigation, crop diversification—were Egypt's real problems; but, as in all emerging nations, psychological imperatives—nationalism, pride, rising expectations—took precedence and dictated policy.

Stevenson talked at length with both parties to the dispute, thought their positions not irreconcilable and told them so. He toured mud-brick villages in blinding clouds of dust, and visited the Suez base—the first American of any stature to do so. And we met General Neguib and (then) Colonel Nasser, who would shortly seize power, something not hard to predict once you had met and talked to him. Unlike the incompetent crooks who ran Egypt under Farouk, the council of officers who now ruled appeared to be incompetent honest men, and also likable.

For me, the best thing about Egypt is that Sim arrived on May 26, a date that sticks in my mind as the high point of the trip. We actually took a day off, saw some sights and called on Foreign Minister Mahmoud Fawzi and his wife, whom we'd met in Paris a year before. When

Stevenson arrived the next day from Saudi Arabia—where the king had talked of nothing but his claim to the Buraimi oasis and gave him a huge rug which he'd carelessly admired—I took Sim into his suite to introduce her. He gave her his automatic bright smile and quick handshake, not knowing who she might be. When he realized it was Sim, he patted her cheek and exclaimed, "Bless you, my dear! We've been chasing you for fifteen thousand miles!" It was typical Stevenson.

The next stop was Beirut, where we stayed at the both splendid and tacky St. George Hotel, later gutted in Lebanon's now permanent civil war. Our ambassador, Harold Minor, gave Stevenson a short but incisive briefing: There was a real danger of the Arab leaders of the Near East telling the U.S. to go to hell because of our automatic support of everything Israel did or wanted. He thought we should put U.S. interests first and occasionally do something that was fair and right even if opposed by Israel. (Minor was clearly no politician.) He predicted more violence otherwise, leading to more Soviet intrusion into the area. That this was said by a senior American diplomat more than thirty years ago is what makes it worth repeating today.

Again and again—in Lebanon, Syria and Jordan—we heard the same arguments that I'd heard ad nauseam in 1951. The only settlement that *might* be acceptable to the Arabs had to embody a rectification of boundaries, the internationalization of Jerusalem, compensation to dispossessed Palestinians and recognition of the refugees' right to return.

Between embassy briefings, meetings with government leaders and visits to refugee camps, temples and shrines, we were on a very tight schedule. From Damascus, where local American residents called on Stevenson in order to urge a more evenhanded American policy in the Near East, we chartered a plane to Amman—a journey that had taken me two days by jeep in 1943. The scenery differed, but not the conversation. The "threat" of Israeli expansionism was the number one topic everywhere. We visited the villages where the barbed wire marking the border separated Arab farmers from their fields and one where the line ran through a hospital, separating the wards from the toilets. And we heard as well as saw absurdities, like the seemingly reasonable editors who inveighed against the "Truman–Wall Street–Communist–Zionist conspiracy."

Only once, at a meeting with three Lebanese socialists, did the conversation momentarily veer away from Israel. "Americans should not talk so much anticommunism," they told Stevenson, "and instead talk about positive social reform. If you did that, the Communists would have no chance in the Arab world." How often we'd heard similar advice on this trip! (And how seldom in the ensuing thirty-three years has it been heeded.)

On our last morning in this Arab world, we strolled in balmy sunshine through the holy places of Old Jerusalem. This is how Stevenson recalled it in the article he later wrote:

> In Jerusalem, walking from the Mosque of Omar and the site of the sacred Hebrew temples down past the Wailing Wall, deserted now, and up the busy bazaar that is the Via Dolorosa to the Holy Sepulcher, I was burdened with the overtones of hate in the city, sacred to Christianity, Judaism and Islam . . . Surely here, one would think, we could settle our differences in the face of peril to our common faith in God. Instead, ill will is growing like the weeds that sprout amongst the rubble of Jerusalem's no man's land.

We walked across that no man's land through the Mandelbaum Gate and into Israeli Jerusalem on June 7. And suddenly, for the first time in three months, we were in a city where no one was barefoot or dressed in rags. We were back in the West. No wonder the Arabs looked on Israel as an alien beachhead, sustained and subsidized by the U.S.

We found almost as much inflexibility on this side of the line, but it was more cocky than vengeful. We were now among the victors, not the vanquished, of the 1948 war. Prime Minister David Ben-Gurion, twinkly-eyed but hard as a walnut, told Stevenson that Israel might consider minor border rectifications and some compensation to deserving refugees—but nothing else. Why should it? As his aide, Teddy Kollek (now Jerusalem's mayor), said, "The Arabs haven't the guts to take us on again."

Fearful that Stevenson had been charmed by the Arabs, the Israelis went all out to win him over. They sometimes went too far. When faculty members at the Hebrew University denounced the demarcation line that separated them from their former hospital on Mount Scopus and asked Stevenson to help them get it back, he replied, "You sound like the Arab farmers who are separated from their fields." This caused some consternation: American politicians were not expected to express any sympathy for the Arabs.

Only once during our stay was mention made of the Soviet Union, which had earlier supported Israel as a "progressive" state in the feudal Near East but had recently severed diplomatic relations. Moshe Sharrett, the foreign minister, told Stevenson he thought the Russians were altering the course of their foreign policy since Stalin. He anticipated less bluster and intimidation and also more freedom of speech within the Communist Party.

I found a current copy of *Look* on sale, with a sinister-looking Senator McCarthy on the cover. Unfortunately, the accompanying article was rather weasel-worded. Stevenson observed wryly, "I'll probably weasel around myself when I write about Israel." (As it turned out, he didn't; his Near East article was a good job of objective reporting that was criticized by both Jews and Arabs.) David Cohn, a Texas friend of Stevenson's, was in Tel-Aviv and told us McCarthy was still a menace and had the financial backing of wealthy oilmen like H. L. Hunt. I suggested to Stevenson it was maybe time he went home and did something about it. He replied jokingly, "Maybe it would be safer not to go home at all if *Look* is willing to support us indefinitely."

After four days of travel around Israel, Stevenson admitted to feeling depressed about the country's chronic economic crisis and consequent dependence on American financial support. Thirty percent of the budget was earmarked for the armed forces, with no relief in sight. And so at his final press conference, he said the biggest problem in the Near East was "pathological"—the fear and hatred poisoning relations between neighbors. He returned to this theme in his *Look* article but had no solution to offer other than to voice the hope that Arabs and Isaelis "might welcome solutions imposed by outsiders willing to be damned by both sides."

It was a vain hope, of course. Decades have come and gone and no solutions have yet surfaced beyond the fragile Camp David accords engineered by President Carter.

We left for Cyprus at 2 A.M. At the airport an Israeli friend confided to me, "Stevenson is too bipartisan for us." During the flight I reflected that the fear and loathing we had found so far on this world tour was seldom directed at what we Americans so feared and loathed—Communist "aggression"—but rather at near neighbors: the Koreans hated the Japanese the way the Egyptians hated the British; the Indians and Pakistanis hated and feared each other, as did the Arabs and Israelis; the Vietnamese hated the Chinese (though we didn't know it then); and the Turks hated the Greeks (and vice versa). And in years to come I would learn that the peoples of Central and Eastern Europe, united in their hatred of their Russian overlords, often despised each other too. Under the circumstances, the "free world" crusade against communism, so dear to Dulles, was a tough show to get on the road.

When we landed in Nicosia at 4 A.M., Stevenson started automatically plying the U.S. consul with questions about the island until I reminded him we were here to rest and to write—but not about Cyprus. I added that Sim would be our typist and, while not as expert as the one we had in Pakistan, was endowed with other intangible qualities.

"I would call them tangible as hell!" Stevenson exclaimed.

The old seaside hotel at Kyrenia was almost relaxing: the British guests all recognized Stevenson but respected his privacy and didn't pester him for autographs or snapshots, as Americans would have. So we wrote, edited, typed and swam, and he occasionally sneaked off to call on the archbishop or to clamber around some ruins. Greek and Turkish Cypriot nationalist associations bombarded him with telegrams, denouncing each other and claiming they were enslaved, oblivious to the fact they were both probably better off under British rule. Some CIA personnel from a monitoring station that tuned in on Soviet broadcasts from Albania all the way to Turkestan came to call. They were quite scornful of Voice of America programs. As one put it, "It's hard to imagine a Bulgarian peasant with a clandestine radio risking jail by listening to a VOA lecture on hemorrhoids."

We flew on to Ankara on June 17 and heard the news of the uprising in East Germany, where Soviet tanks were attacked by young construction workers protesting increased production norms (which translated into lower wages). Workers' committees were briefly in control of most major cities; then the Russians reacted, swiftly but with far more restraint than in Hungary three years later. About thirty Germans were killed, but the production norms were duly cut back.

The events in East Germany, fortunately for the U.S., overshadowed the negative impact of the Rosenbergs' execution for espionage and of Syngman Rhee's attempted sabotage of the Korean armistice talks by unilaterally liberating (instead of exchanging) North Korean prisoners of war.

Remembering Berlin, I wrote to my parents: "It's one of the most exciting and significant stories to come out of Europe since Tito's break with the Kremlin, and I certainly would love to be up there writing about it."

In Ankara, all our talks with Turkish and American officials confirmed what I'd learned in 1950—that the Turks were tough, feisty and deeply distrustful of the Russians (whom they'd fought seventy-seven times in their history). Their army, trained and equipped by a U.S. military mission and battle-tested in Korea, was in a better state of readiness, and a week before they had "proof" that their policy of standing up to the Russians had paid off: Moscow withdrew its claim to Turkish territory in the east as well as a share in the "defense" of the Dardanelles—demands made by Stalin in 1945 and flatly rejected in Ankara.

Democracy also seemed to be sprouting in Turkey, governed for nearly thirty years with an iron hand by Kemal Ataturk's Republican People's Party; to everybody's surprise, a free election was held in 1950 and the Democratic Party won 400 out of 460 seats in parliament.

Don Cook, who was in Turkey on a NATO tour, told me he'd just visited six U.S. embassies in Western Europe and not one had yet dared to report to Washington on the disastrous effects of McCarthyism on our image. I mentioned this to Stevenson, who showed me a note he had just written Arthur Schlesinger, Jr.: "Isn't the time coming when we should launch an all-out attack on McCarthyism, repression, etc.? It recurs in press conferences in Asia constantly. Also the new dispensation in the State Department is having ugly effects." (He was referring in part to the Dulles directive, cited above, purging U.S.I.S. libraries abroad of books and periodicals likely to incur McCarthy's wrath.) Some older Foreign Service officers communicated their dismay to Dulles, but few risked jeopardizing their careers. Conformity reigned and reporting suffered. Not until the following January did five retired diplomats—Norman Armour, Robert Woods Bliss, Joseph C. Grew, William Phillips and G. Howland Shaw—at last speak out in a letter published in the *New York Times* warning that the Foreign Service was being destroyed.

No wonder Stevenson was alarmed. I am reminded of the time eight years later when I interviewed Walter Lippmann in Washington and asked him what had been the greatest American political tragedy in his lifetime. To my surprise, he answered, "I think it was a tragedy that Dewey wasn't elected in 1948. If the Republicans could have come to power then under an able and intelligent man like Dewey, they would have become a responsible party. And the damage of McCarthyism would have been avoided."

Between interviews and receptions in cheerless Ankara, we finished the last draft of the stuff written in Cyprus at 3 A.M. on June 19 and headed west that afternoon. Turkey, Greece and Yugoslavia, despite their ancient and still smoldering hostility, had managed to sign a defensive Balkan pact in February which enabled them to shift troops once facing each other to the more threatening periphery of the iron curtain. The pact gave us a title for Stevenson's next piece: "Building a Balkan Barrier." In the Turkish portion he wrote:

> My guess is that the Turks will be the last people in the world to be lulled to sleep by the Kremlin's current peace policy. . . . Everyone I talked to was pleased that Russia was becoming more conciliatory. But they made it plain that nothing the Kremlin can do will ever drive a wedge between Turkey and its new friends in the West.

Sim and I spent June 22, our third wedding anniversary, in three countries: We breakfasted in Istanbul, lunched in Salonika and dined in Belgrade. At Salonika a group of Greek Princetonians were at the airport with a Class of 1909 banner, along with a Yugoslav newsman named Davicho who told me that when Cohn and Schine came to Belgrade he asked them if U.S. Embassy personnel should ever talk to any Yugoslav officials, since the latter were technically Communists; they said they would give the matter further study.

Belgrade looked like any Western European city, though traffic was lighter and buildings shabbier. We dined with Woody Wallner, the U.S. chargé d'affaires, who said the Yugoslavs literally danced in the streets the day Stalin died. He saw the event as a turning point in postwar Soviet history, as significant as the Tito-Stalin break in 1948. Tito's defiance cemented his popularity; the whole country supported him. Only one senior official, a general, and about two thousand lesser ones opposed him. All were now in exile or in jail.

Wallner added that he had no problem with Cohn and Schine; when they arrived, he just told them, "Boys, welcome to the fightingest anti-Soviet country in Europe," and they seemed satisfied.

U.S. military aid to Yugoslavia was now running at about $220 million a year, and Communist doctrine was adapting to reality. The farm collectives were being rapidly transformed into cooperatives, and the iron curtain between Yugoslavia and the West, which was firmly in place during our 1947 survey, had now been dismantled, and Western tourists had invaded the spectacular Adriatic coast.

At a lunch given by Vice President Eduard Kardelj and attended by most of Tito's closest associates, we were struck by their easy intimacy, forged in their resistance activities against the Nazis and strengthened by their subsequent resistance to the Russians. They were breezy, back-slapping and congenial and, as Americans, we all felt more at home here than in any country we'd visited so far. Milovan Djilas, the author of *The New Class* and *Conversations With Stalin,* said at one point that the proof Yugoslavia was a great country was that "the planners couldn't kill it." Everyone laughed, and Stevenson remarked, "I'm de-lighted to see that you have a sense of humor in Yugoslavia." Alex Bebler, an under secretary of state, replied, "That's why we had to break with the Russians—they have none."

At the end, Stevenson replied to Kardelj's toast with one that de-lighted our hosts. "We should talk less of communism, socialism and democracy," he said, "and pay more attention to friendship and mutual interests."

At Pula, on the coast, a navy launch was waiting to take us out to Brioni, Tito's small private island accessible only to his guests. We had a hotel and beach to ourselves, and security guards patrolled the sur-rounding woods.

A horse-drawn carriage picked Stevenson up in the morning and took him to Tito's villa for a private meeting. The rest of us joined them for lunch. Tito—stocky, trim, tough, a young-looking sixty-one—acted like a man so sure of himself that I couldn't imagine him saying "I don't know" to a question. Stevenson said later he reminded him of the "public utility brigands I used to work for in the twenties"—hard-living, hard-drinking, wisecracking, confident and extroverted.

The talk at lunch was wide-ranging. Tito stressed the significance of the Berlin uprising, especially since the Russians had to resort openly to force, and predicted the unrest would spread (as it did, tragically, in Hungary and later Czechoslovakia). He claimed that his successful de-fiance of Moscow had encouraged this unrest. He expressed sympathy for India, which he said had much in common with Yugoslavia: Both were opposed to Stalinist methods and imperialism, both were steering an independent course in foreign affairs and both were misunderstood in America.

Tito thought the new Kremlin leaders were far more supple and "modern-minded" than Stalin, who was an autocrat. Stevenson re-marked that Stalin could probably be compared to Peter the Great.

"No, no!" cried Tito. "Not Peter the Great—Ivan the Terrible!"

He characterized the Soviet system as state capitalist despotism, which leads to imperialism, and therefore Russia would be aggressive so long as its internal regime was unchanged. "In any case," he added, "we can never trust the Russians one hundred percent."

As for the United States, he said no nation is imperialistic "so long as it gives away more than it takes."

Finally, Tito, Stevenson, Sim and Vilfan, the interpreter, got into his carriage (after Tito asked my permission to "kidnap" my wife) to visit some Roman ruins.

We flew on to Dubrovnik for a day; then, after stopping at Skopje, in Macedonia, for lunch the next day, we changed planes for the trip to Athens. To the Yugoslav officials clustered around the plane, Stevenson said, "I leave you admiring all that you have done and all that you are now doing. I am proud that my country is contributing to the strength and vitality of Yugoslavia."

One of the reporters present, D. J. Jerkovic, wrote later: "No one answered him; there was no need. For during his entire stay he must certainly have become convinced that there is in Yugoslavia a great deal of good will, friendship and respect for his country. He undoubtedly understood that here, confidence in American democracy equaled the hopes which the entire world places in the United States."

No wonder we all felt invigorated by our visit. And in his *Look* piece, Stevenson for the first time conjectured that the death of Stalin was a major event: "It seemed to me that Yugoslavia's leaders are coming around to the view that more consent and less force are better and safer. Maybe the Russians are too."

Starting in Athens, we were back on ground familiar to all of us, so we moved at a faster pace. Stevenson asked me to do a first draft of the Turkish article in Greece, and another about Greece when we reached Rome—a journalistic tour de force, since I barely strayed from our hotel room in Athens, working on Turkey.

Stevenson saw the Greek politicians, who seemed indistinguishable, and also King Paul and Queen Frederica at their palace in Tatoi. I wasn't surprised that Sim and I weren't asked. A couple of years earlier, I'd done a story about the queen for *Life*, and at the end of our talk, when I mentioned King Farouk, another monarch I'd interviewed, she told me of meeting him in Cairo during the war. He had followed her into a drawing room during a party, ordered his wife, Queen Farida, to leave and turned out the lights. "I warned him that my husband was the very big man in the naval uniform outside and that I loved him very much," she said. "Farouk just laughed, turned on the lights and walked out."

King Paul had joined us in time to hear the story and said, "Freddie, I really don't think we want that incident to be published." So I gave them my word I'd leave it out of the story. But when I turned it in to *Life*'s foreign editor, Emmet Hughes, in New York a month later, I told him the anecdote, and without notifying me he inserted it in my piece.

Farouk was enraged, recalled his ambassador from Athens and demanded an apology. A Greek spokesman said the story was "entirely imaginary." So we weren't invited to Tatoi with Stevenson.

John Peurifoy, the U.S. ambassador to Greece, was about to be transferred to Guatemala (a demotion) for having clashed with right-wing Republicans in 1949 about the presence of Communists in the State Department. He had not yet told his staff "since morale is low enough as it is on account of McCarthy." (Peurifoy must have won his cold war spurs back a year later, when he helped engineer the CIA coup that overthrew the legitimate but leftist Arbenz government and installed Colonel Castillo Armas as dictator.) He told us that although we subsidized Greece's huge military budget to the tune of $60 million a year, the standard comic character in Athens music halls was an American with a loud tie and a cigar, twirling a watch chain and announcing, "Hello, boys, I want to make a lot of money."

Like most Americans then (and many even now), Stevenson accepted the prevailing assumption that the Russians were hell-bent to conquer Europe by force of arms; and so he concluded his Balkan article thus:

> Today the free Balkans are solid and strong. Greece and Turkey are ready to give a good account of themselves. Thanks to Marshal Tito of Yugoslavia, the West has driven a bridgehead into Eastern Europe. Where, a few years ago, it looked as though all was lost in the Eastern Mediterranean, the Soviet leaders now face a mighty threat to the left flank of armies headed for the Atlantic.

It was vintage 1950 *Collier's*. Atomic weapons existed but, strange as it now seems, none of us thought much about them.

When we reached Rome, Ambassador Clare Luce had gone to Florence, allegedly "piqued" because Stevenson had declined to be her guest at a dinner party and a Fourth of July carnival. He was still piqued himself at *Time*'s slanted coverage of the 1952 campaign. And so the feud continued, with the next issue of *Time* flippantly suggesting that Stevenson was enjoying a kind of VIP sightseeing junket while Ike was slaving at his White House desk. Blair and I guessed that the president was taking more time off at the golf links, the trout stream and the bridge table in one week than Stevenson had taken during the entire trip.

The political speculation in Rome was about Premier Alcide de Gasperi's center coalition, which had lost votes to the monarchists and the left-wing socialists in the recent elections and no longer had a working majority in parliament. The U.S., and especially Mrs. Luce, were totally committed to de Gasperi's Christian Democrats, which probably was counterproductive. As Giuseppe Saragat, the Social Democratic leader, told Stevenson, Italy's tragedy was that the country had no real democratic tradition and its ruling classes no social conscience.

At a lunch with four American correspondents in the Borghese Gardens, one of them lamented the decline in American influence due to our lack of a policy other than anticommunism and our slack control over foreign aid funds, which tended mainly to benefit the rich. "In 1945 the Italians expected Garibaldi from us," said another. "They would have settled for Jefferson. But all they are getting now is Hoover."

Ed Stevens, a longtime Moscow correspondent, was at the lunch and said we had a chance to seize the initiative right now while the Kremlin was still in flux after Stalin—but only if we had a policy that was not totally reactive. So he figured our inaction would give the Soviet leadership the opportunity to get their act together again.

Stevenson, who had seen the pope, various politicians and even Mrs. Luce, did more listening than talking. But when asked about McCarthy, he attributed his influence to basic American "immaturity"; in other words, the combination of prosecutor, pundit and politician was irresistible to people who view the world in simple, clear-cut, good guy–bad guy terms. But despite all the damage McCarthy was doing to Europe's image of America, Stevenson had such faith in American common sense that he expressed optimism about the senator's imminent decline and fall.

After three days of intensive writing at Positano, south of Naples, we moved on to Vienna, where we heard more speculation about Beria's downfall in Moscow. The most plausible explanation was that he had made so many enemies as Stalin's KGB chief that he was chosen to be the fall guy for the embarrassing East German uprising in June. Stevenson's only comment to the press was, "I'm glad I'm not in politics in Russia today."

The good news we heard in Vienna was that Dulles's February directive banning books by Communist sympathizers, "et cetera" in USIA libraries had been rewritten and toned down, a possible indication that McCarthy's influence was beginning to wane.

Still, I got an earful about sagging morale in the Dulles State Department from Mrs. Llewellyn Thompson, the ambassador's wife, and Bernard MacGuigan, the press attaché, who had tendered his resignation since it had become too risky to display any initiative. Mac told me that Ted Kaghan, a mutual friend of ours and a dedicated anti-Communist, had recently been forced to resign for being discourteous to Cohn and Schine. (He was "forced" in that he was recalled to Washington and told that if he did not resign, the Department would lift his passport and he could not rejoin his family in Germany. Mayor Ernst Reuter of Berlin and ex-Chancellor Figl of Austria had sent letters supporting Kaghan to Washington, but to no avail.)

Austria was still waiting for a peace treaty (which would come in two years) and already beginning to resemble Switzerland; but, as someone said, "more willowy." The local U.S. Army counterintelligence chief, an old wartime buddy, told me the CIA was raiding his detachment and practically supporting the Austrian economy through its apparatus of agents and informers. Our 1950 *Collier's* story, "Vienna's Crimson Shadows," had apparently not yet gone stale.

We flew to Berlin, escorted across the Soviet zone by Russian fighter planes. After lunch with Mayor Reuter, we drove through the Brandenburg Gate into the Soviet sector, stopping near the ruins of Hitler's former bunker so that Blair and I could take pictures of Stevenson walking over the rubble just 200 yards beyond the then invisible iron curtain.

When we returned to the car, with a U.S. flag on its fender, we found it surrounded by a squad of East German militia. We got in, and one of the soldiers stuck his head through the window and said, "You move and we shoot." I'd heard the phrase before but it still came as a surprise. The soldiers must not have recognized Stevenson, or perhaps they were somewhat nervous after the June riots and decided an excess of zeal would not be criticized. Anyway, Cecil Lyon, the U.S. consul, and Major Ed Lumpkin of the Visitors' Bureau, who was in uniform, got out and insisted that the Germans, who had no authority to hold us, go and fetch some Russians.

Our captors wanted to take us to headquarters but finally agreed to send a messenger to the Soviet Embassy, first blocking our car to prevent a getaway.

Stevenson seemed amused by our predicament, and I was hoping the Russians would turn up and give the Germans hell. But after the militiamen lectured us for twenty minutes about fascism in America and the destruction of Berlin by "mercenary" U.S. bombers, a motorcyclist arrived with instructions we were to be released on condition we surrender our film. Major Lumpkin and I were all for holding out—it was a bad precedent—but Lyon was getting nervous, so we gave in and were allowed to leave. Stevenson called it an "advantageous experience."

We went deeper into East Berlin to see the Russian war memorial in Treptower Park. I didn't find the Soviet sector much changed in the past year: fewer propaganda posters, more rebuilding. Some construction workers who saw the flag on our car smiled and waved. A Vopo was taking pictures of the car as we came out of the park, and we told him sternly photographs were *verboten*. He grinned, a bit sheepishly.

Our detention made headlines back home, and I suppose some East Germans were reprimanded. At a press conference afterwards, Stevenson said: "It was a rather important experience for two reasons. One of the militia informed me that taking pictures was not permitted in the United States. Having lived there fifty-three years without knowing that, I was grateful for the information. The second reason was that it gave meaning to the term 'iron curtain.' A few hundred yards away, there was West Berlin—no iron curtain, no restrictions, no threatening with tommy guns."

Back at the hotel, Stevenson told me that after lunch, Mayor Reuter asked him to deliver a personal message to Eisenhower. He knew Ike well and respected him but said he couldn't understand what had happened to him. He wanted Stevenson to tell Ike that "American prestige has been injured almost beyond repair in Europe during the past few months." And he hoped Eisenhower would do something about it, and about McCarthy, while there was still time.

I also heard a now familiar refrain about Cohn and Schine from Major Lumpkin, who said that never in his experience of escorting visitors to Berlin had he been treated so rudely by anyone. (It was hard to find a city they went to where they had made a friend: In Rome, Stan

Swinton of the AP told me that fortunately Cohn was too busy shopping to do any snooping, and Schine was too dumb.)

We paused in Bonn to meet with politicians and newsmen and hold yet another press conference, where Stevenson continued to duck questions about McCarthy but did say he'd been distressed on this trip "by the loss of American prestige and respect as a result of [his] activities."

We took a night train to Paris, where Sim and I slept in our own bed for the first time in months. Stevenson's most interesting meeting was a lunch with Pierre Mendès-France, who would soon be premier, and some of his advisers. While all agreed Indochina was basic to all of France's problems, they told Stevenson France could not carry the triple burden of Western European defense, war in Indochina and economic recovery at home. Mendès-France stated that the Indochinese burden was the one that must be jettisoned. Stevenson disagreed, saying that Southeast Asia was a prime Soviet target, and the French had to win the war by winning over the Vietnamese people with unconditional independence. Mendès gracefully changed the subject, and they speculated about "the fluid situation" behind the iron curtain.

(Mendès, we knew, had favored disengagement from Indochina since 1950. What we didn't know was that on May 8, soon after we were there, Premier René Mayer and General Navarre were discussing how to find an "honorable way out." They had finally faced up to the fact that staying in Indochina would mean a still greater effort and more sacrifice; and so, if it was such a vital front in a U.S.-directed anti-Communist crusade, then France should either withdraw or else be relieved of its military obligations to NATO.)

Later, at a party at our house, Stevenson met with most of the veteran American newsmen in Paris. All thought Soviet imperialism was assuming a new and less military form—outwardly peaceful and aimed at penetrating the more backward nations. The question was, How prepared was the U.S. psychologically to cope with a nonmilitary Soviet offensive?

McCarthyism came up, as always. This time, Stevenson said he wished he were a hard-bitten conservative Republican "like Jim Duff" and could go around the country calling McCarthy "a lying son of a bitch" who was the Kremlin's best friend in America: in short, defeat McCarthy with his own weapons.

Stevenson couldn't explain Eisenhower's inaction but said if political reasons were his motive, then the McCarthy menace could be very great.

Stevenson's meetings in Paris, as well as Rome, highlighted the differences between American and European political perceptions. The presidential candidate widely regarded as a "liberal" in 1952 America sounded quite conservative in Europe. As *The New Republic* said of his Paris visit, "If there were any exception to the general and hearty approbation for Stevenson in France, it existed precisely in those political quarters which expected the most from him, the moderate left."

Paris got so hectic that Sim and I took him to Versailles, where we could write, edit and type in solitude. We stayed three days and went out only twice—to lunch with General Alfred Gruenther, who bemoaned the ignorance of visiting congressmen who were convinced France was "going Communist"; and to see a sound and light show at the château. We took Marie, our cook, along, and I think Stevenson enjoyed the informality of jostling, unnoticed through the crowds, with Marie on his arm.

In his wrap-up article on Europe, Stevenson posed and then answered five questions: 1. Who is winning the cold war? (We are, but let's not become too militaristic or "too inflexible to cope with the Kremlin's changing tactics.") 2. Has U.S. aid served its purpose? (Yes, Western Europe is about ready to stand on its own feet.) 3. Have Soviet intentions changed since Stalin? (Only in that they're less likely to use military force to achieve their aim of dividing the free world and blocking Germany's integration with the West.) 4. What is the matter with France? (Not much that forceful, effective and progressive leadership can't cure.) 5. What are the prospects for European unity? (Dim at the moment, brighter in the long run.)

I joined Stevenson in England after seeing the kids at my mother-in-law's near Lyon and leaving Sim with them. He seemed normally harassed, and disillusioned some of his British admirers at his first press conference with familiar cold war jargon, opposing China's admission to the U.N. because of its actions in Korea and declaring that "the impression that something has changed basically in the nature of Russian imperialism and international communism is both alarming and dangerous."

We hammered out his final article at Herbert Agar's estate in Sussex. It was the kind of place where everybody was Lord or Lady or Sir something, and afternoon tea was followed by croquet. When the AP called one day, Agar innocently told them Stevenson was just "resting, writing and playing croquet." When I told Stevenson, he groaned, as any American politician would. "Why couldn't he have said 'softball' or even 'tennis'? Croquet isn't appreciated in Chicago."

Late one night we somehow finished this interminable assignment. I joined him in the study where he was muttering and sighing as he penciled in the last words on a yellow legal pad. He handed me a sheaf and said, "This is the worst I've done yet. You can try fixing it up or you can just piss on it. I'm all written out."

It wasn't the worst at all; it may even have been the best. I summed up its conclusions in my *Harper's* piece as follows:

> First, a paradox—the danger of World War III is receding, but the threat of Soviet imperialism is undiminished. Second, an explanation—Russia's new rulers have changed their tactics, not their objectives; they are likely to wage the cold war more subtly, with economic and emotional lures designed to divide the free world. Third, an observation—confidence in American leadership has declined as America has seemed to lose confidence in itself; McCarthyism and vacillation in Washington have badly damaged our prestige. Fourth, a warning—mutual misunderstanding between us and our allies is our greatest handicap in meeting the Soviet challenge to us all.

We said good-by outside our London hotel. Stevenson was on his way to call on Arnold Toynbee, and I was headed for the airport. He wondered aloud whether we should "do Africa next year." Surely he was kidding, I thought, but he wasn't.

Sim and I took a leave of absence from *Look* and went off to Mallorca with the children. A note from Stevenson in October asked me to "tell my beloved Sim I haven't had a proper lunch since we left Versailles, or an equivalent hostess!" Later in the winter he wrote, "My life is distracted, as always, and I am now in the throes of trying to contrive some lectures to give at Harvard about International Affairs and I almost wish I had never taken that damn trip. All the same, as the first of March approaches I would be quite willing to start again. But don't worry, there will be no hurry calls for Attwood for the present."

A call finally did come about six years later, but that belongs in another chapter.

Chapter 7

A Change in the Weather

W**E LIVED FOR THREE MONTHS** that fall in a rented house facing a sandy cove on Mallorca's rocky, windswept northern coast. As a mailing address we used a small hotel nearby that had an erratic telephone and a potholed tennis court. Aside from some shepherds and fishermen, the only other residents of Cala San Vicente were two American families and a mysterious German, probably a Nazi fugitive, who lived behind locked iron gates and occasionally ventured out for solitary walks wearing a cape and accompanied by a savage-looking Doberman.

One of the American families was headed by a serious young drinker, like a character in a Fitzgerald novel. The other Americans were Charlie Thayer, a retired Foreign Service officer now writing a book; his second wife, Cynthia, whose father was ambassador to Spain, and their two children. Charlie, though still in his thirties, had had a distinguished career but was now yet another casualty of the Eisenhower-Dulles policy of appeasing McCarthy. Thayer had resigned rather than jeopardize the appointment of his brother-in-law, Chip Bohlen, as ambassador to the Soviet Union. Charlie's offense, which McCarthy would have exploited as an example of moral turpitude, was that he had once lived with a young woman out of wedlock while stationed in Asia. (The fact that he later married her would be irrelevant, he was told.) And so a talented American diplomat and linguist now vegetated in Cala San Vicente.

I vegetated too, but on a temporary basis. I read books about pre–cold war subjects that Joe Barnes, my former boss and now a publisher, sent me regularly for their therapeutic effect. Sim and I swam, got reacquainted with our two small children and took siestas and Spanish lessons. But by year's end we were ready to return to the world. I drove our two poodles back to Paris, speeding up the dusty, winding Costa Brava roads to the border so as to reach a French hotel before nightfall. For in France, the dog is king, welcomed everywhere (except, strangely, in post offices), while in Spain the dog is decidedly non grata, especially in hotels. That is why French dogs strut and Spanish dogs skulk.

Sim flew up with the kids a few days later and found me stoking the rank and belching coal furnace of the rented farmhouse that in September had seemed so quaint and convenient and now so icy and decrepit as France's chilliest postwar winter got under way.

Not much had happened in the glacial cold war soap opera except some sparring over Germany's future and a debate among the Western allies about a four-power conference with the Russians in January. Churchill, who had had a stroke in June, was pressing for summit talks with the new Soviet leadership in which he hoped to crown his career by playing a leading role. Dulles was opposed, and Ike deferred to him. But a foreign ministers' meeting in January was approved.

Life in the *Look* building on Madison Avenue had been far more eventful. Mike Cowles, who disliked firing people face to face, went off on a European trip in January leaving dismissal letters behind on the desks of the editorial director, executive editor and managing editor. (One of the two assistant managing editors, sniffing trouble, had already quit, leaving the other, Bill Arthur, and me as the only people on the masthead besides Cowles himself with the word "editor" in our titles.)

But Mike had persuaded Dan Mich, one of the outstanding magazine editors of our generation, to return to *Look* after three years of running *McCall's*. So I went back to New York to meet him. We hit it off immediately. There was warmth and humor behind his reserve. As I would find out, he was often tough but always fair. Clearly, the magazine was his life, and he ran it with his favorite dictum always in mind: "Nothing we have done in the past will ever be good enough again." He expected us to do the very best work of which we were capable, and, knowing this, we did. He cared deeply about the art of writing clean, uncluttered sentences. He used to say that "mass communications boils down, as conversation does, to one individual talking to another." And that became the *Look* style.

With Dan as editor, there would be no more weasel words about the McCarthys of our society. "The hottest places in hell," he used to say, "are reserved for those who, in times of moral crisis, maintain their neutrality." He was a traditional midwestern liberal whose hero was FDR and whose only abiding interests centered around his magazine, his wife, his dog, jazz and baseball. Dan knew what he wanted but would listen to a strong contrary view and even change his mind if you made a convincing case. He was, in short, the best boss I ever had.

At our first meeting, he urged me to look for good stories in Europe —good not just because of some European angle, but intrinsically good —the kind that would attract readers whatever the locale. For me, this meant that Vienna's crimson shadows were finally fading away and that I'd be writing about more than just the cold war. With the demonic Stalin finally dead and buried and an armistice in Korea, horror stories about the Red Menace were getting stale, except in the *Reader's Digest.* A lull in the cold war seemed to be tacitly in effect; diplomats still convened and jousted, but my assignments in 1954, the last full year I'd be spending in Europe, began to reflect the relatively relaxed mood prevailing in America—a mood I'd be observing at first hand on a cross-country tour a year later.

When I came home to our frigid farmhouse on the outskirts of Paris, Sim had installed bigger porcelain stoves, and the yard was full of coal for me to stoke every morning. So I was glad my first assignment was in Rome, to do a profile of Clare Boothe Luce, then winding up her first year as U.S. ambassador to Italy. It had become the most politically unstable country in Western Europe, with the Communists and their allies holding 30 percent of the seats in parliament.

Meanwhile, the Big Four foreign ministers, who met in Berlin in January and February, managed to reach agreement only on holding another meeting, this time including Red China, in Geneva in April to talk about Indochina and Korea. Eisenhower, alarmed by the explosion of a Soviet hydrogen bomb, had floated his "atoms for peace" proposal —a good propaganda move but a non-starter—while Dulles managed to upset Europeans in December with threats of "an agonizing reappraisal" of American policy if our allies rejected the European Defense Community "European Army" idea (which they eventually did).

Before leaving for Italy, I heard from Cowles that the Russians had invited Mrs. Eleanor Roosevelt to visit the Soviet Union in the summer and that she'd asked to take me along (I gather at Stevenson's recommendation), in addition to her secretary, to help write some articles for *Look.* So a visa application had been submitted for me. It would be a short trip, nothing like our 1953 ordeal, and I looked forward to it.

I found Mrs. Luce reluctant to cooperate, suspecting a hatchet job since she and Fleur Cowles were not the warmest of friends. So it took some cajolery to persuade her my story would be a fair one. And I think it was. "Her voice," I wrote, "is soft but commanding, her manner serene but vibrant. She answers questions quickly, vividly and guardedly. She strikes you as fragile on the outside and flinty on the inside. She smokes almost incessantly. Her nervous tension is contagious; you don't relax easily with her." And I really faulted her only for not having heeded Talleyrand's precept (which was framed on her desk): "And above all, not too much zeal."

But face it, you could not reasonably expect a woman as highly strung as the "Ambass," as she referred to herself, to be nonchalant in the only Western European country where Communist strength seemed to be growing rather than waning—a phenomenon attributable to the do-nothing Christian Democrats, but for which she felt somehow responsible. In point of fact, while Italy had become the last East-West battleground in Europe, the causes of Communist vitality were endemic poverty, the absence of a strong socialist opposition, traditional anticlericalism and the "reasonable" line taken by Communist Party leaders, whose aim, as Mrs. Luce herself recognized, was no longer to take over Italy but to neutralize it as a NATO ally.

The subtitle on my article, when it appeared, alluded to the perennial Communist angle: "Clare Boothe Luce defeats a prejudice against women, and fights to keep Italy anti-Communist." Slaying the Red dragon was no longer the main event, but it still sold some tickets.

Fleur said she liked the piece well enough, but Clare expressed her opinion more obliquely.

"Bet?" she asked me in Rome a few months after it had been published.

"Bet what?"

"That you'll be working for *Life* inside of two years."

I should have taken the bet and made it a big one. I liked *Look*'s easy informality too much to swap it for the pressure-cooker extravagance of what was called the Big Red One. But I was caught off balance by her accolade, as she knew I would be.

My best memories of the Luce assignment were the prolonged nightcaps in the Hotel Excelsior bar with the Humphrey Bogarts. I'd met them through Stevenson, for whom they'd helped raise money in 1952, and we quickly became friends. Bogey had an affectionate sort of respect for writers, and I liked actors who took their craft seriously, as he did. And Betty was just plain extraordinary. Bogey, who was in Italy doing a film with Robert Morley, would preside like an unpredictable and uncensored master of ceremonies over the entire bar scene: no one escaped his attention. Whenever my friend Jerry Goodman ("I Crashed Stalin's Party"), now a Rhodes Scholar on holiday, came into the bar, Bogey would raspingly announce, "Everybody quiet! Our intellectual associate has arrived! Okay, Goodman, say something intelligent, for Chrissake, but don't make it too long."

Betty would get us out of there and to bed sooner or, sometimes, later. They were among the evenings I still like to remember after more than thirty years. There would be other Bogart episodes—with Sim in Paris and in Beverly Hills—but none as high-spirited as the Excelsior follies.

Unlike Italy, communism in France was continuing to lose steam: nearly two-thirds of the Party membership had quit since 1946. Their still sizable vote was clearly more of a protest against living conditions than an expression of faith in Marxism or loyalty to the Kremlin. Yet visiting Americans in Paris never failed to ask me about the "Communist threat". So I decided that the best way to explain the situation was by means of a picture story on a French family who voted Communist. The advantage of the picture story technique, which was perfected by *Look,* was that strong and arresting photographs would induce a casual page turner to stop and read the words that accompanied them. Photojournalism was in fact a blend of text and photographs that flowed together and reinforced each other. It was a far more creative, challenging and effective way of telling a story than was the customary article illustrated by photographs gleaned from the files or bought from an agency. And I think it told a sharper story than today's television documentaries, where the narrative is often dominated and even distorted by the most dramatic film footage. A picture story also required intimate collaboration between writer and photographer, something not always easy to achieve. The writer, usually called producer, was supposed to be in charge, but collaboration was always smoother if no specific instructions had to be given.

This was one reason I was pleased to be working on this Communist story with Kryn Taconis, a Dutch photographer from Bob Capa's Magnum team with whom I'd been on assignment before. I was pleased also to be doing a story that explained something to our readers—that might even educate them—in contrast to the spine-tingling reports of Red Terror that had been the staple of magazine reporting from abroad for more than seven years. Having put the horns and forked tail on the Communists, we now had the obligation to pose and answer questions about their continuing appeal to nice folks like Pierre and Yvonne Gueguen.

Pierre worked on the assembly line of a tractor plant in a dingy factory suburb of Paris called St.-Ouen—only ten minutes by subway from the Ritz bar yet part of another world. Few Americans had ever seen St.-Ouen, except possibly from the window of a car or train headed for Belgium or the channel ports. It was no tourist Mecca but definitely a stronghold of the Communist Party, which regularly polled 60 percent of the vote.

The Gueguens, who had three kids, had lived here two years in a cramped apartment without bathroom or sitting room; previously they'd all been in a hotel room without heat or running water. Pierre bicycled to his factory where he earned about $130 a month, including overtime for a sixty-hour week. Yvonne walked a mile a day to market. There was no money left over, so they never ate out or saw a movie. Sundays they took the kids for a walk in the park.

Their dreams were modest: a cleaner, newer apartment with a bathroom, a small savings account and maybe a car in the distant future.

But after fighting in the Resistance during the war—and killing a German who'd tried to rape Yvonne—Pierre saw former collaborators living it up while he, at thirty-six, had only about ten years of hard labor ahead of him before his muscles and his value to the tractor company were used up. He belonged to a union whose Communist leadership seemed more interested in confrontation than negotiation. No wonder he was bitter: "There's something rotten about the people who run this country," he told me. "I'm not pro-Soviet or anti-American, I'm just fed up. So I vote Communist just to scare the fat cats."

We ended our week with the Gueguens by inviting them for lunch at our old rented farmhouse, which they found palatial and where he confided, after two brandies, that knowing Sim and me had made it impossible for him ever to vote Communist again. I don't know how many *Look* readers we enlightened but at least we made a convert. I ended my piece with this paragraph:

> There are a lesson and a warning in this story. The side that will win the long cold war in the years ahead is not necessarily the side that builds the biggest H-bomb; it's the side that conquers the heart and mind of this one Frenchman and millions like him all over the world.

For a change of pace, and in keeping with Dan Mich's admonition to look for good stories regardless of any East-West angles, Sim and I drove up to Finland, where I remembered once seeing a game of *pesäpallo*—a Finnish adaptation of baseball that had become one of the nation's most popular sports, with more than two thousand teams organized into leagues. My visa to accompany Mrs. Roosevelt to Russia had still not materialized, and a drive through the flowering April landscape of Germany, Denmark and Sweden, and over to Finland by ferry, seemed like the kind of work you feel almost guilty getting paid for.

There is no room in a book of this length to describe all of the finer points of *pesäpallo*, which was introduced in Finland in 1919 by a returning emigrant from the United States. But I can suggest its esotericism by stating that the pitcher (who doubles as catcher) stands across the plate from the batter, who scores by proceeding first to the vicinity of our third base, then to our first, then past the "longstop" to a base located not far from our shortstop and finally around a pole that guides him to home plate. He must take care not to hit a home run, which "kills" him (puts him out), but a pop fly, which only "wounds" him, is not a problem unless he runs on it.

Those are just the bare bones. It made a nice picture story, better than the one we tried to do about saunas (then a rarity in America) because our pert Finnish model could not help revealing more of her anatomy than a family magazine could publish in 1954.

And of course, with the iron curtain so close by, routine reference to the "other side" could not go unmentioned on our trip. My pretext was that Helsinki (and Kabul) were then the only cities outside the Communist club of countries served by Aeroflot, the Soviet airline. So Kryn Taconis, who had joined us, and I met the planes, hoping to find some disembarking passenger (such as a pioneer American tourist) who might make a story for us. But the only Americans were a couple of furtive cheese salesmen and a delegation of astronomers. I did run into a Dane who'd seen commercial jets parked in Moscow's airport, and a group of angry Chinese who objected to photographs, shouting, "You are not in New York now!" (To which I replied, "And you're not in Peking.")

Back in Paris, I found no visas at the Soviet Embassy and was advised to see a Mr. Leonid Ilyichev, the press chief of their Foreign Ministry, who was just then attending the Geneva conference on Indochina and Korea. I could sense the familiar runaround, but Ilyichev, if I could find him, might at least have an explanation. I cornered him at a press conference, but he was no help. "Delays are not uncommon," he said evasively. "Why should there be a problem?"

Why indeed? Did they think the former *Collier's* warmonger would have a baneful influence on Mrs. Roosevelt? Not likely. A similar visa request by her for Whitman Bassow, a Russian-speaking writer, was also in limbo. And so, just hours before her scheduled departure from New York a few weeks later, she held a press conference in the *Look* offices to say she was canceling her trip. "It would be very foolish," she said, "to make the trip without the help of either a trained journalist or one who understands Russian." She did not want to be "left to the complete mercy of Soviet interpreters," and suggested the Russians were trying to force her to make the trip "on their terms."

The only explanation given me on subsequent trips to Russia was that "inefficiency" and "uncertainty" were to blame. And it is possible they hadn't yet drawn up a new post-Stalinist directive on visas for American journalists. But knowing her, I doubt she would have been taken in by any Soviet Potemkin villages, as Alexander Solzhenitsyn implied in a fictional passage in *The First Circle.* I also like to think that somebody in the bureaucracy caught hell after Mrs. Roosevelt's announcement. (She finally went to Russia three years later, accompanied by her secretary and her own interpreter, but by then *Look* had a full-time correspondent in Moscow and we didn't ask to send anyone along with her.)

I stayed around Geneva long enough to watch the conference marking time. (Dulles attended for only a week, but managed to cause an international incident by refusing to shake hands with the Chinese foreign minister, Chou En-lai.) Dien Bien Phu had fallen on May 7, and the French now wanted to turn the war over to the British or the Americans and get out. In London, Anthony Eden turned them down, while Eisenhower overrode Admiral Arthur Radford, Vice President Richard Nixon and Dulles—who favored U.S. military intervention—and decided against our getting involved "in a succession of Asian wars" whose result would be "to drain off our resources and to weaken our overall defensive position." Ike had also taken note of a mid-June poll that showed 64 percent of the American people were opposed to "getting involved in fighting in Indochina." (Financially, we were already involved by 1954 to the tune of $784 million in military aid to the French.)

The conference picked up speed after Mendès-France was chosen France's premier on June 13; a month later, agreement was reached by the participants—France, the U.S., Russia, China, the U.K. and the various Indochinese states and factions—on the withdrawal of foreign troops, a demarcation line at the 17th parallel and general elections in both parts of Vietnam in July 1956. Only the South Vietnamese raised objections, fearing the Viet Minh would prevail in free elections by claiming to be the only true nationalists. But for the moment, Indochina enjoyed a respite from war, a respite that could have come a lot sooner. Back in March 1947, when I covered the war from Paris by translating the Agence France Press news ticker, I reported a broadcast issued in the name of Ho Chi Minh calling for the end of "useless hostilities" and proposing "independence only within the framework of a French federation." The French response was to launch an offensive west of Hanoi. "The operation," I wrote, "aimed at mopping up a large area, was reported this evening to be developing favorably."

Now, more than seven years later, France had settled on less desirable terms after losing 92,000 men of their expeditionary force, 19,000 of them French. But at least they were climbing out of the quagmire; we were just preparing to wade in.

Mike and Fleur Cowles came to Paris in August, and we agree I'd go home in December to become national affairs editor. It was time. I'd lived more than eight of the last nine years abroad, and Sim almost as many, and we both were tiring of the expatriate life. When you weren't explaining to visiting Americans why Europe wasn't headed for perdition, you were reassuring Europeans that America wasn't going fascist. And you were always a stranger, a transient, a renter of houses that were never homes. We had bought some land in Connecticut and were ready to build on it. Our kids would soon need to feel they belonged somewhere. There would still be plenty of travel in our future, but we'd have a base to come home to.

I accompanied Mike to London, where the big political news was how to get Churchill to step down. He had periods of amnesia since his stroke and was sometimes under the impression it was 1938. This had happened a few weeks before when Lord Rothermere came to Chartwell and was mistaken for his father by Churchill, who had moved back in time and began speculating how to bring the U.S. into the coming war with Hitler. It was a difficult evening, but fortunately the old man was back in the present the next morning. However, he refused to set a date for his retirement, in part because he nursed the hope of meeting Malenkov and settling the cold war for good. What he didn't realize, according to our British friends, was that Malenkov was no Stalin and left foreign policy affairs pretty much to Molotov, Andrei Gromyko and Nikita Khrushchev.

The British also expressed annoyance with what they called Eisenhower's vacillating foreign policy, Dulles's obstinacy about China and a spate of statements out of Washington blaming Britain for not backing us up in Indochina (when everybody knew Congress would not have approved direct U.S. intervention). All this grumbling about America, plus what I'd been hearing on the Continent, induced me to write a piece called "Are We Losing Our Allies?" that warned of the widening rift between Europe and the United States. (The EDC, one of our cherished projects, had just been rejected at an allied conference in Brussels and then defeated in the French National Assembly.) Cowles liked the piece, but it kept getting crowded out of each issue by less prosy features and never did get printed. In retrospect, I'm glad it wasn't, for I was mistaking Europe's growing and healthy self-assertiveness and independence vis-à-vis Washington for deeper discord. The time when the United States was omnipotent because of its economic and military might in the immediate postwar years was over. We could still give orders, but they would no longer be automatically obeyed. It was evidence the Marshall Plan had succeeded.

Germany was a good example of this changed relationship, and in October I reported on it from Düsseldorf in a story called "What's Behind the German Comeback?" The answer, of course, was individual initiative and "a passion for hard work and discipline unmatched in Europe." To illustrate it, Kryn Taconis and I used the same picture story technique as we had with the French Communist family; only this time the subject was a small businessman named Carl Gisbert Siebel, down and out in 1946 and now the owner of a factory making injection molding machines. He employed 150 workers, drove a Mercedes and had no time for hobbies. Like most Germans, he suspected the British, considered the French "unstable," loathed the Russians and accepted German rearmament without enthusiasm because less manpower would be available for industry. And like most Germans of his generation, he had supported the Nazis but later blamed Hitler for waging a losing war.

Kryn, who had risked his life in the Dutch underground during the war, did his usual professional job but didn't enjoy the assignment; nor did Siebel warm to Kryn upon learning he'd been in Holland under the Nazi occupation.

But remembering the Germany I'd seen in 1946, I could understand Siebel's point of view and even admire the way he articulated it: "I can tell you that our attitude about work is what saved us after the war. Hard work was a condition of survival then. We had no homes to sit around in. There were no luxuries to buy and our money was worthless anyway. We didn't even have politics to distract us—nothing. It was a question of pride too. Nobody thought we could rebuild Germany. But we did. We're selling our goods all over the world and beating out people who thought we'd be down and out for generations. Sure, we've worked too hard. But it's made us proud to be Germans again."

Another Germany-based picture story I produced that fall (with *Look* photographer Jim Hansen) dealt with a camp near Hamburg where some of the remaining displaced persons were languishing in Spartan conditions—unwilling to go back to Russia or Eastern Europe and unable to go to the U.S. because of bureaucratic obstacles like the McCarran Act, which had been enacted in 1949 over Truman's veto, or health problems, like tuberculosis. We called the story "Our Iron Curtain Is Turning Friends into Enemies"—which was true enough, but who cared about a handful of refugees? Only the CIA, which got a few out who were willing to be recruited and who might prove to be useful.

By 1954, the CIA had become exceedingly active all over Europe (as well as in Latin America, where in July it had managed the overthrow of the Arbenz government in Guatemala). In London in August, I had dinner with Turner Catledge, the managing editor of the *New York Times,* who told me the CIA station chief in New York had called him during the Guatemalan caper to say that two agents posing as *Times* reporters would be calling on a certain Latin American diplomat and asked him to be sure to back them up if challenged. Catledge was so furious he said he'd call the diplomat and warn him any *Times* reporters calling on him would be impostors. In Europe, he'd discovered what many of us knew and deplored—that the Agency had its people posing as correspondents in several countries, notably Germany; that its agents were often spying on each other as well as on agents of other U.S. security services; and that their activities were often ludicrous—such as questioning the German cook of our high commissioner, James B. Conant, about his guests, eating habits and bedtime.

As I wrote Bill Blair in August, "The creeping police state has crept farther than many people realize." And this at a time when the combination of television and boredom was finally discrediting Joseph

McCarthy, the man who had done so much to fan this conspirational mentality. After Dulles yielded once again to the know-nothing vigilantes and dismissed John Paton Davies, General Bedell Smith angrily spoke out against "the Sovietization of our Foreign Service." Its effects are evident even today.

My last long trip before coming home was to interview Nehru in New Delhi. As I wrote in the opening paragraph, "The most significant thing about my visit with Jawaharlal Nehru is that I have met no one who thinks it strange that an American reporter should travel more than 10,000 miles just to ask a few questions of a 64-year-old Indian who was in jail less than ten years ago."

This was a measure of the man's prestige in the world, even though Dulles, along with a good many American politicians, regarded him as an unreliable and possibly two-faced "neutralist."

I invited Sim along as a note taker as well as companion, and we stayed at a now vanished relic of British colonial days—the Hotel Cecil in Old Delhi. Gallons of tea were served daily to old ladies in wicker chairs on the verandah, while an army of turbaned servants crouched and swept all day with their traditional back-breaking short-handled brooms.

Why Sim's pad and pencil and not a tape recorder? For one thing, recorders were almost as bulky as suitcases in those days, and I never used them for interviews—not even later when they were miniaturized. I've noticed that people don't talk as spontaneously when they see a recorder on the table and know their words are being captured verbatim on tape. Instead, I write out the questions I most want answered in a notebook and then get a conversation started. With a little prompting, the answers emerge from the dialogue. I also jot down certain turns of phrase and expressions of anger, humor and emphasis. The interview I then type up is briefer, blunter and more colloquial than anything transcribed from a tape, which is always repetitious. I let my subjects check it out for accuracy, and they've never failed to approve the finished product, sometimes adding a little helpful editing and generally pleased by how clear, grammatical and forceful they sounded. It's worked with Nasser, Ben-Gurion, Prince Sihanouk, Indira Gandhi and Aneurin Bevan, among others, but the first time I tried the technique was with Nehru. Since he'd recently been castigated by *Time,* he wasn't keen on doing this interview and agreed to give me forty-five minutes only because we'd met the year before with Stevenson. So I felt better having Sim there to backstop me while I provoked him into talking.

We were summoned to his office at 7 P.M.—he had a dinner engagement at eight—and he arrived ten minutes late from parliament. I knew I would have to arouse his interest immediately or our ten-thousand-mile journey could barely be justified on the expense account.

So I decided to stir him up by citing the *Time* piece, and then said I hadn't come this far to make polite conversation and so my questions would be blunt; but I suggested that his answers, if equally frank, might dispel some of the misconceptions prevalent in America.

For a moment, the only sound was the whirring of the electric fan overhead. Then Nehru nodded and smiled as if to say, "All right, go ahead."

Now, more than thirty years later, what he had to say makes as much sense as it did then, so I think his responses to my questions are worth excerpting here in some detail. For if more of the superpower statesmen of the time (and of the decades since) had had Nehru's clarity of vision, the cold war might by now already be a memory. But the statesmen were too engaged in the contest to observe it with his detachment.

My first question was: Many Americans feel you are pro-Communist. How would you answer this criticism?

What follows are excerpts of his replies to this and a score of other questions:

> This sort of question strikes me as an example of thinking in clichés. I would answer it with another question: What do you mean by Communist? . . . Take the conflict which divides the world today. I don't agree that it is essentially ideological. I regard it rather as a power conflict in which communism is used as a tool by one side and a target by the other. In any case, however you define the word, the people who feel I am "pro-Communist" are quite wrong. . . .
>
> The basic aim of any policy today should be to prevent war, for war would be disastrous beyond measure. It would not lead to the attainment of any objective; we have reached a stage where war—even for the victor—holds no advantages. . . . During the Munich crisis, I happened to be in Europe and in the heart of it emotionally. I was very much opposed to the Chamberlain policy because it seemed obvious Hitler could not be stopped that way. But conditions are different today. Among other things, war has become an outrageous proposition in the nuclear age. I think this is appreciated by both sides. . . .
>
> Why should America *not* recognize China? Apart from liking or not liking its present government, how can you ignore its existence? Your

anxiety about the future course of events in Asia does not justify your refusal to face facts today. In fact, not recognizing China may well aggravate your problems in Asia, for it makes communications almost impossible. . . . As to the Korean argument, I don't know all the facts and would hesitate to give a simple moral answer. But I can say this much—that the Chinese had a very real fear of being attacked through Korea. When General MacArthur moved north from the 38th parallel and Syngman Rhee spoke of hitting Manchuria, this fear became a certainty. They reacted as you Americans might react to a Communist army approaching the Rio Grande. . . .

I am convinced that this generation of Chinese statesmen, at least, regards war as undesirable. The only thing that might provoke the Chinese is fear of being attacked themselves. That is why the Indochina settlement will eliminate a dangerous situation and lessen fear. . . . What I would also like to see is an attempt to solve the Formosa problem without warfare. The present situation is fraught with danger. . . .

American aid to India has been very helpful, particularly in developing community projects in our villages and in teaching our peasants the skills they need to produce more and live better. But we are anxious not to weaken the urge to work in India. . . . We have staffed 50,000 villages already, and in seven years, we hope to include all 600,000 villages in India in the scheme. Here is where American technical aid and advice have given us the push we needed. We hope they will continue. . . .

The Communists could only be a threat in India if we relaxed our efforts and did not work to improve social and economic conditions. And we are not relaxing. . . . On the whole, the feeling we have about Americans is one of extreme friendliness. But Americans very often tend to look at things from a particular viewpoint and tend to ignore other views which, depending on circumstances, could be right. . . .

I realize that communism is expansionist, but the Communists only go where they can go easily. Steps must be taken to prevent their creeping in elsewhere, but Tibet, on which they have a legitimate claim, is not a problem. . . . You asked for the basis of Asia's undue suspicion of American actions. Perhaps it's because you have become identified with colonialism, by backing the French in Indochina, and with reaction, by supporting discredited and unpopular figures like Chiang and Rhee and Bao Dai. You might call it guilt by association. . . .

Your biggest mistake was underestimating Asia's nationalistic aspirations. The best—or worst—example was Indochina. As late as two or three years ago, the French could have reached a settlement with Ho

Chi Minh that would have been far more advantageous than the one reached at Geneva. But they continued to fight a hopeless, unpopular colonial war with the aid of American money and equipment. As I said before, this is what made Asians identify you with colonialism. You may say that denouncing colonialism is flogging a dead horse—but people under colonial rule don't feel that way. . . . Waving a club will not work because it will just induce your opponent to pick up his own club. That is what makes me wonder whether an organization like SEATO will not do more harm than good in the long run. . . .

My last question to Nehru was, how did he foresee the end of the so-called cold war?

Every generation feels that its problems are the greatest and the most insoluble in history. The French Revolution seemed like a catastrophe in Europe 150 years ago. In Napoleon's day, people did not see how his power would ever be broken. Think of the Crusades that aroused all of Christendom to recover the holy places and destroy Islam. Well, that subsided, too, and both Islam and the Christian world emerged stronger and more tolerant of each other. Europe's religious wars dominated men's minds and passions in the seventeenth century, but these passed away also and were forgotten. Today, some people feel that there is no way out of this conflict we call the cold war except by an inevitable armed clash. But war has become so destructive that both sides are likely to avoid taking the fateful step. I am more inclined to think that with time, both sides will develop a greater capacity for adjustment. As we get used to living together as neighbors and as the fear of war recedes, both the Soviet nations and the democratic nations will modify their policies. In China and the Soviet Union, the patterns that now seem so rigid may well be altered. The areas of agreement will grow, and the areas of conflict will shrink. And eventually, I think, both sides will see that that there was not so much to fight about as they thought. The cold war will just be a phrase in our history books.

When we left Nehru's office, it was nearly nine thirty, his dinner guests were growing impatient and the aides clustered in the corridor treated us with almost deferential respect; we had arrived by taxi, we left by limousine. And for the next three days, while I wrote up the interview, we received invitations to lunch and dinner from editors, politicians and diplomats I'd met the year before on the Stevenson trip. We were always introduced as the American visitors "who spent more than two hours with the prime minister." Apparently celebrity status was instantly conferred on anyone to whom Nehru granted an audience of more than a few minutes.

The year was drawing to a close. While we packed and prepared to leave our farmhouse, the Algerian war broke out, Khrushchev and Bulganin mended fences in Peking and France agreed to let the United States furnish military assistance directly to Ngo Dinh Diem's government in Saigon. They were now only too pleased to let us take over the mess. While there were still only about three hundred U.S. military personnel in Vietnam, this was more than there had been four years earlier.

And yet in spite of gathering clouds in the distance, in spite of Dulles's occasional references to "massive retaliation" (a euphemism for a nuclear first strike) and the need to "go to the brink" to deter aggression, in spite of the start of the cold war's silliest uproar, over Quemoy and Matsu, there had in fact been a relaxation of the tension that characterized the last years of Stalinism and inevitably accompanied the hot wars in Korea and Indochina.

Nehru's moderate tones did not seem as naive and unrealistic in the West as they would have two years earlier; and it was no longer considered heretical in the Soviet Union to say, as Malenkov had in March, that "given modern methods of warfare, [war] means the destruction of world civilization." (The former view, then still asserted by the Chinese, was that only capitalism would be destroyed by nuclear war.)

And the hysteria of McCarthyism seemed to be subsiding at home. Early in 1955, a letter from my friend Bob Joyce, a Foreign Service officer for more than twenty-five years, ended on a hopeful note: "With the appointment of Loy Henderson as Under Secretary of State for Administration and because of other signs and portents, I have a feeling that some of the abuses and inequities which have developed during the past four or five years are on the road to being corrected."

It was somehow appropriate that the last story I produced in 1954 for *Look* had nothing whatever to do with the cold war. It was a delightfully spontaneous picture essay of two seven-year-olds—a French boy and an American girl—engaged in a classroom flirtation in a school near Paris. When I sent the captions, text blocks and contact prints of "Pierre

Loves Nancy" off to Dan Mich, I added a note: "I'm finally following your advice of last winter about looking for good stories and never mind the geography."

But it was not until we got home and began, in January, a voyage of rediscovery across the United States that Sim and I would fully appreciate the extent of Bob Joyce's "signs and portents" nor the changes that had occurred in American society in the years we'd been away.

Chapter 8

Voices of America, 1955

$\mathbf{W}$E DROVE acrosss the country in a British Austin Healey with red French license plates. We figured it would be a conversation starter in the drive-ins and filling stations along the way.

It was. Several times a day we would have to answer questions from innumerable strangers: How many miles a gallon do you get? How fast will it go? What did it cost you? What did you say those license plates were—French?

We would explain that we'd been living in Europe for several years, doing magazine work, and then we'd wait for the questions that seemed inevitable—questions like, "How are things over there?" or "Does it look like war?" Instead we'd hear, "Well, hurry back and see us," or just, "Take it easy, now."

What had happened to the American jitters that we had heard so much about abroad? . . . And what about the sweeping charge that Americans are imperialistic, always reaching out and meddling in other people's business? Plenty of foreigners think that Americans are watching them all the time, and plenty of American correspondents get to feel that their dispatches are the biggest news on Main Street.

Well, we were on the road a month before anybody on any Main Street asked us a question about world affairs. In the previous ten years, Americans may have invested $62 billion and thousands of lives trying to make the world a better place—but the ones we met seemed more interested in our gas mileage than any news we had of their investment.

So we decided that among the biggest surprises of our trip was the relative lack of fear, of curiosity—and of knowledge—about the world outside America.

Thus began the first installment of a *Look* series I wrote soon after getting home. It was Dan Mich's idea.

"When's the last time you went to the West Coast and back?" he asked me the day I reported for work on Madison Avenue. "And I don't mean on a plane."

"In 1945, on a troop train."

"That doesn't count."

"In 1939, in a Model A Ford. It took me two months."

"Too long ago. There've been some changes. Get your car and move out as soon as you can. If you're going to be national affairs editor, I don't want you learning about America here in New York. First place, you won't learn anything. Second place, most of our readers are out there."

So Sim and the children flew to her mother's in Florida and I drove down to join them, marveling en route at the plush motels, many with TV, that had replaced the shabby "tourist cabins" of my youth. And from there, Sim and I set out on January 7, moseying through the Deep South, zigzagging across Texas, taking a detour to Los Alamos, then bearing due west through Arizona to Los Angeles. From there we drove up to Portland, where we shipped the car back, and returned via Salt Lake City, Denver, Des Moines, Milwaukee, Chicago, Detroit, Cleveland and Boston—renting cars in each city for side trips to smaller towns. We left few stones unturned: farms, factories, campuses, trailer parks, movie studios, legislatures, churches, police stations, service clubs, cattle ranches, casinos, white country clubs and "Negro" hotels. (In 1955 Atlanta, there were no other places where you could take black friends to dinner.) All these and more were the sites of long and candid conversations. We had forgotten how open, hospitable and talkative Americans could be, especially on the far side of the Hudson River.

And how friendly. The trip would have taken months had we accepted all the invitations from virtual strangers to stay for supper, for the night or for the weekend. Even the police were pleasant. In the Mojave Desert, the chilling wail of a siren stopped us ten miles from Barstow, and a couple of California state troopers demanded to know what our strange license plates stood for. We began producing documents—two French registrations, each bearing a different address; my driving license, issued in New York, and Sim's, issued in New Jersey; an AAA card, placing us in Connecticut; and an insurance form, showing us domiciled in Florida, where the children were temporarily quartered. We went on to explain that our furniture was still in Europe and our trunks in Long Island. In fact, we did not actually know where we lived.

The troopers studied all our papers, shook their heads and handed them back. "You folks," said the sergeant with a smile, "are *really* disorganized. But I figure you must be honest to get that messed up. Have a nice trip!" They waved us on.

Soon after we got home, in late March, I asked for a six-week leave of absence to expand my *Look* articles into a book called *Still the Most Exciting Country.* I had a 74,000-word diary to work from, and while not all of it is pertinent to *this* book, American attitudes always have been a major factor influencing the course of the cold war. And so some aspects of this journey, insofar as they reflect the national mood of three decades ago, belong among these recollections. While the book was essentially a reportorial portrait of a period, like Bill Moyers's *Listening to America* in the 1970s, parts of some chapters bear recalling and even repeating in this new context.

The first, called "The Start," explained how we went about the assignment. "The Constants" enumerated what hadn't changed—the weak coffee, the empty spaces, the civic spirit and above all, "the friendliness and the haste." In "The Changes," I mentioned my surprise at counting ninety-three motels on the highway into El Paso (where there are probably 930 today), but identified "mobility, standardization and television— and the changes they have wrought" as being the obvious things striking a returning American. "The Prosperity" explored the new nonchalance about owing money: a cafeteria counterman in Louisiana who told us he had a new car, TV, hi-fi and freezer also said, "But if I had to pay cash I couldn't buy a carton of cigarettes." And women seemed just as acquisitive, which is why I reported that "feminism," which encouraged women to build careers instead of homes, had all but died out (a rather hasty conclusion, as it turned out). "The Youth" was upbeat: "I am not worried about them." No one could then anticipate the misnamed counterculture of the sixties. "The Prejudice" was upbeat too. While segregation in the South was still entrenched by a bigotry rooted in fear, the effect of black votes and purchasing power, plus the Supreme Court's decision on separate schools, had begun to revolutionize white southern attitudes even though major struggles still lay ahead and communication was still tentative. Our talks with blacks (a term then never used) often ended like this:

"We certainly enjoyed meeting you. We don't often get a chance to talk to white people this way."

"Why not?"

"You just don't talk this way to a white man, that's all. You tell them what they expect you to say. You don't disagree with them—never. What's the use? They'll just mark you down as a bad—character."

Later in the year I would be supervising a special issue of *Look* entitled "The South Versus the Supreme Court" and would learn a lot more about injustices I had paid little attention to just a few years before but which now seemed intolerable even to those of us endowed with the dominant skin color.

The chapter called "The Ignorance" was equally disturbing, at least to someone who'd been toiling at the task of enlightening his fellow citizens about the outside world. For example, on February 8, the day Malenkov's ouster was announced in Moscow, we were having breakfast in a roadside café near Phoenix. At the other end of the counter a man wearing a windbreaker was picking his teeth over a cup of coffee. The waitress was smoking a cigarette and mopping the counter. Another man, about twenty-five, came in, sat down and ordered a Coke.

"Didja hear the news? They got rid of that guy—what's his name? —Molotov."

"Who's that?"

"The Russian guy. A big shot. He got the ax."

"Whaddaya know? It ain't here in the paper."

"I just heard it on the radio."

The waitress came over and glanced at the paper. "I see where they caught the fella that set fire to that house on East McDowell."

"Yeah, how about that!"

(End of discussion of world politics.)

Three days before, when we were in New Mexico, Mendès-France also fell from power after a no-confidence vote in the National Assembly. I never learned about it; at least it's not in my diary. What is in my diary for that day are the following reflections on the world scene as depicted in U.S. newspapers (TV and radio news then consisted of little more than brief announcements):

> If all my information came from the local press beyond the eastern seaboard, I would think of our allies as flabby, unreliable and irresponsible; some of them, like the French and Italians, no better than the Communists who have infiltrated their governments. Asia, except for

Chiang Kai-shek and Syngman Rhee, would appear as a mysterious and somewhat hostile area dominated by soft-headed double-talkers like Nehru. I'd also be convinced Americans have a monopoly of the old-fashioned virtues and wisdom, the proof being that we live better than anybody else and never lose wars (except in Korea, because Truman was taking orders from the U.N.); that the Russians are the same as the Nazis, only worse, and they usually outfox us; that our only hope lies in our atomic strength and our military bases; that foreign aid was a blunder since no one appreciates it abroad, and that we're lucky Ike's in the White House because he knows what to do.

As for the editorials and columnists, their constant theme was, let's be tough and ready to fight because that's the only language the Russians understand. We found little or no awareness that large areas of the world were in a state of revolutionary ferment over which we had no control. There was no suggestion that military containment alone was not a sufficient policy, nor that we might profitably listen to advice from our friends. The wonder to me was that people had retained as much balance and common sense as they seemed to. Indifference was probably the reason. I was reminded of Artemus Ward's remark, "I'd rather be ignorant than know what ain't so," and decided that the nation might ironically be well served by two phrases we heard over and over: "It's all too complicated for me," and "Ike knows best—after all, he got us out of Korea."

A crisis was percolating in the Far East during the week we were crossing Texas. On January 29, Eisenhower signed a congressional resolution empowering him to use armed force if necessary to defend Formosa and the Pescadores. Quemoy and Matsu were not included unless invaded as a prelude to an attack on Formosa, although Dulles had previously stated that with their capture, the Chinese Communists would "begin their objective of driving us out of the Western Pacific, right back to Hawaii, and even to the United States!"

Nevertheless on January 31, at the height of the crisis, the San Antonio *Express*'s front-page "Top of the News" column led off with: "J.H. Ludlow wants to open an auto agency on the S.W. corner of San Pedro and Santa Monica."

By February 3, I noted that I had not yet found anything in the papers about foreign reaction to the Formosa flap, as if it made no difference what friends or foes thought of it, or us or what we did.

Before we got home in March, Nikolai Bulganin was elected premier by the Supreme Soviet and stressed Sino-Soviet ties, the SEATO Pact went into effect, Israeli forces staged a bloody reprisal raid on Egyptian border posts and Lester Pearson, Canada's prime minister, announced that our old friend and neighbor we always took for granted would not get involved in any conflict over the Chinese offshore islands.

None of this appeared on any front pages we saw, and the first question we were asked about Europe was in Mississippi, where a black service station attendant wanted to know if there was segregation in France. So we started trying to provoke people into talking about the outside world. Sometimes they would listen politely and then change the subject. ("People don't like to talk about things they don't know much about," explained Pat Morin, a Paris AP veteran we ran into in Arizona.)

A few did respond. In Atlanta: "There's a lot less war talk than six months ago . . . People feel things are going to work out all right." (Same observation in Louisiana.) In Austin: "Nobody mentions Joe McCarthy anymore. Television finished him." (Actually just three people mentioned his name in the course of our trip, only one—a Las Vegas press agent—favorably.) In Portland: "An Austrian Peace Treaty? I don't know anything about that. You say you've been to Austria? Did you see many kangaroos?" In Birmingham: "I guess we've got to stick by this fellow Chiang, but I don't really trust him." In Santa Barbara: "The A-bomb? People used to talk about it but not anymore. You can't worry all the time about things you can't do anything about. . . ."

The next chapter, which I called "The Jitters," contained one sentence that summed up our findings: "If the jitters exist, they are harder to find than uranium in your backyard." The things most people worried about were quite personal, such as marital disputes, or quite regional: job security in New England, drought in the plains states, desegregation in the South. Almost every community we visited seemed to have a nucleus of citizens concerned with world affairs, but they were usually a small and exclusive coterie—like chess buffs or balletomanes. I concluded they must have been the only readers of the thousands of words I'd labored over so diligently during those years abroad with *Look*.

One symbol of the Red jitters of the early cold war was the McCarran Act, passed over Truman's veto in 1949. Its intent was to make it harder for spies and other undesirables to gain entry to the United States. Visa applicants were suddenly confronted with prying questionnaires and bureaucratic obstacles. All it accomplished was to make it seem we had something to hide behind an iron curtain as impenetrable as Russia's, since no spy with a grain of sense would fill out an honest visa application listing his place of employment as the KGB, Moscow. (Oddly enough, most Americans we talked to on our trip were surprised to hear that any foreigner needed a visa to come over here and admire the land of the free.)

In Los Angeles, I decided to test my hunch about the McCarran Act by driving into Mexico for a couple of days. Coming back in our conspicuous foreign car, we were stopped at the U.S. border outside Tijuana.

"Where were you folks born?"

"Englewood, New Jersey," said Sim.

"Paris, France," I replied.

"Naturalized?"

"No," I said. "Derivative."

He waved us on.

In El Paso, coming across the bridge from Ciudad Juarez, in Mexico, they didn't even ask for your birthplace, just your nationality. And so any spy, or even a left-leaning Latin American poet, could (and I guess still can) avoid the whole visa hassle by simply learning to pronounce the word "American" like an American when confronted by an immigration officer.

While the jitters we'd anticipated weren't evident, we did detect a sense of disquiet even among people who professed to be carefree. Psychiatrists told us they'd never been so busy and that sleeping pill prescriptions were way up. (Tranquilizers were just coming on the market.) Both the rat race and the arms race had something to do with the tensions people didn't always reveal to strangers—except late at night after a few drinks. But we grew to feel that The Bomb was squatting in people's subconscious minds. This was one reason we decided to make a side trip from Albuquerque up to Los Alamos, the isolated community where scientists worked secretly through World War II to produce the device that wiped out two Japanese cities and changed the world forever.

They called it the Hill—seventy-five square miles of jagged mesa accessible only by air or by a road that wound through forested mountains. Coming in to the airstrip, we could see a town that looked like a hundred other suburban communities with its ranch-type homes, shopping centers, schools and churches. What made it different were the scores of almost windowless buildings from where husbands came home at night unable to talk about what happened at the office, because just about everything connected with the office was top secret. Many of the kids on the playgrounds wore T-shirts stenciled LOS ALAMOS—THE ATOMIC CITY, and some born here during the war, when Los Alamos was so secret its designation was just a postal address, were registered on their birth certificates as having been born in P.O. Box 1663—which came to be known as the biggest box in the world.

The director of the Laboratory was Dr. Norris E. Bradbury, who met us at the Guest Lodge, since his own office was out of bounds to us. I told him the purpose of our trip and said we had some questions about the mysterious nuclear age in which we were now destined to live. "Go ahead—shoot," he said, and for the next half hour he didn't waste a word or duck a question.

Here is a distillation of his answers, and I find it hard to believe they are now more than thirty years old:

> War has become much more unlikely. There may be brush fires, as in Korea, but I think we have seen our last big war. . . . There is no danger to mankind from further tests—not in the way they are being conducted. We wouldn't be making the tests if we thought there was. But the problem of fallout in a major war in which large numbers of nuclear weapons were used would be something else. That is why I said a major war was becoming more unlikely as the weapons are perfected. . . . My guess is that we have a lead over the Russians in these weapons, but it's only a guess. . . . I understand the Russians may have more efficient ways of delivering the bombs than we do. If that's the case, our lead isn't so very important. . . . I think the public should be told as much as possible about this subject—about things that will affect them and they can act on. But I don't see any purpose in releasing technical information. . . . Our security procedures aren't perfect, but people *are* being cleared in substantial numbers, and we are not short of the scientists we need. . . . International inspection, as frequently proposed by our government, would probably be workable—if inspection teams had complete access to all nations. . . . Manufacturing a nuclear device is still too expensive an undertaking for the smaller nations. Even the British effort was chiefly a prestige operation. I doubt if any other attempts will be made. . . . Scientists who work here have no moral qualms about what they are doing. They wouldn't be here if they had.

Bradbury was wrong, as it turned out, about nuclear proliferation and the risks of atmospheric tests, but right about his fellow scientists. That evening, with the help of Dr. David Hill, a youthful physicist, we invited eight of them and their wives to dinner at the Lodge. Most were in their late thirties or early forties, and they enjoyed talking. We didn't break up until after midnight, by which time I had filled pages of mostly legible notes. None of our guests, as Bradbury had said, admitted to having any misgivings about producing weapons that would conceivably destroy civilization and even life on our planet. They were convinced that America's stockpile of atomic bombs had been the biggest factor in preventing Soviet aggression so far and that continuing research was the best insurance against aggression in the future. Some thought the weapons designed and produced here were the most important aspect of their work; others disagreed, saying that the main thing was "advancing the frontiers of knowledge." (But even the weapons enthusiasts regarded the building of the bombs as a necessary prelude to the building of a brighter future—with clean and unlimited fuel for all mankind.) And all agreed with the physicist who said, "American scientists aren't hired hands who'll work for any master, like those Nazi V-2 guys. If we didn't have confidence in the men making the political and military decisions in Washington, we would quit tomorrow."

These men and women of Los Alamos struck us as being more relaxed, more optimistic—you might even say happier—than most of the Americans we had been talking to on this trip. (And, in retrospect, somewhat naive.) They did not share the nagging anxiety that hovered over some people on the outside; their work had a kind of purpose and direction that gave meaning to their lives.

"The fact that war is becoming obsolete will sink into everyone's consciousness—in time," said one of our guests. "War has been part of human experience for so long that you can't expect people to revise their thinking overnight, or even in a decade. I suppose we could hasten the process by holding tests off the New Jersey coast, where everybody could see what these bombs can do, but who knows—maybe they'd be back the next day wanting a bigger bang and more fireworks."

Late—late for Los Alamos, where the only public bar closed at eight-thirty—we all agreed the people who needed to be impressed with the futility of nuclear war were the Soviet leaders. The scientists were hopeful the Russians had drawn this conclusion from their own experiments.

When I asked them whether they could foresee the day when they would be able to sit down and talk with Soviet scientists and compare notes—talk shop, as it were—I could tell it was something they all looked forward to; everyone began talking at once, forming questions, speculating about how the Russians had surmounted this or that obstacle. And the conversation became too technical for Sim and me. All we could gather was that the Hiroshima explosion had given the Russians the big clue they needed, that publication of the Smyth report may have saved them some time and that Klaus Fuchs may have saved them more—if they trusted him.

But it was clear they all looked forward to the day when scientists could join statesmen at the conference tables.

Finally, as we were about to break up, I brought up a question I'd been posing to people all over the country. I asked them what they were most concerned about.

This evening I got different answers from those we'd been hearing. The things that worried them were part of a larger canvas—America's Far Eastern policy, the need for better schools, the prevalence of mental illness, the "lack of leadership" in Washington. And, unanimously, the feeling that America's statesmen "Haven't been using the time we've been buying for them up here on the Hill."

Before leaving, they directed some questions at us which indicated that for all their isolation, these scientists were far less parochial than their fellow Americans: How strong are the Communists in Italy—and why? Aren't we wrong to associate ourselves so closely with Chiang Kai-shek? Who will take over when Adenauer dies? Can we trust the Germans? Will Mendès-France fall? (Fortunately I said yes, since he did —two days later.) What kind of a man is Nehru?

And finally, returning to their concern about "buying time"—what is America doing to combat the Soviet threat on the economic, social and psychological fronts? This question is still being asked today, a generation later, for, strange to say, it's still just as valid.

Three months later, in Wisconsin, I was talking to one of Truman's former cabinet members who had had to deal with the problems of peace in our time. I mentioned the optimism of these scientists who felt they had helped banish war.

"They may be right," he said. "I hope they are. But I can't help worrying that we or the Communists will blunder into a war that would be the ruin of us all. The trouble with scientists is that they sometimes assume that people and politicians are as rational as they are themselves."

At the end of our travels, I set down some of the commonest clichés about America then prevalent abroad to see how they stacked up against our findings on this trip:

Americans were often depicted as scared—of Communists, of McCarthy and of one another; as belligerent and impetuous, ready to plunge the world into atomic war; as hypocrites, preaching democracy to others but denying equal rights to their Negro citizens; as morally lax, breeding a new generation of juvenile delinquents; as reactionary, persecuting liberals at home and making alliances with dictators abroad; as materialistic, too busy pursuing the almighty dollar to appreciate true culture; as immature and overbearing, believing their wealth entitled them to push other people around.

Our trip convinced us these notions were groundless—or largely so. There were civil rights battles still to be fought and we had yet to be humbled in Vietnam in our misguided zeal to police the world. But America's heartbeat seemed strong and its vitality and self-confidence found expression in Ike's irresistible grin. Change was in the air, which is what inspired the title of my book after long experience with hidebound, convalescent postwar Europe.

I doubt if I could give such an upbeat title to a book about my country today. *America Adrift* would be my likelier choice.

But that's for later. At this point in time, as John Dean used to say at the Watergate hearings, in this spring of 1955, the cold war was in transition. The wind from the east was thick with straws, and would be for a year or more. On May 15, the Russians signed the Austrian Peace Treaty, marking the first time that Soviet troops had withdrawn from territory they occupied since the Iranian crisis of 1945. (Later in 1955, they also evacuated the Porkkala naval base and returned it to Finland.) The Austrian accord, after years of deadlocked negotiations, was in part motivated by their desire to persuade West Germany, which became the sovereign Federal German Republic on May 5 and a member of NATO on May 9, to reconsider the advantages of neutrality, Austrian-style. But the Germans had no single, unified government like the Austrians, and it was unrealistic to expect Communist East Germany to be engulfed by the West, much as its people might welcome it. Still, the Austrian Treaty did sever direct lines of communication between NATO forces in Italy and Germany, which was a small plus for the Soviets.

On May 10, the U.S., Britain and France proposed a Big Four summit meeting, something Churchill had first advocated two years earlier, and the Russians accepted. They did sign the Warsaw Pact Treaty on the fourteenth, a natural reaction to NATO, but conciliation was the order of the day. Moscow quickly apologized for shooting down a U.S. Navy plane over the Bering Sea, and we played down the incident as a trigger-happy error; Nikita Khrushchev, now first secretary of the Communist Party, went to Belgrade to start patching up relations with Tito, and even the ruckus in the Formosa Strait quieted down.

The Geneva summit meeting, the first since Truman met Stalin at Potsdam ten years before, lasted from July 18 to 23. I didn't go; it was a spot news story, unsuited to a general magazine, and besides, I was writing my book on the deck of our newly bought and mortgaged split-level home in New Canaan, Connecticut, while Sim and the kids attempted to beautify our wooded acre. But I did go to the Geneva summit more than thirty years later, when Ronald Reagan met Mikhail Gorbachev; and today, looking back, I find the similarities uncanny, considering all that has happened in the intervening years.

Both summits followed a long period of U.S.-Soviet estrangement; both brought together leaders who had never met and who, on the Soviet side, were newly in power, and both reflected a surface cordiality masking underlying distrust.

On his arrival, President Eisenhower pledged to change the "spirit" of distrust: "We are not here to repeat the same dreary excuses that have characterized most of the negotiations of the past ten years . . . We are here to launch fresh negotiations." (Thirty years later, Ronald Reagan was calling for "a fresh start.")

Few observers expected a major breakthrough. James Reston of the *New York Times* called the meeting "an effort to reestablish a system of diplomacy that has been suspended." Congress was skeptical, suspecting a Soviet propaganda show, but the Senate decisively defeated by 77–4 an attempt by their now discredited colleague, Joe McCarthy, to cancel the meeting altogether if the Yalta accords were not on the agenda. Even the usually reasonable *Times* referred to the Soviet "slave system" and warned that "the free world dare not trust anything they say."

As in 1985, some of the president's advisers believed the Russians would be negotiating from weakness. Dulles went so far as to say on July 8 that the Soviet economy "is on the point of collapsing," while Eisenhower was saying "no individual in this government has ever said that the Soviets are coming to this conference weak." He also said on July 7, in his first color telecast, that it was "perfectly stupid" for the world to spend so much on arms. (Little could he anticipate that the U.S. defense budget, then at $42 billion, would have soared to almost a third of a *trillion* dollars by the time Reagan got to Geneva.)

Then, as later, the Soviets were just as preoccupied with being treated "as equals"; and, as today, we favored a go-slow approach in negotiating while they talked in terms of sweeping if impractical agreements aimed at ending the cold war to show they had "changed."

Premier Bulganin was their chief of delegation. Molotov, still the foreign minister, was there along with his deputy, Andrei Gromyko, and Marshal Georgi Zhukov, the recently rehabilitated defense minister, who had known Eisenhower in 1945. (Khrushchev was added to the delegation a few days before the conference, and he and Bulganin scored the first public relations points by driving through Geneva in an open car, waving to the crowds, while Eisenhower was invisibly encased in a bulletproof limousine.)

But while much was the same in 1955, much was also different. There was no talk of Star Wars, since outer space was still out of reach: Sputnik was still two years away. Disarmament was on the agenda, but statesmen then thought more in terms of troop strength and bombers than of missiles and warheads.

The British and French were represented by Prime Minister Anthony Eden (who had replaced an ailing Churchill) and Premier Edgar Faure. Eisenhower, soon to be stricken by a heart attack, radiated confidence. He felt comfortable in Europe. Unlike Reagan, he had served there in both a hot war and a cold one, understood the political currents and knew many of its leaders personally. Khrushchev said later that he underestimated Ike at Geneva because he always consulted Dulles before saying anything. Details were not Ike's strong suit either, but unlike Reagan he did see the big picture clearly. As he wrote to the president of Simon and Schuster in 1956, "We have come to the point where safety cannot be assured by arms alone."

Bulganin's positive response on July 18 to our 1953 "Atoms for Peace" proposal was a hopeful augury that led to the establishment of the International Atomic Energy Agency in Vienna. (It still exists, though not in the forefront of the news.) And Ike had the gift of projecting his fundamental sincerity. In his opening speech, he addressed Zhukov directly as an old soldier and friend who knew he'd never uttered a word of untruth and assured him the U.S. would fight only in self-defense. Even Bulganin seemed to accept this assurance, though he expressed doubts about other members of NATO.

He meant the Germans. For the future of Germany dominated the 1955 agenda and was plainly insoluble. The Western allies wanted a unified Germany tied to NATO (as insurance against a Communist power play), which the Russians, who argued for a neutral, demilitarized Germany, would never accept. Our demands for political freedom in Eastern Europe and for dismantling the iron curtain were equally unrealistic, given the temper of the times. But on July 21, just as the conference seemed to be bogging down, Eisenhower produced a bombshell that made him its star. This was the Open Skies proposal, the brainchild of Nelson Rockefeller and Harold Stassen. It called for an exchange of blueprints and unhampered aerial reconnaissance and photography of each other's military installations. As the boldest scheme yet offered to dispel mutual distrust, it caught the conference by surprise and dominated the news.

Bulganin said he was "deeply moved" by the proposal, that it had "real merit" and that he would give it "sympathetic study." But during a recess in the session, Khrushchev approached Eisenhower. "I don't agree with our chairman," he said, smiling.

In his memoirs, Eisenhower recalled: "But there was no smile in his voice. I saw clearly then, for the first time, the identity of the real boss of the Soviet delegation."

In Khrushchev's view, Open Skies was nothing but a trick to legalize espionage against the U.S.S.R. His reaction typified the suspicious, emotional and impulsive Khrushchev style for which his rule would be remembered and which would eventually lead to his downfall nine years later.

The conference finally disbanded without issuing even a joint statement, as was done in 1985; the participants just passed the unresolved agenda—German unification, European security, disarmament—along to their foreign ministers to wrestle with, in vain, three months later. But at least there had been no name-calling. Ike had even eliminated a reference to "enslaved nations" in discussing Eastern Europe—which the Russians interpreted to mean (correctly, as Hungary was to demonstrate) that we had tacitly accepted the status quo behind the iron curtain. Indeed, as a British delegate put it, "a revival of good manners" may have been the main achievement of the conference. (Thirty years later, one of Reston's post-summit columns was entitled "A Renewal of Manners".) Civility, yes, and a realization by some Western statesmen that maybe the Russians didn't want to go to war after all. The cold war had temporarily been transmuted into a cold peace—or more accurately, in the light of what lay ahead in 1956, a cold armistice.

While all this was happening in Geneva, where I'd been pursuing Mr. Ilyichev a year before, I finished my book and went out to Wichita, Kansas, to produce a picture story on the drought that was lowering the water table and parching the prairie. That done, I took on a four-month assignment with the title "The Position of the Jews in America Today" that took me back and forth across the U.S.A. once again—and gave me a chance to reconfirm many of the impressions I'd gathered in the spring.

I kept up with the news of the world—not always easy in the Wichita *Beacon* or even in Los Angeles, where the LA *Times* was then as provincial in its coverage as it was partisan in its politics. But I gathered the July conference had spawned the "Spirit of Geneva," which led to a further relaxation of old tensions and, in Ike's cheery words, "a new friendliness in the world." Resigned now to the existence of a West German state tied to NATO, the Russians invited Chancellor Adenauer to Moscow in September and established diplomatic relations. In Warsaw, our ambassador started on August 1 meeting regularly with his Chinese counterpart to discuss "practical problems"; five downed American flyers were freed. The Red Army was reduced by 600,000 men. American and Soviet agricultural delegations exchanged visits. The "radio war" was tuned down.

As depicted in a cartoon reprinted in the *New York Times,* the world was now sitting wearily on a rock marked GENEVA from which a steep and tortuous path led upwards past a signpost that read TO PEACE. Few of us who saw this cartoon could anticipate just how steep and interminable this path would turn out to be. All we sensed was that we were in a new and more fluid phase of the cold war. A *Newsday* editorial suggested the Soviets had decided to gain their ends by maneuver rather than by "naked aggression" (without citing any recent examples of naked aggression).

There was no doubt the cold war was in a different mode, but so were many of us who had been immersed in it professionally for nearly a decade. In my own case, though I was still a cold warrior, I was becoming more concerned with the literally vital importance of keeping our ongoing competition peaceful than with preparing for a war that we were beginning to realize would never be fought except by accident. If the security of the United States now depended on our readiness to slaughter tens of millions of innocent people (the really big bombs had not yet been perfected), then it was time to reexamine the moral premises of "security."

But I knew now that ten years of cold war conditioning (and I had played my part in baiting the Russian bear) had left the American people more than ever resigned and fatalistic. Backyard fallout shelters were being advertised. War with the Russians was a possibility which, if not desired, was certainly not ruled out. The dominant mood was, Trust Ike and don't ask questions.

And the arms race was still picking up speed despite the spirit of Geneva. Even so stalwart a hawk as General MacArthur was alarmed. In 1955, in Los Angeles, he warned against "two great illusions"— namely, that both sides in the cold war believed the other was planning to attack. "Both are wrong," he said. "But the constant acceleration of preparation may well, without specific intent, ultimately produce a spontaneous combustion."

What could I do, as a cold war journalist whose job required me to worry more than most of my friends about the state of the world? I could join SANE, along with my neighbor Norman Cousins—and I did. I could contribute speech material to Adlai Stevenson's hopeless 1956 presidential campaign—and I did. But I decided that the most useful contribution I could make was to stay in the mass media where from time to time something I wrote or edited or assigned might dispel some of the confusion about world affairs that was so prevalent all over the country.

In the fifties, the really influential mass media were magazines. Newspapers were mostly parochial; investigative or enterprise reporting was a rarity. And television dealt with news in bulletin form; documentaries, like Ed Murrow's "Harvest of Shame" in 1960, were just beginning to be aired, and seldom in prime time. People watched TV for George Gobel or Jackie Gleason or Sid Caesar—not for enlightenment about the real world. (It's still primarily an entertainment medium, but not, as a generation ago, exclusively so.)

As national affairs editor, I continued my American education but I managed to make a couple of extended trips abroad every year. (In 1956, I returned to the Arab Near East while another *Look* editor went to Israel; later, after the Twentieth Party Congress in Moscow, where Khrushchev confronted and challenged the ghost of Josef Stalin, I made my first of several visits to Russia.) In 1957, I was back in Cairo to see Nasser, and by 1958, I finally had my title changed to foreign editor. I'd been involved with the cold war too long not to follow it all the way to the finish line. But, to scramble metaphors, if I'd known then that I'd still be carrying a spear in this clamorous and seemingly endless pageant thirty years later, I might have eventually chosen a different line of work, such as adding sequels to the children's book I wrote in 1969.

Meanwhile, as 1955 and the Spirit of Geneva drew to a close, the

Russians began shifting their attention to what came to be called the Third World. In November, "B and K," as the two Soviet leaders were dubbed by headline writers, visited India, Burma and Afghanistan, while their Czech allies offered arms to Egypt, where, thanks to Nasser's growing militancy, a new front in the cold war was opening up.

I was briefly in Beverly Hills that fall, working on my Jewish story, and I recall talking to an old friend and film producer, Frank McCarthy, whom I'd known in Paris during the tense postwar years. We agreed that the familiar stereotype of the Russian barbarians probing the defenses of Western Europe was now long out of date, and that the contest for influence was now shifting to Asia, Africa and Latin America. Frank, a Republican, had been General Marshall's aide during the war and knew and admired Eisenhower as a man whose essential decency and devotion to peace was unquestioned. But he thought that we would be better positioned for the contests of the coming Khrushchev era if Ike had a man like Adlai Stevenson as his secretary of state rather than as his presidential rival.

(We were so absorbed in our cold war speculations that evening that I completely missed a hint from one of the other two guests, Grace Kelly, that she was thinking of moving to the Riviera and so attached little importance to her questioning me about Prince Rainier, whom I'd met in Paris. Thus I missed what might have been a scoop; the cold war had distracted me from what was clearly the Big Story.)

The cold war has continued to distract me ever since, perhaps, recalling Joe Barnes's phrase, because it was so central to the history of our times. I have followed it through its alternating thaws and freezes. I even enlisted in those aborted crusades called the New Frontier and the Great Society. And I watched with dismay the squandering of the world's capital resources and human energies on a quarrel that ultimately defied definition but was continually refueled by ignorance, greed and fear.

Now, in the mid-fifties, we were embarked on this new phase of what John F. Kennedy was later to call "the long twilight struggle." In this phase, which came to be known as competitive coexistence, we held all the best cards but didn't always play our hand as though we understood the game.

Chapter 9

Travels in the Khrushchev Era

Nikita Khrushchev was top banana in the Soviet Union from 1956 to 1964, and for the first five of these years he occupied center stage in the cold war follies as well; not until the sixties was he overshadowed by John F. Kennedy. The Khrushchev epoch was marked by what one Sovietologist has called "confusing pyrotechnics," as this essentially crude and impulsive extrovert strutted on the world scene like no other leader in modern times. He boldly challenged the ghost of the great Stalin, he banged his shoe on his desk in the U.N. General Assembly, he tried to bully Kennedy, not knowing the Boston Irish, and while praising peaceful coexistence, boastfully predicted the eventual triumph of the Soviet system. "Whether you like it or not," he told some Western diplomats at a reception in November 1956, "history is moving in our favor, and it is we who will bury you." Whether Khrushchev believed this or not, he managed to anger and alarm millions of Americans who took his words literally rather than as his way of saying that communism would outlast capitalism.

This chapter will deal with the years from 1956—which began in the lingering glow of the Spirit of Geneva and ended in the thunder of gunfire in Budapest and Egypt—to 1959, after which Kennedy was elected president, and the barometer of Soviet-American relations, which had vacillated between variable and foul, began at last to register fair and warmer in the months before Dallas. In retrospect, it can easily be argued that Lee Harvey Oswald's superb marksmanship changed the course of history as much as anything that has happened in this century.

Most of the cold war action during the first four Khrushchev years took place in four areas of the globe: Europe (including the Soviet Union); the Near East; South Asia; and, after Fidel Castro's successful revolution, in long-neglected Latin America as well. And at one time or another during this period, I managed to become involved in some of this overseas action often enough to become a regular visitor to New York's new international airport, then called Idlewild.

Nineteen fifty-six, described as "a troubled year" by one historian, was at the very least eventful. There was Khrushchev's "secret speech" to the Twentieth Party Congress on the night of February 24–25, a documented denunciation of Stalin's abuse of power and "cult of personality" that was doubly shocking to an establishment unaccustomed ever to admit making a mistake. The dissolution of the Cominform in April; the Poznán riots in June that left fifty-three dead and brought Wladislaw Gomulka, a "liberal" Communist, back to power in Poland; the ouster of Matyas Rakosi, Hungary's Stalinist boss, in July; and the popular explosion of anti-Russian violence that wracked that nation in October—all reflected the stresses within a Soviet empire no longer as cowed and prostrate as in the immediate postwar years.

Nasser's seizure of the Suez Canal in July led to the secretive, clumsy and foolhardy Israeli-British-French invasion of Egypt three months later—an operation designed to save the canal and knock out Nasser but which, ironically, saved Nasser and knocked out the canal. In the Far East, the last French troops left Indochina, and the South Vietnamese, under Ngo Dinh Diem, and with our acquiescence, ignored the 1954 Geneva accords calling for nationwide free elections. The first faint signs of discord appeared in Sino-Soviet relations. And Dulles continued to deal with the world's emerging nations as though their leaders were all elderly white Presbyterian corporation lawyers like himself, whereas most (like Nasser) were brash, swarthy professional soldiers with rudimentary academic backgrounds. (The Russians, by contrast, were discovering the so-called Third World and concluding that its leaders were worth cultivating, whether Communist or not.)

No wonder it was a troubled year: the cold war ice pack, now a decade thick, was breaking up, and the noise was sometimes deafening as Stalin's paranoia gave way to Khrushchev's reckless exuberance. More secure now after holding his own at the Big Four Geneva summit and winning his Party Congress gamble, Khrushchev could risk freeing millions of political prisoners for productive reintegration into Soviet society, tour the world like a man riding the wave of the future and, in time, dispense with the services of his more dignified partner, Premier Bulganin.

For me, the eyewitness action started in the winter of 1955–56, in Cairo. The Near East seemed to be percolating even more than usual, and I figured a visit to Israel's Arab neighbors would produce a story to mesh with a simultaneous report from Israel by one of our senior writers, Chet Morrison. Joe Alsop was headed for Cairo, one of the few places he'd never visited, and suggested we travel together.

The old Semiramis on the banks of the Nile was still the best hotel in town, and we got on the phone as soon as we checked in to see if any of our sources knew of a way to get to see Nasser. (In an authoritarian country, one of the rules of the game is to see the top man as soon as possible, and then all doors are opened.) But we struck out. The Israelis had just shelled the Gaza strip, killing four soldiers and fifty-five civilians, and Nasser was in no mood to be interviewed, especially by Americans. So while Joe toured the Western embassies, I saw Gamal Salem, the deputy premier, who suspected Israel of trying to provoke Egypt into starting a war it was still too weak to win. (Some Soviet Mig fighters and Ilyushin bombers had arrived, along with about two hundred Czech and Russian technicians; but for all their new assertiveness, the Egyptians preferred to bide their time rather than risk another defeat.)

So Joe and I saw some sights I'd been seeing since 1942, like the Giza pyramids, where my request for a nonfrisky camel produced a beast so aged and decrepit that he rose up, collapsed and died, but gracefully enough that I was able to scramble out from under him. Cairo at night was no longer the blacked-out city of horse-drawn cabs and raucous Eighth Army "desert rats" I knew in World War II, nor even the crowded but manageable city I'd seen since: now it was all bulldozers and construction cranes and traffic jams, but the belly dancers looked the same, as did the pale, fleshy Greeks and Armenians murmuring over soft drinks and almonds in the Semiramis foyer.

Eventually Joe and I fetched up at the offices of *Al Ahram,* Egypt's leading newspaper, whose editor, Mustafa Amin, was later convicted of working for the CIA, jailed and finally released by Anwar Sadat. Joe, who had just come from London, assured him the British were "quite frantic" about the canal and would "positively" intervene militarily if Nasser nationalized it. While he talked, I noticed that one of Amin's editors, a young man named Mohammed Heikal, quietly left the room. He returned in a few minutes, went up to Alsop and said, "Colonel Nasser would like to see you right away."

I was not included. Nasser obviously wanted a firsthand report from London. But the Alsop warning did not deter him from nationalizing the canal on July 28 after the departure of the British garrison.

Heikal, whom I'd be seeing again, was Nasser's close confidant and later took over *Al Ahram* and made it the biggest-selling daily, as well as Nasser's mouthpiece, in seventeen Arab countries. He was mildly anti-American but chiefly pro-Heikal.

From Cairo I went on to Lebanon and Jordan, where I heard everything I'd heard in 1951 and 1953 all over again. The script never seems to change in this continuing drama. And so when I met Morrison back in New York to compare notes and write our articles, the joint editorial we used as an endpiece sounds almost as valid today as it did then, or would have sooner. We called it "Last Chance for Peace"—something both sides needed desperately, and still do. A truce had been arranged by the U.N., and the Russians appeared ready to help ease tensions in exchange for a voice in Near East affairs.

So we listed the elements of a peace treaty as follows:

1. A compromise between Israel's present frontiers and those of the 1947 partition plan.
2. The right of the Palestinian refugees to be reimbursed for their lost property.
3. A plan to resettle the refugees in Arab states at Israel's expense.
4. Joint use of the Jordan River water for irrigation purposes.
5. Recognition of Israel by the Arab states and the lifting of the economic blockade.
6. An international guarantee of Israel's frontiers.

We concluded that the pressure on both sides would have to come from the U.N., with the tacit agreement of the Asian states and the Soviet bloc. For a stable peace in the area "is not only a problem for Arabs and Jews—it is properly the concern of a world that can no longer risk even a small war."

Our "last chance" lasted until fall. But its general conclusions are not obsolete. That is part of the ongoing tragedy of this corner of the world. By the end of 1956, the Israeli, British and French invasion of Egypt had proved three things: First, that our two old allies could no longer act on their own anywhere in the Third World without our blessing or acquiescence (their troops withdrew three weeks after landing; even if they had taken Cairo, how could they have garrisoned the country?). Second, that Egypt's army was still no match for Israel's (though the

Egyptians fought surprisingly well at Port Said). Third, that the United States and the Soviet Union would henceforth be the only two outside powers to be reckoned with in the Near East.

I lost a friend at Suez, as I had in 1954 in Indochina. David Seymour, whom we knew as Chim, and with whom I'd worked on the Ingrid Bergman and other stories, was killed by Egyptian gunfire as he walked forward of French positions during the cease-fire; earlier, Bob Capa, the founder of Magnum Photos, died when he stepped on a land mine while on a patrol with French troops in Vietnam. Sim and I had spent the afternoon at the races with him in Paris the day before he left on this last assignment. No, the best photographers don't have the worst luck; they just take the most chances.

Looking back on Suez, we were lucky to have been kept in the dark (because our allies didn't trust Dulles), as it made it easier for Eisenhower to press for a cease-fire; and we were lucky, too, as it turned out, to have reneged on our offer to help build the Aswan High Dam. The Russians did instead, at a cost of nearly $5 billion, but when I visited it in 1977, the Egyptians were embarrassed to discuss the flooding and damage to seasonal fertilization it had caused.

The main cold war event in Europe was Khrushchev's shattering of the Stalinist myth: even so celebrated a city as Stalingrad, where the Nazis can be said to have lost the war, had its name changed to Volgograd. And when I applied for a visa to go to Moscow in July to open a *Look* bureau, it was granted without delay. After ten years of knocking on a door, it was hard to believe it had finally opened.

I flew to Paris on a Pan Am Stratocruiser President Special, sharing a berth with my four-year-old daughter, Jan. It was the all-time best flight across the Atlantic—the Concorde included—if you had to take a plane: superb meals, comfortable berths, a downstairs lounge and bar filled with solicitous stewardesses, and no jet lag after sleeping seven or eight of the eighteen in flight. Too bad there's not one still in service: I'd take it.

From Paris, where Jan was taken in hand by an uncle, I flew on to Prague, where I toured the city by cab between flights and found that nine years of Communist rule since my 1947 visit had only made the city shabbier and the traffic sparser. A giant statue of Stalin dominated the landscape but would shortly be removed now that he had been demythed.

An Aeroflot Ilyushin-12, a cousin of the DC-4, took us to Moscow via

Vilnius, in Soviet Lithuania, where the waitress in the airport bar affirmed her nationalism by refusing to bring me a beer when I used the Russian word, *pivo*. She only responded to the German, *bier*.

I spent the long hours flying over the monotonous Russian plain trying to reassure the lone American tourist aboard, whose wife had canceled at the last minute. He finally believed me when I assured him he would not be arrested on arrival. Fewer than fifteen hundred American tourists a year visited the Soviet Union in the mid fifties, and those who did were regarded either as intrepid or as Commies.

Ed Stevens, whom *Look* had hired from the *Christian Science Monitor,* for which he'd been reporting from Moscow since 1947, met me at Vuknovo Airport, today a minor terminal for domestic flights. We drove to the Hotel Moskva near Red Square. Its clientele consisted more of Party big shots than foreigners. In my room, I inspected the thirties plumbing, the tasseled lampshades, the lace doilies and the phone that didn't work and felt that pang of depressive anxiety that I'd anticipated as soon as I got the Soviet visa. Everything was just fine, there was even warm water, but—shades of Leipzig!—when would I be hearing the midnight knock on the door? After ten years of cold war it was hard not to feel that here in the shadow of the Kremlin, you were at last in the belly of the beast.

There was no knock, of course, and in the morning Ed and I talked about what he needed to set up a *Look* bureau. We then called on the editors of *Ogonyok,* the Russian picture magazine, with a proposal for a working exchange involving visiting writer-photographer teams in both our countries. They hedged, not having received instructions, but were interested in my having visited Ernest Hemingway in Cuba a few weeks before. (It had been a short visit: I wanted him to write some captions and a page of text to go with pictures we had of him and his wife, Mary, and at first he begged off; but when I allowed as how 750 words was not a lot to ask of a novelist in a day, the old newspaperman in him was aroused, and he told me to meet him by the pool for daiquiris in two hours. When he arrived he had several typewritten pages of copy —good stuff though not great—and he watched me, seemingly anxious, while I read it.

"It's okay," I said. "We can use it pretty much as it is."

"Okay, is it? It happens to be the best goddamn copy you'll have in your magazine all year!"

Well, all right. He got $6,000 for his efforts and bought Sim and me dinner at the Floridita, with daiquiris en route in an open touring car.

"This is the only thing Scott Fitzgerald ever taught me," he said as we got under way. "How to drink gracefully in an open car."

He asked us to go fishing the next day, but we had children problems at home, and also I think Mary resented our interrupting his work in progress.)

Anyway, the *Ogonyok* editors wanted some new stuff on Hemingway, so I agreed to write them a piece. They said they'd pay me ten rubles (about $12) if I also included a picture of the Famous Anti-Fascist Writer and me together, and I could come and get the money next time I was in Moscow—something I kept forgetting and doubt they remember after thirty years.

Stevens gave a party for me at his home—an old but modernized wooden house in the heart of Moscow—and we had a surprisingly large turnout of Soviet journalists and officials, all of whose names I've forgotten. Conversation with Russians is seldom easy unless they are high enough in the KGB to talk frankly and spontaneously. At this gathering, topics to be avoided were the recent Polish riots and the consequences of the Twentieth Party Congress. Increased technical and cultural exchanges between our two countries was a safe and popular subject, and "What are your impressions of our country?" a stock question without any easy answers.

Coming from the West, you could not possibly praise Moscow with any semblance of conviction. But this austere, charmless, inefficient and relatively primitive city did possess a few redeeming features, so I learned to cheer up my Russian interlocutors by lavishing praise on these—the clean and palatial subways, the exquisite ballet, the tasty ice cream and the proficiency of all the chess players I'd encountered. And of course there was the war—the Great Patriotic War to the Russians, for they considered the western front a sideshow. (It's true that Germany suffered 10 million of its 13.5 million casualties on the eastern front and that forty Soviet soldiers were killed for every American.) So you could also pay sincere tribute to the reconstruction of a country where towns by the tens of thousands had been laid waste and twenty million of whose citizens had died, including virtually all young men seventeen to twenty.

The Russians I talked to also lied about certain aspects of the Great Patriotic War, such as the 1939 Nazi-Soviet Pact. This would come up after they made disparaging remarks about the Allied war effort compared to theirs. I didn't bother to bring up the war in the Pacific—only the fact that Britain fought Hitler alone for nearly two years while the pact was in effect. They would hastily explain it was always Stalin's intention to buy time and then stab Hitler in the back at the opportune moment (which was untrue—Stalin planned to watch the capitalist countries destroy each other, and it was Hitler who did the stabbing). But you were very quickly made aware that it was just as bad form to raise such matters now that we were becoming friends again as it would be for them to mention U.S. military intervention on behalf of the White armies in 1919. A toast to *druzhba i mir* (friendship and peace) was then in order.

I met Bulganin at a diplomatic reception, but not Khrushchev. Smiling, Bulganin said he was always glad to see Americans coming to Moscow so they could discover "we are not such ogres." Stevens told me later that suspicion of foreigners, always endemic in Russia, still existed but somewhat less pervasively. People were feeling more relaxed now that terror had abated, consumer goods were becoming more plentiful and new suburban high rises were easing the housing shortage.

So I toured Moscow on my own to see the city outside the tourist perimeter. I would memorize the name of the subway station nearest to my hotel, so that I'd know how to get back, and ride to the end of the line, or partway. People stared at my seersucker suit but no one spoke to me other than an agitated, elderly little man who tugged at my sleeve as I walked along a station platform, hands in my pockets.

"Nyeh kulturny!" he cried repeatedly until I realized he was criticizing my lack of culture and obligingly let my hands dangle at my sides. This satisfied him and he hurried away. (That evening I looked up "It's none of your business" in my Russian phrase book—*"Eta nyeh vashe dyelo"*—but never had occasion to use it again. He must have been the last Russian left who cared about the etiquette of hands in the pockets.)

One subway excursion took me to the chess pavilion in Gorky Park, where several games were in progress. The unexpected arrival of an American (my suit and loafers identified me) provoked glad cries from players and kibitzers alike. *"Spielen Sie Schach?"* asked one of them in German. I told them I was nothing but a patzer—*ochen plokha.* But I was installed across a board from an older man nonetheless, drew white and shoved my king's pawn out two squares. The rest of the game was deft, swift and decisive: checkmate by black in a dozen moves. I tried to make my getaway but was importuned into another game. This time I decided to play according to no known system. I recklessly sacrificed pawns, offered up a bishop and attacked simultaneously on all fronts.

My opponent, unaccustomed to whimsy, finally gridlocked himself into a draw. The onlookers, by now three deep around our table, regarded me with new respect. *"Kharasho!"* exclaimed my opponent, extending his hand. *"Amerikanskaya teknika!"*

I was urged to stay and demonstrate this unusual technique again but made my escape after much backslapping. Recalling the frosty silence Michel Gordey had encountered as a foreigner in Moscow six years earlier, I concluded that Khrushchev's incumbency *was* making a difference. It had become permissible to act human.

I began to feel comfortable in this city which, physically, attracted me not at all. One day, several blocks around the Kremlin were cordoned off for some high official's funeral procession. My hotel was thus temporarily inaccessible, and no amount of passport brandishing could get me through the police lines. So when I saw a contingent of mourners getting into formation behind a large red banner I simply fell in with them as they marched off toward Red Square. When we came abreast of my hotel, I peeled off and strode purposefully toward the entrance. The militiamen saluted and opened a path through the crowd. I had remembered the lesson of our Leipzig expeditions: in a Communist country, act as though you have official permission and the police generally believe that you do.

Another day I ran into two young *Paris-Match* reporters and their wives, who had driven all the way from France in a Renault. They said the dirt roads, scarce gas pumps and Spartan accommodations made Russia seem like part of a different continent. Their car looked as if it had been in a war. Together with Ed Stevens, who spoke Russian, and his Russian-born wife we went picnicking twenty-five miles out of town on a Sunday, and I saw what the French meant. In a commuting community similar to my hometown, only the wooden railroad station and platform looked familiar. The few state stores were sparsely stocked, the streets unpaved and the bungalowlike houses all about a hundred years old. We knocked on a couple of doors, explaining we were foreigners, and offered to take family snapshots for them. Amid much giggling we were invited to share their black bread and tea. None of the villagers we met had seen Frenchmen or Americans before, so we provided the holiday's excitement. As I learned in all my cold war travels, the friendliness of ordinary people in Communist countries suggested that they either didn't read the vicious anti-American propaganda in their press, or didn't believe it.

Before leaving Moscow, I told Stevens to start making arrangements to go to China in the fall with a *Look* photographer, Phil Harrington. We knew the State Department disapproved of such visits, but Cowles could be feisty where freedom of the press was concerned. We were already preparing a report on China subtitled "The Biggest Problem We've Ever Faced," using German photographs, that referred to "the awakening giant" and warned of the hordes of disciplined "blue ants" now threatening Western civilization. But subtle signs of strain between the Russians and Chinese (who considered Khrushchev too "soft") were now discernible, and we needed more and better reporting from a nation Washington still pretended publicly didn't exist.

As it turned out, Dulles was furious and told Cowles he would be jeopardizing the release of ten American prisoners in China if he didn't recall Stevens and Harrington immediately from Peking. Back in Moscow, they were summoned to the American Embassy, where their passports were taken from them and validated only for travel back to the States. Cowles threatened to take the matter to court, and Dulles eventually backed down. Ironically, he lifted the China ban a year later, but by then the Chinese were no longer issuing visas to Americans.

I got home in August in time to attend the Democratic convention in Chicago with Sim. People asked about Russia—mostly questions like "Were you frightened?" (No.) Or "Were you followed?" (Very seldom, if at all. I took an FBI course in surveillance during the war and can usually tell if I'm being tailed; also, a KGB shadow would have escorted me out of the funeral procession.)

The campaign that followed the convention was a disaster for Stevenson. Not only did he seem groggy from the spring primaries, but he raised issues like ending nuclear testing and the draft that could only cost him votes against a former general who was both trusted and beloved. (Emmet Hughes, one of Eisenhower's speechwriters, told me he couldn't believe Stevenson was so ill-advised politically as to mention a test ban in a campaign—even though the fallout problem was serious and a presidential commission was about to recommend halting atmospheric tests.) And then came the incredible newsreel of events that would have rallied the country around any incumbent president. Consider the chronology:

On October 22, the British foreign secretary and French foreign minister met secretly with Premier Ben-Gurion to coordinate the Suez operation.

On October 23, a popular uprising in Hungary overthrew the existing Communist government, and fighting raged in the streets of Budapest between armed civilians and Soviet troops and tanks.

On October 24, Imre Nagy, a moderate Communist, became prime minister of Hungary and called on the Russians to withdraw from the country. Crowds in Budapest stormed secret police (AVO) headquarters and lynched its occupants.

On October 24, the Israelis invaded the Sinai peninsula.

On October 25, the people's militia was in control of most Hungarian cities as Soviet forces began withdrawing.

On October 28, a cease-fire went into effect in Budapest, but Nagy could not contain the surge of popular emotion pressing for a complete break with the Soviets. He yielded, proclaiming "neutrality," Austrian-style.

On November 4, 200,000 Soviet troops and 2,500 tanks poured back across the border into Hungary to smash the resistance. Nagy appealed in vain for U.N. intervention.

On November 5, British and French troops landed in Egypt, ostensibly to contain the Israeli advance and secure the canal.

On November 6, U.N. and U.S. pressure (and a Soviet warning) brought about a cease-fire in Egypt.

On November 24, British and French forces left Egypt.

On November 25, Nagy was lured out of the Yugoslav Embassy, where he had taken refuge, and abducted by the Russians to Romania, where he was later executed.

The purpose of this book is not to reiterate the history of these turbulent weeks—especially the first six days of November. But certain lessons and consequences need to be cited briefly.

The first week of November 1956 has been called "the week of truth" for four reasons: First, Eastern Europeans learned they could expect no help from the West in a crunch despite the pep talks (such as Henry Cabot Lodge's "We shall not fail them" message to the Hungarian rebels) and other bugle calls broadcast on Radio Free Europe. Second, the Russians learned the postwar status quo east of the iron curtain had tacitly been accepted and their sphere of control was now secure, whatever the occasional political rhetoric about "liberating the captive nations" or "rolling back communism." Third, the French and British learned they could no longer take any major action without American approval and even support. As de Gaulle put it, the world now lived under "the double hegemony of the U.S. and the U.S.S.R." Fourth, we learned that Moscow would go to any length to keep its buffer states in line; and that distrust between Dulles and his British and French colleagues was so profound that they would not even inform him of their disastrous secret enterprise.

Even though the Hungarian tragedy swept away what was left of the Spirit of Geneva, the consequences were not all bad. Even Tito and Gomulka accepted the ultimate Soviet solution as a necessary evil. And as it turned out, Hungary began moving gingerly but steadily toward liberalization under János Kádár, the new Communist leader who was acceptable to the Russians and even to some Hungarians since he had been jailed and tortured during the brutal Rakosi regime. Moreover, had the rebellion been allowed to succeed, all of Eastern Europe might have risen up and been bloodily crushed in a generalized war that just might have drawn in NATO. The cold war would have ended—in a sea of flames.

As it was, the Hungarians' gallant resistance gained them new respect from their Russian overlords. But the last days of the revolt were a nightmare, with children attacking Soviet tanks and the tanks mowing down housewives lined up outside grocery stores. The murders of Imre Nagy and General Pal Maleter were also tragic. Nagy, whom the U.S. Embassy hardly knew because it seemed inconceivable that a Communist should lead an anti-Communist uprising, might at first have kept the uprising within bounds by proposing a form of "Finlandization," but he was himself carried away by the passions of the moment. Maleter, also a Communist, cooperated with the Russians in containing the uprising but fought against them when they broke their word and reinvaded Hungary on November 4; for this he was kidnapped, charged with treason and executed.

Events in Hungary shocked Communists in the West: the Party lost members as well as political credibility. And the cold war turned colder. Yet some old illusions, on both sides, were discarded during that "week of truth," which could not help but facilitate future negotiations. We had a newly reelected president who never believed that the Russians wanted war, and a Soviet leader who was brash, pushy but, unlike Stalin, sane.

As a newsman, I was sorry I missed Hungary's three-week defiance. But events were moving too rapidly then for coverage by a magazine like *Look,* which was printed between three and six weeks before distribution. There was always the risk of running a story that had become dated, silly or downright embarrassing during that long lead time. For example, shortly before Eisenhower's heart attack in September 1955, we published a story called "Five Reasons Why Ike Won't Run Again." It appeared just after he was stricken, and seemed extraordinarily timely. But readers wondered why none of the five reasons included his heart attack.

We now remember 1957, if at all, as the Year of the Sputnik—the year we realized the Russians were no longer the primitive, horse-drawn, vodka-swilling brutes we had pictured them for so long. (They had also produced their first ICBM in August.) Eisenhower's offhand remark after the successful Sputnik launch in October that "it had no military value," which Walter Lippmann sharply challenged, was also unconvincing to the military; crash programs were set in motion, reaching down even to high school curricula, where science courses were suddenly in demand. Then a Soviet dog named Laika went up with the next Sputnik in November, and we redoubled our efforts. Ever since the atomic bomb, the Russians had always been the ones catching up with our technology; now, to our surprise, we had become the catcher-uppers.

But 1957 started not with Sputnik in the fall but in January with the Eisenhower Doctrine for the Near East—a vague sort of commitment on our part to help maintain regional peace and discourage Soviet meddling. Everyone knew the U.S. had only two interests in the area —oil (and denying the Russians access to it), and Israel (both out of sympathy for Hitler's victims and because of the political clout of American Jews back home). Nasser, the only leader with real stature in the Arab world, was annoyed with us—partly because of our support of Israel, partly because we'd backed off from financing the Aswan Dam and partly because he believed we could have stopped the Suez War before it started.

The irritation was mutual. In fact, as I learned before going back to Cairo in March, the State Department had just about given up on him and favored freezing Egyptian assets in the U.S., applying mild economic pressure and biding our time—a policy certain to accomplish nothing except possibly to enhance his prestige among the Arabs, including his own people.

As an old friend and onetime *Trib* colleague put it: The main question was, Could we deal with Nasser? If the answer was "no," then we should have joined the 1956 invasion and overthrown him. Since we didn't, the answer had to be "yes."

I'd written Nasser after the Suez War, suggesting a no-holds-barred interview, like the Nehru one, but got no reply. So when I was introduced in New York to an Egyptian lawyer and self-described "close friend" of Nasser's in January and heard him complain about the bad press Egypt was getting in the States because of the "Zionist" media, I pointed out that I'd offered Nasser a chance to state his point of view, unedited, for our six million readers but never received an answer. In effect, he was turning down about $40,000 in free space at current advertising rates, which indicated he was either totally indifferent to or ignorant of public relations. So I told him Nasser had only himself to blame, not the alleged Zionist media, if he thought he was getting a bad press.

The lawyer, whose name was Hassan El-Aroussy, got quite excited and said he would deliver my message personally to Nasser. Evidently he did, because I got a telex a week later saying Nasser would see me any time I came to Cairo. So it was back to the Semiramis (newer hotels were still under construction) where I settled down for the usual vigil.

Over at the U.S. Embassy, they were curious about my interview, since their own sources in the Egyptian government were drying up. The USIS office was overflowing with thousands of pamphlets entitled "A Vacuum in the Middle East"—hardly a title designed to captivate the millions who lived there. The director agreed with me that making friends with a few key journalists was far more productive than flooding a semiliterate country with pamphlets, but Washington apparently judged a post's productivity by volume rather than results. "I guess the peasants put the paper in our handouts to good use, though," he remarked wryly.

I spent one convivial evening in the company of three bibulous Muslims—an Egyptian landowner and two Palestinian lawyers, the kind who hated America and loved Americans. But after three days of waiting, I called Heikal, now a columnist and personal media adviser to Nasser, who told me to be patient. Three more days went by, and I ran into Senator Hubert Humphrey in the bar on his way to meet Nasser. I told him to let the man know I was flying home the day after next and it would be a very long time before *Look* would again offer him five pages of prime editorial space.

Humphrey forever after claimed he got me the appointment, and maybe he did, for Heikal called that evening and said he'd drive me over to Nasser's villa at two the next day.

And he was on time. I brought an American woman with me as backup note taker, along with a list of forty-two tough questions, several of them supplied to me in New York by friends in the American Jewish Committee and B'nai Brith.

Right from the start, Nasser made it plain he didn't like talking with American journalists anymore. "I saw at least six hundred up until this year," he said as we shook hands, "and nearly all wrote bad things. I don't know why I am bothering to talk to you."

But he did, for two hours, in English that was accented but surprisingly colloquial. And as he talked, fingering his prayer beads, I began to understand why, at thirty-nine, he had come so far so quickly. He had two priceless assets—enormous vitality and great charm. Even when I disagreed with what he said, it was hard not to like him.

I warned him, as I had Nehru, that my questions might sound rude but they were the kind Americans would like to have answered. His smile became a grin and he leaned back in his chair. "Good," he said. "That's fine. Let's get started."

What follows are excerpts from his answers that either are relevant to the cold war or especially valid today. One of my first questions quoted a Soviet expert on Egypt, L. N. Vatolina, who in 1954 called Nasser's regime "madly reactionary, terrorist, antidemocratic and demagogic." Had the Soviets changed or had he?

Only the United States has changed since 1954. We were friends then. But you refused us the weapons we needed, you organized the Baghdad Pact aimed at dividing the Arabs, you withdrew your offer to help us build the Aswan High Dam. So we have drifted apart . . . The Dulles policy was to try to bring down our government. Why must you try to coerce us? We will not accept orders. Don't you understand? . . . The Suez War showed the British also did not understand the change that has come over the Egyptian people in four years. I knew my people; they did not.

I was building castles in the air in my relations with America. I tried in every way to be friendly without being a puppet. . . . But there were strings on practically everything offered us. . . . I mean the Mutual Security Administration with its special military missions, its inspectors, its pacts—all that sort of thing. You would have been controlling us. . . . The Communist countries send in only technicians who come to assemble some of the equipment. Our people go to their countries for instruction. Look—I don't mind missions if I ask for them, but I don't like them imposed on me as a condition of aid. Don't you see the difference? . . . I don't want to say anything about the Eisenhower Doctrine. As I said before, I'm fed up. My advice is ignored anyway. . . . All I will say is that we are at a turning point in our relations with the West. I would suggest that you Americans try to get accurate information about this part of the world. . . . Israel? I have never called for the destruction of Israel . . . As to peace, an overall settlement would have to take into consideration the right of the refugees to return to their land, and the frontier problem. On the Israeli side, it would have to take into consideration the right to use the canal and the Gulf of Aqaba. I do not know when such an overall settlement will be possible . . .

You ask why we didn't condemn the Russians at the U.N. over Hungary. Well, the Soviet Union was the only country in the Security Council that supported us in our dispute over the Suez Canal. So we abstained out of gratitude. . . . Of course, local Communist parties will always work to seize power. They want collective ownership, among other things. I still think their objectives are dangerous—and that is why the Communist Party is illegal in Egypt. But our people do not have to like communism in order to feel sympathy and friendship for Russia. . . . Ben-Gurion? Seven days before attacking us last fall he was saying Israel would never commit aggression. How can you negotiate with a man like that?

One of my last questions was about General Neguib, who was Egypt's leader when I came to Cairo with Stevenson in 1953. Did Nasser ever see him? "He was sentenced to ten years' house arrest by a tribunal. No, I do not see him."

(This was the "hard news" of the interview, in that Neguib's fate had until then been a mystery.)

When Heikal drove me back to the hotel, he said he'd be by at eleven in the morning to go over the text of the interview and check it for accuracy. So I had a long night ahead of me, condensing and sharpening Nasser's answers to keep the copy tight and readable. I finished at 4 A.M. and an obliging embassy secretary came by at seven and picked up the manuscript (my typewriter had jammed). I spent the rest of the day waiting for Heikal and thinking over what Nasser had said. Underlying most of his answers, I decided, was a fear of Israeli expansionism (knowing his army was no match for theirs) and a disenchantment with the West that was driving him to seek security with the Soviet bloc. ("If Israel comes again, with allies," he had said, "this time we'll have allies, too—stronger ones.")

Heikal appeared in his Mercedes late in the afternoon with a casual apology. At his office, he read the typescript, approved it on Nasser's behalf, initialed it and offered me a government car to go to the airport the next day. Why not? Two days later, I reached New York via Rome, Florence and Frankfurt, feeling groggy and feverish, and discovered from blood tests taken at Yale that I'd brought the Asian flu back to the United States along with my exclusive interview.

When the piece appeared in *Look* and was released to the press, it got heavy play worldwide, especially in the Arab world, where the attitude of most editors was: "Nasser really told off the Americans and Zionists. He put Attwood in his place."

In Israel and at home, Jews also seemed to like the interview because, they said, of the way Nasser revealed himself to be a liar, weaseling on all the tough questions.

And *Look*'s circulation department was pleased too, which left only Sim, who promptly caught my flu, unenthusiastic about the assignment.

Having worked the Near East five out of the past eight years, I was ready for a change, especially since the rhetoric hardly ever varied. But, as it turned out, I'd be back again a year later.

The cold war sputtered on. Chou En-lai visited Moscow in January, a gesture he figured would put Khrushchev in his debt, but only friction ensued when the Russians welshed on their promise to deliver a prototype of an atomic bomb to Peking. (Two years later, the Russians secretly abrogated their atomic accord with China.) *Look*'s two stories about China suggested a wider split between the Communist giants was in the offing. Disarmament discussions in Europe got under way despite Dulles's warning there were risks in entering into negotiations "with malignant forces of evil"—sounding much like Ronald Reagan a quarter century later.

In Indochina, the cease-fire held, though overtures from the north in 1958 were brushed aside. As the head of the U.S. Military Mission in Saigon said a year later, "The guerrillas have ceased to be a major menace to the government"—a statement almost as fatuous as Lyndon Johnson's characterization of Diem in 1961 as "a Churchill of the decade."

At home, I found myself deeply involved in covering the often turbulent changes in the southern states, a region which in some respects seemed like a foreign country to the Yankee reporters and photographers we sent there. I'll confine my comments on this undertaking, for which *Look* won several awards, to a letter that James Baldwin, the novelist, wrote his agent from Alabama in October. I'd assigned him to travel through these states, which he had never visited even though he was black:

> The best that I can say is that the South has a Fifth Column and it's found in the goddamdest places. Everyone I met is terribly involved with what's happening down here—of course—and I am, too. But I think Bill Attwood's going to be very pleased and I'm never going to be the same again. Walking through the South is a little like walking through the human heart—if you can imagine walking through so terrible a place—and some of the people I've met down here—not many, but some—have made me very proud to be alive.
>
> I have occasional qualms about life and limb—I am spectacularly visible down here, to say nothing, in such a society! of my social awkwardness; and then keep thinking of a fifteen-year-old boy I met and a twelve-year-old girl who find themselves alone all day, each day, at school, and if all that happens is name-calling, then it's been a good day. I also spoke to the boy's principal, a convinced segregation man, who, nevertheless, loved children—his world was breaking up before my eyes. It is out of this agony that a new country will be born.

Three happenings, none unexpected, got 1958 off to a fresh start. First, the U.S. Explorer satellite joined Sputnik up in the heavens—and henceforth we would always be first in technological breakthroughs of military significance. Second, Sim was elected secretary of the New Canaan Democratic Town Committee in a community where the Republicans outpolled us four to one, which prompted Adlai Stevenson to write her: "Dear Madam: Word has come to the remotest recess of the prairie about your recent elevation. Please know that the most torpid hearts of the democracy are stirred* by the news. Thanks to you, our hopes are boundless! Faithfully, AES. *Mine is still in liquid form from too much stirring." And third, Khrushchev finally pushed Bulganin off the back of the sled in March and assumed the premiership.

My personal recollections of 1958 are of seemingly incessant but always exhilarating travel. I made three trips across the Atlantic in the spring: once to Jerusalem to interview David Ben-Gurion, Israel's prime minister, and twice to London—to interview Aneurin Bevan, slated to be foreign secretary on the next Labour government; to unravel a strange tale of a cockney showgirl who was Princess Margaret's secret stand-in for an official portrait; and finally to talk at length with

Ingrid Bergman, now about to remarry after finishing a film, *The Inn of the Sixth Happiness*, in London. As she and I played marbles on the set, I reflected that, all things considered, my job didn't lack variety.

Finally, in June, Sim and I and the children boarded an ocean liner for a journey around the "captive" nations of Eastern Europe, virtually off limits to Western journalists since our iron curtain series in 1947. The experiences of this trip—grotesque, unsettling and sometimes poignant—plus what we learned about the actual working of Communist despotism at the grass roots were both an education and an adventure, and I don't want to jam it into this already cluttered chapter. "One Way to See the Biggest Prison in the World," which was the title of the piece I wrote for *Look*, requires a chapter of its own—the next.

Meanwhile, the idea of inviting Ben-Gurion to field some tough questions, as Nasser had, seemed only fair. The Israelis were glad to cooperate, and some Egyptian newsmen and diplomats I knew happily furnished me with questions they figured he would have trouble answering—which indicated how little they knew Ben-Gurion.

I got to Tel-Aviv on a Tuesday and was told the meeting with the prime minister was set up for Friday. So I had time to look around and to drive up the coast to Acre with a government press officer. Acre was a city inhabited mostly by Arabs, and the Arab mayor, with whom we lunched, predictably told me his people were better off as Israeli citizens than their compatriots who had fled to Arab countries. His only gripe was that the Saudis wouldn't let them make the pilgrimage to Mecca with their Israeli passports.

The next day I refined and condensed my questions for Ben-Gurion to thirty-one, and on Friday faced him across the desk in his small and rather cluttered office.

He was then seventy-one, and Israel, ten. Yet the two had much in common. Both were small, cocky, energetic and loaded with brains. And, like Israel, born and weaned in battle, Ben-Gurion could also be brusque. He neither minced nor wasted words. When I said something about rough questions, he interrupted impatiently: "Go ahead, go ahead. Ask me anything you want."

Much of our talk dealt with my visit with Nasser the year before.

"Nasser talks as if he were the only one who wants to negotiate. Two years ago, an important intermediary—I can't tell you who—came to me and then went to Nasser in an effort to bring us together. I was willing, but Nasser refused. . . . As to their being afraid of us, look at the figures: forty million against fewer than two million; an area sixty times bigger than ours; at least four times as many weapons, and of far better quality. . . . If the Arabs have any self-respect, how can they be afraid of us? . . . As to the Sinai campaign, I don't regret it at all. Why should I? In reply to the second part of your question—would we strike again if we felt threatened, it is hypothetical, so I would rather not answer it. . . . If Nasser is willing to talk peace, we are willing to discuss the refugees. And we will make constructive proposals to solve the problem for the good of the refugees."

I also threw him a few hard balls: "Just three years ago this morning you personally ordered a military raid on Gaza in which thirty-eight Egyptians were killed and thirty-three wounded. C. L. Sulzberger recently wrote in the *New York Times* that this 'brutal assault' is what caused Nasser to revise his policies and make his arms deal with Russia. Do you agree?"

Ben Gurion replied: "Have you heard of the *fedayeen?* These people, trained and armed by Nasser, were crossing the border, killing our farmers working in their fields, killing our children going to school. There were just three things we could do: We could let them go on killing—but not even Gandhi would have accepted that. We could retaliate in the same way—but why should we kill innocent people? Or we could destroy the *fedayeen* bases. This we did—this was the purpose of our action. And we will do it again if the fedayeen resume their raids."

In closing, I asked if he would consider flying to Cairo to meet with Nasser—assuming the latter was agreeable. Or did he share the opinion of those who refer to Nasser as another Hitler?

"I would definitely go to Cairo, any time he invites me. I really don't know what sort of a man he is, though I suspect his ambition is to be the dominating leader in Africa and the Muslim world. But I have never thought of him as a Hitler; I don't think he would or could do what Hitler did. Therefore I would not hesitate to negotiate with him as man to man."

It was too bad Nasser didn't feel secure enough to take the chance that Anwar Sadat did many years later; for after meeting both Nasser and Ben-Gurion, I believe they would have reacted to each other much more positively in the fifties than their successors did in the seventies.

And thousands of lives would have been spared and vast resources diverted from destruction to development.

My meeting with Aneurin Bevan, a big, tousled, plain-spoken former coal miner, took place in his office at the House of Parliament and is worth citing today because of his refreshing candor and common sense, still untarnished after twenty years.

He said he was depressed during a recent trip to the States by what he called the deterioration of the mental climate: "The attitude of young people used to be a healthy 'Oh, yeah?' but now it's more 'I guess you're right.' You now have a tendency to think in slogans. For example, I was asked again and again what I thought should be done to help strengthen the defenses of the free world. Nobody questioned what the free world consisted of or seemed interested in exploring the concept of defense in the nuclear age."

Of Eisenhower he said: "He was, and is a man of moral integrity without intellectual penetration," while of Dulles he said, "I could not find many people who defended him—apparently his qualities are visible only to the president." He particularly deplored Dulles's moralistic penchant for dividing the world into "God-nations and devil-nations."

On China he was equally blunt: "U.S. policy compels the Chinese to learn Russian instead of English; it has prevented us from influencing the development of the most populous nation on earth. If the Russians controlled your State Department, they could not have adopted a China policy more advantageous to themselves . . ."

Bevan deplored our failure to seize opportunities "to end the cold war" and favored fixing a date for an early summit meeting: "President Eisenhower has been going at it the wrong way—trying to find out first if the meeting will produce results. How can we tell in advance?" He thought limited, modest accords could be negotiated that would "create an atmosphere of trust which the world desperately needs." (Reading his words today, I can imagine him applauding the 1985 Geneva summit meeting.)

He also believed the Russians distrusted us as much as we did them: "Why shouldn't they? Look at the Suez affair in 1956. Khrushchev is convinced that you secretly connived with us . . ." And he deplored the gradual transformation of NATO from a mutual defense pact into an ideological crusade against communism.

When I asked what he thought was Western diplomacy's greatest mistake since World War II, he replied: "The assumption, from 1950 on, that the Russians were preparing a war of aggression so soon after emerging from the devastating war against Germany. This crippled the West financially by forcing us to spend billions on useless weapons . . ."

But he was moderately hopeful about the future: "If mankind survives the next twenty years, it will survive the next twenty thousand . . . The capitalist and Communist nations have, for the first time, a common interest. They must both avoid war. . . . I believe the Soviet leaders know war is impossible. They are not lunatics. Our leaders realize it too, but until they act accordingly and make this fact a principle of diplomatic action, we will all be in danger. That is why the next few years are so critical for mankind."

Unfortunately, Bevan never did become foreign secretary, but we can take comfort in his prediction. Not only have we survived those twenty critical years he mentioned, but we are getting close to thirty; which means, depending on the clarity of his crystal ball, that we'll have 19,970 more not to worry about.

The last cold war occurrence of 1958 was a tripartite conference in November to discuss a nuclear test ban, and then the curtain went up on 1959 with the triumphal entry of Fidel Castro's *barbudos* into Havana. I went down there a week later, and again in July, and again from time to time for the next twenty years. Since I was also involved in some diplomatic initiatives pertaining to Cuba during the Kennedy Administration, it would be best to bypass chronology and tell the whole story in succeeding chapters.

After the Havana visit, I found myself headed for India once again —fortunately, in the temperate month of February—at the request of Averell Harriman, who had contracted to do a series of articles for the *New York Times* and needed somebody to help write them. Dan Mich figured there might be a *Look* story in it as well.

There were four of us, including his late wife, Marie—earthy, irreverent and exuberant—and an earnest young researcher named Walter Friedenberg. Harriman himself was distracted and downcast by his recent loss of the New York governorship to Nelson Rockefeller, a defeat he blamed on bad advice from Tammany boss Carmine de Sapio.

We started our tour in New Delhi with the ritual call on Nehru, who pleased Harriman by expressing apprehension about the Chinese. (He was to assail them publicly a month later over their actions in Tibet.) Like Eisenhower and other American public figures who had visited the Soviet Union, especially during and soon after the war, Harriman did not believe the Russians wanted nor would risk a war. He was a firm believer in hard bargaining and signed agreements ("but never try to push a Russian through a closed door"); however, he neither knew nor trusted the Chinese. And so, after a round of meetings with politicians, diplomats and journalists in New Delhi, I wrote a lead on his first *Times* article that I knew for certain he'd like: "The best news out of India today is that her leaders are finally aware of the menace of Communist China." The piece went on to say this rivalry was crucial since one of these two emerging giants would serve as a model for all Asia, and deplored our tilt to Pakistan, which was a member of the Dulles-conceived Baghdad Pact. (Dulles, as strong-willed as he was wrongheaded, died of cancer that May, and Ike then had to take a more active role in formulating foreign policy.)

In Agra I typed the article in the hotel garden while two snake charmers tried to distract me with their cobras (they did) and the Harrimans tramped around the Taj Mahal in the hot sun. He seemed groggy when they returned for lunch and also bewildered by an American tour group who had arrived in buses that morning and now filled all the tables in the dining room. As we entered, he began dazedly moving from table to table, murmuring, "I'm Averell Harriman and I appreciate your support." Being mostly midwesterners, the tourists reacted as though he was their new cruise director introducing himself, until he reached one table where a man sprang up and cried, "Governor! Great to see ya! I'm from Rochester an' a good friend of Carmine de Sapio's."

Harriman seemed to blink back to reality and joined Marie and me at our table, muttering, "Carmine de Sapio—that son of a bitch!"

After New Delhi, we kept moving—Katmandu first, where the Harrimans stayed at the Royal Hotel, a former palace whose corridors were lined with photographs of maharajas posing with one foot on a dead tiger, and Walter and I at the Snowview, which had one stone bathtub and an Israeli in the lobby giving a slide lecture on his kibbutz. Nepal was then like another planet, though two local Communists did appear to raise loud objections to my taking pictures of women lined up to vote in the country's first free election. They accused me of trying to influence them.

And so to Dum Dum Airport in Calcutta, still teeming and reeking, where the U.S. consul general presented us with a schedule that brought back memories of the 1953 Stevenson ordeal: visit to Indian

Statistical Institute, lunch at consul general's (who warned us against eating at the city's best Chinese restaurant because it was "Red"), tour of the harbor, tea and press conference at the Grand Hotel, visit to the notorious "black hole," meeting with the food minister at his office, followed by meeting with the chief minister at his, and an eight fifteen dinner and briefing at the consul general's before departing for Raipur at 7 A.M. by car with box lunch.

But Harriman, at sixty-eight, was indefatigable. We visited two steel mills in two days, clambering over catwalks while he asked innumerable questions. The first was operated by a private Indian firm; the second was being completed by Russians with financing provided by a long-term, low-interest loan. It was an effective form of economic aid, since the Indians didn't feel they were receiving a handout with possible strings attached.

The chief engineer at the Russian plant at Bhilai was named V. E. Dymshits, and we were treated like VIPs because Harriman had been ambassador to Moscow during our wartime alliance. The Indians I talked to at the reception told me the Russians worked hard but were stern and standoffish. Some of the Russians, sorely tempted by my offer of a drink at our guest cottage after living six months in a dry state, hesitated outside the door and finally turned back, not sure, I suppose, if one of their group might be a KGB watchdog.

We pressed on to Kerala state, whose Communist chief minister, E. M. S. Namboodripad, joined us for dinner and stilted small talk at the State Guest House. (When I went to his office to invite him, I didn't make the mistake my *Look* colleague had the year before when he sat outside the chief minister's office for an hour, waiting for the clerk to usher him in. Finally, he asked when Mr. Namboodripad would be available. The clerk leaped up, eyes flashing. "But *I* am Namboodripad!" he cried.)

And then on to Bangalore and Bombay, where I finished the draft of Harriman's fifth and final article and learned once again that there is no end to surprises in India. . . . At a dinner at the home of a Sikh artist I'd met in New York, I found myself sitting next to a very pretty, demure-looking young woman wearing the usual sari and adorned with a nose diamond and a caste mark on her forehead. While we deplored the fact that American red tape had allowed only twenty Indians to go to the States on study grants last year—far fewer than to the Soviet Union—I noticed that she quietly downed three martinis. She then confided to me she'd been going to a psychiatrist since her divorce and was bored with her job as account executive in an advertising agency. Bombay was a lot closer to Madison Avenue than I'd thought.

I was told by the other guests, who were on the radical fringe of Indian politics, that the Communists were losing strength now that they were split between pro-Moscow and pro-Peking factions. Their strategy of capturing one state government at a time had succeeded only in Kerala, where there was a glut of unemployed intellectuals.

Finally we were on our way home, via Karachi, where the midgets were still operating the elevators at the Metropole, and the Pakistanis still harped on India's perfidy. I was reminded that the world was and is pockmarked with ancient quarrels, like never-quite-extinct volcanoes, which lend a sense of continuity to history and an occasional frisson of anticipation to mothballed foreign correspondents.

In the summer, after a visit with Fidel Castro (to be recounted later), Phil Harrington and I toured U.S. bases in Italy and Turkey as part of an "Americans Abroad" series. We found no great fraternization but no discernible friction either. I did run into the expected hostility toward Greeks in Izmir, where I dined with some local newspapermen and remarked jocularly that Greeks were probably more popular than Turks in America because there were more of them and they operated good restaurants all over the country.

The next day's paper carried my offhand comments on the front page under a headline stating I had "revealed" the existence of a sinister gastronomic Greek plot designed to influence U.S. public opinion. This was still another feud, still another half-extinct volcano, which would probably continue to span the generations.

In September 1959, Nikita Khrushchev came to the United States and appeared to like most of what he saw except Hollywood, where he found *Can-Can* vulgar. Eisenhower so charmed him at Camp David that he left crying, "Long live Soviet-American friendship!" The defunct Spirit of Geneva was now refurbished as the Spirit of Camp David, and Khrushchev proposed a summit in Paris in the spring to discuss banning nuclear tests and also invited Ike to Moscow.

Americans reacted to Khrushchev with curiosity, suspicion and disbelief: this energetic, pudgy performer spouting proverbs and homespun humor hardly fitted our popular image of a stony Soviet dictator. I recall seeing him on TV in a Third Avenue bar one evening after work (people still went to bars then to watch the tube as well as to drink). The comments from the viewers were not unexpected: "You'd think he'd a learned to speak English by now" and "He's got a nerve comin' over here—Americans can't go to Russia" and "If Ike likes him he can't be all bad."

Not all bad, and quite shrewd. At Roswell Garth's Iowa farm, Khrushchev admitted frankly that Russians had a "siege mentality" and were "secretive and suspicious." He said if we want them to try hybrid corn, "make it seem you were smuggling it to us." He recalled that in the czarist days landowners got their serfs to eat cheap and nourishing potatoes only by fencing in the potato patches, certain the serfs would then steal them and acquire a taste for them.

At any rate, the visit helped dispel the residual chill from the May foreign ministers' meeting, which was marked by the usual squabbling over Germany. It was clear the Russians had to find a way to stem the tide of refugees fleeing East Germany to the West—three million since 1948, or more than a sixth of the population. New threats were therefore inevitable. But for the moment, another thaw was on; Anastas Mikoyan, the Kremlin's Great Survivor, came to Washington and sounded conciliatory; and, of course, another Eisenhower-Khrushchev meeting was in the offing.

The new decade, in some ways, had the feel of a new dawn. We opened a year-end issue of *Look* with a piece called "How America Feels As We Enter the Soaring Sixties." The lead I wrote started:

> The next ten years may be the most exciting in mankind's 100,000-year adventure on earth. At long last, we are about to begin the exploration of the mysterious universe that surrounds our planet. At the same time, we are faced with the choice of giving up organized tribal warfare and perhaps ending this long adventure by thermonuclear suicide. Ten years from now, life on earth may have been made intolerable by human stupidity—or it may have been transformed by human intelligence and ingenuity into something better than man has ever known.

In conjunction with the article and picture stories of a cross-section of Americans, we commissioned a special Gallup survey which revealed that people in all parts of the country looked forward with confidence to continued peace and prosperity . . . regarded education as more important than hard work in achieving success in life . . . would like (one in four) to move to California or Florida . . . feared big labor more than either big business or big government . . . took rising prices and high taxes for granted . . . except for farmers, did not worry about the future

... said, if teenagers, that their attitudes and opinions differed very little from those of adults.

The country was in for quite a few surprises during the decade ahead.

And so was I, when Adlai Stevenson asked me in December to take a leave of absence and help him with some speeches in advance of the 1960 presidential campaign. This was to be the decade when I learned how easily one thing can lead to lots of others.

Chapter 10

The Biggest Prison in the World

Sim and I were visiting a state dairy farm about fifteen miles outside of Bucharest, Romania, when I got the idea for a title of the report I'd be writing about this six-week drive through the captive nations of Eastern Europe. One of the government agronomists escorting us asked me for my impressions of Romania. I thought back to the evening we crossed the border from Hungary—remembering the machine guns, the barbed wire, the watchtowers—and I replied, "Well, it reminds me of a prison. You have low-cost housing, good security, free medical care and plain but nourishing food. But you don't elect your warden, you are at the mercy of the guards and you can't get out. So I'd say Romania is really better than some Americans think because a well-run prison can be quite tolerable if you're not too curious or ambitious . . ."

"Of course, we've had a hard time," said another Romanian.

"Sure you have. Thanks to the Russians, you had your Marshall Plan, too, but in reverse."

"I see we are having a frank and intimate discussion," he remarked dryly. "Who told you these things?"

No one had to, I explained, describing the border and citing the drabness, the austerity and the all-too-obvious secret police who infested the hotels. "You can tell when you're in a prison," I added. They fell silent. But as we walked back to our car, one of the group drew me aside. "You're right!" he whispered. "You're right!"

So I called the piece—which was a hard one to write for fear of endangering all the good and brave people who confided in us—"One Way to See the Biggest Prison in the World." It was our first protracted, close-up look at communism in practice and made an indelible impression on us. It did not turn me into a hawk but it strengthened my repugnance for the tyranny and inhumanity that was synonymous, at least in the fifties, with the Soviet system.

I got the idea of exploring Russia's Europe by car early in 1958 when ads urging Americans to visit the Soviet Union began appearing in the *New York Times*. Someone in Moscow had decided that tourism was an easy way to earn hard currency, as the Yugoslavs had discovered, and I figured the Eastern Europeans would soon follow suit now that Moscow had pointed the way.

Dan Mich liked the idea, but only if we got into Russia. I disagreed privately (which was the best way to disagree with Dan) because I knew that communication with ordinary people would be easier in countries where German, French and even English were fairly common than in Russia (as I'd learned in Moscow); also, we had large enough ethnic minorities of Poles, Hungarians, Czechs, Slovaks—plus some Yugoslavs, Romanians and Bulgarians—in the United States so that there'd be more potential readers for a report on their homelands than on Russia. And there'd be variety, which would make for better pictures.

So I told the Cosmos Travel Agency, which had a near monopoly on the new Communist tour market, to make the arrangements, including visas to all Eastern European countries, including the U.S.S.R. but excluding Albania, which was still off limits.

As it turned out, Sim and I must have been put back on the Soviet blacklist, because that's the only visa that didn't come through; which was just as well, despite Dan's grumbling.

For pictures, I invited Dennis Stock of Magnum to come along, together with his then girl friend, Kate Roosevelt, a lovely twenty-two-year-old who proved to be an asset to us in countries where Franklin D. Roosevelt, her grandfather, was revered by the Communist rulers as Stalin's wartime partner. (In Romania, our foursome was even referred to respectfully as "the Roosevelt party.")

I also told Cosmos to pass the word we'd be doing a survey of the tourist possibilities for Americans behind the iron curtain—which in a sense we were.

Our vehicle was a huge two-tone Ford station wagon with tail fins and double headlights and fitted with a special low-octane carburetor and an electrical outlet for our tape recorder and record player—in short a real crowd-pleaser that often made us feel like visitors from a friendly planet driving a spaceship on wheels. Sim and I took off from central France, where the kids stayed at my mother-in-law's, and met up with Kate and Dennis in Vienna. What with suitcases, magazines, records, film, whiskey, toilet paper and assorted sundries we figured might be hard to find, we needed all the car's available space. I say "figured" because we really did not know what to expect. This expedition was, to my knowledge, the first such trip undertaken by Americans since the start of the cold war. The CIA people naturally wanted to meet with us, but I declined. Our rule at *Look* was that talking to the Agency was all right *after* a trip (if only to correct some of their misinformation) but never before. The moment they told you to watch out for something, you became a semi-spy. The CIA did manage to recruit a few journalists but the latter eventually became pariahs among their peers.

We passed through the iron curtain—its barbed wire, minefields and watchtowers—less than an hour's drive from Vienna. The stern Hungarian customs officials delayed us longer rummaging through our baggage. Then we headed east through villages and a landscape identical to what we'd seen on the Austrian side—brick or whitewashed houses, cherry trees, geese and cows in the road—with some differences. Except for a few trucks, vehicles were all horse-drawn, red stars adorned public buildings and people either stared at us in amazement or waved enthusiastically. We paused in Györ for lunch while crowds milled around the car, and reached Budapest and the Margarit Hotel on the Danube in time to meet the guide provided by Ibusz, the state tourist agency. His grasp of English was tenuous and his first question ("Why didn't you help us during the revolution?") either naive or provocative. So up in our room we loudly addressed the chandelier, where we'd heard the microphones were usually concealed, and said he would never do because we couldn't understand him. As the first legitimate American tourists in Hungary since the 1956 "disturbances" (as he told us we were), we deserved a more experienced and fluent guide.

Sure enough, another young man appeared in the morning, just as our dinner guest, the local AP correspondent, had predicted. We drove around the first of our Communist capitals, noting that everything old seemed shabby and everything new, shoddy. Buildings in downtown Budapest also were still scarred and pitted from the 1956 street fighting. Many young people without family responsibilities had fled and others were among the 25,000 killed, so the crowds seemed as middle-aged and slow-moving as the vintage trolley cars.

We had some names and phone numbers, and after the ritual sight-seeing and coping with the red tape of gas coupons and car insurance, I met with some friends of friends. Ferenc Marton, a writer, told me, "If you stay out of politics, you can get along." He felt there were more drawbacks than advantages in joining the Communist Party, which now had about 400,000 members—"perhaps a quarter reliable, the rest opportunists." While membership got you to the head of the line, so to speak, it also meant you were under stricter surveillance, had to attend meetings and were despised by most of your neighbors. "The best thing about the uprising," he said, "is that we Hungarians discovered we all felt the same way about the Russians and the system. Now we are more like a family—we trust each other."

We were under casual surveillance when not accompanied by our guide. One night we took out two young friends of a 1956 resistance fighter who had managed to escape to New York. After dinner at the Kis Royal and listening to good jazz at the Paris Garten (where the vocalists sang in English), we drove them home. A police car was parked across the street. They shrugged. "The police will leave when you do," they said. "It's unpleasant but not dangerous."

The lack of gaiety and animation, even in a cabaret, became oppressive. At the Journalists' Club, conversation was subdued and stilted. "Intellectuals"—especially journalists—were still suspect since most had been in the forefront of the revolt, along with industrial workers. Premier János Kádár was trying to win them back (the club had just been reopened); as for the workers, he had recently stated, with a kind of pathetic candor rare among Communists: "I think I may say without fear of contradiction that a majority of the working people of our country now support their government."

A visit to Budapest's leading magazine, *Orszag Villag*, ended with a surprise. When I noticed their current issue contained the Hemingway piece I'd written for *Ogonyok* nearly two years before, I told the editors jokingly that I still hadn't been able to collect my ten rubles from the Russians, and maybe that's why we were having trouble getting a Soviet visa. They laughed but still seemed embarrassed at having used the article. And the next day a handsome doll in peasant costume, worth about $80, arrived at the hotel with their compliments to my six-year-old daughter. I decided Hungarian editors had more class than their Russian counterparts.

We attended the July Fourth reception at the American Legation residence in the once elegant and now run-down Buda hills. A few

Hungarians came, and I was asked by our political officer to lure a police informer away from a drunken Hungarian writer who was getting too outspoken for his own good. No Russians were invited, a petty and meaningless gesture but understandable in view of the lingering revulsion at home and in Hungary at their behavior in 1956. Other diplomats I talked to at the party about the revolt agreed there was nothing anyone could have done without risking World War III; had the U.N. secretary-general, Dag Hammarskjöld, accepted Nagy's invitation, he probably would have been taken into custody by the Russians "for his own protection" until they'd mopped up the resistance.

As for now, the Indian ambassador told me the best thing we could do was send thousands of tourists here every year to let the people feel they were not totally isolated in their Soviet cell block.

Before leaving for Romania, we drove to Lake Balaton for lunch at the Hotel Tihany, until 1956 a Soviet officers' club. A miniature American flag decorated our table, as at the Margarit, which gave the other guests an excuse to stare at us. At a public beach we played jazz records and took Polaroid pictures, which attracted a huge throng, including a woman who clung to us, sobbing and stammering incomprehensibly. Several policemen watched us but kept their distance until I opened the hood of the car. Then their curiosity got the better of them. The hardest thing for people to accept was that this resplendent vehicle was a lowly Ford—which they knew was a low-cost car, a "worker's car," as I pointed out.

Kate had an accident back at the Tihany, where she used a lakeshore slide that ended in two feet of water. She wrenched her foot badly and was in such pain when we got back to Budapest that I asked the hotel clerk to call a doctor. Since medical care was a state monopoly, the young physician who turned up wore a visored cap adorned with a hammer-and-sickle emblem and was accompanied by two unshaven stretcher bearers in stained white smocks. He gently examined her swollen foot.

"We'd better take her to the hospital for an X-ray," he told me in French. "There may be a small fracture."

"No!" yelled Kate. "Don't let them take me away! You'll never see me again!"

The doctor shrugged. "In that case, crutches and aspirin."

"Where did you learn French?" I asked him.

"As a child," he said, smiling, "I had a French governess."

"I see. And your bourgeois background is not a handicap?"

"Not if you have a skill they—the nation—needs," he replied. *Bonsoir, et bon voyage.*"

The Ibusz people tried to dissuade us from making a detour via the town of Békéscsaba on our way to Romania, but we had arranged to call on the parents of Tibor, our young exile friend. "The road is very bad," we were told. "Your big car will get stuck in the mud."

The road was actually very good. Charley, our part-time guide in Budapest, showed us the way out of town. "This has been like a holiday for me," he said as we parted. "Next week they will probably give me sixty Mongolians to take care of."

There was no traffic other than a few trucks and buses, so it was easy to spot the white Mercedes that tailed us all day. We bought gas (65-octane at 80 cents a gallon) and picnic fixings at Kecskemet, where an inquisitive English-speaking plainclothes cop kept asking us who we were and where we were going. When a crowd of people, including some Russian soldiers, gathered around the car, he tried to disperse them and was angrily chased away.

The Mercedes roared by as we picnicked and then stopped a few hundred yards down the road to wait for us. We waved as we passed but the two occupants didn't wave back.

The picnic was a mistake. Tibor's parents and relatives had a five-course lunch prepared, and it was late in the afternoon before we got away after passing out magazines, taping messages and taking snapshots —and subjecting poor Kate to the ministrations of a Gypsy osteopath, who pronounced her throbbing foot cured.

The border crossing between Hungary and Romania was and probably still is one of Europe's bleakest sites. Treeless, windswept, wired, barricaded and mined, it was not a picturesque place to linger, especially at dusk. But we suddenly found ourselves in a Catch-22, no-exit situation.

I knew something was wrong when the top cop came out holding our passports and frowning. *"Nicht gut,"* he growled.

After some further exchange of fractured German, he explained and I understood that our Hungarian visas stipulated we were to leave via Austria, not Romania. So he could not let us pass.

I pointed out that the visas expired at midnight, four hours hence, and the Austrian border was eight hours away. Therefore, if he didn't let us through he would be an accessory *(ein Teilnehmer)* to our illegal presence in Hungary. This clearly bothered him and he went to his phone, a primitive instrument with a crank, to try and reach headquarters in Budapest (unfortunately our Mercedes escort had gone on back). Meanwhile, we were to wait in the car.

It got windier and darker. Suddenly Kate let out a squeal. A swarthy, leering Hungarian soldier cradling a machine gun was tapping on her window. I cranked it open. *"Was ist los?"* I demanded.

"Sie amerikanisch?" he asked. *"Ich numismatisch."*

It took me a moment to realize this grimy gunslinger was a coin collector, a numismatician.

"Anybody got a penny?" I asked.

Sim did, and I handed it to him. He clutched it happily and even bowed. *"Danke, danke!"*

Then the phone rang, and the head man came out, looking puzzled. It was not Budapest calling back after all. "Roosevelt?" he asked.

"It's got to be your mother insisting you come home right away," I told Kate.

But it wasn't Mrs. Jock Whitney either. It was a Romanian woman across the border asking, in English, what was holding us up. When Kate explained, she asked to speak to the Hungarian. She must have been important or persuasive or maybe he decided that getting rid of us was his safest alternative; because the barrier was promptly lifted by the happy numismatician and we drove out of Hungary, three of us for the last time. It would be twenty years before I returned.

A rather formidable, quadrilingual woman whom I will call Mrs. Maniu was waiting for us at the Romanian customs and whisked us through the formalities. She introduced herself as our "escort" before launching into a diatribe against Hungarian stupidity and inefficiency. (We had heard similar diatribes in Budapest against Romanian deceit and decadence.) She then insisted we were famished and led us to a restaurant in Oradea, the nearest town, before driving on to Cluj, the capital of Transylvania, where we were to spend the night. Her car was a big black Russian Zim, with chauffeur, and she invited Sim and Kate to ride with her. Mrs. Maniu was clearly the take-charge type, as we were to learn during the next few days.

The Continental, in Cluj, was a well appointed but almost deserted hotel dating from prewar times when the city was a convenient overnight stop for the upper classes motoring between Budapest and Bucharest. Travel between the two cities for the contemporary privileged class—the Communist bureaucracy—was usually by plane.

In the morning, we performed the sightseeing routine (including a crowded church where the sermon was given in Hungarian) while mobs engulfed our car to the annoyance of Mrs. Maniu, who found it "undignified." (Her driver was also annoyed, since no one looked at the Zim except with distaste.) But she cheered up when we told her we were mainly interested in folk dancing, holiday resorts and nice scenery; in other words, nothing that might present political problems. And we got what we asked for: Romania's countryside and old cities were truly spectacular. Unfortunately, Mrs. Maniu's running commentary attributed everything that looked clean and modern—like a prewar sanatorium—to "socialist enterprise and discipline," and anything primitive or dirty to "fascism and feudalism." She sounded like the stenciled whitewashed slogans and faded red banners that defaced every town—even more so than in Hungary—extolling the regime and exhorting the populace to still greater efforts. *Traiasca*—long live—seemed to be Romania's commonest word.

We lunched at Sibiu in a two-class restaurant—one section had tablecloths and flowers and the other, none—and stopped for the night in Stalin, formerly Brasov and before that Kronstedt, and soon to become Brasov again now that Khrushchev had consigned Uncle Joe to purgatory. We were assigned a vast suite and were seated at the dining room's most prominent table, decorated with an American flag. As a result, all conversation stopped when we walked in, Kate on her crutches and the surly chauffeur tagging along behind. Sim asked who ate here. Mrs. Maniu replied, "Artists, officers, intellectuals." Any workers? She looked around and pointed to a table: "Over there is a worker."

"How can you tell?"

"That is an indiscreet question," said Mrs. Maniu sternly. "You can tell by looking at his face."

At meal's end, we raised our glasses of *tsuica*, a kind of Romanian brandy, in a toast to the other diners, most of whom toasted us back. On the way out, one man grabbed my arm and whispered, "America —good!"

"As you can see," said Mrs. Maniu, "Romanians are very friendly people."

The next day we crossed the Carpathian foothills; stopped in an ethnic German town where we were invited to drink beer and dance to an oompah band at an engagement party; taped folksingers in a village right out of the old *National Geographic;* picnicked on wine and goat cheese in a grotto with costumed peasants; picked up a hitchhiker so dumbfounded at being in an American car that we gave him some book matches which he could show his friends as proof of his fantastic experience; and wound up at Sinaia in a 1912 spa hotel, now converted to a vacation retreat for deserving workers, where suites had been reserved for "the Roosevelt delegation." The other guests seemed subdued, playing chess or strolling in the garden, probably to escape the incessant noise of speeches and martial music on the loudspeakers. At six, a scheduled conference on "Friendship and Comradeship" was canceled when only two people showed up. During dinner, Mrs. Maniu, to whom we'd been lending American magazines, showed her first symptoms of uncertainty when she admitted that "even under socialism there is considerable discontent with the details of everyday living."

Then, in the morning, at breakfast, she broke down completely.

I triggered it. "What glorious achievements of socialism are you going to show us today, Mrs. Maniu?" I asked her jestingly. She bit her lip and then burst into tears. She was a big woman, and it was unsettling to watch her shoulders heaving and hear her choked sobs as she tried to regain control. Fortunately, the dining room was almost empty. Sim put her arm around her and then the words came tumbling out.

"For three days I have been lying to you . . . Making propaganda for this terrible regime . . . And you have been so nice . . . I just can't keep it up, not anymore. . . . I don't care what happens to me . . . I am a widow, you understand, with three children . . . It was the only work I could find as a bourgeois. . . . Will you forgive me?"

We calmed her down and told her not to worry, to go right on with her spiel in front of officials, only now we would be playing a game. We would pretend to believe her and then we could all relax and be friends and enjoy the rest of our visit.

She dabbed at her eyes and smiled tentatively. "And you understand I am now at your mercy. If you told my employers . . ."

"I will tell your boss the People's Republic of Romania should be proud of you. *Traiasca* Comrade Maniu!"

Then she really smiled and now there were tears in *our* eyes.

We had a good day. A pleasant young French-speaking doctor at the spa noticed Kate on her crutches and insisted she come to the clinic for an X-ray. "It's a good thing you didn't let the Hungarians touch you," he said. "They know nothing about medicine."

It turned out she did have a small fracture, so he put her foot in a cast, compliments of the People's Republic.

While she was being treated, Sim and I were talking to a man named

Jimmy who had come up to the car and told us in American English he'd lived seventeen years in New York, came back to Romania for a visit just before the war and had been trapped here ever since. He had a good job as top comedian in a musical revue but yearned to get away. We gave him some magazines and records, and he introduced us to the director and cast of his show, called *Revista 58*. They'd finished rehearsals and were opening in Bucharest the next evening. He said there'd be complimentary tickets for us at the box office the following night and maybe we could have supper after the performance.

Then we drove him around while he related a few grim details of life in a country controlled by the *Sicuritate*, reputed to be the most repressive police apparatus in Eastern Europe. Driving the car was another passerby who'd told us he would give nine years of his life to be our chauffeur. His expression, as he gripped the wheel of this splendid vehicle, was close to beatific. Yet so pervasive was the miasma of suspicion that I couldn't help wondering later if he wasn't a *Sicuritate* agent assigned to cover Jimmy.

We got to Bucharest the next afternoon via Ploesti, where Mrs. Maniu had to use her authority with a saturnine uniformed cop who tried to arrest us for taking his picture. Like many policemen, he was a Gypsy, therefore less inhibited about roughing up other Romanian citizens.

The Lido Hotel featured a swimming pool with artificial waves and frayed art deco furnishings. But the food was tasty and the city itself reminiscent of Paris without the traffic. As a Latin country surrounded by Slavs and Magyars, prewar Romania had always cherished its French connection and today still regarded its neighbors with the contempt of cultured gentry trapped on the wrong side of the tracks.

In the morning, Mrs. Maniu and I called on the director of Carpati, the state tourist organization, where I praised her skills as a guide, assuring him that she had opened our eyes to the reality of the impressive achievements of the People's Republic under socialism. They both smiled broadly, she with relief and he, no doubt, at my naiveté. Anyway, she would be all right and might even get a raise if, as I suggested, she turned in a detailed report on our activities to the *Sicuritate*.

People still clustered around the car, more furtively, it seemed, than in the countryside. But even in whispers they made no secret of how they felt, especially the young. That evening, we went to the Boema Garten theater and picked up our four free tickets at the box office. They were good seats but flanked on each side by empties. As the lights dimmed, a young man and woman slipped into them and soon informed us in English they'd be glad to translate anything we didn't understand.

The show was lively but second-rate vaudeville with some muted satire about the bureaucracy. (If you know French and Spanish, Romanian is almost understandable.) But Jimmy, though listed in the program, never appeared. And so, trailed by our young *Sicuritate* companions, we went backstage after the final curtain and asked about him. Someone said evasively that he was sick, someone else that he was on holiday. We supped alone.

The next day, I told Mrs. Maniu I wanted to get in touch with him. She made some calls and assured me he was all right. Not good enough, I said. I wanted to talk to him. Finally she produced a phone number. He answered my call, said he was sorry to have missed us but was having his apartment painted. Everything was okay, he added, wishing us a good trip home.

On our last day in Romania, we visited the dairy farm and the Gheorgiu Dej textile factory, where Sim questioned the matron in the day-care center about the bust of Stalin on the shelf. "What do you tell the children about him now?" she inquired.

"They don't ask," was the reply.

Meanwhile I was asking the manager if the workers could strike.

"They don't," was *his* reply.

From other conversations, including an informal briefing at the American Embassy, I gathered that, repression aside, life was hard in Romania. For example, a woman I met who owned an apartment building was not allowed to sell it or even give it away, except to the state. But the authorities had devised a better way of fleecing her. They simply raised her taxes and imposed strict rent controls that, in effect, forced her to operate at a loss and thus pay tribute to the state. Crime, too, was becoming a serious problem, since the people so detested the police they would not even cooperate with them on criminal cases. The consensus among Western diplomats was that there were not more than five hundred dedicated Communists in Romania; the other Party members were either "careerists or idiots."

The current "joke" (there was always one going the rounds in Communist countries as a sanity preserver) was about the three adjectives intelligent, honest and Communist—and why not more than two could ever be applied to one person: One could be honest and intelligent— but then not a Communist; or honest and a Communist—but then not intelligent; or intelligent and a Communist—but then not honest.

To be fair, there *were* things about what was called the "socialist" system that most people liked: free medical care, low-cost housing, paid vacations, public schools and a chance for bright students to go to college, full employment and the end of feudalism and absentee land-lords.

Yet the "revolution" which brought these changes was imposed from the outside, and the changes themselves could have been imple-mented without terror; and unlike most revolutions, this one did not on the whole result in greater freedom, whatever the social injustice and inequality of prewar Romanian society. Between 20 and 90 percent of farms, depending on regions and crops, were now collectivized, and the state could be a harsher landlord than the former aristocrats.

On our last evening, we had a dinner date with a playwright, Aurel Baranga, who never showed up, to Mrs. Maniu's annoyance. So we went to hear Romania's Marlene Dietrich, a lovely, middle-aged folksinger named Maria Tanase. She had once been in love with an American I knew. She talked carefully (not knowing Mrs. Maniu) but did say, in French, "Not everything here is as it should be."

Outside, in the crowd massed around our car, I spotted Jimmy. Moving closer, he whispered, "Everything's okay, it really is. As soon as you leave the country, I'll be back in the show. They just don't want us to talk . . ." And then he was gone.

Mrs. Maniu was less sanguine. "Nothing will happen to him—while you're here," she said.

She accompanied us to the Bulgarian border. We hugged each other, and she was in tears when we drove off, toward the next cell block.

We crossed the Danube on the "Friendship Bridge," heavily pa-trolled by armed soldiers. On the Bulgarian side, a burly customs in-spector made us take everything out of the car. No one was there to meet us, as in Romania, so we complied and watched him churn up our belongings. I asked him in German what he was looking for; he didn't know. Finally he encountered some tampons and began taking one apart. *"Was ist?"* he muttered.

My German was not up to a clinical explanation. *"Für Frauen,"* I said. *"Jeder Monat."* It worked. "For women every month" he under-stood, and a big Bulgarian blush was the result, along with a wave of the hand indicating we should pack up and proceed. He also gave us the name of the best hotel in Russe, the small, dimly lit town beyond the bridge.

There were rooms available at the Duna and a meal of shashlik, red caviar, slivovitz and beer. An English-speaking violinist and his wife, a physician, joined us. They'd come home from Australia after the war and wished they hadn't. As we talked, other diners drifted out to look at the car and decipher our USA emblem—which in their Cyrillic alphabet would have been YCA. We were nearing the Orient: the johns were Turkish-type, stand-up contraptions that soaked your feet when they were flushed and gave poor one-legged Kate a hard time.

After breakfast, with no guide to advise us, we decided to visit the local textile mill, which the violinist told us was managed by a woman. She turned out to be a pleasant, grandmotherly type, a former dressmaker and office clerk fired for Communist activity under the old regime. Her office was decorated with red flags and photographs of Lenin, Stalin and assorted Bulgarian Communists. She willingly showed us around but could not authorize pictures without the approval of the Russe party secretary. So she was called and soon appeared—a severe, buxom lady with medals on her lapels who relaxed only when we gave her Polaroid pictures of herself under Lenin's portrait.

"My wife here," I said, again in rusty German, "is also a party secretary in our town."

She was interested. "Which party?"

"Democratic."

"Is your party opposed to the policies of Eisenhower and Dulles?"

"Yes, indeed."

"You are in favor of peace? It is a progressive party?"

"We're all for peace and progress," I replied.

She beamed with pleasure and relief. I had given the correct answers. We must be fellow travelers. Trays of coffee, cakes and brandy quickly materialized—followed by a bolt of cloth as a "souvenir" of our visit to the factory. We toasted peace and friendship between Bulgarian and American workers, while Dennis took pictures of the two party secretaries and the manager, all wreathed in smiles.

After changing some money, we headed for Varna, on the Black Sea coast, through farm country where the peasants were so eager to meet us they made roadblocks with bales of hay so that we'd have to stop, say who we were and accept their offerings of goat cheese and strawberries in exchange for instant snapshots. Two women laborers needed a ride, and once in the car, held hands with Dennis, Kate and Sim. When they got out, one of them even scraped up a few words of English. "I love you," she said.

The seaside at Varna had been transformed into a modern beach resort called Golden Sands with the help of Swiss architects who had designed and built seventeen high-rise hotels that now earned 25 percent of Bulgaria's hard currency. Along with Western Europeans attracted by the bargain prices ($11 a day per person for a beachfront room, all meals included), there were organized holiday groups from other Eastern European countries—especially landlocked Hungary and Czechoslovakia. A female Czech band played at our hotel, and every table sported its little national flag. I was surprised they had the Stars and Stripes in stock, since we had broken diplomatic relations with Bulgaria in 1950, but they were no doubt planning ahead. (We lifted a travel ban in 1957 and our legation was reopened in 1960 and elevated to an embassy in 1966.)

Bulgaria had the largest number of physicians, per capita, of any European country—and maybe still does—so Kate was inevitably approached by one at the beach. When he learned the cast on her foot was Romanian, he hustled her off to Varna's hospital for another X-ray—and a new cast. "The Romanians have no medical knowledge at all," he explained.

The Bulgarians we met in Varna, including a Balkantourist guide who'd gone to meet us in Russe a day late, did not seem as cowed and furtive as the Romanians. Being Slavs living under a tough Nazi occupation, they had actually welcomed the Red Army as liberators in 1944. A young lifeguard I gave a jazz record to told me life was tolerable so long as you stayed out of politics, but like most of his contemporaries he resented not being able to get out and see the world, especially the glittering, forbidden West.

The regime was also clamping down on manifestations of Western culture such as rock 'n' roll. When a West German jukebox was installed in a Sofia department store that spring, it drew such crowds that the authorities quietly replaced the records, though not the labels. So when the kids came back and pushed the Presley button, out came *La Bohème*. The lifeguard added perceptively, "It's a mistake to allow a little freedom and then take it away."

At our guide's suggestion, we broke the long drive to Sofia at the medieval city of Tirnovo, where the recommended hotel, the Tirnovo Palace (what else?), was the second worst of our trip, the worst still to come, in Poland. Some Russian tourists from Archangel were complaining loudly when we arrived, a bad sign since Russians aren't normally fussy. Bugs were the problem—roaches, spiders, beetles, flies, mosquitoes, ticks—the whole wonderful world of insects. We spent much of the night sitting up swatting, spraying or smoking and leafing through copies of *Look* with the Russians. When I told them this was July 14, my thirty-ninth birthday, they produced a bottle of vodka and woke up the manager. He didn't like the hotel either and at breakfast asked us, first, for razor blades and second, if we would take him with us. I decided the vodka had addled him and suggested he sleep on the idea. So we looked around the old moats and battlements before driving on to Sofia, 150 miles away. We picked up one hitchhiker on the way, who insisted on paying for his ride with a gift of a mackerel wrapped in newspaper that he extracted from his briefcase. It was hard not to like the Bulgarians.

In Sofia—broad avenues and sparse traffic—we were housed in the new Balkantourist Hotel, a grandiose, Stalinist edifice where a truck could be driven through the corridors and banquet rooms—and the bathtub faucets fell off when turned. But then a Mr. Yotov, the burly chief of Balkantourist, turned up with two assistants, and things started crackling: first, a "reception" with caviar, cakes, wine and vodka, where they took notes while we gave them tips on how to attract hard-currency tourists—such as marking toilets with signs in the Latin as well as Cyrillic alphabet and making non-Communist newspapers available in hotels.

Yotov invited us to dinner at the Golden Bridges, a hilltop restaurant accessible by a boulder-strewn dirt road from which our Ford never fully recovered. Sim had her problems as a passenger in Yotov's limousine and had to discourage his advances with a lighted cigarette. Dinner consisted mostly of white wine, and we were easily induced to join a cultural gathering in honor of some visiting Communist writers. The Bulgarian literati, both male and female, looked like professional wrestlers. A Scottish poet sang "Sixteen Tons," which was singularly appropriate in Sofia, since a Communist country is the quintessential company store. Toast after toast was proposed. When my turn came, the Balkantourist interpreter seemed quite nervous, but I simply praised the beauty of Bulgaria and the friendliness of the people and said we didn't have to agree with each other's political systems to join in a toast to *"druzhba i mir."* Everyone looked greatly relieved that I had spoken the proper phrases, including the Russian words for friendship and peace, and more wine was uncorked. Still later I found myself taping a Bulgarian bagpiper beside the car and even later watching Yotov attempting to jitterbug with Sim in a night spot he ordered to remain open past closing time for our "enjoyment." As he proclaimed, "Balkan-tourist is a republic within a republic, and I am its president. The band plays until I tell it to stop."

We turned in at dawn and awoke in stifling heat. The only air-conditioned building in town was Georgi Dimitrov's mausoleum—a replica of Lenin's in Moscow—so we went there and cooled off while leisurely viewing the corpse of the Kremlin's leading international secret agent.

At dinner at the British chargé's apartment, we told him Yotov had scheduled a press conference and cocktail party for us the next afternoon at which we were expected to extol the virtues of Bulgaria and Balkantourist. How could we get out of it? Our host pointed to the chandelier in the living room, so I informed the microphone planted there that I intended to use the press conference to denounce the rotten Communist system.

And sure enough, no one appeared at the appointed time except Yotov and the interpreter. We stood around a kind of wedding cake decorated with crossed American and Bulgarian flags; finally Yotov stomped out, promising he'd have all the press there at 5 P.M. But by then he'd apparently received word; only the interpreter, looking sheepish, turned up saying it was a very busy news day and all the reporters were out on assignment.

We did meet some journalists when we called on the editors of *Our Nation* and *Literary Front*. While we were discussing Hungary, the chief editor remarked, "Whether the Russians were right or wrong, you Americans are doing the same thing in Lebanon."

Having been cut off from the news since leaving Mrs. Maniu (our British host's radio wasn't working), we didn't know U.S. Marines had just landed in Beirut at the request of the Lebanese president after the overthrow of the Iraqi government by radicals and the discovery of an alleged Syrian plot to seize power in Lebanon. (British troops had been sent to Jordan at the same time.) So we joined the Bulgarians in a toast to "friendly disagreement" and hurried back to the hotel. We decided that if the Near East was about to blow up, Bulgaria was not the place for us to be. Within an hour we were loaded up and heading for the Yugoslav border, less than two hours drive away.

Once past the baggage search, barbed wire, plowed fields and watchtowers, we felt we were back in the West, even though the Yugoslav border guard called me *"Kamerad."* At the service station in Nis, there was a poster advertising 1958 Fords, British and Pakistani officers driving to Karachi, French and Italian backpackers hitchhiking to Istanbul and more animation at the hotel than we'd seen since June.

The next day we reached Belgrade, which was considerably spruced up since our 1953 visit. We stayed at a new hotel, the Metropole, where Western papers were for sale at the newsstand, and B-girls were for rent at the bar. We caught up on the news from the Near East. Khrushchev's reaction to the Lebanese operation had been relatively mild. (He simply compared it to the Suez War and Nazi aggression.) Although the Chinese were unsuccessfully pressing the Arabs to accept "volunteers" to repel the "imperialist invasion," the Soviets indicated they'd stay out of the squabbling unless we moved into Iraq. Syria had meanwhile formed a union with Egypt and Yemen called the United Arab Republic, which was to last three years. (On August 21, both the Arabs and the Israelis joined in an 80–0 vote in the U.N. General Assembly calling on the big powers to stay out of the Near East; the U.S. Marines phased out of Lebanon between August and October, having suffered only one casualty.)

I saw some Yugoslav friends while Kate had her cast replaced yet again at the insistence of a Yugoslav doctor who had no confidence in his Bulgarian colleagues. While still a police state, Yugoslavia now seemed on a par with Spain; political repression was homegrown, not Soviet-imposed.

Vilfan, Tito's aide who'd escorted us to Brioni in 1953, seemed relieved when I assured him I was not including Yugoslavia in this Eastern Europe report for *Look* since it was no longer part of the Soviet empire. (In fact, its brand of communism, which now stressed decentralized management and incentives, had become increasingly heretical in Moscow's view.)

He arranged for us to spend a night near Zagreb at a camp for young volunteers working on the Autoput, the new express highway to Slovenia. We got a warm welcome, a good meal and, by chance, an evening's entertainment by visiting troupes of folk dancers. While I taped the songs, the campers crowded around asking questions about James Dean and Elvis Presley. Politics was not much on their minds: those I queried professed to like "Yugoslav communism" and regarded the U.S. and the U.S.S.R. as equally "imperialist." At bedtime, Sim and Kate were offered the commander's hut, while Dennis and I were given cots in a communal tent.

In the morning we found eight young Americans in the area reserved for foreign volunteers. Their chief gripe was that they were at a disadvantage in political discussions—for example, about Lebanon—because they had never thought much about U.S. foreign policy: "We didn't realize how little we knew until we got over here."

Yugoslavia was like a halfway house to the West. People looked at us, waved and smiled, but didn't surround the car or talk in whispers. Still, it wasn't until we crossed into Austria with its traffic jams, neon lights and well-stocked shops that we felt we were truly back where we belonged.

Not for long. We paused in Vienna only to patch up the car and see if our Soviet visas had been granted (they hadn't) and if Kate's and Dennis's Czech and Polish visas were ready (they weren't). So after picking up our mail at the Freidins, who now lived in Vienna, Sim and I drove the thirty miles to the Czechoslovak border and plunged back into the drab and subdued Communist ambience of Bratislava. Fortunately there was no guide from Čedok, the tourist office, to meet us; we were on our own.

So we called on the brother of our hometown druggist, a seventy-year-old Jewish pensioner who was not even allowed to visit his sister in Austria, let alone emigrate. The only explanation was that the regime felt so insecure it could not admit that anyone would want to leave the country—even though desperate Czechs were breaking out week after week; one family even hijacked a train to crash through the iron curtain.

We were told that in one wooded area on the Bavarian border, the Czechs had fabricated a fake frontier about a mile inside the actual border. There, escapees could see a guardhouse topped by a U.S. flag and manned by American soldiers behind a strand of barbed wire. But on approaching, they discovered the soldiers were in fact Czech militiamen in disguise.

Sim was now taking pictures with her Rolleiflex. Whenever we stopped, say to buy gas, the usual crowd would gather—some of them taking risks just to make sure we wouldn't get a wrong impression of the country. "Things are really not so nice here," said a young girl quietly (police informers were always assumed to be nearby). Two young motorcyclists named Joe and Ladislaw offered to show us the way to Piestany, where I'd stayed in 1947, so we drew up to the hotel under noisy escort. This, and the fact we were Americans, induced the manager to find us a nice (and presumably bugged) room in what was supposedly a fully booked establishment.

We bought beers for our bikers, who talked to us in a mixture of German and English at a tavern already jammed with loud drunken Czechs even though it was not yet noon. "People here drink a lot," said Joe, "because it's the only way to get away. When you are drunk you can make believe you are someplace else. Even in Hollywood."

An English-speaking engineer joined us, kissing Sim's hand, a Central European custom that had persisted, despite communism, in all the countries we'd visited. He was now working as a cashier in a café because his "bourgeois background" disqualified him from professional employment. He said that many skills were being wasted for such political reasons, but that it was safer and more relaxing to be a clerk or manual worker than to hold a high visibility job under the present regime.

A group of prancing, playful children—communism's most pampered minority—passed by, escorted by two young women from a day-care center. The engineer remarked, "That's the thing to be under communism—a child. And then, when you grow up, a bird."

At dinner we were seated next to a table of pudgy East German VIPs who drank champagne with every course. This was the New Class, so incisively portrayed in Milovan Djilas's book: thugs and opportunists who had served the Party and the Russians slavishly and who had now become communism's aristocracy. But unlike the decadent old Habsburg aristocrats, they didn't seem to know how to enjoy their privileges. They ate and drank stolidly and silently, belching occasionally and watching us with curiosity. Recalling Herr Dittmar in Leipzig, I was just as glad they didn't strike up a conversation.

While we dined, I'd left one of my notebooks in a flight bag in our room. It wasn't until we got to Prague the next afternoon that I realized it was missing. I should have known the room would be searched. Fortunately, my notes were cryptic, no names mentioned and most of the Hungarian stuff easily reconstructed from memory. But I fired a telegram off to Piestany nonetheless from the Alcron Hotel. (By mistake, I entered the telephone operators' room and was quickly hustled out, but not before spotting a dozen reels of tape spinning over the switchboards—suggesting that in at least a dozen rooms the phones were bugged.)

We called a Czech television technician we'd met at Varna, and he showed us proudly around the old city. He was no Communist but said he loved his country too much ever to leave (he finally did, in 1968). He deplored the fact that many Czechs were so anxious to stay out of trouble that they collaborated with the regime more than they needed to. "If one works hard and doesn't complain and never discusses politics, one can live fairly well," he said. "But I'm glad Hana and I have no children. I worry the children may be corrupted."

A young woman he introduced us to was more eloquent when I asked her how it was possible to live in this suppressed fashion without becoming a little crazy.

"You must accept reality," she replied. "You must never pretend that things are going to be any better. You must do your work, you must be kind to your fellow countrymen, you must try to remain a human being. You must never cringe or try to please the masters. I will meet you and your wife in public any time. Let the police watch us or follow us. It doesn't make any difference. If they want to destroy me, they don't need an excuse. Once you accept this reality, then you never say, 'It isn't fair,' and then you can live."

We had driven to Prague via Brno and told Čedok we'd like to go to Poland via Ostrava and perhaps see some collective farms along the way. No problem. At Kostivice and Olomouc, we tramped around these cheerless bureaucratic farm complexes where a couple of laborers managed to get word to us that this or that building or acreage had once been their family farms. Sim's camera caught the bitterness in their faces just before the local Party secretary appeared and wanted to know why we were here. She got his picture, too, which pleased him even though he looked like a Mafia hit man. It wasn't hard to understand why agricultural production was flagging. A farmer who used to work sixteen hours a day during the harvest on his own place now put in his eight hours as a hired hand and went home to cultivate the vegetables in his backyard plot.

Our visas expired at midnight, and we made Ostrava by eleven. While we dined on sausages from a pushcart, two young men offered to guide us to the border crossing. One said he'd been a prisoner of war in Russia because he'd been drafted into the puppet Slovakian army. "And now, living here, I am a civilian prisoner," he said. (The prison analogy had come up in every country we'd been to except Yugoslavia, where people now felt they were in a kind of minimum security facility.)

The Poles made a polite and cursory inspection of our bags and directed us to the only hotel in nearby Cieszyn. It turned out to be the town bordello, so we had to pay in advance and endure a noisy night. We found a place at dawn where they served bread and coffee and sat with a pilot who'd served with the RAF and been imprisoned in Russia. "They decided I was a spy," he said. "It was worse than Auschwitz." Back in Poland, he was picked up by the U.B., the secret police, who knocked out his teeth and then broke his hands so that he couldn't fly again. He had no objection to our photographing his hands. Now he worked in an office. Things were better. "Two years ago, I wouldn't have dared to talk to you. Now it's all right."

He despised the Czechs: "If they were ever occupied by Arabs, they'd all become Muslims." And he repeated a story we'd already heard in Hungary—that during the 1956 uprising, "The Hungarians behaved like Poles, the Poles like Czechs and the Czechs like swine."

Cracow had not changed much since my 1947 visit. We checked in at a hotel run by Orbis, the state tourist office, where they changed some traveler's checks at a rate so discounted that, much to the glee of the Poles in the lobby, I blew up: "You rob the workers, you rob the peasants and now you rob the tourists! Don't you Communists have any shame?"

So I felt better and we enjoyed meeting the mechanics at a nearby garage who were said to be well versed in American cars. Ours was making strange noises again: Bulgaria had been its undoing. They promised to fix whatever was wrong with the undercarriage by the next afternoon. "You're lucky not to be Russians," said the foreman. "For them we require a week."

I asked him how things were in Poland today. "Better," he said. "We are now at least free to grumble about our low wages."

We walked over to the university (where Copernicus once taught) to meet Professor Karol Estreicher, a delightfully outspoken scholar who told us the young were far more knowledgeable than their elders and by no means taken in by Communist slogans. "We are now half-free," he said. "And that is no small achievement." The existence of a second power center—the Catholic Church—made Poland different and the Soviets cautious.

Estreicher said his students all tried to dress "Western" and most, as we noticed, succeeded. The faculty, not the bureaucracy, decided who would be admitted; unlike Romania, where the Party approved students on the basis of ideological commitment and social origin, the only criteria here were academic.

It was a long drive from Cracow to Warsaw, slowed by innumerable horse-drawn farm wagons along the two-lane highway. Our most unexpected hitchhiker was the wife of the Yugoslav ambassador to Prague, whose car had broken down; our most unusual, a priest who chattered away in Latin. At dusk we reached the new Bristol Hotel—many notches above the Polonia of yore. The city itself was transformed: traffic was plentiful, including taxis and private cars; Western newspapers were available in public reading rooms and, best of all, the medieval Old City, reduced to rubble in the war, had been faithfully restored to its former splendor.

We called Abe Rosenthal, later executive editor of the *New York Times* and then its Warsaw correspondent. We lunched, along with his wife, Anne, and their children, and then strolled in the park. He said that Warsaw's surface bustle concealed a pervasive sadness among a proud people who now knew what they only feared in 1947—that they were irrevocably locked into the Soviet system. Their only hope, and it was a remote one, was that the Russians would change and tolerate more freedom as they became more secure.

"The screws have been loosened a little," said Abe, "but the same people are holding the screwdriver."

He had us to dinner with three editors of *Tribuna Ludu,* the Communist Party organ, and their wives. Marion Podkawinski, who'd rescued us from the Vopos in Berlin years before, was also there, and the conversation, lubricated by wine and vodka, became quite uninhibited. They made no secret of their anti-Russian feelings, while professing support for communism, and said Poland might well have gone to the aid of the Hungarians in 1956 if they'd had a common border. And they admitted to preferring Americans to Russians "because at least you admit your mistakes—they never do." They were critical of the Lebanese operation but conceded that, unlike the Russians in Hungary, we at least didn't shoot anybody.

They took us to the Journalists' Club the next day, where everyone seemed surprised the Russians had refused us visas while all their client states had granted them, at least to Sim and me. At the hotel, American tourists, mostly here visiting relatives, filled the lobby and appeared surprised by Warsaw. One told me they'd expected a city patrolled by Russian troops where starving Poles were marched around in chain gangs. More than a decade's exposure to our free press had not prepared them for reality.

Adlai Stevenson, two of his sons and Bill Blair also turned up after their tour of the Soviet Union. We compared notes and decided to run our pieces together in the same issue of *Look*. He was impressed by Khrushchev but concerned that the Russians didn't fully appreciate the Chinese menace. We all convened at the Mannikin nightclub in the Old City after dinner—a depressing place where young people huddled over tape recorders in a haze of cheap cigarette smoke and complained to us about being bored and confined. One of them finally spoke up and said, "All right, we're in jail. All we can do is make the best of it. Maybe it isn't fair but it's fate. Meanwhile"—bowing to Sim—"let us dance."

Driving to Sopot, a resort on the Baltic coast, we acquired two young hitchhikers, a boy and a girl, who spoke French. At a village called Rypin we had to slow down as the main square was filled with a wedding party spilling out of the church. So we stopped and I put the Polaroid to use, handing out pictures to the bride and groom and attendants.

In a moment an armed militiaman sauntered up and motioned to us to follow him to the "Kommandatura." The crowd fell silent. Meanwhile he took my camera, while Sim kept on surreptitiously recording the proceedings with her Rollei.

At headquarters, the deputy police chief, a real simian type, took our passports and ordered us to wait in an adjoining room. I said in German I wanted to call the American Embassy. Impossible. How about the editor of *Tribuna Ludu,* with whom I'd dined in Warsaw? This seemed to bother him but—impossible. So we sat and waited. A middle-aged man paused in the doorway and said, "How do you do?" in English.

I asked him why we were being detained.

He took out a piece of paper and pencil and wrote, "You do not understand the Communist system."

Oh yes, I did, only too well. I also knew that their goons could be intimidated by a show of authority. When we were called back, the deputy, who had never handled Polaroid film before, was washing his hands.

"Why are we being held?" I asked.

He handed me our passports. "For blocking traffic. You can go now."

"Not until I have your name. We will now be late for our appointment in Sopot. I will have to report you to Orbis for interfering with the legitimate movement of guests of the Polish state."

He was now looking quite pained, sensing he had blundered.

"Please go," he said.

"Where are our young passengers?"

"Upstairs. They will stay."

"Then we will stay. Someone will come from Warsaw soon enough to see what has happened to us. I don't envy you."

Now thoroughly upset, he had our hitchhikers brought down from an interrogation room, and we walked out of the building. The whole town seemed to be waiting around, and a cheer went up as we appeared, and there were waves and smiles as we drove away.

"It's not often they have the pleasure of seeing the police forced to back down," explained one of our passengers.

But I was thinking: What if we'd been Poles?

Sopot, a seaside retreat for beefy Polish bureaucrats and their young mistresses (at least it looked that way) was not worth the trip, nor was the fourteenth-century castle at Marienburg, in what had been East Prussia. A colorful caravan of amiable Gypsies provided some good pictures, and some German-speaking truck drivers a touch of irony. As they admired our car and marveled at the cost (which I always translated into monthly wages), I told them I hadn't found the people's democracies either popular or democratic. All laughed and agreed. "Take me to America in your trunk!" shouted one as they drove off.

And this was the proletariat the regime counted on for support. Like the embattled factory workers in 1956 Budapest.

Sim and I were by now anxious to get home. Constant indignation wears you down, and we missed the children. So in Warsaw we got transit visas for the German Democratic Republic (which the U.S. didn't yet recognize) so that we could make a shortcut down to Switzerland without swinging west. I also reported our detention at Rypin to *Tribuna Ludu,* where the editor seemed genuinely surprised, and to Orbis, where a young woman simply observed, "Freedom is very relative here."

We left for Berlin on a Sunday, so all the gas pumps were closed in Poland beyond Poznań. Across the Oder River, in East Germany, we found none at all, open or closed; so, with the tank empty, we drove off the autobahn at Fürstenwalde, which turned out to be a Red Army garrison town. Squads of Russian soldiers marched past our parked car, heads immobile but eyeballs turned in our direction. No one asked us what we were doing here. Finally, we hailed a civilian on a bicycle and explained our predicament. He told us to follow him, and we wound up in a courtyard down an alley where, for two cartons of Camels, we were given enough fuel out of jerricans to take us to Berlin.

At the border between the Soviet zone of Germany (the D.D.R.) and the Soviet sector of Berlin, we were told to drive around to the check-point into the American sector. The East Germans regarded us with curiosity but no surprise: Berliners were used to seeing American cars, and our D.D.R. visas were like merit badges.

We tarried in West Berlin just long enough to eat our first oranges and bananas in six weeks and to order some good Danish furniture for our new house in Connecticut; and, like old times, to sample some caviar at the Intourist restaurant in East Berlin. (You could still drive back and forth across the sector boundary, which nineteen thousand fugitives from East Germany had crossed in July alone.) But there was no longer any caviar to be had. So we set out in the morning, first changing fifteen West marks for eighty East marks at a *Wechselstube,* or currency exchange booth, for buying food and gas in East Germany. We passed through the U.S. checkpoint and pulled up at the East German border crossing. The customs official asked what currency I had with me, and I produced all my cash, including the East marks. When I told him I'd obtained them from a West Berlin exchange office, he summoned two Vopos who escorted me past the car (Sim looked alarmed, so I winked) and over to a wooden building occupied by a dozen uniformed officials, seven of them sitting on a raised platform.

I was informed this was a people's tribunal and that I was being charged with illegally obtaining eighty East marks at a black market rate and importing them into the D.D.R. Then a clerk began the usual Teutonic routine of filling out a long printed form with the names and birthplaces of my parents and children, the value of my house, the number of my driving license and other irrelevant data.

When it was my turn to speak, I decided my best posture would be to combine aggrieved innocence, respect for the law and indignation at the hotel porter who had recommended the *Wechselstube.* After hearing me out, the tribunal adjourned to another room to deliberate. I was sweating a little, not only because we were totally at their mercy, but also because of the many notebooks and rolls of film in the car.

But my craven defense seemed to work. When the tribunal emerged, I was informed that in view of my ignorance of the law, my sentence would be a mild one—a fine of only one hundred West marks, plus the loss my eighty East marks (for a total of about $30). I suspect the abundance of Eastern European visas in my passport may also have led them to believe I might be some kind of American fellow traveler.

Anyway, as I bid them *"Auf Wiedersehen"* and headed for the door, a Vopo with a gun stopped me in midstride. *"Ein moment,"* he said.

Now what? I sat down and was handed a document to sign. Was this the confession that I was in fact a CIA saboteur? No, it was a statement that I acknowledged my right to appeal the sentence by appearing in court in Magdeburg on August 27—two weeks hence. There's nothing like German bureaucracy, East or West.

Nearly two hours had elapsed, and Sim was getting worried. A Norwegian woman in the next car had been body-searched and her husband interrogated for four hours. So we could consider ourselves lucky on our last day behind the curtain.

We paused for beer and wurst at a truck stop, where people stared at us but didn't speak, and then pushed on down the all but deserted autobahn and later through some depopulated villages where we actually saw garages converted to stables. A few pedestrians gaped as we drove by. I took no chances and therefore no pictures—luckily. When we reached the border at Juchhöh, cameras were inspected before we were allowed into West Germany. There was a nice little hotel in Hof, and we slept soundly until 5:30 A.M., when the police informed us our car had been broken into and whatever baggage left in it spirited back across the border.

After stops in Munich, where we stayed with the Thayers, our neighbors in Mallorca; and in Bern, where we met the Stevenson party again and he persuaded me to do a "draft" of his *Look* piece on Russia from two pages of scribbled notes, we picked up our kids and relaxed with them on a drive through Normandy before flying home.

So Dan Mich was pleased with the summer's work even though we never got to Russia. I wasn't too pleased with the headline that introduced the package—Stevenson's four pages and my nine (with three of Sim's photographs): "Our Enemy's Two Faces. Why the Russians Smile. Why Their Captives Don't." The word "enemy" harked back to the darkest days of the cold war. We were rivals, adversaries, competitors, even opponents. But an enemy was someone to be destroyed, and that was something neither side could any longer safely contemplate.

Otherwise, the package was a good mix of words and pictures. Stevenson said of his trip that he'd been both exhilarated (by the warmth and friendliness of the people) and depressed (by their ignorance of the outside world). I couldn't help but recall my own feelings after driving around America in 1955. And after meeting Khrushchev, Stevenson was satisfied he sincerely wanted peace but that the Soviet leader also believed the world was inevitably going Communist. Khrushchev froze when Stevenson brought up Hungary, indicating that what went on "between Communist parties" was none of our business, "though he regards events in the non-Communist world as very much his business."

At the end of my own report, in a postscript headed "What Can We Do?" I wrote:

> Liberation by force is out; nuclear war won't solve anybody's problems. . . . We can encourage Communists to see America instead of keeping them out . . . We can take advantage of every chance to get behind *their* iron curtain. . . . We can make our propaganda more effective. . . . We can silence Communism's propaganda guns with an up-to-date foreign policy that would convince a war-weary world we are really for peace. . . . We can do some homework on Communism, current events and geography. . . . The day we left East Germany, the Soviet Army newspaper bragged, "In our time, the East Wind is blowing harder than the West wind" . . . What can we do? We can do everything in our power to make sure they're wrong. I've felt that East wind, and I'm still shivering.

And, figuratively speaking, I was. For no amount of reading or guided tours can make a Westerner as fully appreciate the grim reality of communism in action as seeing it close up and unchaperoned the way we did, on what turned out to be an educational adventure.

The day this article appeared, on November 10, Khrushchev declared the 1945 Potsdam accords were "out of date," called for the end of the four-power occupation of Berlin and precipitated what the historian André Fontaine called "the greatest crisis of the cold war." It would last four years, long enough to become one of those gestating crises, like Cuba and Vietnam, that, as John F. Kennedy was to discover, came with the presidency.

Chapter 11

New Frontier in Africa

T HE MORNING AFTER President Kennedy was shot, I started writing a personal kind of tribute to him that *Look* needed two days later to meet a deadline. In it, I expressed my gratitude to the man "for having made me and my generation—some of us, anyway, feel alive, exhilarated and prouder to be Americans than we've ever been before. This is no small thing. It takes a lot to give you this kind of feeling when you're past forty and have, as they say, been around."

So the Kennedy years, however fleeting, made an indelible impression on those of us lucky enough to have served on the New Frontier. It was an exciting time to be alive and a wonderful time to be an American abroad. Most of us were sustained by the sense that we were taking part in some kind of crusade, not that the word was ever invoked. But the intervening years have diluted the magic of that brief interlude, and perhaps a retrospective piece I wrote for *Newsday* ten years after Dallas more accurately reflects the reality as most surviving New Frontiersmen now perceive it:

> The real Kennedy legacy . . . is a vague sort of inheritance compounded of a sense of adventure, a quickened pulse, a lot of hard work, renewed pride in our country, a willingness to experiment, a sparkle of memories, a lump in the throat. For the enduring actions of Kennedy's thousand days, once you filter out the rhetoric and emotion, won't amount to more than a few paragraphs in tomorrow's history books: the Bay of Pigs, the Peace Corps, the Nuclear Test Ban Treaty, the Cuban missile crisis, the start of some civil rights legislation—as well as the start of deeper involvement in Vietnam . . . Ten years tomorrow. My God,

what's the point of looking back to how it was or how it might have been? Better to get on with what needs doing now and recognize the Kennedy years for what they were to us who lived them—a recollection of style and grace and courage and unfulfilled hope—a poignant memory, yes, but still and all, and essentially, an insubstantial pageant faded and—let's face it—such stuff as dreams are made on. Or so it seems today.

My involvement in politics and then diplomacy came about when Stevenson asked me in December 1959 if I could take a leave of absence and "assemble some speech material" for him just in case he was once again nominated for president. He wouldn't go after it this time, but if a deadlock developed and the convention turned to him, he wanted to be "better prepared than last time." Losing to Ike was bad enough, but to be defeated by Nixon, a man he detested, would be heartbreaking; so if he thought I might help him avoid some of the chaotic improvisation of his 1956 campaign, I could not refuse. Money to match my *Look* salary was available, and Dan Mich granted me a leave until November.

Stevenson had eight or nine speaking engagements that spring, the most important at the University of Virginia. His political supporters—those who wanted him to seek the nomination actively—included George Ball, Tom Finletter, Agnes Meyer, Senator Mike Monroney, John Sharon, Tom Finney and, eventually, Hubert Humphrey and Eleanor Roosevelt. They kept pressing me to toughen up his speeches, and in Virginia I succeeded in converting a scholarly appraisal of Thomas Jefferson into an assault on Nixon. The next day's Washington *Post* headline, ADLAI LASHES OUT AT G.O.P., pleased his loyal following but bothered him. He simply wanted to remain a passive candidate, available on request but not soliciting support.

It was a difficult position that made him seem both indecisive and disingenuous. Kennedy, who believed in either going for it or else supporting another candidate, found it incomprehensible. And after Kennedy's primary victories over Humphrey in Wisconsin in March and in West Virginia in April, Stevenson's aloofness was hard to justify even by his own rationale.

Then, in May, the Russians shot down one of our U-2 spy planes and captured its pilot, Gary Powers, just before the opening of the Paris summit meeting. At home, the political effect was to breathe new life into Stevenson's noncampaign.

The aircraft was downed on May 1. On the fifth, NASA said a Turk-

ish-based U.S. weather plane had gone astray. Khrushchev then glee-
fully revealed the truth to the Supreme Soviet. Two days later, the State
Department conceded the aircraft was probably on an intelligence
mission. On the fourteenth, Khrushchev arrived in Paris to meet with
Eisenhower, de Gaulle and Harold Macmillan. He promptly demanded
an apology, a condemnation of the flight and punishment of those responsible. Meanwhile, he said, the conference should be postponed and
Ike would not be welcome in the Soviet Union, which he had planned
to visit.

When Eisenhower replied the U-2 flights had been suspended,
Khrushchev wanted to know for how long. "As long as I am President,"
replied Ike. This wasn't good enough. Enraged, in part at Eisenhower's
candid but undiplomatic admission he knew of the flight and in part at
the false impression he claimed Ike had given him at Camp David that
a deal on Berlin was possible, Khrushchev threatened retaliation
against our Turkish bases and demanded Western forces get out of
Berlin. Two days later, his fury apparently spent, he said the U.S.S.R.
would never do anything to bring back "the unhappy period of the cold
war."

In blowing up, which he probably did as much for domestic political
reasons and to silence Chinese criticism as from wounded pride,
Khrushchev regrettably missed a chance to start serious disarmament
talks with an American president who was deeply committed to arms
reduction. But the U-2 overflights at such a time, given Soviet missile
capability, were as inexcusable as Khrushchev's reaction was predictable. After Eisenhower blamed him on May 25 for the summit's collapse,
Khrushchev retorted that he should "head a kindergarten" when he
left the White House. And he resumed jamming the VOA and the BBC.

The day after the conference broke up, I wrote a memo for Stevenson suggesting a reaction speech, showed it to Ball and Walter Lippmann, added their comments and flew to Chicago the next morning.
Stevenson liked the memo, and that night at his farm in Libertyville,
I did a speech draft on the gardener's typewriter. He edited it, and then
we watched Khrushchev's May 18 press conference on the flickering
TV. "I never can fix this goddam thing," said Stevenson, sitting on the
floor and twirling the dials.

He delivered the speech the next day. The key passage was:
"Khrushchev wrecked this conference. Make no mistake about that.
But we handed him the crowbar and the sledgehammer."

The speech got good play on radio and TV that night, overshadowed
Kennedy's flabbier statement ("I would certainly express regret at the

timing and give assurances that it would not happen again") and thrust Stevenson back into the running for the nomination. With the collapse of the summit and a possible cold war crisis brewing, Kennedy's relative inexperience in foreign affairs had become a major handicap. Lippmann proposed a Stevenson-Kennedy ticket. Mrs. Roosevelt phoned Stevenson while we were at Libertyville urging him to become an active candidate. "She wants to throw me to the wolves," he told me afterward; and then, almost plaintively, "How can Kennedy be stopped?" and "I'm not sure I can beat Nixon."

As it turned out, Kennedy could not be stopped. Had he been, his forces would have sat out the campaign, the Democratic Party would have been perceived as anti-Catholic and Stevenson would have been beaten once again. There was certainly no doubt in my mind about Kennedy's attitude after dining with him and his wife at Ben Bradlee's Washington home on June 14. Kennedy was understandably curious about "what Adlai was up to." When I explained his posture of passive availability and cited Lippmann's call for a Stevenson-Kennedy ticket, Kennedy broke in.

"I'm running for the presidency, period," he said in a flat, hard voice.

Jacqueline was more vehement. "I will slash my wrists and write an oath in blood that Jack will never run for vice president!" she cried. "We'd let Adlai go down to defeat alone!"

She was very convincing. Fortunately, the July convention nominated the one man who could unite the Democrats and delay, at least for eight years, Nixon's capture of the White House. Fences were quickly mended. Stevenson agreed to make at least ten major speeches on behalf of the candidate and asked me to prepare drafts. Meanwhile, I joined Kennedy's speech-writing staff in Washington, and was part of his airborne entourage in California and the Southwest. But by September it was clear that Stevenson's loyal legions (cultists, as Kennedy staffers called them) were not yet fired up, and Stevenson's ten scheduled speeches ballooned to more than seventy-five in thirteen states. So I was detailed to accompany him on the swing, where you could tell from his crowds that they wanted to hear it from Adlai himself that Jack was okay.

In retrospect, I think Stevenson's active campaigning (which mobilized the liberals for Kennedy), along with Kennedy's Texas speech to the Protestant clergy (which defused the Catholic issue), his phone call to Mrs. Martin Luther King, Jr. (which crystallized the black vote), and the first debate (when many voters were able to compare him, favorably, with Nixon for the first time) were the chief factors that together produced his narrow margin of victory.

Until a pre–Election Day rally in Los Angeles, the only contact between Kennedy and Stevenson during the campaign occurred on October 22. A memo from Kennedy's headquarters implying support for an invasion of Cuba by exiles (an operation then being prepared by the CIA) had surfaced in the press; and Stevenson, who was due to be interviewed by Walter Cronkite the next day, wanted some guidance from the candidate on what to say. I managed to get through to Kennedy on the phone (we were in North Carolina and he in Minnesota), and he told Stevenson the memo was a mistake and asked him "to get us back on the high ground." So we took the position on TV and in a later speech in Maryland that Cuba was a problem to be dealt with by the Organization of American States and not by the U.S. acting unilaterally. It's too bad Kennedy didn't reread that speech before ordering up the Bay of Pigs invasion.

While we campaigned, a flamboyant Khrushchev was raising hell and losing friends at the United Nations. On September 20, he went to the Hotel Teresa, in Harlem, where Fidel Castro had chosen to stay, and gave him an embrace that would later prove costly to the Soviet Union. He called for the dismissal of the U.N. secretary-general and his replacement by a three-man body—a troika—that would effectively paralyze the organization; on October 7, he followed up earlier threats to Berlin in January and February by threatening to sign a peace treaty with East Germany unless the U.S. agreed to another summit meeting after the election to discuss it. After having accused the Chinese of "madness" in June for saying that war with "imperialism" was inevitable, Khrushchev called for their admission to the U.N., declaring on October 11, "We are producing missiles like a chain of sausages—the arms race is going to come to a head and in that war we will crush you." He interrupted speakers, repeatedly waved his shoe and once hit his desk with it. Even his own delegation was said to have been mortified.

At least the Sino-Soviet split was now out in the open. In August, Soviet technicians were recalled from China, whose leaders were accused by *Pravda* of "Communism of the left," and Albania, a Chinese ally, was soon to be expelled from the Warsaw Pact.

On the Monday after Election Day, I was back in my *Look* office feeling, I don't know, back in civilian clothes—the banners furled, the trumpets muted. My first assignment was a piece previewing

Kennedy's foreign policy, which necessitated trips to Washington and talks with Ted Sorensen, Dick Goodwin and members of the transition team. The gist of my article was: "If there is one thing his advisers all agree on, it is that the new President will make his own decisions—and that their keynote will be action." In the cards were renewed efforts to negotiate a nuclear test ban (which Kennedy felt would lessen chances of a Berlin showdown); a reassessment of our China policy; a revamped foreign aid program stressing economic development, especially in Africa and Latin America; and strengthened relations with Eastern Europe (whose "liberation" hinged on winding down the cold war) and Russia, where Kennedy considered the political atmosphere "more fluid and rational" since Stalin's death.

Friends from the campaign sounded me out about working for the government, but Washington didn't appeal to me any more than the U.N., where Stevenson asked me to be his public affairs officer; nor was the pay equal to what I was making. But, half in jest, I did write Chester Bowles, now under secretary of state, to let me know if he was looking for an ambassador to Guinea. In mid-January, he phoned one evening while Sim was ironing and I was reading to say I was all set for Guinea. After I hung up, I asked Sim, "Do you want to go to Africa?"

"Sure," she said, "when do I start packing?" I decided I had married the right woman.

We were snowed in and missed the inauguration. But watching it on TV with Sim and the kids and hearing Kennedy's vibrant summons, I felt good knowing we were going to be part of the action. The lassitude of November was gone. The crusades beckoned.

Significantly, Kennedy's speech did not refer to the Russians as the "enemy" (which *Look* did, to my discomfiture, in 1958), nor even imply, then or later, that they might be. Instead, he spoke of "those nations who would make themselves our adversary"—a nice distinction that did not go unnoticed in the Kremlin. The barrage of verbal attacks against the United States and its leadership that had started at the aborted Paris summit meeting in May and continued through 1960 abruptly ceased after Kennedy became president.

Why had I chosen Guinea, of all places? Other, pleasanter posts were offered to me. At a Washington party, a columnist jokingly suggested, "You must have written some lousy speeches for Jack to be sent to that dump." Well, a dump it wasn't; but a dilapidated, tropical, tragicomic circus rife with cold war intrigue it certainly was. Guinea in 1961 was a perfect setting for a Graham Greene novel.

It was also a challenge, to use one of Bowles's favorite words, as well as a chance for me to test my theory that Third World leaders, no matter how radical their rhetoric, would rather work with us than the Soviets, provided we dealt with them sympathetically and showed some understanding of their problems.

Guinea, abandoned by the French in 1958 for having chosen independence in a referendum, was promptly invaded by Soviet bloc missions. (The first ambassador to arrive in Conakry, the capital, was Bulgarian.) By 1960, even Mongolia had opened an embassy, its only one outside the Soviet orbit. So there was work to do if, as we then feared, the Soviets were planning to establish a showcase/beachhead—an African Cuba—from which to spread the Marxist gospel throughout West Africa. Today we have all grown wiser—except the so-called neoconservatives—and know that no outside power has a prayer of "taking over" this huge, diverse, tribally splintered continent—or even pieces of it, like Angola. And especially not the generally ham-handed Russians.

But in 1961 we overestimated the appeal of communism, the skill of Soviet bloc personnel, the efficacy of their aid programs and the quality of the equipment they lavished on target countries like Guinea. In another book I cataloged some of their most egregious failures in a chapter called "Malice in Blunderland."

There were other reasons than just sidelining the Russians for our making an effort in Guinea. The country was estimated to possess a third of the world's known reserves of bauxite, plus vast deposits of iron ore and potential hydroelectric power to spare. An American firm, Olin Mathieson, with a $75-million investment in an upcountry alumina plant, faced expropriation if we continued to follow France's policy of ostracizing Guinea. And Kennedy himself was intrigued by the prospect of dislodging the Soviets; he agreed with my hunch that Guinea's charismatic president, Sékou Touré, valued his reputation as an African leader too much to tarnish it by becoming a Soviet stooge. When I called on him before leaving Washington in April, he suggested I size up Touré, look over the situation and return in a few weeks with some recommendations.

The mood at the State Department was different. There was a disposition to "write Guinea off" as being "hopelessly down the drain"—an attitude about problem countries that has surfaced time and again in later administrations, always to our detriment. According to this reasoning, since Touré had accepted aid from the Communists, he must be pro-Communist. But I never could accept the defeatist view that any country was down any drain just because the Soviets got there first, unless they brought the Red Army with them as in Eastern Europe. I felt that if the New Frontier meant anything, it meant that America had stopped acting rigid, tired and querulous when problems got difficult. The Dulles era was behind us. What distinguished Kennedy appointees from many career civil servants in 1961 Washington was their inclination to say "Why not?" instead of "Better not" when a new initiative was proposed.

Ironically, the disastrous Bay of Pigs gamble occurred as we were crossing the Atlantic by ocean liner—ironically, because, while I was on my way to see how we might counter Communist influence in Guinea by diplomacy, an operation had been launched to achieve the same objective in Cuba by the use of force. But everything that could have gone wrong at the Bay of Pigs did go wrong. And even if the landing had succeeded, the operation would have been a failure. For Castro, again a guerrilla fighting the gringos and their puppets, would have become an instant martyr and hero all over Latin America. But people in Washington who should have known better were victimized by their own enthusiasm and faulty intelligence reports. Hardly anyone stopped to think that no counterrevolution mounted from abroad has ever succeeded against a mass movement headed by a popular leader. Only Senator Fulbright, Chester Bowles and Arthur Schlesinger among Kennedy's close advisers opposed the invasion—and were overridden.

And today, twenty-five years later, a new generation of Washington strategists are stubbornly committed to the same foredoomed policy of trying to bully another small country, Nicaragua, into saying "uncle"— as Ronald Reagan put it—for accepting Soviet aid and mouthing Marxist slogans.

The one beneficial consequence of the Cuban fiasco was a presidential directive in May placing CIA personnel abroad under the jurisdiction of the ambassador, as head of the "country team." This meant they had to keep us informed in a general way about what they were doing and reporting.

My first priority in Guinea was winning Sékou Touré's confidence and convincing him our policy toward Africa would henceforth be made in Washington and not in London, Paris or Lisbon. I decided that a low-key, relaxed approach would work best, especially if I encouraged him to do what he liked best, which was talk. So I did a lot of listening in his unpretentious office over in the former French governor's palace. And I left him with the impression we were prepared to help Guinea's economic development if he was genuinely nonaligned and his aid requests geared to the real needs of his people; also, that his relations with the Soviets didn't bother us so long as he didn't take orders from them. In one conversation, I said that if they ever gave him a hard time, he had only to pick up the phone and call me. He smiled and said, "I might do that."

It was clear to me he wanted to avoid becoming wholly dependent on his Communist benefactors, who had already co-opted most of Guinea's export crops in barter agreements favorable to them. And the fact we didn't appear upset about all the Soviet bloc missions in town surprised him as well as his associates, who thought of Americans as rabid cold warriors with a phobia about Russians. At a May Day celebration, I was invited to a reception given by the Ministry of Information, an entity infested with East German and Chinese "advisers." A Soviet-made film about the Congo was shown in which Tunisian troops serving in the U.N. peacekeeping force were identified as "American imperialist intruders." Afterward, Guineans crowded around me, wondering why I hadn't protested or walked out. One asked me what I thought of the film. I just shrugged and said it must be embarrassing for them to have to borrow a foreign propaganda film about the Congo for their celebration instead of producing their own film about their own country, with Guinean talent. I could tell this was the right answer, and I knew it would get around. In a small city like Conakry, where the phones seldom worked, almost everything got around, by express grapevine.

Philip Habib, a State Department officer in charge of "Communist economic affairs" came over for a week, and together we wrote a report for President Kennedy assessing the situation and recommending a modest but practical aid program and an expanded American presence, since none of our Western allies except Germany was paying much attention to Guinea. Back in Washington we navigated through the bureaucracy's cumbersome procedures after getting the nod from the president. I also got his approval to have Sargent Shriver, his brother-in-law and director of the Peace Corps, come to Conakry for a visit in June as his stand-in—Touré having extended an invitation to Kennedy himself.

Shriver's stumbling French, infectious good humor, obvious sincerity and easy informality made a great hit with Touré and his cabinet, accustomed as they were to the stern and often patronizing French and then to the stiff-necked Communist envoys, who rarely unbent enough to join in the joking, backslapping repartee that Africans enjoy.

Human relationships are a vital element in diplomacy, nowhere more so than in Africa; and this is where straight-talking Americans had an advantage over the dour Communists and the former colonial masters. We could be as frank as we pleased—a sign to the Africans we weren't currying favor. For example, in reply to Touré's chip-on-the-shoulder remark that Guinea was a "socialist" country, Shriver pointed out that America really had the most socialistic society on earth because our workers had the highest standard of living and there were fewer class distinctions than in any other country, whether called socialist or not.

The next morning, when Touré took Shriver for a tour of the countryside, the roads were lined with schoolchildren waving plastic American flags. Guinea's economy may have been a mess, but its political organization was superb.

I attended a conference of our West African ambassadors in Nigeria in July, where I was assigned to draft a memo summing up our views on southern Africa. We predicted the early end of Portuguese rule in Angola and Mozambique (which Henry Kissinger ten years later believed would endure), and warned that the Soviets would exploit any sign that we were backing the racist regime in South Africa. It was clear even then that they hoped to maneuver us into supporting the doomed white minority government while they became the champions of the black liberation movement. It is still their plan today; the only difference is that the Reagan Administration now seems to be following the Communist script by a futile policy of "constructive engagement" with the enforcers of the apartheid system we keep piously deploring.

Someone at this conference pinpointed the South African issue, as it concerned us, in one sentence: "You can go with the tide of history and against morality—and you might win; or you can go with morality and against the tide of history—and you might win; but if you go against both, then you're sure to lose."

Driving back through Ghana and the Ivory Coast, I felt dizzy and feverish. In Conakry, a French doctor decided I had malaria. Then I suddenly became paralyzed and was flown to a French military hospital in Dakar, where my problem was diagnosed as polio. After nearly four months of intensive therapy at Bethesda Naval Hospital I returned to Guinea in December on crutches. By March I was walking without a cane. In the end, polio left me with a slight limp (but what adult really needs to run fast?) and greater equanimity: the recollection of what it feels like to be immobile and helpless gives you permanent immunity to many of the minor vexations of life.

I also caught up on the news in my hospital bed. August 1961 was the month the Berlin Wall went up. Hints that the percolating Berlin crisis would bubble up again surfaced at the Kennedy-Khrushchev meeting in Vienna in June, when the latter said he would sign a peace treaty with East Germany before the end of the year, after which the Western powers would have to leave Berlin. Kennedy replied dryly, "If that is true, it will be a cold winter."

The Vienna meeting was a standoff. Both men sized each other up. Khrushchev decided Kennedy was tougher than he'd expected him to be after the Bay of Pigs, while Kennedy was only surprised by Khrushchev's belligerency over Berlin, which could lead to a confrontation if he meant what he said about a separate peace treaty.

Berlin made the headlines on August 3 when barbed wire was strung along the Soviet sector boundary, followed ten days later by the construction of a wall. It should not have come as a surprise. More than fifteen thousand East Germans fled to the West through Berlin in the first ten days of August, and four thousand more on August 12 alone. The Wall was a defeat for the Soviets in that it was tangible proof, visible to all, that Eastern Europe was indeed a prison from which people risked their lives to escape.

But the Wall shocked some Americans, who thought we should somehow have prevented its erection. Bob Moskin, my successor as foreign editor of *Look,* did a story in 1962 called "Retreat in Berlin" saying just that. On his return, he was told by Pierre Salinger at the White House that the president didn't feel that way at all. When Bob reported to Dan Mich that Kennedy disagreed with the article, Dan replied, "So did I."

"That was the greatest compliment Dan could have given me," Bob said later. "He published my article even though he disagreed with it . . . That was what *Look* was all about . . . [it] was a reporter's magazine."

And yet, imperceptibly, another thaw in the cold war was getting under way. On September 29, Khrushchev initiated a private correspondence with Kennedy that lasted until the assassination. The two men exchanged more than forty letters that bypassed official channels (they were delivered by hand) and were never made public. So they were able to communicate frankly and at length. This channel undoubtedly helped defuse the last really dangerous confrontation of the cold war—the 1962 Cuban missile crisis. As for Khrushchev's threat to sign an East German treaty, the December deadline passed quietly. There was a symbolic reinforcement of the U.S. garrison; otherwise, nothing happened.

We returned to Guinea in December just two days before the Soviet ambassador, Daniel Solod, was declared persona non grata and sent home. My Yugoslav colleague told me cryptically he had been caught "red-handed." What had apparently happened was that Russian teachers and technicians, in an excess of zeal, were fraternizing with their students after hours, cultivating "intellectuals" and organizing Marxist study groups—all of which Touré understandably regarded as political meddling with the aim of creating centers of subversion. And our presence in Guinea, especially our assurance of support in a pinch, no doubt emboldened him to take drastic action.

Solod's deputy, a genial, tousled man named Ivan Marchuk, occasionally came over for dinner or a swim on the strip of beach we shared with the Chinese, Hungarian and West German ambassadors—and the Texaco representative. Marchuk, like most Russians, hated Guinea (and the Guineans sensed it), and he couldn't understand why I'd requested this assignment or why I'd returned with a lame leg. I explained that it was a good place to continue my therapy, both on an outdoor exercise table and in the ocean. But I wondered why the Chinese ambassador never returned my greeting when we met on the beach.

"What do you expect?" said Marchuk. "Those people aren't even human." The freeze in Sino-Soviet relations was no longer a private affair.

There were a good many members of the Conakry diplomatic corps who weren't on speaking terms, and this could create problems at receptions. One New Year's Day, when the corps assembled at the palace to greet Touré, the Swiss consul was snubbed by the North Korean envoy (who mistook him for an American); the North Vietnamese dean of the corps had neglected to invite the French ambassador, who arrived—late and furious—in a sports shirt; the chief of protocol confused the East German with the West German; Marchuk introduced the new Lebanese chargé as an Indonesian to the Dutch consul, who began talking about West Irian; Topaloski, the Yugoslav, and I were seated next to the rigidly hostile Chinese, and the Moroccan next to the Israeli. By the time Touré appeared, an hour late, no one was talking to anyone else.

So we plugged away through 1962, keeping an eye on the opposition and getting our aid program on the tracks with projects that were practical (like irrigation, crop management and vocational training) rather than grandiose, like the Russian-built luxury hotel that started crumbling away soon after its grand opening. Some required prodding our Agency for International Development bureaucracy: a simple palm oil processing plant was hamstrung by red tape until Kennedy himself, during my October trip to Washington, called the AID director for Africa and told him he wanted it to be "a crash program."

Our country director, Gene Abrams, was an activist like me, with the additional talent of being able to explain the intricacies of our aid procedures to Guinean ministers. He and his wife, Monique, spoke impeccable French, and when she and Sim became volunteer workers in the Donka hospital's understaffed maternity ward, the whole town knew about it. Much later, I was told by a Guinean minister, "We appreciated your efforts to help us, but the work of your wife and Mrs. Abrams did more to build friendship for America among our people than all your development projects." Wives of Soviet bloc diplomats never ventured far from their air-conditioned villas.

The importance of having even a small aid program in an African country was that it gave us a pretext to call on various ministers, as well as the president, and talk about a variety of things, such as U.N. issues they might be unfamiliar with. It also gave us some leverage—preferably understated. For example, when the government radio station, which was manned in part by Chinese and East German technicians, broadcast malicious attacks on the United States, I simply remarked to a few key people that while I personally couldn't care less about what the *"Voix de la Revolution"* said about us, these attacks unfortunately made it harder for us to get foreign aid appropriations approved in the Congress. This usually worked, whereas a protest would have been regarded as interference and therefore been counterproductive.

The informality of Conakry is what made it bearable. When our junior economic officer, Bob Strand, married Penny Packard, an American teacher at the high school, the captain of an Egyptian dredge offered us his launch to take the wedding party to a small Anglican church on a nearby island. So we invited him and his officers to the reception at our house in the evening. Penny had asked all her fellow teachers—Czechs, Bulgarians, Israelis, Russians, French, Haitians and even our one resident American Communist—along with officials from the Ministry of Education. We dug pits in the garden and roasted four lambs; several cases of champagne and a four-piece Congolese band soon turned the reception into the liveliest party of the season. Egyptian dredgers twisted with Israeli teachers, Russians with Americans, Penny's father, a Harvard professor, with the wife of the minister of education. Sometime after midnight, two unsteady Bulgarians led me outside to reassure me that "none of us are Communists, not even the Russians." I told them it didn't matter. "But it does matter," they insisted, swaying in the moonlight. "We do not want you to think we are Communists."

"Let us have a toast," I suggested, and we went back and drank to President Kennedy.

It rains most of July and August in Guinea—nearly 200 inches—and anybody who's able to leave, does. Sim and I took the children for a drive through Switzerland, Austria and Bavaria, but after battling traffic and arguing with the managers of overbooked hotels, we headed for Czechoslovakia. Peter, then eleven, was especially keen on finding a hidden microphone in a chandelier, and we'd written ahead to our friends Joe and Hana (from 1958) about our arrival. A strange, formal letter came back from him, addressing me as "Dear Sir," and assuring us he would be at our disposal during our stay.

At the Czech border, our passports were taken by a uniformed guard and returned almost immediately with a bow by the officer in charge, who smilingly wished us a pleasant visit. The border looked like the iron curtain but felt like a red carpet.

In Prague there was a message from Joe at the hotel. We called him, and he arrived a few minutes later. "Let us go for a drive," he said.

In the car, out of earshot, he explained that the security police had called him in after intercepting my letter from Conakry. They wanted to know how he happened to be acquainted with an American ambassador. Satisfied with his answer (we met on the beach at Varna), they then asked him to "take charge" of us while we were in Czechoslovakia and make sure we got a good impression of the country and had no problems getting choice hotel rooms or anything else we needed. He was also told to invite us to his apartment, which would be bugged in advance, and ask us three questions about Guinea. For this service, he was given an expense account and time off from his job.

It turned out to be an ideal arrangement for all parties concerned. Joe earned some brownie points with the police, we got splendid accommodations at Karlovy Vary's Hotel Pupp—where we'd been told no rooms were available—and the police were surely commended for eavesdropping on a U.S. ambassador. I also enjoyed their three questions, which Joe worked into our table talk by prearranged signal: What do you think of the effectiveness of Czech aid programs in Guinea? How would you rate the caliber, performance and morale of Czech personnel? Are they liked and respected by the Guineans?

That's all they wanted to know. Possibly they reasoned that these were the kinds of questions to which I *would* give them straight answers.

At our embassy I was told the Russians compelled the Czechs to mount aid programs in Africa they couldn't really afford; also, that Africans sent here on scholarships were generally discontented and came around asking us to help them go home.

Peter never did find a bug in our hotel room even after prying the floorboards loose. The authorities probably figured on getting all they wanted from Joe; or maybe the bugged rooms were all booked.

We reluctantly put the children on a plane to the States, where they could stay with family and attend school. (They had to have a tutor in Guinea.) And we returned to Guinea just a few weeks before Sékou Touré left, early in October, to attend the opening of the U.N. General Assembly and to see President Kennedy. His trip almost coincided with the Cuban missile crisis, which lasted from October 16 to 28. During these thirteen days, the two superpowers were to come closer to war than at any time since the Berlin blockade of 1948. At the outset, we underestimated Khrushchev's willingness to gamble, while the Soviets underestimated Kennedy's willingness to fight. When it was over, the two men and their advisers realized they had peered into the nuclear abyss; when they stepped back, it was tacitly understood by both sides that the cold war had moved into a new and less dangerous phase. Whatever insults and threats were to be exchanged in the years to come, the men who later came to power in the White House and the Kremlin would remember October 1962 and never again allow such a confrontation to occur. Dangers would persist, but those caused by human error or miscalculation would subside. Indeed, the first genuine détente in the cold war got under way not long after those fateful two weeks.

Because of the timing of Touré's visit, I reached Washington just before the crisis started, and went with George Ball, now under secretary of state, to the National Airport to join Kennedy in greeting the Guinean leader. The visit went well: after a motorcade to the White

House, Kennedy took us to the upstairs terrace for sherry and then introduced Touré to his wife and young children in an adjoining room. This small gesture made a deep impression on Touré: like most Africans, he attached more importance to being received by family than by regiments of honor guards. It may have impelled him to tell Kennedy, in a luncheon toast, "Africa is independent today thanks to people like yourself." He wanted us to help him repair his relations with the French and sought to reassure the president that he was no puppet of the Soviets, whatever his detractors said. At a press conference across the street at Blair House, he declared, "Don't judge us by what others say, or what we say, but by what we do."

Kennedy did not see photographic verification of the Soviet missile sites in Cuba until October 16, and the story of his skillful handling of the ensuing crisis has been told at length and in detail. Security was so tight that even though I was in Washington and New York seeing such inner circle advisers as Secretary of State Dean Rusk, Ball and Stevenson, I didn't know anything about Khrushchev's dangerous gambit. In fact, it was not until I reached Dakar on the twenty-second that I saw the advance text of Kennedy's speech quarantining Cuba—just received by Phil Kaiser, our ambassador to Senegal. In my diary that night I wrote, "A bold move and a damn good speech—and we're on solid ground here. Glad he did it, but worried, too. That and mosquitoes kept me awake."

Senator Allen Ellender of Louisiana, who was also staying with Kaiser, slept well. "I've been to Russia," he told us, "and they're real nice people. They won't create any trouble." And then he began quizzing us on how we were wasting the taxpayers' money in Africa—which, along with taking color slides, was the purpose of his trip.

On the twenty-third, Stevenson effectively confronted the Soviets at the U.N. with evidence of their deception. On the twenty-fourth, the crisis peaked as the quarantine went into effect with the Soviet ships still steaming toward Cuba. Back now in Conakry, I asked for and received firm assurances from the Guineans that no Soviet planes en route to Cuba would be permitted to land and refuel at Conakry. (I recalled Touré's remark in Washington about judging them not by what they say but by what they do.)

On the twenty-fifth and twenty-sixth, while contradictory messages from Khrushchev arrived in Washington, I had to take care of Ellender, still concerned solely with possible embassy extravagance. He was traveling in an Air Force C-47, and in the morning, when we went to the airport to see him off, a big Russian Ilyushin-18 was parked next to his plane. It was heading west, that's all anyone knew. To Cuba perhaps? We had a spurious maintenance man with a Geiger counter circle the aircraft but it seemed clean.

While I walked with Ellender to the runway, Sim was greeted cordially on the terminal terrace by the second secretary of the Soviet Embassy.

"I wonder if you could tell me," he added, "who that gentleman is and what your aircraft is doing here?"

Sim explained that the senator was on a routine inspection of African posts and was now on his way to Freetown and Monrovia.

"Thank you very much," said the Russian. "And now I will tell you something. Our Ilyushin is leaving for Brazil tomorrow to pick up the body of the Soviet ambassador, who was drowned while swimming last week. It is not flying to Cuba. Your husband may be interested to know this." I was. So was the State Department. And the plane did go to Brazil. At times like this, Conakry's informality saved everyone a lot of trouble.

That day, some of the Soviet ships stopped. The crisis seemed to be easing. Yet a Khrushchev message suggesting a swap (we had missile bases in Turkey which were later dismantled) sounded like stalling. We were still eyeball-to-eyeball. It was not until the next morning, Sunday the twenty-eighth, that the ships turned around and Rusk could say to Kennedy, "I think the other fellow just blinked."

Less than a month later, we lifted the quarantine and assured the Russians we had no intention of invading Cuba, a face-saving gesture that cost us nothing and paved the way for the coming thaw.

There were no real winners in this test of wills, though Kennedy's display of coolness under pressure was widely admired. Khrushchev could claim he had saved Cuba from a U.S. invasion and had also kept his cool. Castro had acquired a big brother to keep his economy afloat —and his impulses in check. In 1975, he told Senator George McGovern: "I would have taken a harder line than Khrushchev. I was furious when he compromised. But Khrushchev was older and wiser. I realized in retrospect that he reached the proper settlement with Kennedy. If my position had prevailed, there might have been a terrible war. I was wrong."

So why did Khrushchev risk so much for so little? There were a number of plausible reasons which together may have driven him to do it: he needed a foreign policy success after a year of reverses in Africa and Latin America and even Berlin, where the Wall was hardly a monument to the glories of communism; he may have been trying to bring the wayward Chinese leaders back into his fold with a display of toughness; perhaps he hoped to break the deadlock on disarmament and Berlin by an action that would shock but not provoke Kennedy as it did, and he was persuaded by Castro early in 1962 that the Americans were planning to avenge their defeat at the Bay of Pigs.

And so the crisis, ironically, cleared the air. It demonstrated once again that intelligence services can fail, that statesmen can lie, that seemingly rational men can behave recklessly and that a conflict is often resolved most successfully when there are neither winners nor losers.

Cuba, which I visited five times after Fidel Castro's revolution, is a story in itself—frustrating, tragic and also comical—and will be dealt with in the next chapter. It was also one of those foreign policy problems Kennedy inherited from the previous administration. The others were Berlin and Indochina.

Berlin, long a menacing flashpoint, faded away during 1962 and 1963 as Khrushchev began to understand our determination to stand firm (as well as our readiness to discuss reasonable solutions) and was no longer under pressure from the East Germans to seal off the Berlin escape route that was draining their manpower: the Wall secured the prison and the wardens were satisfied. In June 1963, Kennedy received one of the greatest ovations of his career when he told a vast, cheering crowd outside the Berlin City Hall, "Two thousand years ago the proudest boast was *'Civis Romanus sum.'* Today, in the world of freedom, the proudest boast is *'Ich bin ein Berliner.'* "

The Indochina crisis, unlike the others Kennedy inherited, was entirely of our own making, did not directly affect our national interest and got worse instead of better during his presidency—though not as bad as it would get after his death.

Indochina—or Vietnam, which is where most of the action took place initially—was not uppermost in our minds in 1961. Even though I'd reported France's war from Paris in the forties, gone there in 1953 and attended the Geneva conference winding up French involvement, I don't recall thinking about Vietnam at all in Guinea until the son of Mac Walling, the Olin Mathieson representative, was shot down dropping leaflets over Viet Cong territory. Yet U.S. troops were trickling in and U.S. casualties inching up—from 14 in 1961 to 109 in 1962 to 489 in 1963.

Kennedy was ambivalent about what we should do to help Diem. Like many of us, his judgment was clouded by three assumptions—first, that Chinese expansionism was the driving force behind Communist aggression from the North (in October 1962, after seizing Tibet, the Chinese killed six thousand Indian troops in Himalayan border fighting, and an invasion seemed imminent); second, that the domino theory, to which Kennedy subscribed as much as had Eisenhower, meant that all of South Asia was in jeopardy if South Vietnam were overrun ("If we permitted Laos to fall," said Ike as he left office, "then we would have to write off the whole area"); and third, that the partition line drawn across Vietnam at the 17th parallel was in fact an international boundary, and the southern part of the country consequently a sovereign state.

But he had nagging doubts, having visited Indochina in 1951 and been persuaded the French effort was hopeless. He tried to resolve these doubts by sending one "fact-finding" mission after another out there—the most important being the Walt Rostow–Maxwell Taylor trip in 1961. With rare exceptions, all came home optimistic; none confessed, like poor George Romney later on, to having been "brainwashed" by the military. The consensus of the missions was that the South could win with just a little help from its American friends—who would not be perceived, like the French, as fighting a colonial war. (Generally overlooked was the fact that all white men looked alike to the Vietnamese and were rightly considered intruders in what was a civil war.)

In January 1962, Kennedy went so far as to say, "The spearpoint of aggression has been blunted"—one of the first of many such expressions of wishful thinking we would hear over the next decade. His reliance on hawkish reports from the military and the CIA was surprising in light of the bad advice they had given him during the Bay of Pigs and Cuban missile crises. Blunt warnings about the Vietnam quagmire from Senator Mike Mansfield and John Kenneth Galbraith, then ambassador to India, were brushed aside, and by the end of 1963, seventeen thousand Americans had already been sent into the quagmire.

Why didn't Kennedy wind down our involvement when he was riding a wave of popularity after the missile crisis? It would have been easy enough: our military prestige and sacred honor had not yet been committed to Vietnam; a negotiated settlement had been worked out in Laos by Averell Harriman; Cambodia was still peaceful and unscarred; the French and Russians could have been helpful. The erroneous assumptions cited above were the obstacle. I know, because I was myself caught up in the New Frontier's stampede to stop Chinese "aggression." I remember agreeing with Rusk in 1962 when he once asked me how a "liberal" could justify delivering fifteen million people in Vietnam to the Communists. (Rusk, who had discounted the possibility of Chinese intervention in Korea in 1950, was especially anxious not to make that mistake again.) And as late as 1966, I was making speeches defending our policy of protecting the independence of small countries like South Vietnam. Not for another year did it dawn on me that "the best and the brightest" had been deceiving themselves and the American people.

Hindsight is okay if you don't pretend you had foresight when it mattered.

In March 1963, Kennedy did tell Mansfield he was beginning to agree we should withdraw but that this would not be possible until after the 1964 election, for fear the Republicans would charge him with "losing Vietnam." Barbara Tuchman, the historian, and Kennedy's own associates have also said he was determined to get out of Vietnam before we were irrevocably committed—and that he would have, early in 1965.

If true, and I'm inclined to believe it is, this was not Kennedy's finest hour. Waiting for nearly two years to do the right thing while thousands died may or may not have been smart politics; but inspiring leadership it wasn't.

In 1963 Guinea, we Americans basked in an era of good feeling. Touré now felt he had a friend in the White House. He had told Kennedy about subversion by Russian "political agents" and how he'd learned the Soviet system was not right for Africa. So we pushed our modest aid projects through the Guinean and U.S. bureaucracies (ours was the more cumbersome), and traveled around the back country, often seeing no white faces for days on end except for some American missionaries and a few lonely Soviet bloc doctors, midwives and geologists.

We had visitors—G. Mennen (Soapy) Williams, the assistant secretary of state for African affairs, who logged thousands of miles in Africa, everywhere popular with the leaders because he enjoyed talking politics as much as they did; Chester Bowles, now a special presidential representative, fretful at being out of the chain of command; Senator Vance Hartke, who helped us get a generator for an upcountry hospital from AID after we'd taken pictures of him holding African babies in the dim, lamplit maternity ward (pictures sure to help him politically in Gary, Indiana); and even Dick Watts, the New York *Post* drama critic, who arrived unannounced one evening from Upper Volta and informed us on the terrace, while we watched the fruit bats silhouetted against the violet sky, that you could get a better martini in Bobo-Dioulasso than in Ouagadougou, the capital.

The Russians contributed to good Guinean-American relations by some heavy-handed behavior. When a pretty young Russian teacher named Svetlana Ushakova ignored her embassy's warning to stop dating one of her Haitian colleagues, Moscow ordered her home on the next Soviet plane. With no time to get her an exit visa, the embassy gave her someone else's passport and sent her to the airport with two escorts. The Guinean security officer looked at the passport, then at her.

"But this is not your photograph, mademoiselle," he said.

"It is not my passport either," she replied. "These two men are forcing me to leave. I want to stay in Guinea."

The airport commander, Commissaire Paul, was summoned and sent them away, saying Guinea was a sovereign country with its own regulations.

Moments later, Paul looked at the Russian crew walking out to their plane and noticed there was an extra stewardess. He stopped them and recognized Svetlana. Angrily, he posted guards on the plane and tried to phone police headquarters in Conakry, but the phone was dead, as usual.

Meanwhile, Svetlana vanished again. But just before departure, an ambulance drove up. A Russian got out, produced a passport and asked permission to drive to the plane and put a patient aboard. Paul looked inside, recognized Svetlana again, though she was swathed in bandages, and took custody of her. When the Soviet ambassador himself arrived, Paul later told me, "My African blood began to boil." Svetlana was taken to town in a Guinean police jeep and placed under the protection of the Ministry of Education. A final attempt to kidnap her in a restaurant was foiled by Guinean detectives sitting with her, and she was finally lodged in a villa under guard—and in time married the Haitian, with Commissaire Paul as best man.

The story was all over town the next day, with some racial embellishment (since the Haitian was black), and Touré came close to expelling the Soviet ambassador. But he thought that might be overdoing it, since Solod had been sent home only seventeen months before.

A U.S. Trade Fair—with gadgets, tools, photographic panels, go-carts, a push-button Q and A console and Guinean students operating simple machinery and answering questions—was the big event of the spring season. It compared very favorably with a Soviet fair a year earlier that resembled a tacky department store where nothing was for sale, not even the fur hats. At our opening—to which Sargent Shriver came on Pan Am's inaugural flight, along with a CBS film crew—Sékou Touré praised America in terms not often heard in nonaligned Africa. "Every African leader with a conscience," he declared, "must now recognize the value of cooperation with the United States and that American assistance, contrary to what we were told, is the most disinterested, the most effective and the most responsive to our real needs."

Even Mamady Kaba, the trade union boss and leading anti-American in the Guinean power structure, seemed to have mellowed. When Shriver and I called on him, he seemed stiff and nervous. Then Shriver, who'd picked up some Communist pamphlets in the waiting room, switched to English. "You tell him," he said to me, "that the things I've been reading here and have in my hand are all a pack of goddam lies!" As usual, frankness broke the ice; Kaba and his staff laughed, saying their reading matter was perhaps dated, and we wound up having a useful talk.

I recalled the collective wisdom of most of the State Department's Africanists in 1961 that we should "write off" Guinea as being "hopelessly down the drain." And now the Guineans were negotiating with American firms like Alcoa and Harvey Aluminum for mining rights to the rich bauxite deposits north of Conakry.

The French, sulking over their own failed policy of ostracism, boycotted the opening of our fair (and then claimed we hadn't invited them), and later fabricated a story sent out by Agence France Presse about Touré sharply criticizing Kennedy for the racial violence in Alabama. (Whatever their motive for this story, it boomeranged, since Touré issued a statement a few days later supporting Kennedy's handling of racial strife "without any reservations.")

Before leaving for a Pan-African conference in Addis Ababa on May 20, Touré asked me for a figure encompassing total U.S. assistance to Guinea—past, present, projected and probable—and said he hoped it would exceed $30 million. By throwing in everything from estimated spare parts to undelivered rice, we came up with a $31.5 million figure. The midday radio news report identified this as a "new" U.S. grant. So I set the record straight with wire service stringers and other embassies all afternoon. That night, at the airport, he summoned me to his private departure lounge, causing speculative murmurs among the assembled diplomatic corps, and I told him I'd been correcting the "news" all day. Grinning broadly, he said fine, that was my job, as a diplomat, to correct wrong impressions. But he, as a politician, needed the figure as reported. And no harm was done, he added, so long as Washington understood: after all, the Guineans were happy, the Soviets upset and our own prestige enhanced. So what was there to be concerned about? I couldn't argue, especially after he presented me with his picture inscribed, "To our brother and friend."

Before our departure a week later, I invited some Czech teachers whom I had permitted to use our beach to stop by for a drink in the garden. They were painfully grateful for this small favor and congratulated me on all America had accomplished in Guinea. I thought how unusual it would be for Americans to say the same thing to a Communist ambassador; and I wondered how anybody could still believe that communism was the wave of the future when its leaders couldn't even count on the loyalty of the people they sent abroad.

What next? The *New York Times* announced in May that my next post would be Yugoslavia—which turned out to be a Bowles idea quickly shot down by the State Department, which had its own career candidate. Looking for clues on my return to Washington in June, I checked out other published reports that I was headed for Mexico, Indonesia and even Argentina. At the Department, I was told my destination was Bolivia—which *I* shot down by pointing out Sim was pregnant and La Paz 13,000 feet high. Harriman suggested Nigeria; Ball, Panama; Ralph Dungan, at the White House, Brazil; Williams, Zambia. All I found out for sure was that you had to know what you wanted and then lobby for it, preferably at the summit.

So when I found myself sitting next to the president at a party at Joe Alsop's, I said I'd like to see him about whether to stay in the government—or not. He told me to bypass channels and gatekeepers and call his secretary, Mrs. Lincoln, directly. The next day, after twenty minutes in his office, we agreed I'd be going to Colombia in January after serving under Stevenson on our U.N. delegation during the General Assembly in the fall. Kennedy wanted to get the Alliance for Progress moving and promised me there'd be plenty to do in South America. (My Spanish was even rustier than my German but could be lubricated during the summer.)

Kennedy was having a good month: soon after his Berlin triumph, he gave the best speech of his presidency at the American University on June 10. He spoke of peace, "not merely peace in our time but peace for all time." He said that Soviet and American attitudes must change, for in the nuclear age, peace had become "the necessary rational end of rational men," and "no government or social system is so evil that its people must be considered as lacking in virtue." (It would be many years yet before an American president would speak of "the evil empire.") And Kennedy ended with a plea for halting an arms race bred by mutual suspicion: "If we cannot end now all our differences, at least we can help make the world safe for diversity. For, in the final analysis, our most basic common link is that we all inhabit this small planet. We all breathe the same air. We all cherish our children's future. And we are all mortal."

Khrushchev was profoundly impressed; he called it "the greatest speech by an American president since Roosevelt." And he finally responded positively to our proposal for negotiating a limited test ban treaty. On July 5 Harriman went to Moscow, and a month later a treaty banning atmospheric testing was signed. It coincided with Khrushchev's denunciation of the Maoist heresy and the "anti-Marxist, anti-Communist and anti-human" character of Chinese foreign policy. Peking replied in kind, and the Sino-Soviet split was now final.

The treaty—which Kennedy hoped would lead to a comprehensive one banning underground tests as well—was also important symbolically, as was the hot line that was installed between the White House and the Kremlin after the missile crisis. And the phrase in the American University speech about making the world "safe for diversity" was and still is the most succinct and appealing expression of what the goal of our foreign policy should be.

The cold war was now on hold. Kennedy spoke of "a pause." André Fontaine called it "a provisional termination." In short, the stage was set, during the last few months of Kennedy's presidency, for a major shift in U.S. relations not only with the Soviet Union but with the developing world. Kennedy had mastered his job, and the evidence was apparent from Berlin to New Delhi. As I wrote in an article for *Look* that fall, "On balance, the state of the world, as seen from Washington, looks considerably more hopeful than it did three years ago."

I got a note from Kennedy a few days later, three weeks before his death, saying, "That was a first-class article you wrote for Look. I think it will be of major assistance. Many thanks."

When he was shot, Khrushchev is said to have wept. Sékou Touré said, "I have lost my only real friend in the outside world." Castro was stunned (and the next chapter may help explain why). And in the hasty memoir I composed for *Look* on that rainy assassination weekend, I wrote: "Jack Kennedy was so much a part of everything we did in Washington that the day after his death, waiting at the State Department before going over to the White House, I still found it hard to believe, impossible, really, that the President would not be there to greet us in his office. He had been dead, after all, less than twenty-four hours. It wasn't until I walked into the darkened East Room and saw the flag-draped casket that I fully realized we had lost him—and what an unexpectedly personal loss it was for someone like me, who had known him so fleetingly."

Chapter 12

The Cuban Connection

CUBAN DICTATOR FULGENCIO BATISTA, his U.S.-equipped army utterly routed, fled to the Dominican Republic on December 31, 1958. Five days later, a revolutionary government, headed by Dr. Manuel Urrutria, was formed. On January 8, Fidel Castro, supposedly killed, according to the United Press, when he landed with eighty-two companions on the coast of Oriente Province two years before, led his ragtag, bearded soldiery into Havana for the most tumultuous welcome since the liberation of Paris.

I arrived on the nineteenth and found the lobby of the Hilton swarming with foreign correspondents, American PR men looking for business, clusters of bewildered tourists, furtive figures from the Miami underworld in conference by the roulette tables, Representative Adam Clayton Powell issuing slurred pronouncements to a bevy of Puerto Rican courtesans, and wandering bands of amiable *barbudos*—the bearded ones—slung with weapons and puffing enormous cigars amid the joyful bedlam.

Two days later I saw Castro for the first time, at a distance. He was delivering one of his nonstop extemporaneous speeches in front of the presidential palace, where the crowd was so dense I came close to being crushed against a building. In panic, I yelled *"Prensa norteamericana!"* and was immediately hoisted up to a balcony so that I could "see and hear the truth." I finally made it to the roof of the palace, overlooking the speaker's platform, after shouting *"Prensa!"* and submitting to some casual frisking for weapons.

The next day I saw Castro again when he strode into the hotel, followed by his usual surging retinue of amiable brigands, and proceeded to hold an impromptu, strolling press conference in the lobby for an hour while his escorts scratched themselves, combed their shaggy locks and examined each other's hardware as though they had just taken the Hilton by storm.

I went to see an old school friend, Alberto Fernandez, who had just been made responsible for sugar production. "How long can this go on?" he moaned. "They're all so disorganized. And nothing happens without Fidel's say-so."

"What did you expect?"

"We didn't expect chaos. This revolution was made by the Rotarians, the Lions—and the peasants. Not only the middle classes but even some of the big landowners and businessmen like me supported it because we were fed up with the corruption and brutality of Batista's rule. It was an uprising of decent people against indecency. But Fidel won't last if he tries to run the country like this . . ."

The man has lasted nearly thirty years. Among chiefs of state, only Kádár of Hungary, Hussein of Jordan and Stroessner of Paraguay have been in power as long. (So have Emperor Hirohito and Queen Elizabeth, but they have no power.) He has survived one U.S.-sponsored invasion, numerous sabotage raids from U.S. territory, U.S. economic sanctions and several assassination attempts, mostly dreamed up by agents and alumni of the CIA; and though he runs a country of only 10,000,000 people, he has gained greater worldwide name recognition over the years than any other contemporary leader. Passionate and impulsive, he engineered the only thoroughgoing social revolution in the western hemisphere and, in the process, managed the impossible: he made North Americans really begin to pay serious attention to Latin America. Warts and all, Fidel Castro is indisputably one of the most interesting public men of our time. This chapter is about his role, as I observed it between 1959 and 1964, in the continuing pageant of the cold war.

In a report for *Look* after my January visit, I wrote, "We can thank our lucky stars that Castro was no Communist." This statement may sound naive today, but it was valid then. CIA Director Allen Dulles told the Senate Foreign Relations Committee in January, "We do not think that Castro himself has any Communist leanings," but warned that he could lose control of the situation and that his brother Raúl was "more irresponsible." Vice President Nixon, after meeting Castro in Washington in April, also said he was not a Communist but "a captive of the

Communists." I doubt he was ever anyone's captive but he did publicly embrace Communist doctrine in 1961, after the Bay of Pigs, though not Soviet discipline. That June, Khrushchev told Kennedy that Castro was "not a Communist but U.S. policy could make him one."

In the spring of 1959, when he came to the States at the invitation of the American Society of Newspaper Editors, he got something of a hero's welcome. Even the Eisenhower Administration was prepared to discuss economic aid to Cuba, but his finance minister, Rufo Lopez-Fresquet (who was to resign a year later), was instructed by Castro to reject any offer. "We did not come here for money," he loftily told the assembled American editors.

No one quite like him had yet appeared on the world stage, and I was curious to find out more about the man. So Sim and I and Andy St. George, a free-lance photographer who had covered the December fighting, flew to Havana on June 22 and stalked Castro until July 1, when we boarded his private plane and talked with him during the four-hour round trip to Camaguey. As I wrote later, "In some ways it's harder to find the man, now that he's prime minister, than it was a year ago when he was an outlaw hiding in the Sierra Maestra mountains. He is seldom in his office. His daily schedule changes from hour to hour as he rushes around the city and countryside. He sleeps when he feels like it, at odd hours and in a variety of beds. Sometimes he just disappears. I pity any Martian landing in Havana and asking a Cuban, 'Take me to your leader.'"

He was touring the provinces when we arrived, so I talked with a variety of people ranging from the rabid dowager crying, "I want to kill!" at a fund-raising party to hire assassins, all the way across the spectrum to Carlos Franqui, the bitterly revolutionary but anti-Communist editor of *Revolución,* who believed in Fidel (as everyone called him—and still does) but worried about some of his new associates, like the Communist leader and later vice-president, Carlos Rafael Rodriguez. Among the moderates still in the government, like Lopez-Fresquet, who felt *he* should be running Cuba, I found more alarm about inefficiency and chronic disorganization than about communism, although brother Raúl was suspected of helping the formerly anti-Castro Cuban Communists to infiltrate the power structure.

On the night of June 28 we got word that Fidel was returning to Havana at 2 A.M. and would be staying with his Girl Friday, Celia Sanchez. We went to her apartment building at nine, learned he was still asleep, fraternized with the languorous *barbudos* and eventually headed for the presidential palace, where he had scheduled a cabinet meeting for 1 P.M. We settled down for an all-day vigil in the company of hangers-on, favor seekers, vagabond Nicaraguans and genial but heavily armed guards. Just to fill time we visited with the president, Dr. Urrutria, who, as a reformist, deplored the radicalization of the revolution. He was forced to resign nineteen days later by Castro, who explained quite accurately that Urrutria was "not a revolutionary." Urrutria wisely sought and was granted political asylum in the Venezuelan Embassy.

Castro barged into the palace about 10 P.M. and told us to follow him. We got our car and sped off in pursuit of his, stopping as he did at red lights, and trailed him to the Hilton—where he showered in a suite and again dashed off into the night, suggesting we meet at Celia's in the morning.

But he never got there. A *barbudo* on duty said he might be at the Agrarian Reform Institute, where we found a roomful of impatient people waiting for him. He finally burst in, harangued them for an hour and stalked out, with us, a *Prensa Latina* reporter and two *barbudos* close behind. Out at Air Force headquarters, which turned out to be our destination, all was confusion. The Air Force commander, Major Pedro Diaz Lang, had just resigned (he later fled to the U.S.) in protest at Communist infiltration. Fidel, Raúl, Camilo Cienfuegos and Armando Hart of the inner circle were in conference. We kept getting arrested and released by long-haired teenagers in green fatigues. Some pilots we talked to told us, sotto voce, that they agreed with Diaz. Finally, we gave up on Fidel and went back to the hotel to make plane reservations home.

At eight the next morning, Andy woke us to say a reporter from *Revolución* had located Fidel at 4 A.M. and persuaded him to take us along to Camaguey, a two-hour flight in the presidential DC-3. We were at the airport at nine and took off when he appeared at noon. We started talking in a mix of Spanish and English as soon as we were airborne, but he seemed nervous and distracted and after a while suggested we resume on the way back.

At Camaguey, we squeezed into the bodyguards' car—where Sim was more welcome than Andy and I—and lunched at Major Huber Matos's house, where Fidel and I got into a discussion of the Okinawan campaign and the efficacy of flamethrowers, while Matos, who had fought with him against Batista, was having his hair cut by a daughter. (Three months later, Matos, an outspoken anti-Communist, resigned when Raúl was put in charge of the armed forces, tried for treason as a "false revolutionary" and sentenced to twenty years' imprisonment; after his release he came to the United States.)

There followed a two-hour speech to a throng of cattlemen, worried landowners and adoring youths, after which our two-car caravan roared off to another meeting before reaching the airport after dark. On the way, a car cut in between Fidel and us bodyguards, but all our companions did was honk the horn, yell and pound the outside of our car with their guns. I asked why they hadn't shot out the tires of the intruding vehicle. It hadn't occurred to them; besides, the occupants turned out to be young fans who only wanted Fidel's autograph.

It had been a long day and, for him, a long night before. But in the plane he found the energy to talk with me at length. And some of what he said is worth repeating today.

He started (as he would in later talks we had over the years) by asking me questions. How many other chiefs of state had I interviewed? He stopped me when I mentioned Nasser and wanted to know if I detected a resemblance between them. "You seem to be a lot alike," I said, "except that you're much more disorganized."

He leaned back and nodded. "I know," he said. "I try to do too much." His cigar glowed in the dim light of the cabin. Then he bent forward and gripped my arm. "But remember, I am an emotional man!"

He also wanted to know if I'd been to Russia and other Communist countries, and how people fared and how officials lived.

When I told him at least 90 percent of the people in countries like Poland hated the system, he wanted to know why. I explained what a real police state, imposed by the Red Army was like. I mentioned the collective farms, where the state robbed farmers of their land and livestock, and the Communist elite, who lived like privileged despots.

"That's terrible," he said. "We don't want anything like that here. People must have something to call their own. Their leaders must live simply. We want Cubans to feel free."

Was it true, he asked, that people in Communist countries couldn't get out? And wasn't an American who went to Russia accused of being a Communist when he came home? When I told him the Russians were in effect prisoners in their own land and that fifteen thousand American tourists would be going to the Soviet Union in 1959, he seemed genuinely surprised. "This is very, very interesting," he said. "I should have more time to talk with people who travel and who know about these things."

I decided that Castro's knowledge of the outside world, like his grasp of economics, was rudimentary—and understandably so. He started out as a young lawyer with a gift for words and now, at thirty-two, had been a professional revolutionary most of his adult life. He'd seen little of the world. Perhaps he felt overwhelmed by it. Twice, he referred nostalgically to the Sierra Maestra, like Robin Hood dreaming of Sherwood Forest. His uniform, beard and .45 had become symbols and reminders of happier, simpler times.

He fielded my own questions adroitly. He did not want to fix "an exact date" for elections, but claimed 90 percent of the people supported him: "You could call this government a regime of public opinion. If Americans do not think I am right, I will be glad to invite any public opinion institute to come to Cuba and make its own independent survey."

Should he die or be killed, Castro foresaw group leadership by his "companions," among whom would be his brother Raúl. About his visit to the States, he said he found Americans "more sensitive than I thought . . . When I spoke there, I felt the same as when I speak in Cuba. I found much kindness and sympathy, and I have a good impression of the American people. I am very sincere when I tell you this."

Castro claimed it was his nature to be opposed to all dictatorships, of the right or the left. He also said he intended to have diplomatic and commercial relations with Communist countries "mainly because we are interested in trade with all countries. But now is not the opportune moment. . . . Our ideas are very clear. They have nothing to do with communism. And the complete responsibility of power is in the hands of the 26th of July Movement. But we do not persecute any other political idea . . . We are not afraid of other ideologies."

We talked on until the plane began its descent over Havana. Then Castro said, "There is one more thing I want to say to Americans: Do not be deceived by the propaganda of our enemies. Keep in mind the efforts we are making for the prosperity and happiness of our country. Let us be friends."

It was late when we landed. As the door swung open, he put a hand on my shoulder. "I wish we had more time to talk," he said. "I need more time." Then he was off, trailed by a cohort of guards, a big man in sweat-stained fatigues with a pistol on his hip.

I wrote up the interview the next day and then put in another day searching for Fidel, to whom I'd promised to show the text, for accuracy. Phil Bonsal, our ambassador, told me he thought the situation was deteriorating but not yet hopeless: the Russians had not appeared so far, and there were still decent, serious men working in the government. But he thought the revolution could go either way. In the evening, already packed to leave the next day, I spotted Castro striding through the Hilton lobby toward the kitchen. I followed, greeting a couple of bodyguards, to whom I was now a *compañero,* and located the boss in a back room working on a steak dinner with Cienfuegos, who was cleaning his pistol, and some other pals I didn't recognize. He read and approved the interview, shoved some cigars into my shirt pocket and urged me to come back.

My last stop was at *Revolución* to thank Franqui for his help. In another nine years, he would go into exile, a revolutionary still but too undisciplined and humanistic for the kind of revolution that the Communists then advising Castro had in mind for Cuba. Trusted comrades and early supporters who opposed the developing trend were elbowed aside, and perhaps worse. Cienfuegos, one of Castro's closest friends and associates along with Che Guevara, disappeared without trace on October 14, 1959, while flying from Camaguey to Havana on a calm and cloudless day. Guevara, an active revolutionary too impetuous finally to submit to Communist discipline, was killed while trying to foment rebellion in Bolivia in 1967 by security forces working in conjunction with the CIA and, allegedly, Bolivian Communists, who resented mavericks, especially from abroad. In a brief talk with a friend of Guevara's I learned something about how a man can become anti-American (though not necessarily pro-Communist). An Argentine, Che was a young man in Buenos Aires in 1945 when a U.S. naval vessel was in port. He still recalled a "very big" American sailor coming up and grabbing his girl in a dance hall. When he protested, the sailor put his hand on Guevara's head and said, "Sit down and shut up, you little nigger." Ever since, the word "America" made him think of a huge hand pressing down on his head and the word "nigger." Thus are lifelong guerrillas often created; yet we tend to forget that humiliation always arouses stronger and more lasting emotions than ideology or even injustice.

In the piece I wrote on my return, called "The Tragedy of Fidel Castro," I said that he had swept into Havana like a knight in shining armor leading an army with banners; but that now, eight months later, "the armor is tarnished, the banners wilting." Former supporters were calling him a Red and plotting his assassination; others were disenchanted by his slapdash military rule and government-by-crony. Cuba was still quite a way from being a Communist dictatorship but "when you sniff the air, you can smell a police state in the making."

I summed up my impressions by writing, "The saddest thing about Castro's slowly curdling revolution is that no one is really to blame but Fidel himself . . . trying to be the one-and-only ringmaster in a circus too big for him to handle." And while I saw no advantage in U.S. intervention—military or economic—which would merely rally the Cubans against "Yankee imperialism," I held out some hope that he might be persuaded to mend his ways, for the revolution's sake. If he just restored the rule of law, moderated the pace (and injustice) of agrarian reform, broke with the Communists (who were latecomers to his cause) and set a date for elections, Cuba's future would be bright and American support a distinct possibility. But it seemed more likely he would prolong "this reckless, hoarse and turbulent spree." In that case, I concluded, "Fidel Castro will become the world's likeliest target for an assassin's bullet between now and the end of the year."

My crystal ball was clouded—in part because of the lax security that I'd witnessed. (How easily I could have gunned him and his companions down with a silencer in the back room of the Hilton kitchen on my last night in Havana—and walked away unnoticed.) Also, on my return to New York, Julio Lobo, Cuba's wealthiest sugar magnate, who had wisely chosen exile, told me flatly Castro would be dead in six months; the assassins had been recruited and the plans finalized.

Whether Lobo's operation was ever mounted I don't know. If so, Castro survived it and many others over the next five years. The story of our clandestine efforts to bring him down, beginning in 1960, cannot make an American proud. (Nor, I venture to say, will our association with the Nicaraguan Contras many years later.) But our Cuban follies are worth citing if only to reveal our paranoia about Cuba and to acknowledge Castro's virtuoso performance in the role of a Latino David with a charmed life standing up to a gringo Goliath with the instincts of a bully.

The decision to help Cuban exiles overthrow the Castro regime was taken in the spring of 1960 after one final stab at accommodation. In January, the deputy CIA director told a Senate committee there was no evidence Castro was a Communist, even though he had delegated power to persons linked with communism. But the pressure to "do something about Castro" mounted as more exiles made their way to

Florida, there to dream of revenge and scheme for returning to their homeland, much like the White Russian exiles in Europe in the twenties. Meanwhile the Soviets moved in, first with a trade mission in Havana and within a year with embassies from most Communist countries, even including a leftist rebel faction from the Congo. U.S. relations with Cuba progressively deteriorated, starting with our ban on purchases of Cuban sugar. When the Russians sent Cuba oil in exchange for the sugar, U.S. companies refused to refine it, and were nationalized. In October, we prohibited most exports to Cuba and in January 1961 broke off diplomatic relations, three months before the Bay of Pigs. As the secretary of defense, Robert McNamara, was to testify later, "We were hysterical about Castro at the time of the Bay of Pigs and thereafter."

This hysteria at what seemed to be a calculated Soviet penetration of the western hemisphere led to a bizarre series of plots and dirty tricks organized for the most part by the CIA in collusion with Cuban exiles. There was Operation Mongoose, there was AM/LASH, there were sinister underworld connections, there were hit-and-run raids and attempts on Castro's life—twenty-four by his reckoning, in nine of which the CIA admitted being involved. Some of these were grotesque: the exotic seashell, rigged to explode, to be deposited where Castro commonly went skin-diving; the diving suit, contaminated by a tubercle bacillus, to be delivered to him as a gift; the cigars treated with a potent botulism toxin; the poison pills to be administered by a German girl friend, and so on. Some schemes were designed simply to tarnish Castro's public image, such as dusting his boots with thallium salts, a strong depilatory that would cause his beard to fall out if he stroked it after putting on the boots, or spraying his broadcasting studio with an odorless chemical that produced effects similar to LSD. All are set forth in a 346-page report of the U.S. Senate Select Committee to Study Governmental Operations with Respect to Intelligence Activities, dated November 20, 1975.

"The most ironic of these plots," says the report, "took place on November 22, 1963, the very day that President Kennedy was shot in Dallas—when a CIA official offered a poison pen to a Cuban for use against Castro while at the same time an emissary from President Kennedy was meeting with Castro to explore the possibility of improved relations."

Castro survived the plots, of which neither President Eisenhower, Kennedy nor Johnson was apparently aware, nor even their CIA directors. Richard Bissell and probably Richard Helms, successive deputy directors for plans, appear to have been the most senior officials to know about these murderous shenanigans; they evidently thought they were carrying out presidential wishes.

And Cuba survived the hit-and-run raids that started in earnest in 1962. A blown-up bridge or a burned-down sugar mill did not cause unrest and disaffection among the people, as intended, but rather strengthened their sense of patriotism and loyalty to Fidel. So our covert activities were dismal failures even if less embarrassing than the Bay of Pigs. The squabbling exile factions in Florida were infiltrated by Castro informers, so the Cubans were generally alerted in advance and waiting for the would-be saboteurs; when captured, these were put on display, along with their U.S. equipment, C-rations and all. In short, we handed Castro a propaganda bonanza, while the constant harassment from the mainland made it easier for him to create a siege mentality and blame most of Cuba's economic woes on the Yankee colossus. And of course his own anti-Yankee prejudices were reinforced. As he once remarked to Herbert Matthews of the *New York Times,* "You Americans keep complaining that Cuba is only ninety miles from your shores. I say that the United States is ninety miles from Cuba, and for us that is worse."

What if some of our cockeyed hugger-mugger had succeeded? What if the exotic seashell had been successfully planted and blown off Fidel's head?

On April 21, 1963, McGeorge Bundy, Kennedy's national security adviser, wrote a memorandum entitled "Cuban Alternatives" that made the point, heretofore overlooked, that Castro's death would lead to "singularly unpromising" consequences for U.S. policy, since he would almost certainly be succeeded by his brother Raúl. And there was little doubt that Raúl was far more likely than Fidel to follow the Soviet script to the letter.

Bundy's memorandum also identified three possible alternatives to continuing futile plots and pinpricks indefinitely: (a) forcing "a non-Communist solution in Cuba by all necessary means"; (b) insisting on "major but limited ends"; (c) moving "in the direction of a gradual development of some form of accommodation with Castro."

The last alternative, which grew out of a January proposal from Bundy to Kennedy about exploring the possibility of communicating with Castro, was then accepted by a new committee, the Special Group, which had assumed responsibility within the White House for reviewing and approving covert actions in Cuba. Sabotage had all but ceased early in 1963. Yet in June—the same month Kennedy delivered his famous speech on making the world "safe for diversity"—a sabotage program designed to "nourish a spirit of resistance and disaffection" was approved in the White House, and thirteen major operations planned for the November 1963–January 1964 period.

What could we—or should we—have been doing instead?

Four realities had to be kept in mind, and weren't:

First, Fidel Castro's one-man revolution was improvised, erratic, whimsical at times, but pervasive—and fueled by passionate popular support. Politically, he was an impetuous radical revolutionary—too undisciplined to be the Communists' satrap but not averse to using them and parts of their doctrine, nor to turning to the Soviet Union for the aid and trade he needed to keep going. His avowal in December 1961 that he'd always been a Marxist was believed by no one who knew him well; but his pride compelled him to say he was neither an opportunist nor some wet-behind-the-ears recent convert to Lenin's teachings.

Second, the revolution he'd set in motion could never be reversed after 1959. To turn the clock back, as the exiles hoped to do, would have meant closing schools and clinics, taking shoes away from children, returning most sugar plantations to absentee landlords, reopening Havana's casinos and notorious brothels and denationalizing expropriated firms whose owners had by now fled. There was just no way. The social and economic transformation of Cuba was too far advanced. Even if the revolution was mismanaged, as it was, the Soviets seemed willing to bail out their protégé indefinitely by buying his sugar above market prices and selling him oil below market prices. As a result, Castro has cost them billions of rubles over the past quarter century; but why should this concern us?

Third, the Cuban exile community, augmented annually by Castro's shrewd policy of letting the disgruntled leave—with one suitcase each —created a voting bloc in Florida and some northeastern states that soon carried weight with politicians. Denouncing Castro became a ritual for candidates in certain congressional districts, even though there were more brutal and corrupt dictators then in power all over Latin America.

Fourth, the only identifiable U.S. interests in Cuba were to retain our naval base at Guantanamo Bay (which we have) and to prevent Cuba from becoming a center for Soviet subversion of Latin America.

As it turned out, the Soviets preferred using traditional (and obedient) Communist parties for this purpose, and Castro's forays in the area were such failures that he all but gave up trying to export his revolution in mid-1964, by which time it had become somewhat tarnished by economic failures. Che Guevara, more restless and romantic, carried his revolutionary torch a while longer until his death in the jungles of Bolivia in 1967.

My hunch, buttressed by what I've read and heard, is that by mid-1959 it was too late for us to influence the course or the pace of the Cuban revolution. Castro, like a runaway horse with the bit in his teeth, was going all out. He barely found the time to see our able and generally sympathetic new career ambassador, Philip Bonsal, who replaced two successive pro-Batista political envoys, Arthur Gardner and Earl Smith. Bonsal hadn't given up on Castro in July, as I said earlier, but that was before Cienfuegos's mysterious disappearance, Urrutria's ouster and Matos's arrest and conviction.

In 1958, imaginative diplomacy on our part might have succeeded in persuading Batista to leave (as Marcos was persuaded twenty-eight years later) and allowing the democratic reformists to set up a government while Castro was still in the mountains—a government, backed by the army, in which his 26th of July Movement could play a role but not a commanding one—certainly until elections were held. I was told just such a course of action was proposed in Washington but flatly rejected by Ambassador Smith.

But if Fidel Castro was in fact committed to an anti-American policy, why did he sound so conciliatory in his talk with me? Indeed, why did he even bother to see me? The answer, I think, is that he had not yet turned against us (as he did, understandably, in 1960, when he learned of the Eisenhower Administration's preparations for the Bay of Pigs). He plausibly wanted normal diplomatic and trade relations with us, provided we didn't interfere with his revolutionary programs or even protest—as we did in May 1959—the seizure of U.S. property without compensation under the new Agrarian Reform Law. Castro was erratic and, as he confessed to me, emotional. It was in character for him to say, "Let us be friends"—and mean it—even while taking economic and political actions in the name of the revolution that were certain to anger us.

My own view today is that our wisest policy would have been to accept the fact that Castro was firmly in control and treat him with benign indifference, letting him know our door was open if he wanted to talk (as I once told Sékou Touré). Harassing or insulting him served no American purpose and was also an unbecoming stance for a great power. After all, we held on to Guantanamo, even though he refused to accept the annual rental payment; we didn't need his sugar, and he was never a threat to our security except in our fevered political rhetoric. The missile crisis was a U.S.-U.S.S.R. stare-down, with Fidel as a bystander, furious when Khrushchev backed off; it was never a *Cuban-*American crisis. As for the lure of Castroism in Latin America, his efforts in that direction finally fizzled out in Caracas, and Castro turned his attention to agronomy. *Look,* which had opened a South American bureau in 1963 to cover the expected Fidelista penetration of the continent, closed it down two years later. Absent the specter of Fidelismo, readers of American mass magazines couldn't care less about that part of the world.

To sum up, our national interest was not served by a policy of unremitting hostility any more than it was in the eighties in Nicaragua. It merely isolated us progressively from the Organization of American States and, on the trade embargo, from our European allies, who continued to do business with Cuba. Even the Vatican has kept a papal nuncio in Havana through the years. We have managed to look both surly and scared and, since the Bay of Pigs, vengeful. Europeans often told me we kept slapping at Castro because he'd had the effrontery to thumb his nose at us, *just ninety miles from our shores.* All we really accomplished was to dispel the myth (to which some Americans still cling) that we are both innocent and omnipotent.

The foregoing considerations made me receptive to some signals I began picking up in September 1963 at the United Nations, where I was assigned to our delegation as special adviser on African affairs. Among my duties were keeping in touch with African delegates and trying to mitigate the effects of our frequent votes in favor of South African or Portuguese positions. (The lawyers who dominated our delegation persisted in viewing the General Assembly as a tidy parliamentary chamber or judicial body, which it certainly wasn't, instead of an unruly political convention where no one ever got nominated and scoring publicity points was the name of the game (along with letting off steam.) Even President Kennedy questioned our almost automatic support of Portugal, something the Pentagon insisted on to safeguard our bases in the Azores. (When I once mentioned to him that backing Portuguese colonialism hurt us in Black Africa, he mused aloud, "The navy keeps saying the Azores are vital to our security. But I bet they'd find an alternative if the Azores disappeared in a tidal wave.")

Anyway, on September 5, I was talking Africa with Lisa Howard, an ABC correspondent, who told me she'd recently interviewed Castro in Havana and was convinced he'd like to restore communications with the U.S. She offered to arrange a social gathering at her apartment where I could meet casually and informally with Carlos Lechuga, Cuba's representative at the U.N.

I told her I'd let her know, on the understanding that she would keep all such contacts confidential in exchange for exclusivity if there should be a story to be told somewhere down the road. But her impression reminded me of something Sékou Touré said to me during the 1962 missile crisis: "I'm sorry for Castro. I think he is a nationalist and a neutralist at heart, whatever he sometimes says. But he had neither the intellectual training nor the ideological experience to understand the Communists. I did—in the trade union movement—so I know how they operate. But Castro is naive and has allowed himself to be used by them. Even so, if you are flexible, I think he can be brought back to a neutralist position."

This could be the moment to be flexible, and in Washington a week later I mentioned the possibility of sounding out Lechuga to Averell Harriman, then an assistant secretary of state. He was intrigued and asked me to do a memo on it. Ken Galbraith, back from India and returning to Harvard, told me Harriman, rather than Stevenson, was the man to see in order to get the president's attention.

On September 17, I ran into Seydou Diallo, Guinea's ambassador to Cuba, in the Delegates' Lounge, and he volunteered the information that Cuba's economy was in a slump and Castro would soon be amenable to some sort of agreement with us. "He is salvageable," he said. "Give him another three months." Other Africans I talked to expressed generally the same view.

That day I wrote a "Memorandum on Cuba," based on the premise that the policy of isolating Cuba not only intensified Castro's desire to cause trouble but froze the United States before the world "in the unattractive posture of a big country trying to bully a small country."

The memo went on:

According to neutral diplomats I have talked to at the U.N., there is reason to believe that Castro is unhappy about his present dependence on the Soviet Union; that he does not enjoy in effect being a satellite;

that our trade embargo is hurting him—though not enough to endanger his position; and that he would like to establish some official contact with the United States and would go to some length to obtain normalization of relations with us—even though this would not be welcomed by most of his hard-core Communist entourage . . .

All of this may or may not be true. But it would seem that we have something to gain and nothing to lose by finding out whether in fact Castro does want to talk and what concessions he would be prepared to make . . .

What I am proposing is a discreet inquiry into neutralizing Cuba on our terms. It is based on the assumption that, short of a change of regime, our principal political objectives in Cuba are: a. The evacuation of all Soviet bloc military personnel. b. An end to subversive activities by Cuba in Latin America. c. Adoption by Cuba of a policy of non-alignment.

I suggested the time and place for this inquiry were the current session of the U.N. General Assembly and that, having visited Cuba and talked with Castro in 1959, it would be natural for me to meet informally with Lechuga. If Castro was interested, one thing might lead to another: "For the moment, all I would like is the authority to make contact with Lechuga. We'll see what happens then."

The next day, I showed the memorandum to Stevenson, who liked it. "Unfortunately," he said, "the CIA is still in charge of Cuba." But he offered to take it up with the president. Harriman was in New York on the nineteenth, so I gave him a copy too. He said he was "adventuresome enough" to be interested but urged me to see Bob Kennedy, whose approval would be essential. I called Kennedy and got an appointment to see him on the twenty-fourth.

Meanwhile, Stevenson told me he had talked to the president about the Cuban initiative when he came to New York on the twentieth to address the General Assembly, and got his agreement to go ahead. For some reason, Stevenson was not keen on my seeing Robert Kennedy, but I trusted Harriman's instincts. Bob had been deeply involved in our Cuban relations and would expect to be consulted about this gambit; also, he had his brother's ear as did no one else.

I did tell Lisa to organize her cocktail party, and on the twenty-third Lechuga and I found ourselves talking about Fidel and the revolution in a corner of her apartment. He said Castro had hoped to establish some sort of contact with Kennedy after he became president in 1961, but the Bay of Pigs ended any chance of that, at least for the time being. But Castro had read Kennedy's American University speech in June and had liked its tone. I mentioned my Havana visit in 1959 and Fidel's "Let us be friends" remark in our conversation. Lechuga said another such conversation in Havana could be useful and might be arranged. He expressed irritation at the continuing exile raids and our freezing $33 million in Cuban assets in U.S. banks in July. We agreed the present situation was abnormal and we should keep in touch.

On the twenty-fourth I flew to Washington, gave Bob Kennedy my memo, which he read, and told him of my talk with Lechuga the night before. He said my going to Cuba, as Lechuga had mentioned, was too risky—it was bound to leak—and if nothing came of it the Republicans would call it appeasement and demand a congressional investigation. But he thought the matter was worth pursuing at the U.N. and perhaps even with Castro some place outside Cuba. He said he'd consult with Harriman and McGeorge Bundy.

On the twenty-seventh I met Lechuga in the U.N. Delegates' Lounge—always a good place for discreet encounters because of its noise and confusion—and said it would be difficult for me, in my present capacity as a government official, to accept an invitation to Cuba; however, I was authorized to talk to anyone who came here from Havana. He said he'd pass my message along. Meanwhile, he warned me he'd be making a tough anti-American speech on October 7, but not to take it too seriously.

On October 2, Bundy called to say that Gordon Chase, one of his deputies, would be my White House contact and to keep him informed.

The next day, I lunched with an old friend, Jean Daniel, the editor of the French socialist newsweekly *L'Observateur,* who said he was going to Washington and then Havana to see Castro, who he had reason to believe would now be receptive to some bold diplomacy from our side. I called Ben Bradlee, then *Newsweek*'s Washington bureau chief, who knew Daniel, and suggested he try to get him an appointment with the president.

On the seventh, Lechuga made his speech, denouncing our trade embargo and the exile raids as warlike acts. It got a lot of applause, even from the moderates, who instinctively sympathized with a small country standing up to a superpower. Stevenson had asked me for a draft of a reply, in which he said that Castro could have peace with all his neighbors if he stopped trying to subvert other nations and taking orders from Moscow and instead started honoring the original democratic pledges of his revolution.

On October 19, a Greek town planner named Doxiades, just back from Havana, dropped in to tell me Castro was sincerely interested in normalizing relations with us.

Two days later Chase called and I told him the ball was still in Lechuga's court.

On the twenty-fourth, the president saw Daniel after Bradlee told him of his forthcoming trip to Cuba. Kennedy blamed our pro-Batista policy in the fifties for "economic colonization, humiliation and exploitation" and added, "We'll have to pay for those sins." But he said the Cuban problem now had a Soviet dimension in that Castro was doing the Kremlin's bidding and acting as its agent in Latin America: "The continuation of our economic blockade depends on his continuation of subversive activities." But as Daniel wrote later, "I could see plainly that John Kennedy had doubts and was seeking a way out."

On the twenty-eighth, Lechuga told me Havana didn't see how formal talks could be useful just now but he'd be glad to continue chatting with me anyway. Lisa Howard had meanwhile been in touch by phone with Castro's personal aide, Major René Vallejo. He told her Castro did want to talk personally and privately to us about improving relations and was glad we were ready to listen. She told him about our proposal for a meeting at the U.N., but Vallejo said Castro couldn't leave Cuba just now.

On the thirty-first, Vallejo called her back and said Castro would like a U.S. official to come and see him alone. He appreciated the importance of discretion and therefore offered to send a plane to fly the official to a private airport near Varadero, where no one else would see him. She told him I was the official concerned and would get in touch.

I kept Stevenson informed and also called Chase, who told me on November 4 to come to the White House the next day. There, I briefed him and Bundy on Vallejo's message to Lisa. Bundy said the president was more interested in this Cuban exercise than was the State Department. (I knew he could see the political advantage of possibly weaning Castro away from the Soviet fold.) He asked for a chronological memorandum describing all the exchanges that had taken place since my first talk with Lisa.

On the twelfth, she told me Vallejo had phoned again suggesting I come to Varadero from Key West on an American plane, which was bound to attract less attention than a Cuban plane in Florida. Bundy then called, reiterating that the president favored a preliminary discussion about an agenda, perhaps with Vallejo, at the U.N.—and to call Cuba and tell him so.

During the next four days I tried to reach Vallejo but either the circuit was out or he was. Finally, on the eighteenth, I spoke to him at 2 A.M. and told him the White House position. He said Castro would send instructions to Lechuga to discuss an agenda with me. He spoke fluent English and called me "sir." (Many years later, Castro told me he was listening in on our conversation.)

I reported to Bundy in the morning. He said once an agenda had been agreed upon, the president would want to see me and decide what to say to Castro. He said the president would be making a brief trip to Dallas but otherwise planned to be in Washington.

Meanwhile, in a speech the day before, the president said of Cuba that it had become "a weapon in an effort dictated by external powers to subvert the other American republics. This and this alone divides us. As long as this is true, nothing is possible. Without it, everything is possible." Arthur Schlesinger, Jr., who helped in the preparation of this speech, said it was intended to help me by signaling to Castro that normalization was possible if Cuba simply stopped doing the Kremlin's work in Latin America (such as trying to sabotage—vainly, as it turned out—the upcoming Venezuelan elections).

Daniel saw Castro on November 20 and told him of his meeting with Kennedy. He found the Cuban leader thoughtful and attentive; he had Daniel repeat what Kennedy had said about Batista. "He has come to understand many things over the past few months," Castro concluded, adding, "As a revolutionary, the present situation does not displease me. But as a man and a statesman, it is my duty to indicate what the bases for understanding could be."

They met again on the twenty-second, just as the news of Kennedy's assassination was broadcast. Castro seemed stunned. *"Es una mala noticia,"* he murmured. "This is bad news. This is a serious matter, an extremely serious matter. There is the end of your mission of peace." And later: "At least Kennedy was an enemy to whom we had become accustomed."

He also predicted to Daniel that the Cubans would be blamed for it, as they were for several days after the murder. What Fidel did not know was that Desmond FitzGerald, a senior CIA official, was on that very day, in Paris, giving Rolando Cubela, whose code name was AM/ LASH, a poison pen with which to kill Castro. There is no evidence that Kennedy knew this either. And indeed, what motive would either of them have in plotting the death of someone they were planning to communicate with?

One thing was clear: Stevenson was right when he told me back in September that "the CIA is in charge of Cuba"; or anyway, acted as if it thought it was, and to hell with the president it was pledged to serve.

After November 22, the Cuban exercise was gradually laid to rest by our side. On the twenty-ninth, I told Lisa, who was seeing Lechuga, that I had no instructions yet to call it off. On December 2, Lechuga confirmed getting a message from Vallejo authorizing him to talk to me "in general terms"—and had I heard anything from Washington? I called Chase and said the next move was up to us.

Two days later, Lechuga approached me in the Delegates' Lounge to say he now had a letter from Fidel himself, instructing him to talk with me about a specific agenda. I called Chase, who replied all policies were now under review and to be patient.

Jean Daniel returned from Cuba that week, convinced that Fidel wanted to reach a modus vivendi with us. I phoned Schlesinger and Chase at the White House and arranged an appointment for Daniel with Bundy.

On the twelfth, I told Lechuga to be patient and that so far as I knew, we weren't closing the door. (Neither of us knew then that it would be six years before we would meet again—in Havana.)

The General Assembly was coming to an end, and the next day I finally had the satisfaction of casting a vote in the Fourth Committee against South Africa on the question of self-determination for Namibia, which was (and still is) illegally occupied by the South Africans.

President Johnson came to New York and lunched with our delegation after reassuring the General Assembly that he'd be carrying on Kennedy's policies. At lunch, he told me he'd read my chronological account of our Cuban initiative "with interest."

And that was it. I was named ambassador to Kenya in January, and during my Washington briefings I saw Chase, who told me there was apparently no desire among the Johnson people to do anything about Cuba in an election year.

On April 7, Johnson did decide to discontinue the CIA-controlled sabotage raids against Cuba, which John McCone, the CIA director, interpreted as giving up our long-standing objective of overthrowing the regime. Later, Johnson was quoted in an interview as saying that when he took office he had discovered that "we had been operating a damned Murder, Inc., in the Caribbean."

What part, if any, our Cuban gambit played in Kennedy's assassination is the kind of question that now seems pointless to raise. While we kept the exercise under wraps (apparently not even the secretary of state was fully apprised), the CIA must have had an inkling of what was happening from phone taps and surveillance of Lechuga. The news could then have trickled down to the frustrated Bay of Pigs veterans still huddled around their CIA case officers, still hoping for another invasion attempt. An accommodation would have dashed these hopes. Many Cuban adventurers like Frank Fiorini, alias Frank Sturgis, who would wind up working the catacombs of Watergate, could easily have been aroused by what Schlesinger has referred to as "a broadside of unknown origin that told Cuban exiles in Miami that 'only one development' would return them to their homeland—'if an inspired Act of God should place in the White House within weeks a Texan known to be a friend of all Latin Americans.'" Aroused enough to help perform the "act"? I don't know and don't care to speculate about it.

What I do know is that I did not get to Cuba in 1963, contrary to a Tass dispatch from Tokyo in 1977, quoting a Japanese newsweekly's rehash of the assassination: "The CIA, then under John McCone, found that Kennedy was considering détente with Castro in 1963 and even tried to pass Castro a gift of a poison-coated diving suit through unwitting United Nations representative William Attwood, who went to Cuba that year for talks with the Cuban premier."

Seldom have I read a sentence containing so many errors. Which makes it a fitting conclusion to a chapter recalling an episode in American foreign policy best described as a comedy of errors that wasn't always very funny.

Chapter 13

From the Rift Valley to the Mekong Delta

T HE QUICKEST WAY TO FEEL OLD without trying to run upstairs is to engage someone about twenty-five in a discussion of recent history—that is, of events you recall as having happened only yesterday and thus still memory-fresh. Korea? No reaction. Vietnam? Yes, there have been books and films about it and their fathers may have been involved. But what about the Spirit of Glassboro and the Six-Day War in 1967? the Prague spring in 1968? and going back further, to 1964, the Stanleyville rescue mission? the Zanzibar coup? *Zanzibar?*

Yes, Zanzibar, that clove-scented, cigar-shaped island off the coast of East Africa made the front pages so often in February 1964 that the State Department hustled me out to Kenya after a Washington *Star* editorial demanded to know why, as our newly named ambassador to Kenya, I was not at my post doing battle with the Communists who had allegedly taken over this "strategic" island as a springboard for the conquest of the dark continent.

Mutinies that same month over low pay and promotions in the Kenyan army were quickly put down by some remaining British units, but the mutinies, along with the overthrow of the docile old sultan in Zanzibar, only contributed to the general apprehension in Washington that East Africa was heading straight down the spout.

The British were characteristically more relaxed, even phlegmatic, about these happenings. On March 8, when Bill Leonhart, our ambassador to Tanzania, Frank Carlucci, our consul in Zanzibar, and I met with Colonial Secretary Duncan Sandys and his aides in Dar es Salaam, he responded to our dire warnings of Soviet beachheads like a character in an Evelyn Waugh novel. He seemed especially intrigued with a wild-eyed African gunslinger who dubbed himself General John Okello after deposing the sultan and his entourage of wealthy Arabs and massacring hundreds of others. He later fled to the mainland when a Marxist conspirator nicknamed Babu took charge and invited the Chinese to open an embassy.

"Perhaps that beggar Okello's our chap after all," suggested Sandys. "Why don't we send him back to Zanzibar and let him blow it all up again? The pieces might come down in a different shape, what? Where do you suppose we could find him?"

Not only the Chinese but the East Germans opened shop in Zanzibar, which gave the State Department reason to refer to the "Sino-Soviet threat"—a phrase still being used by our bureaucracy even though the Chinese and Russians had scarcely been on speaking terms for years.

Back again in Washington, I told a press conference on April 2 that it was obvious the Chinese were trying to set up a "non-African type of regime" in Zanzibar, and the East Africans ought to be on their guard; I wanted to stress it was *their* problem more than ours, even though Babu's crowd shut down our satellite tracking station (which we were planning to move anyway), allegedly as a result of my remarks.

And the Great Zanzibar Crisis fizzled out less than three weeks later, and four days after Cy Sulzberger, in his *New York Times* column, scolded our "feckless fleet" for cruising by the island while the tracking station was being dismantled instead of, presumably, giving the wogs a whiff of the grape. Babu was eased out, and Sheikh Karume, an unsophisticated fisherman but no Communist, agreed to join Tanzania in something called URTZ (the United Republic of Tanzania and Zanzibar). The East Germans went on building their cheap, low-rise, Berlin-style apartments, the Chinese experimented with some agricultural projects and the island went back to sleep.

My rushing out to East Africa in late February (something Harriman and Soapy Williams favored, but which the latter's deputy, Wayne Fredericks, considered a panic button reaction) did serve some useful purposes: It got me out of a full term at the Counter Insurgency School, a new and perfectly useless interagency course sold to Robert Kennedy as essential for overseas-bound government personnel; it enabled me to see the president on a more than pro forma basis, thanks to Bill Moyers, his press secretary; and it gave me a chance on my return to report on Kenya's needs and light some fires under the bureaucracy, as I had in 1961 on returning briefly from Guinea. (Kenya's main problems in 1964 were unemployment, education and land—and we could do something about all three: a National Youth Corps, like the New Deal's CCC, for the idle young people, Peace Corps and AID teachers for the schools and Peace Corps agronomists to help Africans manage the farms bought by the government from former white settlers.)

President Johnson approved of this kind of aid, but his chief interest in talking to me was that he'd heard I'd written political speeches for Stevenson and Kennedy—and would I send some stuff to Moyers for the fall campaign? I had already agreed to write a piece for the Democratic Convention Book reviewing a century of unbroken Democratic successes and unbroken Republican failures in foreign policy (not an easy assignment), and political speeches were not traditionally an ambassadorial function—but what the hell. Goldwater worried me too; and LBJ promised he'd back me up on the Kenya National Youth Service. While we talked, one of his beagles, muddy-pawed, jumped up on my lap and had to be carried away by Moyers. A picture of this mishap got a lot of front-page play (it was the beagle Johnson claimed liked to be lifted up by its ears) and as a result a lot of our friends found out we were going to Kenya. So this was a plus, too, saving us considerable postage.

By the time I returned to Nairobi on April 15 with Sim, Jan and our new daughter, Susan (Peter was in boarding school), I'd presented my credentials—addressed to Queen Elizabeth, since Kenya, though independent, was not yet a republic; knew the staff and had an idea of what we had to do. For the purpose of this book, I simply want to cite some of the highlights of what were, in retrospect, two of the most satisfying years of my life.

The cold war, while defused by the Cuban missile crisis, was still going full blast in what was now being called the Third World. Andrei Gromyko, the Soviet foreign minister, made it plain in a speech a few months earlier that we were still competing vigorously for influence in this "world," of which Africa was an integral part: "We, the representatives of the world of socialism," said Gromyko, "have indeed waged and will go on waging an unremitting struggle for the triumph of the ideals of socialism and Communism . . . It is not divisions of soldiers but legions of books, not nuclear bombs but the ability to produce more of the common benefits and to redistribute them more equitably that must constitute the weapons in the fight between the two philosophies."

The sparring in Kenya started soon after *uhuru* (independence) in December 1963, when various competing countries, like Nationalist and Communist China, and East and West Germany, scrambled for recognition by Kenya. (In those days, it was one or the other, not both.) A North Korean mission, twenty-seven strong, arrived and rented a house, assured by their Chinese sponsors they would be accredited. But one of our enterprising CIA employees got two personable South Koreans, one a general, to fly in from Seoul and hustled them over to meet Mbiyu Koinange, an old Kikuyu crony of Jomo Kenyatta's who'd been assigned certain diplomatic chores. Koinange, the son of a distinguished tribal chief, lived on a farm in nearby Kiambu with numerous relatives, including his father's six surviving wives, aged twenty-two to eighty-six. When our man introduced him to the South Koreans, he explained they'd come out to pay homage to his father, the great chief, whose grave, he knew, was on the premises and whose exploits had long been admired and celebrated in South Korea.

At the gravesite, the Koreans donned silk robes, lighted some incense and prostrated themselves on prayer mats, chanting unintelligibly before the old chief's tomb while our man intoned the Lord's Prayer. The assembled widows began weeping and ululating; Koinange, deeply moved, wiped the tears from his eyes—and the next day Kenya recognized South Korea and sent the North Koreans packing, minus the deposit on their house. I don't recall the general and his sidekick doing anything while I was in Kenya except play poker and golf (at which they became very proficient), but at least we didn't have twenty-seven mischief-makers roaming around.

I had had one CIA man on my staff on Guinea to keep tabs on the activities of Soviet bloc personnel upcountry via a network of Lebanese merchants for whom he did a few favors. In Kenya we had a larger contingent, but their work never included dirty tricks. (Of the thirty-six employees of the Soviet Embassy, we identified seventeen as KGB agents, which was about average for them; the proportion of CIA people in our mission was less than one in ten.) We cooperated with the Kenya Special Branch by providing information about many of the Soviet bloc and Chinese visitors who turned up in Nairobi. In 1965, a Soviet military mission headed by a KGB general arrived in town to supervise the delivery of weapons (requested by Vice President Oginga Odinga while visiting Moscow) from a freighter, the *Fizik Lebedev,* in Mombasa harbor. With information we were able to provide, the Kenyans investigated the matter and sent both the ship and the Russians home. About the same time, a convoy of Chinese arms was intercepted on Kenyan territory en route to Uganda. Kenyatta, who didn't like things going on behind his back, naturally suspected his chief rival in the government, Odinga, a crafty but basically silly man who was heavily subsidized by both the Chinese and Russians. When Odinga became vice president in 1964, they had assumed he was in line to succeed Kenyatta, apparently overlooking the fact that the Kikuyus would never permit a Luo tribesman like Double-O, as the British called Odinga, ever to take power. And the Kikuyus, backed by us and the British, were the toughest of all Kenya's tribes. The so-called Mau-Maus were Kikuyus.

All sorts of cold war games were played and replayed in those years, and in time Kenyatta and his chief aides became convinced our policy was to help them create a stable, nonaligned, prosperous multiracial society that could be a model for Africa. And so, eventually, a 1965 verse by Ogden Nash in the *New Republic* finally came true:

> Oginga Odinga, Oginga Odinga
> In Kenya's black pie he is Mao's red finger.
> Though his name leads me into this frivolous jingle,
> Not one to laugh off is Ogingle Odingle.
> I hope that Kenyatta, the lion of Kenya,
> Will settle the hash of this mirthless hyena.

The last line was unfair to poor Double-O. He loved coming to meals and parties at our house because, as he once told me, "With Americans I can laugh and relax. You are like the Chinese. But the Russians—they are stiff and formal, like the British." Words failed me.

Money was passed around in Kenya, but fortunately Kenyatta called me in soon after my arrival and said he didn't want any subsidies going to individual politicians: All requests for emergency funding would henceforth come from him and be collected by his most trusted advisers —Charles Njonjo, the attorney general; Bruce McKenzie, the minister of agriculture; and James Gichuru, the minister of finance. Tom Mboya and a few others had been receiving indirect CIA stipends but I cut them off. Tom, a Luo, was practical and intelligent, but his close rapport with Kenyatta was resented by Kikuyu extremists. And so he was eventually murdered, along with Bildad Kaggia, a turncoat Kikuyu, and Pio de Gama Pinto, a bright Marxist adviser to Odinga. Suspects were always arrested but the cases were never satisfactorily resolved and public interest gradually waned. There was a Cosa Nostra quality to Kenyan politics, and partly because I hinted at it in a book I later wrote, I was declared a prohibited immigrant in 1967 and the book banned.

Ironically, Njonjo, who banished me, approached me at a garden party in March 1966 to ask for a $15,000 loan to stage some weekend political rallies. He said his regular British contact was unavailable, but that we'd be repaid the following week. Well, why not?

The oddest request I got for funds came from Albert René, now the president of the Seychelles, but in 1965 merely the leader of the local leftist United People's Party. The main party on the Seychelles—then accessible only by boat or by a lumbering U.S. Navy seaplane that covered the thousand miles in seven hours and serviced our new tracking station—was the Democratic Party, headed by Charles Mancham, a Chinese African who was embarrassingly pro-American. After I'd seen both of them during a visit to the exotic islands, René called on me one day in Nairobi and asked for $1,500 to buy some new office equipment. I pointed out that his party regularly staged demonstrations against our tracking station—so why should we help him?

"Ah, but we don't *have* to oppose your facility," he replied. "We could change our policy and support it!"

My CIA station chief was tempted—it was a bargain price for a growing political party—but the Seychelles were then a British colony and therefore off limits to our spooks.

Sino-Soviet relations were getting worse by the month, as we could tell in Africa. In June 1964, the Russians accused the Chinese of trading secretly with South Africa, while the Chinese issued a warning to all new nations that Soviet aid meant political control. In Nairobi, Wang, the Chinese ambassador, and Lavrov, the Russian, seldom spoke to each other, though Lavrov took me aside at my July 4 reception to join him in a "special toast" to friendship and peace. The Pakistani envoy kept trying to get me and Wang together for drinks at his house, but Wang could never get clearance from Peking, probably because Mao's cultural revolution was about to erupt.

As I prepared to leave Africa in 1966, I could detect a lessening of interest in the continent on the part of the Russians, perhaps because they had been singed so often, most recently by the coup in Ghana that ousted Nkrumah. In Kenya, they reneged on financing an irrigation scheme in the Kano Plains, Odinga country, probably because they sensed the Chinese, bracing for an upheaval at home, were losing interest too. Even so, Mao's protégé, Lin Piao, did say in September 1965, "In the final analysis, the whole cause of world revolution hinges on the revolutionary struggle of the Asian, African and Latin American peoples who make up the overwhelming majority of the world's population

. . . [This area is] the main battlefield against U.S. imperialism and its lackeys." But in Africa's case, Peking was becoming too preoccupied just now with the home front to bother lavishing fortune cookies on dubious clients. Savimbi, Mugabe, Nyerere and Touré—and even Karume of once frenzied Zanzibar—were getting used to seeking other benefactors.

Thanks to the CIA, we had a pretty good pipeline into the Chinese Embassy, as well as a few others, and probably knew more than even the Kenyans did about whatever cold war skirmishing was going on. But we also had a procession of American reporters in transit who knew little of Africa and were interested only in finding or fabricating evidence of race violence or the Red threat. When the *Wall Street Journal* published a story from Nairobi in October 1964 headlined WHITES FLEEING KENYA IN FEAR OF BLACK RULE ADD TO ITS PROBLEMS, I felt impelled to write a letter setting the record straight—such as the fact that seventeen new American businesses had been established in Kenya in the past six months and that many more whites were staying on than "fleeing." The British press was no better. The London *Sunday Telegraph* headlined a story about a few confiscated weapons: RED TAKEOVER IN KENYA. The same Commie power grab line was echoed in *U.S. News and World Report,* to the point that I was asked by a cabinet minister if this was an official U.S. Government publication.

Cy Sulzberger was a special case. When he strode into my office in 1964 and said he wished to see Kenyatta, I knew that the old man, who was resting at his farm and had probably never heard of Sulzberger, would be otherwise occupied. And so he was, according to his private secretary.

But Sulzberger, who was accustomed on arriving in any world capital to being whisked from the airport straight to the prime minister's for a lunch in his honor, would not accept my explanation of Kenyatta's inaccessibility. "If he knew I was in Nairobi," he said, "he'd see me. If he can't be bothered, then I don't see why we should bother giving a penny to the old bandit. And I'll damn well say so."

We had a problem. I could see us losing the two million bucks for National Youth Service tents, uniforms, tools and vehicles on the strength of a blast on the *New York Times* editorial page, and the Soviets then picking up the project. Fortunately, I ran into Jimmy Gichuru at a party that evening and filled him in. He understood right away. "Leave it to me," he said.

The next afternoon, Sulzberger, all smiles, reappeared in my office.

"You were wrong, Bill," he said. "Kenyatta just hadn't been told I was here. Early this morning, the minister of finance himself came to my hotel to apologize and drove me out to see the prime minister at his farm. We had a very pleasant and informative visit."

And thanks to Gichuru, Cy wrote a favorable column and our aid program was unscathed.

The only real crisis we experienced in Kenya spilled over from the Congo (now Zaire) in the fall of 1964. The full story has been told elsewhere, so I'll confine this account to the outlines of a very complex pattern of intrigue that culminated in a mass murder and a dramatic (and all-but-forgotten) rescue operation code-named Dragon Rouge.

The Congo had been a mess since the Belgians pulled out in 1960, leaving just thirteen African college graduates behind to administer a heterogeneous country as big as the United States east of the Mississippi —and smack in the heart of Africa. Tribal warlords masquerading as politicians proceeded to carve it up. Mineral-rich Katanga, under Moïse Tshombe, almost managed to secede. In the northeast, an area as big as France called the Congolese People's Republic was set up in Stanley-ville (now Kisangani), with the aid and encouragement of Algeria and Egypt (then in a meddlesome phase) and probably the Chinese and (indirectly) the Russians as well. What they seemed to share was a common interest in chaos. The "Republic" eventually declared itself a Communist state, hoping for massive Soviet bloc support, but by then it was falling apart and a rather poor gamble.

Our involvement started with the sequestration on August 5 of Michael Hoyt, our consul, and his four-man staff; and the detention and subsequent sentencing to death for espionage of an American medical missionary, Paul Carlson. They all became hostages, along with about thirty other Americans, mostly missionaries, six hundred Belgians and perhaps a thousand other foreigners, including Asians and Africans. (Their gruesome ordeal was later recounted in David Reed's book *111 Days in Stanleyville*.) The crisis developed when Tshombe, a realistic but unpopular African, decided to unify the country by force with the help of trigger-happy white mercenaries and black Katangese gen-darmes, which he dubbed the ANC (Congolese National Army), and some U.S.-donated B-26 and T-5 planes piloted by anti-Castro Cubans, presumably on the CIA payroll. By October, an ANC column com-manded by "Mad Mike" Hoare was hell-bent for Stanleyville after sav-ing some white hostages from execution at Kindu. No one, not even Tshombe himself waving a stop sign on the road, could have stopped this force now. But Kenyatta, like most African leaders, believed

Tshombe was our puppet who would and could do anything we asked. Meanwhile it was certain that the Stanleyville hostages, all threatened and many mistreated, would be massacred by panicky rebel mobs when Hoare's desperadoes neared the city. We had to find a way to rescue them first.

The reason I got thrust into this donnybrook was that Kenyatta was named chairman of a committee of the misnamed Organization of African Unity whose mission was to save the hostages by stopping the fighting, and I was picked by Washington to negotiate with him in this capacity. But I knew the only way to save the hostages was to rescue them before the inevitable bloodbath. And so October was a month of maneuvering in a morass of lies, intrigue, deceit and propaganda— much of it orchestrated by a glib trilingual doctor of psychology named Thomas Kanza who claimed to be the rebel government's foreign minister. But after October 7 he kept away from Stanleyville, where at least one official had been eaten by young *simbas* (rebel soldiers), who figured it would enhance their *dawa* (magic protection against bullets). Kanza, who was charming and totally unscrupulous, and I had several talks, culminating in a final meeting on November 23 at Kenyatta's farm at Gatundu, where I told him the only thing to be discussed was the freeing of the hostages. He replied he could not discuss what he called "prisoners of war" until all military operations and air raids were halted. (An arms airlift from North Africa was under way, and the rebels were trying to buy time.)

I knew, but Kanza didn't, that six hundred Belgian paratroopers had been flown from Brussels to Kamina air base, in the Congo, via Ascension Island, in U.S. Air Force C-130s, and were now waiting for our final talks to break down before dropping on Stanleyville early the next morning.

So I told Kanza and the OAU representative (who hitched a ride out of town that afternoon in a U.S. attaché plane) as well as the other Kenyans present, including Kenyatta, that I would have to report to Washington before giving him a reply.

I knew what it would be, but surprise was essential.

At 7 A.M. I got word the Belgians had landed just before dawn and rescued all but twenty-eight hostages, two of them Americans (including Carlson) who were murdered seconds before the Belgians reached them. Many hostages, including children, were wounded when the *simbas* went on a shooting spree before fleeing from the paratroopers. Only one trooper was killed.

When I broke the news to Kenyatta at ten-thirty, he seemed stunned and glowered at me. He felt I had betrayed him by pretending to negotiate in good faith. This was a case where it would have been wiser to send a special negotiator from Washington rather than jeopardize the relationship of trust he and I had built up over the year. Leaving his office, I brushed past Odinga and met Kanza in the hall. "When are we meeting again?" he asked jovially. I handed him the bulletin announcing the parachute drop. I had never seen an African blanch before, and I confess to enjoying his reaction, as I did his later reference to me at a press conference as "my good friend."

In the next two days, other foreigners were saved at Paulis, an hour's flight from Stanleyville; but more were killed in remote areas when the Belgians decided to wrap it up and return to base.

The reaction to Stanleyville was predictable. The Africans were humiliated: the white man was back, doing what he pleased, as he always had, this time with a handful of troops. But they had asked for it by refusing to look at the facts, blinded by their hatred of Tshombe. At the U.N., only the Nigerians, among the Africans, defended the rescue mission. Kenyatta had even refused to receive a Swiss Red Cross delegation on their return from Stanleyville in October, believing Kanza's charge that they were "Western spies," even though the Red Cross could have evacuated the hostages without bloodshed.

The episode taught me an important lesson: that in diplomacy rational argument is worse than useless against unbridled passion—worse because it only makes you sound hypocritical to those who have accepted lies, forgeries and rumors as fact. In such situations, silence, patience and a low profile are the best tactics.

The "radical" triumph was short-lived. On Thanksgiving Day, returning to the embassy from a church service, my deputy, Jim Ruchti, and I were stopped by a white police officer with a bullhorn who told us a crowd was approaching and to use the back entrance. A mob soon blocked the street, and we watched from my office while rioters set fire to cars with diplomatic plates—one British, one Swedish, one Indian—before being finally dispersed by two truckloads of white riot police that Kenyatta apparently held in reserve for real emergencies. A Chinese embassy car parked across the street served as the demonstrators' command post. After an hour's shouting, the mob surged to the Asian part of town, looted a few shops and went on home, high on beer and *bhang,* a popular local drug.

"How do you feel?" asked a British reporter also trapped in our embassy.

"Sad," I replied. "And also sore at missing my Thanksgiving turkey."

They had overplayed their hand and alarmed Kenyatta, who had not authorized this violence. And by keeping our cool, by showing our displeasure by calculated indifference, we eventually got our relations back on the even keel where he wanted them. Still, it was important to keep them guessing, and let them realize that Kenya needed the United States more than we needed Kenya—a fact that invariably surprised Africans, who figured all the big powers still lusted after them.

Odinga tried to get me expelled—he had produced a dossier full of wild charges at a cabinet meeting—but by mid-December even Double-O and I were shaking hands. Lavrov was barely civil to me for a time after Stanleyville but warmed up again in the spring when he was satisfied I was no longer in the Kenyan doghouse.

Out of this flap, I detected three factions forming in the State Department with respect to Africa. Williams and Fredericks considered Africa important and deserving of our sympathy and understanding; Harriman considered it important and therefore a place to demonstrate our toughness; and Rusk and Ball considered it of secondary importance and consequently a candidate for selective disengagement. I could see merit in blending the first and third approaches.

While we worried about our hostages, Nikita Khrushchev was finally relieved of his functions on October 15—a day after China exploded its first atomic bomb. He had been top dog for a decade and would spend the rest of his life in anonymous retirement in his dacha on the outskirts of Moscow. He was succeeded by Aleksei Kosygin as head of government and Leonid Brezhnev as party boss (the better job). Khrushchev's style—free-wheeling, at times even clownish and bombastic—disturbed the Bolshevik old guard, some of whom never forgave him for debunking Stalin (which they called "spitting on the history of our country"). And his determination, expressed at the twenty-second Party Congress in October 1961, to reform the sclerotic Soviet bureaucracy alarmed a power structure jealous of its privileges. Yet thousands of innocent prisoners were freed and overdue reforms carried out under his leadership, and he and Kennedy came closer to ending the cold war than have any of their successors; the day after Kennedy was shot, a somber and shaken Khrushchev was the first Russian to sign the memorial book at the American Embassy.

The year 1965 was a time for repairing the Congo damage for those of us stationed in East Africa, and we sensed the healing would be hastened if we let the African firebrands know that by allowing their

Arab and Soviet backers to use them politically, they may possibly have alienated the only countries—Britain, the U.S. and West Germany— which could provide the capital and expertise for their national economic development. One way to keep them wondering was for our ambassadors to Kenya, Tanzania and Uganda to return to Washington for "consultations." This took some arranging, but we flew back early in February and managed to see the president—thanks to Jack Valenti —on our very last day for that essential photograph of us "consulting." He did read a memo we gave him and wished us well, but when we asked State what our African policy was these days we were told, "If you find out at the White House, let us know." So we decided that maybe we should make policy in the field and then sell it to Washington. For the moment, as the Congo emotions subsided, our posture—which I described as benevolent indifference—was just as important as our policy.

The Russians, after briefly helping the Congolese rebel gang, were also prudently disengaging and cutting their losses. (The ANC on April 7 found a cache of 240 Soviet vehicles, 900 small arms and 20,000 gallons of fuel at Watsa, near the Uganda border.) The Yugoslav ambassador, one of my best sources, along with the Israeli envoy and the British high commissioner (few of the other diplomats in Nairobi really exerted themselves), told me the Russians had decided to support existing regimes and let the Chinese play at revolution with the crazies. They had realized, like us, that the real division in Africa was not so much between "moderates" and "radicals" as it was between "modernizers" and "agitators." (Later on, the Russians would get involved in a limited way in Africa—in Angola, Ethiopia, Somalia and Mozambique —but always at the invitation of legitimate governments.)

My personal relations with Kenyatta healed slowly. *Mzee* (Swahili for old man, and his nickname) was not used to being challenged. But on May 5 he called me over the State House, held out his hand and said, "The Congo is finished. Now we can be friends again."

And 1965 was also the year of massive U.S. escalation in Vietnam. Knowing not only what I know today but what I already knew then, I find it hard to believe that as late as March 24, 1965, I was defending our Vietnam policy before the Nairobi Lions Club—and a year later calling on Kenyatta with Soapy Williams to solicit his support for our efforts to end the war "honorably." (He was sympathetic and did have Mboya speak to the Russians in Moscow; but they did not trust our "sincerity" and saw no way to force Hanoi to negotiate.)

Three factors influenced my thinking and that of a good many of my liberal friends: first, that we were simply fighting for principle by helping a small country (South Vietnam) defend itself against aggression from the North—as we had in Korea; second, that this aggression was directed from Peking as part of a master plan for subjugating Southeast Asia; and third, that our intentions were selfless and noble, and the men in charge back in Washington for the most part rational, well informed and peace-loving.

Still, an entry about Vietnam in my diary for February 2 suggests some developing doubts: "What a hideous mess. No foresight, no sense of history."

But we were too busy to think much about Vietnam yet, and the Africans were largely indifferent to events that didn't affect them directly. Even the landing of two U.S. Marine divisions in the Dominican Republic in April 1965 (as insurance against another Cuba) passed almost unnoticed in Nairobi.

A speech I made about there being strings to our aid got much bigger press play, understandably, since it was customary for diplomats to deny that assistance to poor countries came with any conditions. But I carefully described what the strings were: "We expect countries receiving our assistance to be serious about preserving their freedom and respecting the freedom of others. And we expect them to be serious about rational economic development so that the benefits of our aid are shared by the whole nation and not by just a favored few."

Peace Corps volunteers were now at work all over Kenya, most of them in schools and on farms, and dispelling whatever lingering hostility existed toward Americans, especially among the British. Redundant Communist charges that they were CIA agents in disguise were unconvincing; had they worked for the CIA they'd have been far less effective than they were. As it was, they kept their distance from our embassy, though I did mobilize a few nimble-looking ones when the Czech Embassy challenged us to a volleyball game. We were trounced, which gave the Czechs something to cheer about. Three of their staff were summarily expelled from Kenya early in 1966, along with the first and second secretaries of the Soviet Embassy and a Chinese diplomatic clerk. (This action, an indication of how much had changed in East Africa since the Zanzibar panic of 1964, was ignored in the Western press: the next day's *International Herald Tribune* featured a story about Luxembourg's two-battalion army. Editors seemed to distrust or discount good news out of Africa.)

I got ready to leave Kenya, and the Foreign Service, in 1966. After Adlai Stevenson's death, Arthur Goldberg, who succeeded him at the U.N., wanted me to become his deputy, but five years of diplomatic acrobatics and bureaucratic jousting had left me weary and my family homesick for our own turf. Nor is there much security in an appointive job in government. (Had I stayed on, Nixon would have canned me in 1969 anyway.) And the job was done. U.S.-Kenyan relations were harmonious, American firms were making Nairobi their African headquarters, and even Lavrov invited me to be his houseguest if I came back for a visit. (I couldn't help noticing that the security men at his residence looked more like male fashion models than the baggy-trousered thugs that used to patrol Soviet installations.) Odinga, too, was personally friendly, though politically emasculated. He resigned as vice president on April 14 and two weeks later formed an opposition party which was praised in *Pravda* and later banned in Kenya as subversive. According to Soviet bloc diplomatic reports, to which we often had access, Odinga's failure was the result of our handing out more bribes to our African clients than they had to theirs. This betrayed both their contempt for Africans and their ignorance of the psychological factors involved in dealing with people who were far less naive than they seemed.

Thomas Kanza, of the Stanleyville days, turned up from time to time, usually job hunting. He once even asked me for a recommendation. Kenyatta finally deported him in April at the request of Joseph Mobutu, the new Congolese honcho.

Before leaving, I thought it might be both fun and appropriate to visit Zanzibar; so Sim and I hitched a ride on an itinerant U.S. Air Force plane, along with our ambassadors to Uganda, Somalia and Tanzania. After playing golf at Zanzibar's nine-hole People's Golf Club, deserted except for a lone East German, we toured the island, including the V.I. Lenin Hospital, and chanced to meet Sheikh Karume outside his residence. When he learned he was confronted with a gaggle of American ambassadors, he retreated behind his garden gate, looking bewildered and apprehensive until our consul explained in Swahili we'd be gone by nightfall.

After the usual farewell parties, I had one last private talk with Kenyatta out at his Gatundu farm. We talked about some of the problems I'd encountered on my arrival—unemployment, education, land —and what had been done to solve them. And for the first time since the 1950s, the inflow of whites to Kenya exceeded the outflow—a sign that, contrary to the alarmists, a multiracial society in a black-ruled African country might not be so wild a dream.

On the way home, I stopped in Guinea to call on Sékou Touré. Little had changed. He had expelled the Peace Corps but now regretted it. The economy was still mismanaged, but the bauxite project with American financing was still on the tracks. In Paris, where I met up with Sim and the children and reported on Guinea by confidential telegram (nothing else got any attention in the State Department), I saw our ambassador, Chip Bohlen, a friend since the 1946 peace conference, and other old Paris hands who asked me seriously the name of Kenya's president and its capital. I'd forgotten how parochially European some of our career Foreign Service officers could be.

In Washington, I paid a farewell call on President Johnson before going home to write my book and start a new job in New York as editor-in-chief of Cowles Communications—a publishing conglomerate of which *Look* was now the flagship.

Johnson did most of the talking, as was his custom. I could tell Vietnam frustrated him, but he seemed to exempt the Russians from blame; in fact, he had recently made a speech about "peaceful engagement" in Eastern Europe—which implicitly accepted the division of the continent five years before the Helsinki accords. And the Glassboro summit with Kosygin was just a year away. He devoted a good deal of time to denouncing the wealth and arrogance of the Kennedys, which I let pass, but when he dismissed foreign aid as a futile cause without popular or congressional support, I broke in—what did I have to lose now?—and pointed out that Americans were compassionate people but that foreign aid had never been properly explained to them or to the Congress by the timorous bureaucrats who dominated AID. I cited the $3,000 incubator presented to Conakry's hospital by the citizens of my hometown after we sent pictures of Sim working there; the electric generator given to the clinic at Maseno, Kenya, by my father's church on Long Island; the building materials for a self-help Kenya school donated by the town of Russell, Kansas. My point was that Americans weren't against helping the needy and deserving if they knew how their money was being used, but were often influenced by uninformed cartoons like the recent one in the St. Louis *Globe-Democrat* showing Uncle Sam on his knees begging a contemptuous dictator to accept a sackful of gold. We needed better public understanding of an issue that had cold war as well as philanthropic aspects.

At least the president listened, or appeared to, and he sent me a picture of me talking and him not, signed "With appreciation."

Look's coverage of the Soviet Union had always been continuous and comprehensive, but we decided, late in 1966, to put out a special issue marking the fiftieth anniversary of the Bolshevik revolution in October 1917. It took some arranging: meetings in Washington with Ambassador Anatoly Dobrynin to enlist support at the top and with Georgy Isachenko of Novosti, the Soviet feature agency whose job was to "facilitate" the work of visiting foreign journalists—for a fee.

Ten of us gathered on May 9 at the venerable National Hotel— Moscow's best at the turn of the century and still the most desirable. Sim and two other wives—Senior Editor Chris Wren's and Norman Rockwell's—were also part of our group. We had commissioned Rockwell to do one painting especially for this issue, and after circulating around town for a couple of days, he settled on an elementary school classroom. I saw nothing exceptional about it—just rows of of well-scrubbed, attentive, uniformed kids seated at desks, with Lenin's ubiquitous picture on the wall. But his finished painting was touched with the Rockwell magic; he altered the scene so that one boy, in the next to last row, was gazing out the open window—a Russian Penrod daydreaming in the warm spring breeze.

The warm spring breeze had come as a surprise. In London's airport, I had asked the Aeroflot clerk about the Moscow weather, and when she told me the temperature was 30, I dashed out of the terminal and bought an overcoat and mufflers for us both. On arrival at Sheremetyevo airport, Sim and I were so bundled up the stewardess helped us down the ramp, thinking we must be terminally ill. It was 30 degrees, all right—Celsius—which translated to 86 degrees Fahrenheit.

Moscow had changed considerably in eleven years. People no longer stared at foreigners—just a passing glance now and then at a chic dress; they were more interested in the foreign cars parked outside the hotels (tourism by car in Russia was now permitted). There was soap—the size of a pat of butter, but still soap—in the bathroom. The phone worked. There was even a radio. On the first floor there was a snack bar where you could buy high-grade caviar and imported liquor and beer with foreign currency.

At the popular restaurants, if you were seated at a table with Russians, they were always eager to talk in scraps of English, German or

French. At the Praga one evening, Sim and I communicated quite successfully with a young couple using only sign language and simple drawings. After a toast to peace, he gave me his fountain pen; Sim gave her some French perfume.

Traffic on the broad avenues, now flanked by modern high-rise buildings, was still light by our standards, but a private car was no longer a rarity. Women were still plump, but less dowdy; more men wore ties. And you no longer felt watched or bugged. With 25,000 American tourists expected in 1967, keeping tabs on all of them would have strained even the KGB's vast resources. As for the phone, it was prudent to assume the tap was still working on certain extensions.

We had an Intourist guide this time—a pleasant but rather formal young woman named Lydia; she answered our questions but shied away from any political discussions. At meetings with officials, we heard a lot of what George Orwell called duckspeak—prefabricated Marxist jargon —but many of the younger people talked more spontaneously. On park benches, teenagers listened to jazz on transistor radios. In the train to Leningrad, we offered an English-speaking fellow passenger a copy of an American newspaper. He thanked us and slipped it quickly into an inside pocket. Tipping was still officially frowned on, but it was the only way to get quick service.

Our first formal meeting (green baize tablecloth, soda water, pads and pencils) with the top brass of Novosti started with introductions. Len Gross, *Look*'s European editor, was team leader: Sim and I were staying only a few days before heading home via Vietnam—which, coupled with Russia, would give me something to speak about at *Look*'s annual series of lunches for advertisers in June. I told Comrade Burkhov, then head of Novosti, that he must already know about me from reading that morning's *Pravda,* which carried a front-page story quoting Charles Njonjo's order banning me and my book from Kenya. *Pravda* embellished the story somewhat with oblique allusions to my alleged CIA activities—all, I presumed, rather gratifying from the Soviet point of view. But our Russian hosts only seemed embarrassed and eager to change the subject.

We enumerated the stories we wanted to cover—education, mountain climbing in the Caucasus, three weeks in a Russian town, meetings with artists, open-heart surgery, a motor trip to the Black Sea, a jazz festival in Estonia and a survey about what Russians knew about the United States. (Later, we would add pieces by Doak Barnett on tension with China, by Harriman reviewing Soviet diplomacy from Stalin to Kosygin, by an old Moscow hand on the KGB—and a page of Russian humor.)

Everything was approved. While we waited for arrangements to be made, we all fanned out, explored Moscow and its river (from where you could marvel at the new six-thousand-room Rossiya Hotel), visited the seminary at Nagorsk and talked to the priests, saw the ballet in the vast Kremlin auditorium, met with diplomatic and press sources and attended parties. Among the Soviet newsmen we talked to, jokes about the Chinese were in fashion. The younger ones, like Vladimir Posner, the editor of *Sputnik,* said Lenin would be proud of his country today but also shocked—for the selfless "Soviet man" on which the Marxist system depended had not yet evolved. Posner, who'd lived in New York as a child and teenager, said most Russians understood that "you can't walk away from Vietnam," and I gathered they weren't too unhappy about our being stuck there, on China's southern border.

(Yuri Zhukov, the *Pravda* correspondent I'd known in Paris in the forties, had recently told Michel Gordey and *France-Soir*'s publisher, Pierre Lazareff, that the Soviets were really concerned only about the Chinese, and in fact had been telling the Japanese not to press us to close down our bases in Okinawa. Fear of the Chinese explained in part their uncharacteristic cooperation with our *Look* project and certainly was their chief motive for the Glassboro summit meeting a month later. On March 31, the U.S. and the U.S.S.R. also signed their first consular treaty since 1917—one more straw in the wind.)

The meeting I remember best in Moscow was with Leonid Zamyatin, then press chief of the Foreign Ministry. He spoke of cooperation with the U.S. in trade, arms control, space and culture, and he too understood our dilemma in Vietnam. But he pointed out that it was becoming a powder keg now that we were bombing the north while Soviet supply ships were in Haiphong harbor—as they would continue to be. "If you hit one and kill some of our sailors," he said, "we would have to react—and then what?"

I remember looking out his window at the springlike panorama of Moscow far below. I thought fleetingly of mushroom clouds exploding here and in American cities. But no: we had learned that lesson, surely, in 1962.

"Why don't you stop the bombing, at least below the twentieth parallel? That would spare Haiphong."

"Why are your freighters there?" I asked.

"A socialist country is under attack. It is our fraternal duty to help. Why are your troops there?"

"A free country is under attack."

He added, off the record, "By the way, we are not really impressed by your peace demonstrations."

We smiled and talked of China. He didn't know what was happening, he said, except for "collective" madness. "The Soviet mission in Peking is like a prison. We are isolated."

He praised Kennedy because he had an "objective" attitude but disparaged Johnson as a man "who talks peace and wages war."

Leaving, I glanced at his wall map of the Soviet Union and reflected that, seen from this perspective, this huge nation did seem to be surrounded on all sides by hostile forces—especially now that China was no longer an ally. For us, it would be rather as if Canada were an avowed enemy, a billion strong, and Mexico a Soviet ally (as Turkey was ours), bristling with hostile military bases. We might well be nervous.

Zamyatin noticed my pausing before the map. "To really understand us," he said as we shook hands, "you have to know our geography and read our history."

When our special issue came out in October, Gross's piece about his three weeks in a Russian city, Bratsk, with photographer Paul Fusco, was the most readable and informative segment. The Russians he spent time with were not selected by Novosti; he met them at random, turned up friends who helped out as interpreters and formed some close if temporary friendships. To his surprise, he learned that most people trusted their rulers and believed the official line; also, that they were not afraid to talk frankly about what they didn't like. He concluded, as did the other reporters working on this project, that the much publicized dissident movement in the Soviet Union had no mass base; with a few notable exceptions, like Andrei Sakharov, most of its activists were romantic intellectuals. In an introduction to a paperback reprint of the *Look* articles, Gross wrote a summary of what fifty years of communism had done in Russia. It remains valid today. He said, in part:

> It works. Ponderously, fitfully, unevenly. But little more than 50 years after the revolution that changed the world forever, the system it fostered wheezes with life . . . Most Soviet citizens think they have a good thing going for them. They feel safe. They don't worry about hunger or loneliness or calamity. Raised in a controlled environment, they are without objective measure, but by their own meager reckoning

of what constitutes freedom, most of them now feel free. . . . The current love affair with profit is one more Marxist concession that ego cannot be subdued. But if the Soviet man is not what the Communists set out to make him, he is in some ways different from you and me. He has blended the demands of ego and the discipline of sacrifice so that group instincts prevail over self. He wants a lot, but not an awful lot. Independent thought makes him uncomfortable. He may bellow his disagreement on a local matter, but when it's Russia against the world, he naively, uncritically—and patriotically—follows the leader. Age has not mellowed the Soviet sense of righteousness; there is no more illuminating, or infuriating, experience than to suggest that Western actions since 1945 have been a response to hostile communist threats—only to have Russians laugh in your face . . . For the moment, at least, the people have the ear of the mighty: consumer goods, not industrial-military power, have priority. And as long as they concentrate on domestic concerns, the mighty cannot be too adventurous abroad. But the mood in the Kremlin could change overnight, and with it, our chances for peace.

(That last sentence was not appreciated among the Soviet elite. After it appeared, a letter came to me from a Professor Vladimir Mishvenieradze saying, "These words are aimed at stepping up tension in the relations between our two countries." I hardly dared show it to poor Len, the very antithesis of a warmonger.)

The title of the paperback was kind of silly: *Red Russia After Fifty Years.* There was no other Russia than the "red" one. But as late as 1967, the word still sold tickets, or so it was assumed.

On May 19, Sim and I flew over Afghanistan's wrinkled landscape to New Delhi, mainly to see Chet Bowles, exuberant still despite the progressive symptoms of Parkinson's disease. The various Indians I talked to all seemed to favor a bombing halt in Vietnam—or at least restricting it to supply routes. Also, since we had proved we wouldn't be forced out yet couldn't defeat the Vietnamese, they thought we should cut risks and losses and find a way out by letting Hanoi know we would respond to peace with peace just as we were responding to force with force. This, they said, would be easier for Asians to understand than our bombing a small country that couldn't bomb us back.

In Saigon, I found Ambassador Ellsworth Bunker almost as cautious as the Indians. It was clear to him that Ho Chi Minh would never settle for less than all Vietnam, but he thought Ho might allow us a graceful way out if we were both firm and prudent. Meanwhile, he saw no early end to the fighting.

"It's dangerous for us to say let's hit 'em and get it over with," he said. "Remember Korea—and MacArthur's impetuous dash to the Yalu."

Bunker also thought it was dangerous not to take the Chinese and Russians seriously when they said they'd back Ho all the way. "We and the Russians, certainly, both have bears by the tail," he said, "and neither of us can let go."

Sim and I were housed in the Caravelle Hotel in the center of Saigon. The city was even shabbier than the one I'd seen in 1953. Its charm, fading then, had by now vanished in the sputter of Hondas, the blare of rock music on the once tree-shaded rue Catinat, the pathetic teenage whores and crippled beggars, the truckloads of ARVN (Army of Vietnam) soldiers cruising with no apparent destination.

I had an appointment the next day with General Westmoreland and was kept waiting in his reception room for forty-five minutes along with four impatient generals while he worked his charm on Ann Landers. She had been expressing dovish sentiments in her column and had to be brought to her senses. When she finally emerged, we agreed to meet for dinner, and I tried to persuade the generals to go in ahead of me.

"You have a war to fight," I said. "I'm just wasting his time."

"After you, sir," the ranking general replied to former Sergeant Attwood.

I kept my interview short. Westy, as everybody called him, said he was concerned with "superhawk" editors who thought we should "clobber them once and for all." He said only patience and perseverance would prevail. When I told him what Zamyatin had said, he assured me our air force was very careful about Haiphong harbor (though we did hit some ships later, by mistake) and seemed interested in the Russians' 20th parallel proposal—which LBJ implemented less than a year later. He was more cautious than I'd expected: I think a good many American generals remembered MacArthur's ill-fated advance to the Yalu and didn't want to risk an invasion of North Vietnam that might bring the Chinese swarming across this border. When he got out his pointer and dutifully walked over to a wall map, I excused myself, pointing out that there were several generals outside with more important matters to discuss than I.

It was clear a major effort was under way in 1967 to keep our wavering press toeing the administration line on Vietnam. Landers (whom we knew by her real name, Eppie Lederer) was everywhere escorted by a solicitous chicken colonel who could have been actor Brian Donlevy's understudy except that he had nothing to say. "The army has no opinions," he would answer when we asked him a question. He was upset that we insisted on eating at a Chinese restaurant "downtown." He had never had a meal off base and was convinced the place was infested with Viet Cong agents. "I'm out of my depth in a place like this," he said, selecting a table near the rear exit.

Elinor Green, an old friend who worked for the vast U.S. information bureaucracy in Saigon, was with us, and after dinner we took two cabs to the home of the embassy's minister-counselor, John Calhoun. And we naturally got lost. The colonel panicked, sure we were being kidnapped, while I pored over a street map with the driver, who spoke some French. But we got there eventually, ahead of Sim and Elinor, who had gone even farther astray.

Harry McPherson, a special counsel in the White House, was seated in a circle of embassy and CIA people being the devil's advocate. His questions were certainly unexpected: Why are we in Vietnam anyway? How is our national interest being served? Does our side have any chance at all of winning? Why don't we pull out now and let them fight their own war? Do we plan to stay here indefinitely? How long do you think the American people will stand for it?

The answers he got were honest but with few exceptions would have brought no comfort to our hawks. No one thought the war could be "won." All felt the military were fighting it "by the manual," without imagination and with the stubborn conviction that if we just persisted, more firepower was bound to prevail sooner or later. No one denied that the South Vietnamese government was corrupt, apathetic, warweary and rife with intrigue or that we blundered in 1962 (after the Maxwell Taylor mission) in mistaking what was always primarily a popular radical nationalist movement for an offshoot of that worldwide monolithic Communist conspiracy—which was so much simpler to understand.

It was a stimulating evening that shook up the group and cheered up a few who inferred that perhaps the president was looking for a way out of the swamp. But McPherson told me later the idea for raising fundamental and unorthodox questions was his alone.

The staff reaction to McPherson that evening was more thoughtful and perceptive than what I encountered a few days later in Hong Kong, where the China-watchers in our consulate-general couldn't imagine our pulling out of Vietnam without a worldwide loss of face. "It would be the end of a twenty-five-year history of keeping our word and carrying out our promises," said one. Well, it finally happened, and it wasn't. But too many experts were looking at the world through lenses distorted by years of cold war conditioning. Even Dean Rusk could still say, as late as October 12, 1967, "U.S. security is at stake in Vietnam." George Kennan's 1947 containment policy, designed for Europe, had been gradually extended to Southeast Asia; and then, when more than fifty thousand American lives and those of uncounted Asians had been expended, and America was torn asunder, the region was perceived to be peripheral to the national interest after all. Out of fear of Communist ideology, the ideology of America was itself being changed.

Before leaving Vietnam, Sim and I were invited to make the obligatory visit by helicopter to a village in the Mekong delta that was "pacified," the operative word in a program of resettlement then costing us $1 billion a year. Except for an occasional billow of smoke indicating an air strike, the view of the lush green carpet of foliage below was peaceful. But the machine gunner crouched in the open door of the chopper peered carefully around the clearing where we got out quickly before our aircraft whirred and chattered up and away.

We lunched on C-rations with a RevDev (Revolutionary Development) team headed by three American officers and a Vietnamese major. Later we visited the militiamen guarding the perimeter and some silent bearded elders smoking in a kind of pagoda. The team was helping the villagers build a road and dig a canal. Kids scampered around our jeep and women looked up, expressionless, from their washtubs. "It's quiet duty," said the American officer in charge. "Now and then the VC probes our defenses at night, but they pull back in the daytime. That's when the villagers work the fields. The people are friendly enough. They seem to like us, the kids anyway, but you can't ever tell." The Vietnamese major said little but smiled a lot. We later learned this village was overrun and occupied by the VC a week after our visit.

The chopper came back for us in the afternoon and we were back in Saigon for dinner on the roof garden of the Caravelle. We had visited the war. I could see how people who were strangers to war and to the Orient would have been impressed. What struck me was that the Viet Cong seemed to be roaming and raiding these pacified areas at will.

We were back in New York May 31, and a couple of days later I was actually telling a luncheon audience in the grand ballroom of the

Waldorf-Astoria that the world would someday be grateful for our taking a stand in Vietnam. Of course I warned against any escalation that might bring in the Chinese or invite a reaction from the Russians, and I even confessed to regretting our initial involvement; but still—I was defending what in retrospect was an indefensible policy. Why? Essentially, I think, because like so many of my friends I was convinced that we were contending not so much with Vietnamese nationalism as with Chinese expansionism.

What everyone overlooked was that, like the English and the Irish, or the Russians and the Poles, the Chinese and the Vietnamese had lived too close to each other for too long ever to trust one another.

At least I wasn't so naive as to yield to the urging of a leading Washington pundit that *Look* print a piece he had just written asserting that we would win the war in Vietnam before the end of the year. He said his evidence was irrefutable, his sources unimpeachable and his conclusion unequivocal. I don't think any other publication published it either, but that's the kind of propaganda the Pentagon was still peddling.

I continued to travel in 1967 but only in the United States, speaking at *Look* lunches and flogging my new book, as they say in the trade. Sim and I heard about the Six-Day War on the car radio, driving to Peter's school, and it was easy to be stirred by Abba Eban's eloquent defense of Israel's action. (Much later I learned that Harry McPherson had stopped in Israel on his way home from Saigon and was invited by General Moshe Dayan to go for a drive early one morning. Next thing he knew he was riding into Egypt with an Israeli tank column. He got out in time. It was not the place for LBJ's special counsel to be photographed at that moment.)

The Israeli strike was predictable after U Thant had withdrawn the U.N. peacekeeping force from the Israeli-Egypt border on May 18 at Nasser's request. When Nasser then moved up his troops, his stated intention—to protect Jordan—was unconvincing to the Israelis.

It had been nearly eleven years since Nasser was last battered in the Sinai, so it occurred to me I might try for a repeat of my 1957 interview —sort of a Nasser-in-Defeat-Revisited piece. I wrote Heikal in August and, for all of Nasser's anger at the U.S. (he'd broken off diplomatic relations, charging we'd participated in the devastating Israeli attack on the Cairo airport), I got a reply inviting me to come on over during the winter. A heart attack in September grounded me for a few weeks and delayed my departure until late January.

Meanwhile, Soviet-American relations were undergoing one of those periodic thaws that usually lasted until another unforeseen crisis put everything back in the freezer. Premier Kosygin and President Johnson met with no fanfare and little advance notice at a small college in Glassboro, New Jersey, partly to get acquainted and partly to talk about banning antiballistic missiles—the Russians then favored them and we then opposed them as leading to an escalation of offensive weapons systems. Secretary of Defense Robert McNamara argued the case against an ABM defense, but LBJ wrote in his memoirs that "the point did not get across—or Kosygin chose not to understand it." Still, the "Spirit of Glassboro" was now part of the cold war's lexicon, and a year later the Kremlin changed its collective mind and agreed to enter arms control talks. Johnson was even planning to go to Moscow in October of 1968 to sign an ABM treaty. Then the talks, the trip and the Glassboro mood were all wiped out by the Soviet bloc invasion of Czechoslovakia in August 1968. Not until 1972, during the Nixon Administration, was an ABM treaty finally negotiated. Ironically, President Reagan actually cited Kosygin's initial ABM arguments eighteen years later in seeking to justify Star Wars.

Soon after the Glassboro meeting, Zamyatin came to lunch at *Look* along with Viktor Sukhodrev, the handsome, youthful interpreter for all Soviet leaders from Khrushchev up to Gorbachev. Viktor spoke six varieties of English flawlessly: American (southern and northern), British (U and non-U), Irish and Australian. His memoirs could doubtless make him a millionaire—probably a dead one.

They asked about our special Soviet issue and then started in on the Chinese, who had exploded their first hydrogen bomb a week before. They pointed out that China was now almost totally isolated in the "socialist camp," with only Albania and the tiny New Zealand Communist Party in its corner. (Kenya, I noted, had broken relations with China on June 29.) But we agreed the Chinese could not be underestimated, if only because there were so many of them. The tumult of the cultural revolution—which they saw as a power struggle between the modernizers and the Maoist "permanent revolutionaries"—would eventually subside, and China could then become a *real* problem. These Russians sounded almost like our old China lobby of the fifties.

Anyway, we also agreed on the importance of vigilance and toasted

Glassboro. When I asked them about getting an exclusive interview with Kosygin, Sukhodrev suggested we wait a while and then try for Brezhnev, who, as Party boss, was certain to become number one before long.

Going back to Cairo to see Nasser was like reenacting a show that had played well once but might not again. Heikal, a bit grayer at the temples, was still on hand to greet Sim and me, but our hotel was now the new high-rise Shepheard's and we felt like the only Americans in town. Since the Six-Day War and the diplomatic break with Washington, free-spending Western tourists had been replaced by tight-fisted Soviet bloc technicians—to the dismay of guides, dragomen, B-girls, shoeshine boys, shopkeepers and beggars. So we were greeted everywhere with open arms, outstretched palms and glad cries of *"Baksheesh!"* A phalanx of waiters and bellboys brought in our breakfast, and three other waiters took turns serving us in the all-but-deserted dining room that evening, planning to split the tip.

While waiting, as before, for the Nasser appointment, we accompanied some professors from the American University—which seemed immune to political eddies—to the Dahshur pyramids, south of Helwan and off the tourist track. They were small enough to climb, but our guide protested vehemently when we started up; he finally looked the other way in exchange for a few piasters, and we saw the reason for his agitation. From the top one could look over a fence to a Soviet missile site under construction (Soviet because the stenciled words on the crates were in the Cyrillic alphabet).

Soon after this excursion into antiquity and the cold war, the summons came from Nasser. He received us, all smiles and charm, at his villa east of the city. While Sim took notes and pictures, he answered my questions for two hours. Nasser was now fifty and a grandfather, but otherwise I had a feeling of *déjà vu, déjà entendu.* As before, the No. 1 topic was Israel. As before, I told him my questions might seem rough. As before, he grinned and said, "Go ahead."

What follows is a digest of some of his most newsworthy remarks. First off, I wanted him to admit he'd been wrong in accusing us of participating in the Israeli attack in June—which was his pretext for breaking relations. So after he said that the chief obstacle to normalization was "your support of Israel in the United Nations," I asked him why he made his unfounded accusation about our alleged air attack, an accusation which angered a lot of Americans. He replied:

There were so many planes coming in from the sea—where your carriers were—more than we thought the Israelis had. And you remember the time before, in 1956, they had not attacked alone. . . . On June 6, I received a phone call from King Hussein, who said he was being subjected to heavy air attack from the sea—400 planes against Jordan alone. So then we issued a statement. . . . Later, Johnson called Kosygin on the hot line to say only two of your reconnaissance planes were flying to investigate the sinking of your ship by the Israeli navy. He told Kosygin to inform us, and he did.

Then I asked Nasser, "In other words, your accusation resulted from a misunderstanding based on suspicion and faulty information?"

He nodded and murmured, "Yes," but when I showed the typed copy to Heikal later, he struck out the question and the answer—which were the guts of the interview. I could have used it anyway but preferred to have his initials on each page so that it couldn't be denied later. So I suggested we have Nasser reply, "*You* could say that, yes," implying that was merely my interpretation. Heikal thought about it and approved the quote. But of course when it appeared in print, the sentence, "You could say that, yes," was in effect an admission that he had been misled, misinformed or mistaken. It got extensive play outside Egypt, where no leader can ever admit to having erred. In the end, even Heikal recognized that Nasser's seeming candor did him more good than harm.

On other matters, I asked him if he thought Soviet motives in the Near East were purely commercial, as he had suggested. He replied:

> Their motives are also political, of course. They want to reduce Western influence and domination in the Middle East. Formerly, the West had been our sole supplier of goods, including arms. And that's another thing—America and Britain attached conditions to their arms deliveries. The Russians do not.

What of the future?

> It is not only our objective but our duty to get the Israelis out of our country. And it is the right of the Palestinians to resist—just as people resisted the German occupation in Europe. It is only human that the inhabitants of any occupied territory have the right to resist . . . The Israelis had and have air supremacy. Yet, in America, you are planning to give them Skyhawks and maybe Phantoms—more than they had before. To be effective here, you must not take sides. . . . But don't

misunderstand me. It has never been our intention to be hostile to the United States. It is Israel that has always been the obstacle to our friendship. How would you feel if foreign troops were occupying a part of the United States?

Nasser's most perceptive remark was in response to my asking how he had retained the loyalty of his people despite all the hardships and the setbacks of the past decade.

> I confess I was surprised by the reaction of the people when I offered to resign on June 9. I felt we had failed, and we had to go . . . But the people, by their insistence that I stay, were trying to explain that we might have lost our army but not our will.

Perceptive, because he was acknowledging, indirectly, what everyone who has lived among the Arabs knows: So massive is their inferiority complex, particularly vis-à-vis the Israelis, that they would rather go down with Nasser (or any charismatic leader), shouting defiance and shaking their fists, than display the weakness associated with compromise by negotiating with the hated foe. Anwar Sadat, a realist, dared to try it a dozen years later—and was killed for his courage.

Before leaving Cairo, we were taken by Heikal on a tour of *Al-Ahram*'s new seven-story plant, still under construction; he would not long occupy its executive suite: After Nasser's death in 1970, Heikal lost his influence. We also called on Mahmoud Fawzi, as we had in 1953. The old pro was still foreign minister, and when we met his pretty teenage daughter, wearing jeans and playing Beatle records, I thought of Naomi Eilan, the daughter of my Israeli colleague in Kenya. They were brunette look-alikes who even talked English with the same inflection. And Naomi was now probably wearing the same clothes and playing the same music. Would they ever meet? Could they ever correspond? I suggested to Fawzi they use me as a forwarding address, but he was hesitant and I suspect they were both too shy. Those girls symbolized for me the hope and the tragedy of this corner of the world, where I had been coming for so long and leaving with the same litany of fear and hatred to report.

Our next stop was Cambodia, which had also broken diplomatic relations with Washington when we hedged on recognizing its present frontiers (since both our South Vietnamese and Thai allies claimed parts of Cambodian territory). Sim and I went at the invitation of Prince Norodom Sihanouk, who had written me in the summer of 1967 protesting a *Look* article that referred to him as the "playboy king" of "tiny Cambodia." In my reply, I admitted the clichés were unfair: he did play jazz piano and the saxophone for relaxation and enjoyed parties, but I knew from reliable sources that he was one of the hardest-working chiefs of state in office; also, as he pointed out, Cambodia was about the size of Oklahoma (which no one called tiny) and bigger than many of our NATO allies. Nor was he even king; he had abdicated in 1955 and was now an elected head of state. *Touché.* So why, I asked, didn't he invite me to Phnom Penh so that we could set the record straight for *Look*'s seven million readers? He did, and early in February, we checked into the old and spacious Royal Hotel in Cambodia's capital.

It was early evening, yet the city was fragrant and quiet: you could hear the tinkling bells of the pedicabs as they glided through the tree-shaded streets. We took one to the Lotus d'Or, a floating restaurant moored to the bank of the Mekong River, and dined on succulent crayfish stew served by the world's most charming waitresses. The rape of this lovely city was one of the Vietnam war's most tragic side effects. I'm glad we saw the city in time.

As for Sihanouk, he had an aide meet us with a Russian car in the morning to tour the town before lunching with him and Princess Monique at their villa near the former palace (where, years before, Stevenson had watched the royal ballet). Now that he was no longer king, Sihanouk was addressed as *Monseigneur*—My Lord.

Our interview, which took place the following morning, is worth a partial reprise here because what he said about Vietnam reflected the views not only of many influential Asians but of more and more Americans. For 1968 was the year when the tide of opinion at home began turning suddenly and decisively against the war.

Words burst out of him in both French and English during our four-hour talk; I could well understand his reply to a physician who told him he would feel more dynamic if he slept more than his usual three or four hours a night: "*More* dynamic? I would explode—just like dynamite!"

> Vigilance. That's important . . . In 1954, at Geneva, the Communists wanted a divided Cambodia, part of which they would rule. We refused, but their agents are still active, and I must go out among the people myself and frustrate their subversion. Vigilance on all sides! Do you know that when Eisenhower was receiving me in Washington with a 21-gun salute, Allen Dulles and the CIA were trying to buy my delega-

tion at the U.N.? Yes! One whom they did bribe was later court-martialed and shot. . . .

The situation in Vietnam is very complex, and you Americans are not realistic. You say you are fighting communism, but in fighting Ho Chi Minh you are pushing North Vietnam into the arms of China. And the Chinese are imperialists—just as you are. Not in the same way, of course. You demand advanced bases all over the world for your security —in fact for white security, for capitalist security—while the Chinese are ideological imperialists. . . . That's why the Russians are nervous about China. And so is Ho Chi Minh, though he would not admit it. Mediation by me? No, not any more . . . My solution—military neutralization of the whole area—is no longer acceptable to either side. . . .

Don't you see that I'm caught in the middle? If I take your side, the Communists will move in massively and organize an unmanageable rebellion against my government; and if I side with the Vietcong militarily, Cambodia will become a vassal of Vietnam—or China—and will get bombed by your air force in the bargain. . . .

I agree you have sacrificed Johnson's Great Society for this war. But is it for Asiatics you are fighting? Why don't you take care of your own Negroes first? Believe me, the Vietnamese people don't want you to continue fighting this war on their land. What are you defending there, anyway? Democracy? What democracy is there in Vietnam—or in Korea, Taiwan, Thailand—all those places where you are supporting corrupt, unpopular regimes? As for aggression, there was no North Vietnamese aggression until you Americans arrived in force in the South. I am not a Communist but a neighbor of Vietnam, and I know what goes on there. I know you came originally not to stop some mythical aggression but to prevent the unification of Vietnam under Ho Chi Minh. There were supposed to be elections in 1956, according to the Geneva accords of 1954, but your man Diem knew Ho Chi Minh would win, so he refused the elections and called on you to prop him up. You should have stayed away and let the Vietnamese work things out by themselves. It might have been possible to neutralize the area if you had, but it's too late now. . . .

What now? Well, you must realize by now you aren't really winning this war that you never should have gotten into. So if I were president of the United States—and I certainly wouldn't want to be—I would dare to do some things which may sound dangerous but would bring the only solution. First, I would stop the bombing of the North—unconditionally. That would at least open the way to negotiations. Then, as de Gaulle did in Algeria, I would deal directly with the National Liberation Front—

the Viet Cong. I used to tell that to the French when they were fighting what was essentially a nationalist movement: the longer you wait, the more you lose. The so-called government of South Vietnam? Forget it. It doesn't represent anybody but a handful of generals and politicians who are using you just to stay in power. They are just a hollow shell, and what's worse, they are using American troops to fight and die for them. The elections? A farce. There are only two parties in South Vietnam— the Viet Cong and the Army. And the Army would melt away if you weren't there. With the Viet Cong you could discuss a cease-fire and phased withdrawal. . . . You can afford to pull back, to admit you were wrong. People know you are strong. It's only if you try to hang on and suffer more setbacks that you will lose face. Recognize the Viet Cong now, deal with them, and the world will applaud you. Asia will be grateful, believe me . . .

I don't know if the North Vietnamese would try to dominate all of Indochina if you withdrew. What I am for is national independence— which the Vietnamese now don't have with you Americans and your stooges there. If the Vietnamese Communists later tried to take us over, we would fight for *our* independence from them. Yes, we would ask for help, for planes and weapons from other countries, from America per- haps. But we would not ask for troops. We would do our own fighting. We wouldn't ask you to die for us, like the Saigon government does . . .

I don't disagree with the domino theory. Of course the Chinese are too smart to move in with their own army. But if you withdraw, there's no doubt they will become more active all over the area through their own agents and local Communist parties. But that will be our responsi- bility—coping with this sort of subversion. And we will, for nationalism in Asia is stronger than you think . . .

Looking beyond this tragic war, I would suggest to Americans that you help us in Asia only when asked—and never with bombers and tanks and divisions of troops. The people worth supporting are those who will fight for their own freedom from other imperialisms, who can't be bought. And the kind of support we need is not expensive—as I told you, bulldozers, small factories and some technicians to instruct our own agronomists and engineers. Wouldn't you rather be doing things like that in Asia than what you are doing in Vietnam?

Sim had to see the temples at Angkor Wat, and for this trip, Sihanouk provided us with a Mercedes and driver. For two days, we explored the whole complex, including the outlying temples, and in the evening I typed up the interview. Back in Phnom Penh, I had to wait around for

Sihanouk's editing, so Sim flew home to be with the children. A cockroach that bit—perhaps indigenous to the Royal Hotel but the only one she'd ever encountered—also speeded up her departure. When the typescript arrived from Sihanouk by motorcycle messenger, I found his editing and inserts helpful and accepted most of them.

On the way home I paused at New Delhi and stayed with Chet and Steb Bowles. His Parkinson's had progressed markedly during the year, but he could still move around. I suspect he dreaded going home and fading away. Writing memoirs, for a man like Bowles, was no substitute for being a part of the action.

Prime Minister Indira Gandhi's press secretary, George Verghese, was a longtime friend and arranged for me to interview her. She was so masterfully evasive and noncommittal that I can't remember spending a more fruitless hour in my variegated journalistic career. The only direct answers I extracted from her were an endorsement of Sihanouk's view that "by fighting Ho you are driving him into China's arms," and her belief that a bombing halt should be "step one" on the road to a Vietnam settlement. Beyond that, her words were as bland and humorless as her personality.

I slept badly my last night in New Delhi. Indigestion and psychosomatic chest pains—not unusual soon after a first coronary—kept waking me up until the dawn departure of the Air India flight to London via Moscow. I curled up in a blanket and asked the stewardess to let me sleep through the Moscow stopover. But a gruff voice shouting "*Gospodin* Advud!" roused me from my stupor, and there was a looming, fur-hatted, gun-toting Russian soldier motioning me to follow him. What now? Years of this sort of thing had still not inured me to the twinge of apprehension I had always felt in the presence of the Great Bear's jaws.

As usual, the upshot was uneventful and even pleasurable. A British diplomat with whom I'd chatted in the New Delhi airport had been invited to the Moscow VIP lounge by some Soviet Foreign Ministry officials, and when he told them a former American ambassador was also aboard, I was sent for and became the excuse for a third round of vodka toasts, which helped wash down the caviar canapes as well as cure my indigestion. In fact, I remember it as the most enjoyable of all my visits to Moscow, and we were all a bit sorry when our flight was called.

The spring of 1968 was a time of turbulence as well as transition in the saga of the cold war. The Tet offensive, the seizure of the American Embassy in Saigon by an enemy supposedly on the verge of collapse, the appointment of Clark Clifford as secretary of defense, the strong primary showing of antiwar candidate Eugene McCarthy, President Johnson's decision on March 31 not to run (coupled with a partial bombing halt in Vietnam), the start of peace talks with the North Vietnamese in Paris in May, polls that reflected mounting opposition to the bloody Vietnam stalemate—all those portents overshadowed the dispatch of 10,500 more combat troops in January and the launching of something called Operation Complete Victory by 100,000 U.S. and ARVN troops on April 3. We were on our way out of the Vietnam quagmire, and more and more people sensed it and approved it. On May 1, I wrote an editorial for *Look* (one of the few we ever ran) that concluded: "The most important national business before us in this year of political debate is to wind up our involvement in the Vietnam war as quickly and as honorably as possible, and to go on from there to the creation of a world order in which America's ingenuity will truly serve the cause of peace."

The assassinations of Martin Luther King, Jr., in April and of Robert Kennedy in June further shook a nation whose traditional self-assurance had been imperceptibly eroding ever since that fatal motorcade in Dallas. I didn't know Bob Kennedy well, but he had joined my family for lunch after my swearing-in ceremony in 1964, and I can recall his eyes filling with tears when Jan, then eleven, started recalling her efforts on behalf of JFK among her third grade schoolmates in 1960. And now I remember changing the blurb on a *Look* issue that pictured Ethel and her ten children on the cover. It was in late April, and the words—"Will there be room enough in the White House?"—seemed appropriate since he'd just announced his candidacy. But Pat Carbine, the managing editor, and I felt they were too flip and changed the line to "Ethel's Kennedys—How She Manages Them." The cover was printed six weeks before the on-sale date, and when this one appeared, Bob Kennedy was dead. I guess *Look* might have been, too, had we kept the original words.

Another *Look* story that underwent a last-minute change that year was Len Gross's report on the "Prague spring"—that heady interlude in Eastern Europe's postwar history when the Czechoslovaks, under their new Communist Party leader, Alexander Dubček, decided to dismantle the political remnants of Stalinism and see if a free, democratic society could be built within a socialist framework. They had no intention, like the Hungarians in 1956, of leaving the Soviet bloc; they knew what the Russian reaction would be. The Czechs simply wanted to test the proposition that repressive measures are not essential to socialism; they were groping for a utopian vision expressed in the early writings of Karl Marx—that the State should exist for the individual, not the individual for the State. "Socialism with a human face," became a slogan of the reformers; by midsummer their experiment seemed to be succeeding. Len's piece, "Last Try for Utopia," was scheduled for our first September issue.

But it was an experiment the Russians finally decided they could not tolerate. On August 20, Russian, Polish, East German, Hungarian and Bulgarian troops invaded Czechoslovakia to "save socialism." (Interestingly, the Romanians, who a year later called for the independence of individual Communist parties, did not participate in this military charade.) Len rewrote his piece under a new title, "Lament for a Lost Revolution," and gradually the reforms and freedoms were snuffed out, the "liberals" replaced by Soviet henchmen (Dubček himself lingered on as an impotent Party secretary until April) and Czechoslovakia henceforth relegated to a status more servile than any of the client states. And yet, for the first time, a "socialist" power led an invasion of another "socialist" country without being able to quote any stooge requesting "brotherly help."

In fact, the Czech experiment posed no real threat to the Russians. Even had it spread to the other Eastern European countries, there was never a risk of their deserting the fold and defecting to NATO or even neutrality. Everyone knew the Red Army was always a few hours away and ready to roll. The most plausible reason for the Soviet move in August was that the Russians mistrust everyone, including themselves, and Brezhnev did not yet feel secure enough on his throne to take any chances. Too bad about the Spirit of Glassboro and too bad about the comrades in the West who had hailed the Prague spring. He saw Dubček's tinkering with Marxism as heresy; worse, as an infection which—perish the thought—might even spread to the Soviet Union itself. So he called for the tanks.

On October 31, just before Nixon squeaked past Humphrey in the election (thanks in large part to Gene McCarthy's indifference), Johnson halted all bombing of North Vietnam as the Paris talks inched forward. I flew over in December and talked with Harriman and his deputy, Cyrus Vance, and both were guardedly hopeful. (Harriman was replaced in January by Henry Cabot Lodge.) Had Nixon moved forcefully when he became president in January, we'd have been out of Vietnam on the same or maybe better terms than we eventually settled for. But Nixon worried about our looking like "a pitiful, helpless giant" and believed against all evidence and common sense that gradual "Vietnamization" of the war would bring both U.S. disengagement and victory.

Fewer and fewer Americans did. In October 1969, I requoted our editorial in *Look* and added:

> Eighteen months, scores of meetings, hundreds of speeches, thousands of deaths, millions of tears and billions of wasted dollars later, we think these words are worth repeating in the hope that someday soon, someone in Washington will have the courage to say: We made a mistake. This is not our war. Let's stop it—now.
>
> Simple? Yes. Politically risky? Perhaps. Humiliating? No—because that would be a new kind of American victory—a victory won over our own willful and self-defeating pride. A victory the whole world would applaud.

A second heart attack early in 1969, a mild one and, as I write this, my last, kept me home two months, long enough to write a children's book, a good antidote for depression. In March I attended a dramatic meeting at the Council on Foreign Relations, where Clark Clifford explained how he had painstakingly become convinced a year earlier that the Vietnam war was unwinnable and that "henceforth . . . our primary goal should be to level off our involvement and to work toward gradual disengagement." His generally conservative audience gave him a standing ovation, something that two years before would have been inconceivable.

Soviet-American relations were taken out of the freezer again as Czechoslovakia receded from the front pages. In March, the U.S. Senate ratified the Nuclear Non-Proliferation Treaty, which we signed with the Russians in November. On July 10, just a month after Soviet and Chinese troops clashed in northwest Sinkiang, Gromyko called for closer ties with the U.S. On November 17, we opened the first Strategic Arms Limitation Talks with the Russians at Helsinki. Soon after, a West German delegation went to Moscow for talks on renouncing the use of force.

There's no question the yellow peril so preoccupied the Russians that an accommodation with the United States had become an elementary precaution.

In September, Ivan Marchuk, my tousled Soviet colleague in Guinea, called from the U.N., where he was on temporary duty with the Soviet delegation to the General Assembly, and we made a lunch date.

There was a bond that transcended politics among those of us who had shared the hardships and the follies of Conakry, and we enjoyed reminiscing about those days. He suggested we invite Viktor Sukhodrev, who had a night off from interpreting the following week, so I drove them out for dinner at my home in Connecticut. As usual they brought gifts of vodka and caviar (from Zamyatin) and by the time we switched to bourbon, after dinner, we had pretty well liquidated the cold war. We agreed we both had our hawks and doves and that they reinforced their transatlantic counterparts. "We who understand the insanity of modern war are in constant struggle with those who still believe in an arms race," said Marchuk. "When you are aggressive it makes our task harder."

"And vice versa," I said.

We toasted the international brotherhood of sane folks, and I quoted Eisenhower's January 1960 farewell speech: "We must guard against the acquisition of unwarranted influence, whether sought or unsought, by the military-industrial complex."

We acknowledged that his warning had not been heeded in either of our countries. And in China, Sukhodrev added, the militarists were clearly dominant. He told me that when Kosygin had stopped briefly in Peking a few months earlier, he cautioned the Chinese that they were "in no position to fight a modern war."

"They knew exactly what he meant. We have their nuclear installations targeted. It would take only a few minutes to eliminate China as a nuclear power. But they needed to know we were serious. Now, I suspect, they will make overtures to you. Be careful of them."

He was a good prophet. In less then two years, Henry Kissinger would be on his way to Peking; stranger still, Sim and I would beat him to it.

Chapter 14

China, 1971 B.K.

IN A 1986 *NEW YORKER* CARTOON, a matronly woman confronting her husband at the dinner table says, "I ran into Ruth Hagerstrom this afternoon. Now *everybody's* been to China except *us.*"

Sixteen years ago, Sim and I, in the same situation, could almost have said, *"Nobody's* been to China except *us.*" Almost, because in June 1971 (the "B.K." stands for "Before Kissinger"), we did run into two other visiting American journalist couples in Peking, to our mutual surprise. But there had been no others except for Mao Tse-tung's old friend Edgar Snow. And so China had become a country that for most Americans was as mysterious as the Land of Oz.

Sim and I were there at the invitation of Prince Sihanouk, who had been living in Peking since being deposed in 1970 while visiting Moscow. But Sihanouk can wait. To recreate the mood of those days, this chapter has to start with our feelings as we arrived in Shanghai on the weekly eighteen-hour flight from Paris. This is how I described them in *Newsday,* the paper of which I'd become publisher the previous fall:

> After Rangoon, we were the only Westerners on the plane except for a Yugoslav delegation headed by Mirko Tepevac, the foreign minister, and two quiet Algerians.
>
> It was funny about the Yugoslavs. Tepevac recalled that only a couple of years ago they were being denounced in China as "running dogs of U.S. imperialism" and worse; and here we were, imperialists and running dogs together heading for Shanghai . . .
>
> They got the big welcome: crowds waving flags, musicians with giant cymbals, an honor guard—the works. Sim and I ducked behind the

soldiers (the rear ranks all twisted around—in China a woman in an American dress outshone a delegation in Yugoslav suits) and reported to customs.

First surprise: the men and women officials (who all looked alike in their baggy khaki uniforms) didn't expect us. After passing the health and visa inspections and a big box full of little red Mao books ("Help Yourself" in four languages), we ran up against a polite but perplexed bureaucracy. We weren't a delegation, the China Travel Service had sent no guide to shepherd us; what to do?

An older man who spoke some French appeared and read my telegram from Prince Sihanouk inviting us to Peking. Great relief—the mystery was solved: We were simply in the wrong city. A plane was leaving for Peking in the morning, so we could spend the night in the airport guest house. Meanwhile we filled out declaration forms, but none of our bags were opened. Much staring and smiling and we were led to a concrete building past a huge sign urging the people of the world to defeat "U.S. aggressors and their running dogs." No porters, no elevators, no lock on our door, no hot water except in a large thermos jug on the night table. A portrait of Mao on one wall, a slogan in Chinese on the other.

We washed up and returned to the cavernous airport restaurant, past the stacks of Communist literature in all languages, including Albanian, Swahili and Esperanto. A pleasant young waiter brought us an assortment of Chinese dishes and cold beer, all for four yuan (about $1.50); a few diners glanced up and returned to their bowls of rice. The loudspeaker blared a cacophony of shouts and noises; soon the lights dimmed, and the last customers drifted away.

We strolled back in the hot, humid night. Far down the runway we heard the whine of the Air France 747 taking off. (It would be the last sound of a plane until morning, even though the airport served a city of 10,000,000.)

Up in the room, with the plane gone, we looked at each other, thought of our family back home and wondered why the hell we were here—and what was going to happen next. Somehow, we felt like astronauts whose spaceship had left them stranded on the moon.

Why *were* we here? The story properly starts in 1968 when the Chinese condemned the Soviet invasion of Czechoslovakia, a gesture that did not go unnoticed by Richard Nixon, soon to be president. When he moved into the White House, he confided to his national security adviser, Henry Kissinger, that he thought the time might be propitious for improving our relations with China. Events in 1969 confirmed his hunch: Verbal salvos between Moscow and Peking escalated in March into bloody armed clashes along the Soviet-Chinese border and culminated in a harsh, impromptu meeting at Peking airport between Kosygin and Premier Chou En-lai—the one I'd heard about at home from Viktor Sukhodrev. Also, the chaos of the cultural revolution—essentially an ideological power struggle between Mao and his less revolutionary associate Liu Shao-chi—was now subsiding, with Mao triumphant and the army reining in the young Red Guards who had spun out of control.

During that summer, Nixon dropped hints to de Gaulle and Romania's boss, Nicolae Ceauşescu, that he'd welcome talks with the Chinese. He also passed the same message, more directly, to the Pakistanis and encouraged U.S. diplomats to manifest our interest in such talks during chance encounters with their Chinese colleagues. (There were ten such encounters in 1969–70.) Finally, at a reception on December 3, our ambassador to Poland, Walter Stoessel, literally cornered the Chinese chargé, Lei Yang—who, without instructions, nervously tried to avoid him—and said we were prepared for "serious talks." He suggested they be held in Warsaw since there had already been 134 meetings between our envoys to Poland between 1955 and 1968—though only to discuss minor issues like repatriation of nationals.

The response from Peking was favorable, and U.S.-Chinese meetings took place in January and February 1970, at which Stoessel conveyed Nixon's interest in sending a personal envoy to Peking. A third meeting, scheduled for May 20, was abruptly canceled by the Chinese because of our "brazen" invasion of Cambodia in April. But Nixon persisted, letting Peking know, through the Pakistani "channel," that he planned to evacuate U.S. forces from Indochina and reiterating his interest in talks.

(During the summer, I'd written Sihanouk in Peking, asking if I might come and interview him. He replied promptly, welcoming my suggestion, but in a second message reported "regretfully" that the Chinese could not grant me a visa "at this time.")

In November, at a White House banquet for Ceauşescu, Nixon referred to "the People's Republic of China"—the first time an American president had used the term publicly, and, so far as Peking was concerned, a significant move in our careful, ongoing minuet. A few weeks later, Mao told Edgar Snow he'd be glad to talk to Nixon and that his

Foreign Ministry was "studying" the matter of issuing visas to Americans. Meanwhile, the Pakistanis reported to Kissinger that the Chinese were prepared to invite him as Nixon's emissary. It was now our move again, and in March 1971, Washington lifted the ban on American travel to China. The Chinese responded on April 6 by inviting an American table tennis team then playing in Japan to come to China. Our players met Chou En-lai and issued their own invitation to their Chinese opponents to come to the United States. It was quickly accepted. And the ice was broken.

I'd made my own move by writing Sihanouk again on February 11, repeating my request to visit him. I knew he and Chou had become close friends, that he wanted to tell his own story and that he trusted me because of our 1968 interview. So I was not too surprised when he notified me on April 19 that he'd have an answer for me in a week. But it was still exciting to get a second message from him on April 26 telling me to come ahead and that my Chinese visa could be picked up in Paris.

Three days before, Chou officially informed the Pakistanis that a U.S. emissary—even Nixon himself—would be welcome in Peking. He proposed mid-June; Nixon replied that Kissinger would be the emissary and suggested July 9, which was acceptable. *That* invitation was somehow kept secret for nearly three months; mine was not, and the news was greeted joyfully at the Los Angeles *Times,* which, like *Newsday,* was owned by the Times Mirror Company and operated a news service jointly with the Washington *Post.* Dreams of exclusive journalistic plums danced in our heads since we didn't know at the time that visas were also being granted to *New York Times* and *Wall Street Journal* representatives—who harbored the same dreams, not knowing about me or each other.

Sim was included in Sihanouk's invitation, but I told her *Newsday,* unlike *Look,* didn't underwrite spouses, so she made a deal with *McCall's,* which offered her $4,000 and expenses for an article on Chinese women; and with CBS, which promised to buy any usable television footage she could shoot with one of their cameras.

We had traveled together to many distant places in twenty-one years of marriage, but no prospective trip had ever thrilled us as much as this one. Today, when "everybody" goes there, it's hard to overestimate or even imagine the lure and the fascination of "Mainland China" to us Americans. It was a vast area of the earth we had not been allowed to see for more than two decades. The iron curtain was grim but never quite airtight—and by now even porous; but the bamboo curtain since 1949 had been virtually impenetrable to Americans.

In Paris, we picked up our visas on June 4, and Sim was given a two-day crash course by CBS in the use of a hand-held TV camera that looked like a sawed-off bazooka. I called on Secretary of State William Rogers, who happened to be in town, and from the way he talked, I gathered—correctly, as it turned out—that he was as unaware of Kissinger's forthcoming mission to Peking as I was. This was understandable. Secrets told to the State Department don't stay secret long, as Kennedy knew during our 1963 Cuban probe.

And so back to the Shanghai airport. In the morning, we asked to visit the city but were told it was off limits to us since we were supposed to be only in Peking. So we waited for our flight in the departure lounge, commiserating with two homesick African diplomats and with the French Air France agent, who gladly drove out from the city to see us: like all foreigners then in China, he lived an isolated existence, sealed off from any social contact with the Chinese.

At last we took off. To minimize accidents, Chinese planes departed only when weather conditions were just right and never mind the schedule. In Peking, a Mr. Chu from the China Travel Service was waiting to meet us and take care of our paperwork and baggage while we drank jasmine-flavored tea dispensed gratis by smiling young girls in army uniforms. In addition to our suitcases, cameras and a typewriter, we had three crates containing a complete stereo system—speakers, record player, tapes and all—as a gift for Sihanouk. But the customs officials waved us on, and soon two Polish-made cabs were taking us and our stuff to the Hsin Chiao Hotel, where we were to spend the next two weeks, much of the time awake.

Let me explain. The six-story Hsin Chiao was where most transient foreigners were lodged in the city, the more elaborate Peking Hotel being reserved for dignitaries and delegations. It had no air-conditioning (just a thermometer to remind us the room temperature was a steady 85–90, day and night), but it did have a kind of tacky charm and whimsical efficiency now all too rare in our increasingly Hiltonized world. Our wakefulness had many causes: the stifling heat, the lingering jet lag, the interminable Slavic (or Romanian) beer-and-card parties down the hall, the noisy nocturnal excavations (for a subway or air raid shelter) across the street, and the bugles, organized calisthenics, honking buses and tinkling bicycles that started at 5 A.M.

So we were chronically tired, though exhilarated. And how could we complain when a load of laundry came back the same day (for forty cents), when a repairman fixed the phone before we knew it was out of order (he knew because it was bugged), when room service (usually cold beer), telegrams and messages were delivered fast and when our weekly bill—all meals included—came to less than $25. It was cheaper than staying home.

There was a Chinese dining room on the ground floor where we always ate too much and a "Western" one on the top floor, where we could start the day with toast, eggs, tea, yogurt and canned pineapple. Downstairs, below the 30-foot Mao portrait on the stairs and the 15-foot Mao statue in the lobby, a poster informed us that "the east wind is prevailing over the west wind," while upstairs the bleary-eyed breakfast trade was exhorted to "unite and win still greater victories."

The upstairs regulars had their own tables—the Japanese traders with their own instant coffee, tea bags and condiments; the dour East European technicians, who usually began the muggy days with quarts of good cold Beijing beer; the stout and sad-eyed Pakistanis, with their bored and squirming children; the long-haired Scandinavian youths wearing red Mao buttons; the convivial East and West German correspondents (no Berlin wall here); the shy Zambian and the genial Irishman; the lonely young Canadian diplomats (Peking was no place for a bachelor), and now we Americans, who provided the regulars with a fresh topic of conversation.

But whatever curiosity we evoked at the Hsin Chiao was nothing compared to the sensation we created outdoors. After unpacking in our cramped quarters, Sim and I decided to stretch our legs. First we asked Mr. Chu—the only person in the lobby who spoke English—to notify Sihanouk and the Information Department of the Foreign Ministry of our arrival and to set up appointments, which he did with the same smiling courtesy we were to encounter everywhere.

There was a small neighborhood park not far away, and as we walked toward it people stared at us as if we were a couple of bright green space aliens—three eyes, webbed feet, antennae and all. It had been a long time since most Chinese had seen foreigners (many never had), and the mere fact we wore different clothes made us conspicuous. Today, they have fashion shows in China, and I read that girls wear makeup, bright skirts and blouses and go to hairdressers. But in 1971, there was one costume for both sexes—a tunic, cap and baggy pants— that came in two colors, blue and olive. As for hair styles, women also had two choices—braids or bangs. No wonder we were stared at, or that some children shyly reached out to touch our strangely pale skin.

In the park there were sedate couples on benches, sweating badminton players and some amateur gymnasts who paused and looked at us, deadpan, when we passed by. Were they hostile or just afraid? To find out, I brought my instant camera the next afternoon, snapped a picture of two little girls and presented it to their astounded parents. Pandemonium! Half the park converged on us. Gasps of astonishment and delight. More pictures, more children, more excited laughter.

Was it just the magic of instant snapshots? I don't think so. To the Chinese we must have seemed like fearsome creatures—tall, big-nosed, hairy, ungainly, garishly dressed. But as soon as we smiled at the children and took their pictures we became human—these Martians liked kids! And everybody could relax. (Later on, when we were issued Foreign Ministry press passes, and displayed them, they relaxed even more, seeing that we had official sanction and thus could not be spies.)

Back at the hotel that first evening, we met Audrey Topping, the wife of Seymour Topping, then assistant managing editor of the *New York Times.* She had been visiting China with her father, Chester Ronning, the former Canadian ambassador, and had persuaded Chou En-lai to grant Top a visa too. He was now touring Manchuria. Although we were glad to see each other, we were both a little disappointed to discover we were not the only astronauts, so to speak, on the moon. And Audrey informed us that Bob Keatley, diplomatic correspondent of the *Wall Street Journal,* and his wife were here as well, having received visas in May after applying since 1965. I suggested that if this kept up we could start an American press club and elect officers. Anyway, I still had Sihanouk to myself—he was granting no other interviews—and we were invited to his residence the day after next.

On our first full day in Peking I was wide awake before 5 A.M., thanks to jet lag, so set forth on a stroll through the old "legation quarter" that adjoined the hotel. Only the Romanians still occupied their former building. Sihanouk was housed in the old French Embassy residence. The other villas were either government offices or abandoned and unkempt, like the padlocked Protestant church. I followed a procession of schoolchildren chanting some patriotic songs and brandishing their little red Mao books, and then I was lost. A soldier standing by a sentry box eyed me warily (or was he glaring?), and suddenly and inexplicably I felt terribly apprehensive—more so even than during my postwar encounters with the *Volkspolizei* in East Germany. It was the China syndrome, the reaction to being alone in the forbidden city of a long forbidden land. I got over it by approaching the soldier boldly but affably and saying, *"Nihau. Hsin Chiao?"* He smiled and pointed to where I should go. *"Sheh-sheh,"* I added, using up my entire Chinese vocabulary. After "good morning" and "thank you," I did learn three more words—*tsai-jen* (good-bye), *pijiu* (beer) and *wai-xien* (outside line), which I always mispronounced as *wei-xian* (danger) to the unflappable hotel operator.

It took us a few days to realize we were in an environment unlike any we had known. For example, nobody would accept a tip: a cab driver once kept me waiting five minutes while he tracked down two cents in change that I was trying to persuade him to keep. Nothing was ever stolen or even accepted as a gift (unless symbolic): I remember a factory worker chasing me half a block to return a half-used matchbook I'd left behind on a table. And everyone was polite in this city without traffic jams, drug problems, strikes, pornography, litter, panhandlers, taxes, unemployment, medical bills, advertising (except for Party slogans) or night life. At 3 A.M. the only sounds were the hoofbeats of farm wagons bringing produce to the markets.

Of course it was also a city without elections, unions, freedom to quit a job or move, cultural activity other than what the Party rigidly prescribed, foolishness, bright lights or colors, variety or . . . fun. This was the price paid for security, a price the Chinese then seemed willing to pay after decades of upheaval, famines, epidemics, warlords, vice lords, landlords and the recent excesses of the cultural revolution.

After my early morning reconnaissance, Sim and I went over to the Information Department of the Foreign Ministry, where Ma Yu-chen and his deputy, Chi Ming-chung, who watched over foreign journalists, received us cordially. We were handed large porcelain mugs of tea (you could drown in tea in China by calling on enough people, and I learned that only by saying something that sounded like "koala" often enough could I stop refills). Then we discussed our "program" once we had finished our Sihanouk meetings. It was mutually agreed that visits to a large people's commune, a couple of factories, Tsinghua University, the Anti-Imperialist Hospital and the ballet—along with sightseeing at the Great Wall, the Ming tombs, the Summer Palace and the Forbidden City (not yet open to the public)—would keep us productively busy.

Mr. Ma, who had been stationed in Burma and spoke with a British accent, added—seriously and I thought unnecessarily—"We have no hatred of Americans, nor of you." Then he smiled and asked, "By the way, what is Bill Moyers doing now? I've been reading his book." (Bill had been my predecessor at *Newsday*.)

It soon became clear to us that they were trying to learn as much as they could about the United States in order to make up for years of near-total estrangement. Chi asked us what American newspapers and magazines they should subscribe to ("We need to find out more about your press"), and Ma wanted to know the difference between our three major networks. It was also obvious that the word was out, loud and clear, that it was okay to be nice to Americans; in fact the Party organ, *Jen Min Jih Pao* (*People's Daily,* and pronounced "Renmin Ribao") actually reminded its readers in April that "the American people have a revolutionary tradition." Praise indeed.

We found out a few days later how much top officials still had to learn about our press after we were invited to a private lunch at the Peking Hotel by Peng Hua, chief of the Information Department. Chang Wei-ching, then in charge of Western European and American affairs, and six or seven other officials and interpreters were there, and the talk was frank and freewheeling. We discussed the status of Taiwan, relations with the Russians and instability in the Near East; U.S. politics, the Pentagon papers and the mood of our youth; the state of the arts in China (moribund), the prospects for large-scale tourism (remote) and table tennis (a Chinese team was definitely going to the United States). All in all, it added up to what diplomats would call a fruitful exchange, enhanced by the fact that it was so unusual. I was especially struck by their outspoken hostility to the Soviet Union, which they referred to as a "bourgeois" country practicing "social imperialism" to achieve "hegemony."

Afterward, Chi phoned to give me the correct spelling of the names of those present. So I figured they expected me to write about our meeting, since no one had said it was off the record.

I filed a story early the next morning, and we then drove out to visit the university. At noon, I was called to the phone. It was Ma. He was wondering if by chance I was planning to write about yesterday's lunch. (I knew he knew I had—there was no actual censorship but every dispatch was screened by the Information Department.) I had already done so? Most unfortunate. While of course I was free to write what I wished, still, some of the quotes might be, well, not quite accurate, since they all assumed it was a private talk . . .

I told him I'd send a wire to *Newsday* blocking the story.

"Good," said Ma. "A car is already on its way to the university to pick up your message." And he apologized for not knowing when to say "off the record."

It was hardly surprising that we and the Chinese had much to learn about each other. To the Chinese, spoon-fed for years on a diet of propaganda, the outside world, especially the U.S., must have seemed like a brawling, crime-ridden inferno. And many Americans still thought of pigtails, rickshas and opium dens when they heard the word "China"; or perhaps of a horde of murderous, blue-clad robots poised to swarm over the globe. Until you see them, how can you picture the merriment of the world's cutest kids or the glowing grace of Chinese girls, baggy clothes notwithstanding?

Today, fifteen years later, we still have much to learn. The Chinese are both complicated and . . . different. A British diplomat in Peking told me that after twenty years of studying the Chinese and their language he thought he was finally beginning to understand them and how their minds worked.

"The only trouble," he added, "is that back in London they say my reports don't make sense anymore. Understanding the Chinese is hard enough; explaining them is almost impossible."

I had an inkling of what he meant since we were talking at a garden party at the British Embassy celebrating Queen Elizabeth's birthday. The embassy had been sacked by a mob of officially sanctioned Red Guards during the cultural revolution, and here we were, three years later, at a sedate reception where ranking Chinese officials joined diplomats in solemn toasts to Her Majesty's health. My presence caused some speculation, especially since the British kept introducing me as "ambassador," and I could see the Soviet envoy eyeing me with unfeigned curiosity. I let him guess but accepted a luncheon invitation for Sim and me from the Dutch ambassador and assured him and other NATO envoys present that my visit was quite unofficial. There wasn't much diplomatic reporting out of Peking, and I could see why the sudden appearance of Americans was a juicy tidbit.

The Chinese at the party did express quiet satisfaction with the June 10 White House announcement liberalizing trade with China—another symbolic gesture in our diplomatic maneuvering. As I wrote in my first story out of Peking: "Despite the Taiwan impasse, some trade, more two-way visits and better mutual understanding seem clearly in the cards. The bamboo curtain is slowly lifting now that the turmoil of the recent cultural revolution is over and China's leadership feels more secure."

Sim and I had lunched with Sihanouk the day before at the mansion he occupied with a retinue of fifty, including three chefs—one for Chinese dishes, one for Cambodian and one for French. He wasn't suffering, except from frustration, and seemed as hyperthyroid as before, and Monique as serene and charming. We arrived with our crates of musical paraphernalia, and his cousin, Prince Sisowath, offered to hook everything up with the help of a transformer. When he was done, I handed him a tape at random, and we waited for the sound. When it came—in an ear-splitting blast—the whole legation quarter was treated to a totally unexpected Benny Goodman rendition of "The Stars and Stripes Forever." Sihanouk thought it very appropriate, so we left it on but lowered the volume.

While Sim and Monique inspected the garden and discussed Chinese women for the *McCall's* piece, Sihanouk and I talked in his study. He thought better U.S.-Chinese relations were far more likely than a reconciliation between China and Russia. His own situation pointed up the Sino-Soviet rivalry. While the Russians and their client states now recognized Lon Nol and denounced Sihanouk, whom he overthrew, as a reactionary royalist, China recognized Sihanouk's shadowy government (whose French acronym was GRUNK) as a kind of tacit ally of the North Vietnamese and the Viet Cong. The reason, he told me, was that he was in Peking, and the Russians couldn't support him without appearing to endorse the Chinese version of communism.

It was all as complicated as the problem the Chinese were having that week drafting a joint communiqué with a visiting Romanian delegation. The Chinese wanted to include an attack on "social imperialists" (their code name for the Russians), but their guests, who were neighbors of the Soviet Union, refused to go that far.

Sihanouk was bitter. He suspected us, falsely, of engineering the coup that elevated Lon Nol (who, as someone remarked, was nobody but Lon Nol spelled backwards), with the result that two-thirds of Cambodia was soon overrun by the rampaging Communist Khmer Rouge, who could tolerate Sihanouk but not an out-and-out pro-American regime.

"Nixon has turned my country into the number one Indochina battlefield," he said, "and the end result will only be a Communist Cambodia." He was just as prophetic about "Vietnamization," on which U.S. troop withdrawals were predicated: It would fail "since the South Vietnamese troops have no patriotic ideal."

He also predicted there would be no bloodbath in South Vietnam after a Communist victory and that North Vietnam would play "a preponderant but not commanding role in Indochina." Nor did he think China would try to occupy or "satellize" the area.

I could tell that more than a year of enforced exile, even with three cooks and the trappings of a chief of state, was making him nervous, though his eloquence and perspicacity seemed unaffected. In discussing U.S. intervention in Vietnam, for example, he drew a parallel to our Civil War: "How would you northerners have felt if the British, say, had come in and kept the Confederacy going with a huge expeditionary force just as it was about to collapse? Can't you see that's what you've been doing in Vietnam all these years—spending your money to kill and die for a lost cause?"

A visit with Sihanouk was never dull. And you also ate well.

We saw him twice more before leaving Peking—once to check the accuracy of the quotes I was using in my account of the interview, and once to lunch again and say good-by. (A French Embassy officer, trying to find out what we had found out in Peking, was the other guest.) At this meeting, Sihanouk assured me the Chinese would never join the United Nations, even if invited, as long as the Taiwanese were members, whatever they called themselves. This was an interesting news item, since Washington was still contemplating a "two-China" solution to the U.N. impasse. I also remember asking Sihanouk why he hadn't returned to Cambodia from Moscow when Lon Nol had staged his coup. (The Russians had even offered to fly him back.)

"I knew Lon Nol well," he said. "He had been my police chief. I knew he was ambitious and could be ruthless. And I had reliable information he was planning to meet me at the airport, pretend to drive me to the palace and then take me to a wooded area in the other direction and have me shot. I could believe that. So I came to Peking instead."

He did go back eventually and was placed under house arrest by the infamous Pol Pot. But we would be meeting again, twice, in New York; so it was good-by but not farewell to a nice guy who seemed destined to finish last.

With my Sihanouk business out of the way, the Chinese took charge of our days and evenings and assigned a young English-speaking guide named Yang Shan-hu to escort us. Our program started with a gala performance of a "ballet" called *Red Detachment of Women,* in which an evil landlord was pursued and done in by a bevy of lovely ballerinas twirling wooden rifles and dressed in what we then called hot pants. It was produced by Mao's wife, Chiang Ch'ing, who was later tried for treason as a member of the Gang of Four. The show blended modern music, Soviet-style ballet and melodramatic gestures carried over from the old Peking Opera and ended, finally, with everybody singing the "Internationale."

Tsinghua University (where Ma phoned me about my indiscreet dispatch) was just coming back to life. It had been shut down during the cultural revolution in 1966–68 before the army finally moved in and clamped down on rebellious students. "People were killed," we were told, "and even state property was destroyed." Now there were 2,700 students, all freshmen, compared to an enrollment of 10,000 in 1966.

Sitting around a conference table with the university's administrators, we heard enough to picture the confusion that prevailed—and to appreciate the British diplomat's remark about the difficulty of understanding the Chinese: "Liu and his ilk wanted a spiritual aristocracy, a new bourgeoisie ... Mao knew that education must be combined with productive labor ... We put up posters calling on others to dare to unhorse Emperor Liu. ... As Red Guards, our enemies were both outer rightists and outer leftists ... We lost our heads, we took up spears and swords and homemade weapons and used radios and loudspeakers ... When the army came, five soldiers were shot by students. But the worker-soldier teams didn't shoot back. ... Instead, propaganda teams organized study groups ... They helped us criticize outer leftists and the no-center theory ... Many learned for the first time that to make a revolution we must first make a revolution against ourselves."

And so it went around the table while we all downed gallons of hot tea. Everybody took turns—former Red Guards; the ex-steelworker who was now "chief of the reforming group" of the university's ruling Revolutionary Committee; and Professor Chien Wei-chang, the smiling, soft-spoken physicist who was at Caltech in the forties. His confession—recited in Chinese although he spoke fluent English—was both poignant and absurd: "I didn't understand why I should be reformed ... In time I realized I was imparting erroneous ideas to my students. I thought my job was to turn them into engineers and scientists. I thought theory was supreme and pure science nonpolitical." After nineteen "re-education" sessions, some lasting all night, Chien was sent off to a factory "where I learned from the workers, lost my arrogance and became modest." Now he was teaching again.

During the lunch break, he and I fell back as our group walked over to the refectory, and he said in English in a low voice, "Everything will be all right. The very fact that Americans like you were allowed to come here and listen to all this—well, that is further evidence to me that the bad times are over."

We visited a class in computers: The Chinese-made machines were in the only air-conditioned room we found in China; and we were shown books printed in the eleventh century—four hundred years before Gutenberg—I suppose as a reminder that China was already a civilized, inventive nation when Europe was barely emerging from the Dark Ages.

Over one last mug of tea, Liu Ping, the vice-chairman of the Revolutionary Committee, admitted there were still "adjustments to be made." As he put it, "New and different textbooks, students coming from different cultural levels, relations between teachers and students, the proper balance between theory and practice, the role of politics in scientific research—these are some of the problems we must grapple with. But we are sure to overcome them, with Chairman Mao's teachings to guide us."

We gave him a book of photographs of New York in appreciation of our visit. He could not accept it unless we were presenting it, as a delegation, to the university. So we did. It was placed on the table and no one looked at it, feigning indifference. But at the door, I looked back and could not see the book for the people crowding around it.

Early one steamy morning, Yang roused us for an all-day tour of the Evergreen People's Commune about twenty-five miles outside Peking. In those days the word "commune" in America connoted an abandoned ranch occupied by a dozen shaggy youths living naked and smoking pot. In China, a commune was then the nation's basic economic, social and political unit. At least eighty thousand had been organized in rural China since 1958.

The forty thousand residents of Evergreen did all sorts of things. They produced fruit, vegetables (a hundred different kinds), poultry, eggs, rice, barley, pigs—you name it—on about 7,000 acres of land. They also raised stud horses, recapped tires, ran two secondary and seventeen primary schools, eight factories, a small coal mine, a hospital and 107 clinics which took care of minor ailments and ardently promoted family planning. Mrs. Wang Ung-wu, chairman of the commune's governing Revolutionary Committee, told us we were the first Americans to visit the place since the nephew of a Communist visitor dropped by a few years back. So this, she said, was an especially enjoyable occasion. Then the ritual, which was repeated at every institution we visited, got under way: briefing with tea, a walk around, a delicious lunch, another walk around, questions with tea and a farewell with photographs.

Another pattern—and this was much more interesting—was that the formality and memorized phrases of the first briefing gradually gave way to spontaneity and laughter as the day wore on. And so afternoon tea was always a more jovial and relaxed affair than morning tea. This was in contrast to Eastern Europe, where rigid Party discipline and Orwellian blather generally prevailed throughout approved visits to factories and collective farms.

We were deluged with statistics that are no longer relevant today, entertained by schoolchildren and plied with gifts of peaches, apricots and strawberries—a welcome change from the Hsin Chiao's everlasting canned pineapple. At the final stop of the day, at a clinic, we were served hot water, which our hosts considered refreshing on a warm day, and exchanged questions. We asked about recreation (mobile film vans, sports and theatrical troupes), crime (very little that couldn't be handled through "discussion and repentance") and even sex ("What if accidents happen?" "They don't—it would be against Chairman Mao's teachings." "What if they did anyway?" Titters from the young nurses. "Well, *if* one did, the girl would have the choice of abortion or adoption —keeping the baby would disgrace her"). They asked questions, too, and when we left I had the feeling that even though such visits were partly stage-managed, these people *had* built something that worked and gave them security and pride. This you could tell from the look in their eyes—not the look we'd seen, for example, in Czechoslovakia.

Of course the communal life was dull by our standards, and those born here were likely to die here. But as a wise Frenchman told me in Peking, "Freedom means nothing to people who have had nothing."

A Canadian TV crew visiting the same commune a week later had an interesting experience which I'm glad we missed. A cameraman stepping backward at a pigsty to get a better shooting angle fell into a deep vat of liquid shit. He was fished out, washed off and his camera dismembered, meticulously cleaned, part by part, and reassembled. Then his Chinese escorts thanked him for having inadvertently illuminated a serious shortcoming: the absence of a fence or wall around the vat of pigshit. This would be corrected the very next day; thanks to him, similar mishaps would not occur in the future.

On subsequent days we were taken to Peking Textile Factory No. 3, where we trudged past endless, deafening rows of spindles and automatic looms which turned out more than 100,000,000 yards of cotton cloth annually; and to the Semi-Conductor Factory No. 1 of the Western District, where once illiterate women workers had been given crash courses to enable them to read the manuals. After a delicious eight-cent lunch at the textile factory canteen, we were invited, as usual, to offer our "criticisms" so that our hosts could benefit from them. Sim suggested the girls at the spindles be given face masks, goggles and ear plugs as protection against lint and noise; this was duly and gratefully noted. At the factory day-care center, the kids sang and danced for us. Other visitors had told me they'd seen an anti-U.S.-in-Vietnam skit performed here, but we were treated to scenes from classical opera. This was typical Chinese tact. Not once in China—until we met Chou En-lai—did anyone mention Vietnam unless we did first.

And there was sightseeing. On the parapet of the Great Wall that coiled over the hills like a giant stone snake, I collected a crowd simply by displaying the contents of my wallet. A stamp that slipped out was retrieved by a small boy, intrigued by the glue (Chinese stamps were nonadhesive); I tried to give it to him but he gravely handed it back. Two students to whom I gave instant snapshots stammered out some English words—"Welcome to China" and "Thank you." Sim, scrambling up to yet another watchtower, pointed her camera at a group of soldiers, who cowered against the wall, not knowing what weapon this mad foreigner might be toting.

At the Ming tombs we joined a throng deep in the cool crypts staring wide-eyed at the bright colors of the imperial ornaments in glass cases. (In a society where everything is drab and utilitarian, anything gaudy and useless holds a special fascination.) In the Forbidden City—vast, deserted and awesome with its succession of musty throne rooms and acres of weedy courtyards—we were told that during the cultural revolution many antiques and "other old things" were considered subversive and destroyed by the Red Guards. The complex of small palaces was then shut down. Now everything was being repaired and spruced up and it would soon be reopened to the public. At the twelfth-century Summer Palace on Kunming Lake, workmen had already restored the colors on the wooden friezes under the covered promenade; they had been whitewashed and defaced but fortunately not smashed by the Red Guards (who seem to have "guarded" precious little). At the Park of Culture near the great Tien An Men gate, women swept and swept— you never saw so much as a scrap of paper on the ground in Peking— and when we passed a group of obviously Russian tourists, our guide, Yang, muttered scornfully.

And eventually, at dusk, we would get back to the hotel in our official car, modeled on a Checker, and go for a final stroll past the family groups fanning themselves on their stoops, smiling when you smiled, staring when you didn't. Back also to a welcome gin-and-tonic with the Canadian diplomats upstairs, jotting down as yet unanswered questions:

Why no dogs in the city? (Unnecessary and nonproductive, use up food and space.) Why no flies? (All swatted to death years ago in a massive clean-up campaign.) And why no kissing or even hand holding in all these romantic parks and gardens? (We never did find out, but I'm told young people in today's China are less inhibited.)

All the climbing around the Great Wall had given Sim a sore back, so Yang proposed a visit to the Anti-Imperialist Hospital (renamed the Friendship Hospital in September), where he would find her a good acupuncturist. I went along, and for the first and only time in China was asked not to take a picture. It would have been a beaut. The doctor, a Fu Manchu look-alike, was bending over her, prone on a table, and preparing to plunge a six-inch needle into the back of her thigh. His other hand held a flaming wand with which he planned to apply suction cups to her lower back. As I unslung my camera, he cautioned, "No pictures."

Yes, her pain was relieved, and we also got a chance to talk with some of the doctors, two of whom had studied in the U.S. Dr. Lim Chau-chi, a pert and lively lady of seventy who was chief gynecologist, had worked here when it was the Union Medical Hospital—supported by Rockefeller funds. We were swamped, as usual, with hot tea and statistics before visiting some neat but austere wards and, after donning smocks and masks, watching an abortion and a gall bladder operation performed with only acupuncture as an anesthetic. (The needles were inserted in the cartilage of the ears and in the feet.)

On June 18, the program completed, we were making plans to leave when Ma called to ask us to stay another couple of days as there was a chance we would have a meeting with "a very important person."

At dinner that night, we were surprised to see Topping, who had left Peking two days previously to go home. Then the Keatleys turned up, also unexpectedly. It took us until morning to realize we'd all been advised to stand by for the same meeting with the same very important person, who could only be Chou En-lai.

It was good planning by the Chinese. Their purpose, of course, was to expose American public opinion to the reality of Mainland China and the views of its leadership in advance of the Kissinger trip—which we naturally knew nothing about. By inviting the three of us, they were assured access to the *New York Times* news service; the Los Angeles *Times*/Washington *Post* service, of which *Newsday* was a part; and the Dow Jones service, which included the *Wall Street Journal.* This guaranteed that any story filed by us three would appear in roughly two-thirds of all American dailies—with the AP and UPI excerpting our stuff for the remainder. Television was left out, probably because our meeting with Chou was meant to be low-key and also better suited to words than pictures.

And so, resigned to the prospect of nonexclusivity, we devoted the next day to preparing a scenario for the meeting. By deciding in advance who would ask which questions in what order, we could make the most of the time available.

On June 21, after two days of guide-less moseying around the town and picture taking, we were alerted by Mr. Chi at 4 P.M. to stand by at the hotel, where limousines would pick us up at six fifteen and take us to dinner with the premier.

Our destination was the Great Hall of the People, where Chou and a retinue of six officials and an interpreter were waiting. We were all introduced to him individually, posed for the traditional group photograph and strolled past a spectacular lacquer screen to a round table set with blue and white porcelain, place cards, ivory chopsticks and glasses for Chinese wine, beer and mou t'ai, a 120-proof sorghum brandy.

"We'll eat Chinese-style," declared Chou through an interpreter, which meant we were seated on one side of the circular table and our hosts on the other. As soon as we sat down, he remarked that this was the first time in twenty-five years he'd dined with a group of Americans. Judging from his expression—you could detect a twinkle in his eyes behind a mask of formality—I think he was relishing the occasion as much as we were.

The menu, hand-printed in English, promised that the meal would be leisurely: Hors d'Oeuvre (sic); Silver Agarie Consommé; Sea Cucumbers, Abalone and Meat Balls; Chicken slices, shrimp and green peas; Shad; Mushroom and Lima Beans; Bean Purée; Pastries and Fruits. Everything was delicious and, except for the abalone and sea slugs, not beyond our dexterity with chopsticks.

None of us were quite sure about the protocol of taking notes during a Chinese banquet, but Chou took care of that. As we began juggling pencils and chopsticks while balancing unobtrusive notebooks on our knees, he said, "First I would like to propose a toast to the end of American intervention in Vietnam."

We had no trouble with that. So we sipped our fiery mou t'ai and were smilingly assured by our host that even though you can set fire to it, "mou t'ai won't make you drunk or even give you a hangover" because of the purity of the water it's made with.

The toast out of the way (the test given and passed), Chou then said, still smiling, "I have two more suggestions—first that we remove our jackets so that we will be as comfortable as the ladies, and second that you put your notebooks on the table so that you can write more easily."

He spoke in Chinese through Nancy T'ang, his American-born interpreter, but we could tell from his reaction to our questions before they were translated that he understood English perfectly well.

We took turns asking the questions. While they—and his answers— are now dated, it bears recalling that the messages that came through most clearly at this preview of the coming meetings with Kissinger and Nixon—the messages that he wanted Americans to hear—were: First, China would never compromise on the status of Taiwan, which was an internal Chinese affair; second, Taiwan's reassociation with the mainland would be accomplished peacefully, and its inhabitants would enjoy an even higher standard of living; third, China expected to be consulted on all "superpower" decisions affecting the Far East; fourth, China had no intention of invading other countries, but did reserve the right to send arms and money to "oppressed people" struggling for "liberation"; finally, the chances of an accommodation with the United States were better than chances for a reconciliation with China's ideological enemies and next-door neighbors, the Russians—in fact, China was not even interested in the new Soviet proposal for a five-power nuclear conference, which smacked of a "superpower club."

As for a Nixon visit to China, Chou said he or his emissary would be welcome but only on condition it was understood "under what circumstances the visit would be made"—meaning, presumably, Nixon's acceptance of the fact that China's only capital was Peking, not Taipei.

Chou's contention that Taiwan was not such an insuperable obstacle as it then seemed has been borne out by events. But in 1971, his saying that even Chiang Kai-shek agreed with him that there was only one China sounded like a fresh insight after years of blather about Quemoy, Matsu and a two-China solution.

Beyond these and other weighty matters, the talk ranged far and wide—from China's assiduous efforts to promote birth control to the women's liberation movement, which called for another toast.

The small talk was more revealing of Chou's personality than the heavier stuff. At seventy-three, he looked trim, his eyes sparkled under dark brows and his quick wit made it seem plausible that, when asked by a Western diplomat how history would have been affected if Khrushchev and not Kennedy had been assassinated in 1963, Chou allegedly replied, "Mrs. Khrushchev would not have become Mrs. Onassis."

When I mentioned Barbara Tuchman's new book about wartime China, he told Ma Yu-chen to get it and have it translated. Ma was pleased to report he'd already ordered it.

At one point, Chou spoke approvingly of a *Newsday* editorial he had read which opposed U.S. actions in Vietnam. Topping and Keatley were quick to point out that their papers, too, had advocated phasing out our involvement.

"I'm very glad to hear that," said Chou, "but the *Newsday* editorial happened to be the one I saw."

Later, around bean purée time, I told Chou that when Sim and I were married I promised her that one day we would go to China. So I was especially pleased to have been able to keep my promise on the eve of our twenty-first anniversary.

"And what day is that?"

"Tomorrow," I replied.

"And have you enjoyed your visit?" he asked, turning to Sim.

"Very much," she said, "Except that we aren't getting much sleep. There's a subway being built outside our window, and the drilling doesn't stop even at night."

Someone explained the subway was in fact an air raid shelter, and the conversation shifted to the Soviet military threat as seen from Peking.

It was after ten when Chou rose and proposed the seventh and final toast of the evening—this time to improved Sino-American relations. He knew what we didn't—that Kissinger would be arriving eighteen days hence to set the stage for the Nixon trip in 1972.

A few minutes later, in three rooms of the Hsin Chiao, three electric fans were switched on and three typewriters began clacking away. Chou had been right about the mou t'ai—we had no trouble composing our stories or finding the keys. I don't know who finished first, but around midnight I was barreling along Peking's deserted streets in a taxi whose driver presumably understood the Chinese characters on a slip of paper that spelled out "Foreign Ministry."

Top and Bob had just arrived with their copy. Ma was waiting in his office, where he informed us we'd be called the next day when the quotes were checked out for accuracy—I gathered by Chou himself—and we could then file our stories. The world would not know of our dinner party for another twelve hours or so. The Chinese would learn about it the following day in a six-inch front-page story in *Jen Min Jih Pao* that stated the premier had dined with us and had "a friendly talk." We got the same space and position in the paper, it turned out, as did Kissinger when he met Chou a couple of weeks later.

It was a long morning for all of us. Whoever's story was cleared first would go out first, and for all of our fraternal feelings, we were, to say the least, competitive.

We lunched together and waited separately. Finally, at 4 P.M. I called Ma. "I've been trying to reach you," he said, "but your phone has been busy or out of order. The others are here with their stories, but I told the Central Post Office to send nothing out until all three of you are there."

Bless Mr. Ma. I collided with the phone repair man at the door and sped to the Foreign Ministry. Our stories went out simultaneously and I got back to the Hsin Chiao in time, I figured, for a quiet tête-à-tête anniversary celebration, quiet at least until the bulldozers started clanking and grinding away at the air raid shelter.

At 6 P.M.—surprise. Ma and Chi phoned from the lobby. Could they come up? Of course. We ordered some cold bottles of Beijing *pijiu,* inferring they didn't want to meet in the restaurant, where there would be no hidden mikes to record our conversation.

They walked in bearing a long, flamboyant bouquet of red flowers —the kind you see nine-year-old Czech or East German girls handing Communist Party dignitaries at airports.

"For your anniversary," explained Ma.

Chou En-lai had remembered.

While we drank the beer we talked politics; Sim said she thought communism could only work in have-not countries, where life had always been harsh. I doubt if they agreed: They changed the subject. Of the cultural revolution, they said it was drastic but necessary to check the growth of a privileged class separated from the masses—such as existed in the Soviet Union.

"We are still backward," said Ma, "but at least today a person has security and dignity in China. A peasant doesn't have to sell his daughters to rich men to keep his family from starving."

We didn't try to argue about which way of life was right. I told them ours was right for us, given our cultural and historical experience, and maybe theirs was right for them just now, given China's experience.

They didn't disagree. We finished the beer. Outside it was getting dark. We parted—I think friends.

Another surprise. We skipped dinner and packed for the morning flight to Canton. Seven, eight, nine o'clock went by—and the only sounds from the street below were the tinkling of thumb bells from some of Peking's million bicycles.

And later, silence—the whole blessed night long. What a nice present for a couple of imperialist strangers! That's why Sim and I will always recall our twenty-first anniversary with a warm spot in our hearts for old Chou.

Would Russians have sent flowers and silenced the construction work? I think not. And it occurred to me that the charm, the humor and the courtesy of the Chinese are what have made it easier for us Americans to shed our hostility toward *these* Communists and embrace them, so to speak, in a span of just a few years; far easier than for us to smile at, let alone embrace, the Russians, even though our two nations have never fought a hot war as we did against the Chinese in Korea. Perhaps the experience of American missionaries in China and our traditional down-home image of the Chinese as hardworking, cheerful, pigtailed laundrymen and dispensers of delicious food have played a role too. Kissinger, with whom I exchanged impressions a few weeks later, summed it up by saying, "The Chinese are civilized people, the Russians are thugs."

Civilized may not be just the right term, given the massacres that followed the Communist victory in 1949. I suspect that what most differentiates the Chinese and the Russians is that the former are more relaxed because they have always felt superior to all the barbarians who populate the earth; while the latter are still striving for equality and acceptance in a Western world which not so long ago sneered at the crude Muscovites as "baptized bears."

And so to Canton. If Peking was like a dry sauna, Canton was a steam bath. A flock of guides escorted us and the Toppings to spacious hotel suites. Our dinner with Chou En-lai had apparently given us VIP status. We trudged around the wet, tropical city—crowded arcades, barges and sampans on the yellowish Pearl River, vegetable plots in the gardens of the once-swanky old consular district.

On our return, a delegation headed by the vice-chairman of Canton's Revolutionary Committee was waiting to see me, alone. Oh boy, what now? Even after weeks of exposure to Chinese charm, I experienced what Ed Murrow used to call the clangs, which he defined for me as "a rush of cold shit to the heart." We adjourned to a small salon to drink tea while the vice-chairman relayed a request he had received from the Information Department in Peking to obtain my permission to reprint excerpts from the *Newsday* editorial Chou had praised. His manner was deferential, almost humble, and his thanks profuse when I gave my consent. (This was another point of contrast: I couldn't imagine Russian officials asking any such permission; they would simply reprint what they wanted.) But there was more. After an eight-course feast with some Canadians, we tumbled into bed, and at 2 A.M. the phone rang. Who knew I was in Canton? Who, if they did, would want to call me at this hour?

It was Ma, of course. He was proofreading the editorial and thought he'd found a typographical error. Would it be all right to correct it? He read it to me. It was a typo, sure enough, that we had missed. He thanked me and wished us a good night's sleep. I decided it was impossible to overestimate, let alone understand the Chinese.

At 9 A.M. we boarded a spotless and unexpectedly air-conditioned train that glided past miles of rice paddies and pulled up at the China–Hong Kong border.

Processing was speedy—no baggage inspection, and a soldier helped us lug our stuff to the Lowu bridge, past a huge wall poster, slightly faded now, that read: PEOPLE OF THE WORLD, UNITE AND DEFEAT THE U.S. AGGRESSORS AND ALL THEIR RUNNING DOGS! Up ahead we could see the Union Jack and the British train.

"Well," I said to the soldier, *"Tsai-jen* and *sheh-sheh."*

"Tsai-jen," he replied with a smile.

On the other side, we boarded the train. On the way to the city we looked at the cars on the roads and litter in the backyards; at the first station, boys with long hair and women in split skirts came aboard; local newspapers were passed around (HONG KONG DUMPING OF SEWAGE PRIMITIVE was one banner headline, while the tabloid's back-page feature under a "Showbiz" logo was an interview with an Oriental starlet telling how she'd discovered her "real self"). At Kowloon station, jostling crowds, inquisitive newsmen, aggressive porters, honking cabs: "Watch your bags—keep an eye on your bags!"

Across the bay the high-rise buildings gleamed in the noonday sun. We were back in the world, out of Utopia, and it felt good.

In Hong Kong I refiled the story I'd held up at Ma's request, since it had now become an elaboration of Chou's remarks, and was "debriefed" at our consulate general. The China-watchers were intrigued by minutiae I'd have overlooked, such as the fact that the reprinted

Newsday editorial, in which I'd commented on our February invasion of Laos, contained this paragraph:

> Of course this latest adventure won't work. Nothing we have done in Indochina has worked. Not even last May's "incursion" that turned placid Cambodia into a slaughterhouse. A Reuter's news dispatch from Cambodia last week quoted "senior Cambodian officers' as saying that "the Viet Cong were returning to sanctuaries cleared by South Vietnamese and U.S. troops last summer and building new ones opposite South Vietnam."

Apparently this was the first time the Chinese had admitted, even indirectly, that there were Viet Cong troops in Cambodia.

We came home June 25 on a direct flight to New York. On the way, I jotted down some thoughts about China's future, three of which are worth repeating sixteen years later:

1. Materialism, individualism and personal ambition will adulterate "pure" Chinese communism as they have already modified some of the European varieties.
2. China is likely to play an increasingly active role in world affairs. It will take its United Nations seat when it's offered but won't beg for it or accept any two-China compromise.
3. U.S.-China relations will move toward normalization as we get better acquainted—whether or not the Nixon visit takes place.

And I couldn't disagree with Topping's conclusions, written in Hong Kong and published in the *Times* June 27: Access to China is essential if the country is to be understood and intelligent policy toward its government formulated. China is on the way to becoming a first-rate power. The Chinese Communist society is disciplined, militant and committed by its leaders to the ultimate goal of world communism, with Peking as its ideological center.

Sim and I both had more writing to do, and her TV footage was good enough for CBS to pay her $2,000 for it. Had we known that on July 15 the announcement of Nixon's forthcoming trip to China would be made, she could have waited and then sold it for much more. There didn't seem to be any up-to-date film about China in the United States —certainly none shot by Americans.

I phoned Kissinger when he returned from his secret mission, and he invited me to the White House July 27 to compare notes and impressions, off the record. We sat on a couch in his office, and he suggested that since we had forty minutes available, I should go on first for twenty minutes. Just as I was finishing my account, the phone beside him rang.

"I'm sorry," he said, putting down the receiver. "That was the president. He wants to see me right away. We'll talk again some other time."

No one will ever convince me that call wasn't prearranged with his secretary. No matter. What would he have told me that didn't turn up in his memoirs?

In fact, we did talk again less than a month later on the deck of Otis Chandler's beach house at Dana Point, just south of Laguna, California. Chandler was then publisher of the Los Angeles *Times* and had asked Kissinger to come up for a drink from nearby San Clemente. Chandler's parents and another couple were there, along with Sim and me, but Kissinger quickly took over the microphone, so to speak, to talk about Vietnamization, the latest gimmick that was going to bring our "boys" home without losing the war.

It was a difficult strategy to explain, let alone defend. Our one bargaining chip with Hanoi was an offer to withdraw troops unilaterally. But in April 1970, Nixon destroyed our leverage by announcing major troop withdrawals (150,000 by the end of the year) and then indicated he planned a phased evacuation of *all* U.S. forces. He and Kissinger seemed to believe that our bombing would meanwhile force Hanoi to its knees. It didn't, and when Kissinger finally cashed our chip in the fall of 1971, it was too late to extract any concessions from the other side. Hanoi knew all it had to do was stall negotiations until the American army had gone home—the bombing didn't intimidate them—and then sign an agreement that would ensure its victory over the South Vietnamese.

Which is what eventually happened. Rather than use our bargaining power while we still had a strong military presence in Vietnam, we spread indiscriminate carnage with bombers while bringing the army home. Defeat was thus effectively assured.

As George Ball wrote later:

No one but our soldiers, sailors and airmen who did the actual fighting emerged free from blame. The Eisenhower Administration promised limited aid for the Saigon government; the Kennedy Administration provided military equipment and greatly increased the number of military advisors; the Johnson Administration turned our limited commitment into an all-out engagement; and the Nixon Administration kept

America in the war a further four years at a cost in lives of 20,000 young Americans and several hundred thousand Vietnamese.

Kissinger must have sensed Vietnamization wouldn't work. If we couldn't prevail with 500,000 soldiers, how could the ARVN possibly prevail alone? Yet such was Kissinger's prestige that the people gathered at Dana Point that afternoon listened to him like a guru. I was reminded of what used to be said of Marshall McLuhan: He's not meant to be understood, he's meant to be respected.

Only Sim had the *chutzpah* to challenge Henry by posing the obvious question: How could the South Vietnamese possibly win alone when they couldn't win with us?

The only result of her question (which received an answer both sonorous and patronizing) was that she then got more attention from Kissinger than anybody else and was regarded by our hosts with a mixture of astonishment and awe.

Meanwhile, Washington had announced it wouldn't object to Peking's admission to the U.N., provided Chiang Kai-shek somehow retained his seat. This was in response to a joint resolution calling for Peking's admission that was sponsored by seventeen U.N. member countries on July 15—the very day Nixon's China visit was announced. A showdown was inevitable, since we'd been told in Peking a two-China membership formula would be unacceptable. This question came up every year and we had always managed to muster enough votes by cajolery and arm-twisting to exclude Peking and keep Taiwan in the Chinese seat. What was different this year was that it was harder for us to go on treating China as a pariah now that we were publicly edging toward a more cordial bilateral relationship.

Knowing how much importance Nixon attached to his Peking trip —now planned for February, followed by a Moscow visit in May—I couldn't believe we'd raise more than token objections to admitting the People's Republic to the U.N. on their terms. For if we succeeded in blocking Peking once again, the Chinese might conceivably react by canceling the Nixon visit.

But I gathered that George Bush, then our representative at the U.N., was fighting tooth and claw for a U.S. resolution stating that Taiwan's "expulsion" was "an important question" that, under the rules, required a two-thirds majority in the General Assembly. At a small dinner party Bush gave on October 17 in his Waldorf suite, Sim and I were amazed to hear him announce fervently, "I told the president today that I'm going to win this one for him!" He even emphasized his determination by striking his left palm with his right fist.

The vote came a week later, while Kissinger was making a second trip to Peking and after much counterproductive pressure in the U.N. by the U.S. delegation. When our "important question" resolution failed, 59–55 with 16 abstentions, it was all over, and there was literally dancing in the aisles. The next vote, on inviting Peking to occupy China's seat, was more lopsided—76–35 with 17 absentions. Even our traditional allies, like Britain and France, voted against us on both ballots. Although Bush referred to the outcome as "a moment of infamy," it was actually a vote in favor of realism and against fantasy. Since both Peking and Taipei agreed there was only one China, the subsequent uproar in Congress and the press over the "expulsion" of our gallant little Taiwanese ally was mindless, since Taiwan did not exist as a nation or U.N. member; its ousted delegation simply represented a defeated government that ruled over less than two percent of the Chinese people.

In a piece for *Newsday* that emphasized this distinction, I concluded by saying that George Bush rated a restful vacation "for having worked like hell against hopeless odds for a losing cause."

My guess is that the White House might well have passed the word quietly to our allies that the Bush effort was essentially a propaganda exercise directed at a public conditioned to be sentimental about Taiwan. Even the *New York Times* deplored the outcome, while admitting the vote was actually a plus for Nixon and would facilitate his negotiations in Peking. As Scotty Reston pointed out, "No doubt he agrees, at least in public, with Secretary of State Rogers that the vote in the U.N. is regrettable"; however, Reston added that in fact the U.N. had done Nixon a favor.

And perhaps George Bush, too. Three years later, he was named our special envoy to the People's Republic of China by President Gerald Ford, the "moment of infamy" long since obliterated from everyone's memory.

An era that cost us billions of dollars and thousands of lives was ending at last, and it's fair to say Nixon deserves much of the credit. He saw an opportunity and seized it. Had FDR not been preoccupied with Europe twenty-seven years earlier and done likewise, much postwar history might have been different. At the end of 1944, Mao Tse-tung offered to fly to Washington and reach a post–World War II agreement

with Roosevelt. The message was transmitted over U.S. military channels on January 9, 1945, from Mao's headquarters in Yenan.

But the overture was ignored. As a result, the U.S. became deeply
involved with the losing side of the Chinese civil war; Mao then made
up with Stalin, who in turn felt free to act more aggressively in Europe;
and North Korea, confident of Chinese support, saw no reason not to
attack South Korea.

All history is replete with "what ifs," but the years of our feud with
China seem to have produced far more than their share.

Chapter 15

Razryadka and Venceremos

WE AMERICANS ARE PRONE to characterize decades the way we do nations. Just as the Germans are stolid and the French frivolous, so are the 1890s supposedly "gay" (in the older sense of that word), the twenties "roaring," the thirties "depressed," the forties "fabulous," the fifties "flabby" and the sixties "turbulent." But the seventies are as yet undefined. True, the decade really didn't get started until 1974—after Watergate and Vietnam, which really belonged to the sixties; so it's hardly surprising the next six years are remembered, if at all, for little else than jogging, cocaine, the disco beat, CB radios and the Ayatollah.

But as a chapter in the seemingly interminable saga of the cold war, the seventies loom large. This was the decade that coincided almost exactly with the rise and fall of détente, a French word often confused with entente and never popular with Americans. President Gerald Ford formally jettisoned it from his political vocabulary in a speech in Peoria, Illinois, on March 15, 1976, figuring it would be safer to campaign that fall with the familiar old "peace through strength" slogan.

Two days later, I happened to leave on a prearranged trip to Moscow with David Laventhol, *Newsday*'s editor, and Bill Sexton, our associate editor, to see how the Russians viewed détente, which they called *razryadka,* a much more easily understood word meaning an easing of tension, an unwinding, like what you do at home after a hard day's work, or after a long cold war.

So we'll stay in Russia for a few pages and return later to the origins and unfulfilled promise of détente, a policy contrived by Nixon and Kissinger, starting in 1969 and never really scuttled until the end of the Carter Administration.

In a preliminary meeting with Ambassador Dobrynin in February, I explained we weren't doing an "inside Russia" series but wanted only to meet with officials "in a position to speak frankly about Soviet policy." As a result, we circulated mainly among what is called the *nomenklatura,* or "designated list"—an elite of probably not more than a million Communist Party members in all segments of Soviet society who are selected early in their careers to become an informal ruling class in the manner of Britain's onetime "old boy" network of Eton, Harrow, Oxford and Cambridge alumni.

First, some impressions: The changes in Moscow in the nine years since my last visit were even more striking than those I'd noted between 1956 and 1967. The airport, even in this chill and somber March, was choked with foreign tourists, part of the three million who now come here each year. A Novosti Press Agency delegation met and drove us past a forest of tall new apartment buildings to the twenty-story Intourist Hotel—a high-rise replica of an American motel with wall-to-wall carpets, functioning bathrooms, ample soap and a TV set in every room. I picked up the phone and was talking to my Long Island office in fifteen minutes. Credit cards were accepted. Tipping was taken for granted. Cafeteria-style breakfasts had done away with phlegmatic waitresses. Some non-Communist Western papers were now and then available at the newsstand.

Out on Gorky Street, the traffic was dense, the neon brighter, the crowds indistinguishable (except for fur hats) from any in Western Europe. On the train to Tallinn, a Russian lawyer borrowed our copy of *Newsweek* and read it openly, lying on his berth. In Leningrad, a TV drama looked like a fast-moving Italian movie with a Russian background. Among the youth, boys' hair was longer, blue jeans were common and they told us good grades and technical skills now counted for more than being a dutiful Party member.

Was anything outwardly the same? Well, the streets were just as safe at night, the air smogless, the subways palatial, the lines outside Lenin's mausoleum as long as ever, and hotel receptionists still looked and acted, as one travel writer put it, like women "who had all suffered long and harrowing love affairs."

Our days were filled with meetings—at Tass, *Izvestia, Pravda,* the Foreign Ministry, Moscow University and the three-year-old Institute for USA and Canada Studies, where a staff of 320 worked full-time studying developments in North America and reported directly to the Party's Central Committee. (Thanks to the Institute, the Soviet leadership was better informed than ever before about the United States.)

In all our talks, détente and China were the chief topics, and the prospects for the SALT II Treaty under President Ford the number one concern. The Russians wondered at our insistence on building the Cruise missile. Radomir Bogdanov, the Institute's deputy director, put it this way: "Ever since the last day of World War II, we've been running to catch up with you. We always do. It's a vicious cycle. Take the Cruise missile. We can make them, it's no problem at all. In fact, they're a lot cheaper and simpler than most of the weapons we build these days. The problem is that these missiles are a destabilizing factor. They put us back in the cycle—in the deadly spiral."

We soon discovered that "peace with America" was the uppermost concern of the average Russian and, among the elite, second only to the perpetuation of their own power. In some ways, the Russians we met knew more about our society than we did about theirs; in others, less. The Watergate scandal was frequently cited to us as a plot by enemies of détente to get rid of Nixon—a predictable if naive reaction of people long conditioned to conspirational politics. Thus we heard both sense and nonsense. But their emphasis on *razryadka* was insistent and plausible. In a world of nuclear weapons, we were repeatedly told, "the U.S. and the Soviet Union must agree to coexist in order to survive. There is no sane alternative . . ." At one meeting, Lev Tolkunov, a member of the ruling Central Committee (which elects the Politburo), leaned across the table to stress the Kremlin's stake in a more stable relationship: "I can assure you I speak for the entire Central Committee when I tell you we have a great many internal problems which can be solved only by peace and stability."

What they apparently had in mind was a Hertz-Avis kind of competition with plenty of hustle but a tacit understanding that nobody's cars would get smashed up.

We got the feeling from talking to this Soviet aristocracy that their country, for all the seeming rigidity of its orthodoxy, was a society in transition. Where conversation from their side once consisted largely of memorized Marxist phrases, there was now an effort at genuine communication (frequently in English). At a meeting with Foreign Ministry officials, we mentioned Angola—where Soviet aid to one of the three tribal factions had incensed American public opinion. The ensuing exchange went something like this:

"You were upset because it proved we were now a big power that could intervene in Africa, like you in Vietnam."

"Not at all. Americans just figured you were trying to pull a fast one after giving us a lot of sweet talk about détente."

"But we had an obligation to the MPLA: We supported their movement for many years. It's always been our policy to encourage national liberation movements. Anyway, why worry? Angola's too far away to be one of our client states."

"Okay, if those liberation movements are more important to you than relaxation of tensions, we can always resume the cold war."

"Now wait! You bombed Haiphong in 1972 and hit a Soviet ship and still we didn't cancel the Moscow summit. Why are you so touchy about Angola?"

"Americans don't like to feel they've been taken advantage of, especially by Cuban mercenaries."

"But what about Iran, where you're giving the Shah six billion in arms, maybe even a nuclear capability? We don't make a fuss over that. And now you have lured Sadat over to your side!"

"It's just going to save you some money you would have wasted on arms for Egypt."

Wry grins all around, while everybody expressed the hope that the process of détente wouldn't be held up by any more "miscalculations."

We also became aware of a widening generation gap in the power structure. The younger breed seemed more interested in Russian nationalism (and material progress) than in "proletarian internationalism." More inquisitive, too. After one long-winded meeting with a senior editor at *Izvestia,* his young deputy told us with surprising frankness it had been a waste of time. "All you got was the standard speech—none of us learned anything. Now let's have a drink and you can tell me more about China."

What was *not* different were the ingrained Russian characteristics that I'd noted before and that predate communism: intense patriotism, suspicion of foreigners, a collective inferiority complex and a preference for authority, even tyranny, to the only imaginable alternative—confusion and chaos. Time and again we heard about the Great Patriotic War: "We have more war victims buried in Leningrad's cemetery alone than you lost in three wars. What do you Americans know about suffering?" And time and again we noticed the chips on their shoulders: "Why are you going to Eastern Europe from here?" asked a TV commentator in Tallinn. "Just to show the Soviet Union in a bad light?" We gave a copy of *Time* to our interpreter, an attractive young woman named Ludmilla (who was thrilled to accompany us to meetings with celebrated Soviet journalists, like Viktor Nekrasov of *Pravda*). "I know this magazine will be filled with anti-Soviet propaganda," she said, "so

I will read it simply to practice my English." She added that most of the Americans she piloted around resembled Russians more than any other nationality but were "terribly uninformed." (One couple had recently asked her where the government kept the iron curtain.) We refrained from telling her she was too.

At the Institute for USA and Canada Studies, the talk was about our November election. Like most Soviet officials we met, the America-watchers favored Ford as "a known quantity and Nixon's choice" but figured that with Reagan and Wallace eliminated they'd anyway be dealing with a "reasonable president." They seemed astonished when I predicted Jimmy Carter would be Ford's opponent. Having met Carter the summer before at a publishers' convention and seen the mostly Republican audience give him a standing ovation, I decided then he was the man to watch. I'd also dined with him in Washington a few days before this trip and watched him charm and impress the thirty-odd guests—all members of the Georgetown establishment—simply by letting them do most of the talking and nodding agreement.

But the Russians had very little information about him, and when I produced a copy of a speech he'd just made on foreign policy, they reacted as if it were the Rosetta stone. "May we copy it?" asked the chief of the U.S. Domestic Politics branch. When I told him he could have the original, we were invited to lunch.

Before leaving Moscow for a few days' travel, we called on Walter Stoessel, the U.S. ambassador, who seemed to share the Russians' desire for a mutually acceptable SALT II Treaty. He also felt they were beginning to realize that détente was a process rather than a sudden change of course, given the decades of distrust we had lived through ever since 1918, when American troops landed in Archangel and Siberia in support of the White forces (an episode no Russian will let you forget).

Stoessel agreed with the Canadian ambassador, an old Moscow hand, that the Angola adventure was a Soviet blunder. Right in assuming we'd stay out of it (though the CIA had long backed the defeated Holden Roberto faction), the Kremlin was wrong to think American public opinion would not regard it as a violation of détente. Both envoys also thought the emerging, younger Soviet leaders were far more pragmatic than ideological in their approach to problems.

And the problems were plentiful: an economy hard to manage because not governed by supply and demand; a burdensome military budget; China—perceived as overpopulated and therefore expansionist; a succession of foreign policy setbacks—in Portugal, in Egypt and in West Africa; the prospects of confronting foreign Communist heretics reminiscent of the papacy during the Reformation; and restive ethnic minorities within the U.S.S.R.

We visited one of their ethnic republics, Estonia, whose capital, Tallinn, is one of Europe's most attractive small cities. The Hotel Viru, designed and built by Finns, could compete in style and service with any back home; a convention of architects in well-cut business suits and a nightclub floor show (all in English, German or Estonian) that rivaled Las Vegas, created an illusion that we were no longer in the Soviet Union, still drab despite all its cosmetic changes. Here you felt . . . well, almost in Europe. Even the TV antennae were extra tall in order to receive broadcasts from Finland, whose language is related to Estonian. This unusual privilege had been authorized by Moscow both as a safety valve and as a reward for high labor productivity.

We got a glimpse of the economic benefits of the velvet glove at the Kirov Kholkoz—a fishing collective east of Tallinn that encompassed entire villages in an area a hundred miles long. The director, with his limousine and paneled dining room, reminded us of an American corporate executive. He ran the place like the CEO of a subsidiary of a big corporation (in his case, the state) and reported to Moscow on a quarterly basis just as his American counterpart normally reported to his Board of Directors. (I knew the routine.) A native Estonian, he attributed Kirov's success to "our German attitude toward work," along with incentive bonuses, the right to own a home and a paternalistic policy that cared for Kholkoz members from kindergarten to retirement homes. I reflected that capitalism and communism might still be antithetical in theory but were more and more alike in practice.

We went on to Leningrad by overnight train. Seeking a dining car, I wandered into a third-class carriage. The scene was Hogarthian—dim, smoky, overcrowded, acrid, noisy and alcoholic. Someone challenged me and I shrugged, adding, *"Ya Amerikanski—nyeh panemayoo po Russki."* This was an error, since I was promptly seized, pulled into a compartment where an unappetizing flask of vodka was shoved at me while voices shouted *"Kharasho!" "Mir!" "Freundschaft!"* and "America good!" Détente in action at the grass roots could be unnerving, and I had a hard time escaping back to the sober serenity of first class.

After some further scouting and interviewing around Leningrad, we took the midnight express to Moscow. It was just as plush as when Sim and I took it in 1967, but I noticed it now departed in two sections— one at 11:59 P.M. and the other at 12:01 A.M. I asked about this, since

Dave and I had been put on the first and Sexton on the second. We were told there were no berths left on our train (there were), but not to worry, the sections arrived almost simultaneously. Then why two? The explanation was both halting and revealing. I knew a bureaucracy always takes care of its own, but only in a country where it is all-powerful can it adjust train schedules to its own benefit.

Here's how the two-train system worked: Moscow bureaucrats on a trip to Leningrad got a per diem allowance for each day they were there. So they returned to Moscow on the 12:01, since the one minute in Leningrad counted as a full day on their travel vouchers. But the Leningrad bureaucrats going to Moscow took the 11:59, sufficient evidence they were out of town on the day just ending. In Moscow, the process was reversed: the Leningraders took the later train and the Muscovites, the earlier one. And everybody made out at the expense of the state.

Sexton's assignment to the 12:01 was otherwise motivated. The passenger sharing his compartment turned out to be a comely young woman who happened to speak fluent English and traveled with a bottle of vodka. Bill looked sheepish enough in the Moscow dawn for us to assume it had been an enjoyable trip. The KGB had delicately chosen the only unmarried member of our group for this special treatment, and the young woman, who wanted only to hear Bill's impressions of the Soviet Union and of our "program," got what she wanted and maybe more—such as a commendation from her superiors.

Spring came to Moscow all of a sudden: On March 31, the sun was out, the snow melting and the fur hats put away. As we packed to leave, a call came from Victor Louis, a shadowy newspaperman used by the KGB for overt, purportedly journalistic assignments. Could we come to lunch at his dacha in Peredeliniko? His driver would take us from there directly to the airport. Why not? First, we asked Ludmilla to call Andrei Sakharov, then still in Moscow, for an appointment. She did so reluctantly, and, as we expected, he couldn't receive us. But we knew it was always helpful for the KGB phone-tappers to report that Western visitors had not forgotten him.

Viktor Sukhodrev was the other luncheon guest at the dacha, whose bar was stocked with Western liquors and whose garage contained a Mercedes and a Porsche. For a man who was ostensibly the Moscow correspondent for a second-rate London daily, Louis lived well. He told us Khrushchev had had a dacha nearby where he had lived in comfortable oblivion from his downfall in 1964 to his death in 1971.

It was soon obvious that the purpose of the lunch was to interrogate us about Jimmy Carter—not that we had much to tell them—and China, which Dave had recently visited. Sukhodrev seemed concerned about the influence of a viscerally anti-Soviet "Polish" academic like Brzezinski in a Carter Administration (as it turned out, with good reason). We naively reassured him by saying Zbig didn't have Kissinger's chutzpah and bravura and could be kept in line by a strong secretary of state.

Sukhodrev felt the "pragmatists" in China now had the support of the army and were prevailing over "the wild men of Shanghai." But he foresaw no Moscow-Peking détente for a while. With respect to the word, he remarked that "Americans should really look it up in the dictionary—for example, Merriam-Webster." The definition of détente therein is surely succinct: "a relaxation of strained relations or tensions (as between nations)."

And this is what more and more Americans were then turning against, to the point that Ford dared not use the term. So what did they want instead? More strain? More tension? Clearly not. Yet we now know that a period of jingoism and unreason, when even support for the carefully crafted Panama Canal Treaty was mindlessly attacked as practically treasonable by Ronald Reagan, Jesse Helms and others, was not far away, and is not yet over.

In a concluding editorial to our series of Soviet articles, *Newsday* deplored the "outdated perceptions" Americans had of the Soviet Union and suggested the U.S. was pursuing obsolete policies "such as equating national security with defense spending" even though the other side invariably caught up with us in a race no one could win. And the paper pleaded for "hard thinking" during the forthcoming national political campaign—something that had never happened before and of course did not happen in 1976.

From Moscow, Laventhol and I flew to Belgrade, while Sexton headed for Helsinki, East Berlin and Budapest. Dave went on to Paris, while I visited Bucharest and Rome. We found living standards had risen all over Eastern Europe—especially in diligent, disciplined East Germany. Nationalism was flourishing, and the iron curtain had rusted. Détente was popular, but many Europeans, east and west, feared a superpower deal at their expense; a détente between both halves of Europe seemed to offer them more tangible rewards. Recent remarks by Helmut Sonnenfeldt, a Kissinger aide, endorsing what he called "organic unity" between the Soviet Union and its client states, had evoked anxiety and bitterness, especially in Romania and Yugoslavia, countries that cherished their independence (very relative in Romania's case) from Soviet dictation.

In short, Eastern Europe was a far different place from the cowed but seething "prison" I remembered from our station wagon expedition in 1958.

There was no guide, like Mrs. Maniu, to meet me in Bucharest. The new Intercontinental Hotel's snack bar served cheeseburgers, its newsstand sold Western papers and a sign in the lobby announced the day's television movies in English. Dacia cars and taxis clogged the once empty streets. At my hotel, a renovated old inn called the Hanul Manuc, the wooden balconies overlooked a medieval cobbled courtyard, but the carved peasant-style chest in the bedroom concealed a TV set.

Just as surprising was the frankness with which officials, editors and the diplomats and professors of ADIRI (the Association of International Law and International Relations) talked with me—usually in French. Gone was their former reticence about discussing relations with the Soviet Union, although they evaded questions about the Ceauşescu regime. They now bragged about being the only Soviet bloc state to recognize Israel and Cambodia, to maintain cordial relations with China, to allow unfettered Jewish emigration, to remain on good terms with all the Arabs and to refuse to take part in the 1968 Kremlin-ordered fraternal invasion of Czechoslovakia. They saw their role as being that of a catalyst for global détente. But they knew how far they could go: Romanians never challenged Russian hegemony or internal repression.

The ADIRI people talked of real problems, of disarmament, trade, energy, the underdeveloped world and even ecology. They looked forward to the dissolution of both NATO and the Warsaw Pact ("ghosts —structures without substance") and hoped for an all-European security system within the framework of the 1975 Helsinki accords (which had been variously interpreted and applied by the thirty-five signatories).

Despite the stimulating conversation, three days in Bucharest were plenty. Harry Barnes, our able, Romanian-speaking ambassador, was good company but swamped with social obligations, so my evenings dragged. Aside from the wan jezebels in the expensive bars, Romanians were far more careful than Russians about associating with foreigners in public, and I was glad to catch the weekly Tarom flight to Rome. My last recollection of Bucharest's airport was a poster, in English, urging passengers to "come to Marlboro country" while a loudspeaker blared out "A Slow Boat to China." It would have been more accurate if the poster had read "Nixon country." For his visit there in 1969—the first by an American president—was still talked about with gratitude in this isolated Latin nation.

In Rome, an Italian friend took me straight from my hotel to Communist Party headquarters, where Paolo Bufalini, a member of parliament and of the Party's ruling directorate, gave me plausible reasons why they were now ready to renounce violence and enter a coalition with the Christian Democrats. (The French Communists took the same line with Laventhol in Paris.) The lead of my story from Rome summed it up:

> Italy's Communist Party—the biggest in the West—says it is now ready, willing and able to share in the fruits and responsibilities of power, to play by democratic rules and to permit NATO installations to remain in Italy.

What was happening in these countries, and in Spain as well, was that the Communists, who after the war hoped to seize power by staging paralyzing strikes and violent demonstrations, had seen their strength and influence begin to decline. It was now time to discard "proletarian internationalism" (the code phrase for "the Kremlin knows best") in favor of adjusting their tactics to local conditions. So I ended the piece thus:

> Are the Communists willing to play the game according to parliamentary rules, as Bufalini assured me? The answer is—they probably are, if only because it would be smart politics to do so and because the Red Army, far to the east, would not be in a position to back them up if they didn't.

For three more days in Rome, I holed up in my Via Veneto hotel writing my portion of the series we'd be collaborating on for the paper. It was a depressing interlude for me because the city was so full of memories—of Igor and our *Trib* jeep, of Lilo, of the camaraderie at the Stampa Estera, of the Bogarts in the Excelsior bar, of days and nights with Bergman and Rossellini and Bob Capa, of premarital excursions with Sim, of Adlai Stevenson and Claire Luce, of that vast, shifting cast of characters now either dead or dispersed. I called some old phone numbers that had been disconnected and looked in at the press club—

deserted but for a leftover drinker from the fifties who fortunately no longer recognized me. Walking back, up the Spanish Steps, I quickly realized I was now twice as old as when I used to commute effortlessly up and down these steps between my hotel and the *Herald Tribune* office. I paused twice, to catch my breath, then ate alone in a small trattoria and caught the next day's train to Venice, writing en route and hoping Sim and Suzy would be waiting for me there after a ski trip. I'd talked to enough Communists in the past three weeks and was ready for the gondolas and the pigeons of St. Mark's.

We must now backtrack to keep the rise and fall of détente during the seventies in some kind of orderly sequence. It won't be easy, because a period so dominated by men as complex as Nixon and Kissinger abounds in intricate maneuvering, rampant egomania, grand designs, petty rivalries, panache and deceit. We started in 1976 because that year heralded one more turning point in U.S.-Soviet relations. The code of conduct both powers had warily subscribed to when détente was launched four years earlier was starting to crumble. As Americans saw it, the abrasive issues were Soviet interference in Angola in 1975 and in the Near East in 1973, during the Egypt-Israeli "Yom Kippur" war, as well as attempted Communist subversion in Portugal. For their part, the Soviets resented our excluding them from a Near East settlement, interfering in their domestic affairs (notably human rights) and obstructing trade by linking credits to the rate of Jewish emigration.

This chapter promises to be long enough without trying to analyze all the twists and turns of this phase of the cold war. One book, Raymond L. Garthoff's *Détente and Confrontation*, devotes no fewer than 1,147 pages to it, about a quarter in six-point-type footnotes.

What follows, then, is simply a drastic condensation of events that have already been dissected not only by scholars but in the often conflicting memoirs of several participants. Your librarian can give you a list.

The high noon of détente lasted from 1972 to 1974. Nixon's first priority by 1970 was to get our troops out of Vietnam "honorably"; he knew Americans would not reelect him if he didn't. He figured both the Russians and the Chinese might be helpful with the Vietnamese, hence his overtures to Peking and Moscow in 1971 and his trips there in 1972. He liked the idea of a triangular diplomacy manipulated to American advantage. Arms negotiations didn't interest him as much as domestic politics, but he appreciated the appeal of the peace issue. I remember

Chief Justice Earl Warren telling me at a private lunch in his chambers in June 1970 that Nixon "thinks only of the next election" and therefore "spends most of his time reacting to Teddy Kennedy." (He also criticized him for being out of touch with America's youth, whom Warren called "reformist and radical but not revolutionary or destructive.")

Kissinger's interest in détente was to use it for building "a structure of peace" inspired, it would seem, by Metternich's success at the 1815 Congress of Vienna in achieving a diplomatic détente that ushered in several generations of relative stability, at least among the major powers. But the globe's power brokers, who in 1815 could all sit comfortably around one table, had by 1970 proliferated to the point that no single virtuoso could keep the first, second, third and fourth worlds in any sort of sync. Kissinger did try, even though he knew little of Africa and Latin America, but in time he came to resemble a frantic circus ringmaster trying to preside over so many acts that he couldn't prevent the lions from jumping off their stools or the bareback riders from falling off their horses. SALT, Vietnam, Berlin, China, the Near East, Portugal, Cuba, Angola, the Indo-Pakistani war of 1971, East-West trade—this welter of problems and a host of minor crises were just too much for any one man to handle.

Nixon gave him free rein and kept just about everybody else in the dark, especially the secretary of state, William Rogers, and his Department. When Kissinger flew to Moscow with Dobrynin in April 1972, for four days of talks with Leonid Brezhnev (to seal SALT and schedule the next summit), the U.S. ambassador, Jacob Beam, never even knew he was in town. At successive summits, Nixon would meet alone with Brezhnev and Sukhodrev without his own interpreter to record the conversation. So Kissinger himself was on occasion kept guessing. No wonder their memoirs (and those of others) often have such different emphases and contradictory perspectives.

There is no point in cataloging all of the errors of judgment—such as Kissinger's dismissal of Mario Soares (now Portugal's president) as the "Kerensky" of the 1974 democratic revolution. But, it was clear the indefatigable and peripatetic Dr. K. was not always in control; small wonder his nerves became as frayed as the fabric of détente itself.

When a *Newsday* editorial on April 16, 1975, called for his resignation because he had "misled the world for two years about secret understandings between Richard Nixon and Nguyen Van Thieu," Kissinger blew his top. I got a call that morning from Bob McCloskey, the State Department spokesman and normally reasonable, that was peppered with loud expletives and complaints about "the boss" being "on my ass." But, contrary to his flat denial, there was indeed an exchange of letters between the two leaders committing the U.S. to send more aid to Saigon and to "react vigorously" to violations of the Paris peace accords.

Kissinger never forgot that editorial. Two years later, after Ford's defeat, we met at a party and he remarked sardonically, "Well, I finally took your advice." And even later, he told my teenage daughter at a reception, "Every week for four years, your father demanded my resignation."

We digress. I've cited Nixon's reasons for supporting détente and also Kissinger's. What about the Russians'?

Their aim was basically to achieve parity with the U.S. This is why they liked the SALT Treaty, which became known as the "flagship of détente." Khrushchev had affirmed parity a decade earlier by bluster and bluff. Brezhnev didn't have to; for all practical purposes both nations now had the capacity to destroy each other and most of the world. This was the new and unprecedented reality. And Nixon, who said in 1957 that parity would create "a crisis of the first order," had quietly accepted reality.

And so, because Europe was ready for it, because West German and Berlin treaties were signed in 1971, because we had alarmed the Russians by making up with China, because peace in Vietnam was now in sight, because of promising arms talks and a Soviet desire for trade with the West—because of all these converging factors, détente was launched at the Moscow summit in May 1972, in the form of twelve accords, both military and civilian, including "détente's charter"—a document called Basic Principles of Relations between the USA and the USSR. This was a call for "peaceful coexistence," to which the Soviets attached great importance since they interpreted it as a license to support "national liberation movements" wherever no direct confrontation with us was likely.

In the brief golden age of détente, three more summit meetings were held—in 1973 in the United States, and in 1974 on the Black Sea and later, after Ford had replaced Nixon, at Vladivostok. Nixon, facing impeachment, was understandably distraught at his last meeting with Brezhnev but still prescient enough to warn the Russians, in urging more Jewish emigration, that "if détente unravels, the hawks will take over in America, not the doves."

Meanwhile, our involvement in Vietnam came to an end, Sadat

expelled the Soviet military mission from Egypt, we established diplomatic relations with East Germany and even considered lifting the trade embargo on Cuba, a U.S.-Soviet rendezvous was set up in space, a Prevention of Nuclear War agreement was signed along with the thirty-five-nation Helsinki accords, and the dominoes didn't fall as predicted in Southeast Asia—except later and against each other, when Communist China invaded Communist Vietnam because Communist Vietnam invaded Communist Cambodia.

But the unraveling of détente was under way by the time South Vietnam collapsed in April 1975, an event that brought home on our TV screens the futility of our longest war. As Averell Harriman wrote me, "I think that everything that was done by the Nixon Administration in Vietnam was wrong . . . Humphrey would have settled the war in 1969; whereas Nixon carried it on for three years, during which time we lost 40 percent of all those Americans who were killed in the war."

Our national ego needed a lift, and Ford provided it in May when he ordered air strikes on Cambodia and sent marines to rescue thirty-nine crew members of an American-flag freighter detained by the Khmer Rouge. He probably remembered the *Pueblo* incident in Korea, but that ship, unlike the *Mayaguez,* was on an intelligence-gathering mission. Anyway, we lost forty-one men attacking an island while the crew was being voluntarily released elsewhere—and later, went ahead and hit the town of Kompong Son with yet another air strike. It was not our most glorious military operation, but Ford's popularity soared in the polls. Nothing stirs our patriotic juices more than having marines storming a beach under fire, even when the beach is on the wrong island and their mission already accomplished.

Really good news was unexpected. When the Portuguese Socialists foiled an attempted Communist coup in 1975, Vermont Royster, the sage of the *Wall Street Journal,* expressed the surprise "of almost every outside observer," even though self-proclaimed Communists never had seized power west of Russia unless the Red Army was within driving distance.

One last vignette of this time sticks in my mind. After Lon Nol was overthrown in Cambodia in 1975, Sihanouk, as nominal chief of state, was sent to New York in October to plead the new coalition regime's case at the U.N. He was staying at the Essex House with Monique, and invited us to call on them one morning. (We had corresponded ever since Peking and he regularly sent me messages to forward to the president.) Sim couldn't come, so I brought Jan, then living on a farm in Delaware and up for a weekend visit wearing blue jeans and work boots. In his suite we sipped champagne and talked Cambodian politics: He had no illusions that, as a non-Communist, he would exert much influence, but he clearly underestimated the ruthlessness of Pol Pot. Meanwhile Jan and Monique chatted in French. When we finally took our leave, Jan impulsively kissed him, which he minded not at all, and we boarded the elevator. All eyes were riveted on us: What was this middle-aged man in a business suit doing here with this gorgeous, scruffy and slightly tipsy teenager? (She was twenty-three but looked sixteen.) Then she exclaimed, "How about that! Guzzling champagne with the prince at ten A.M.—and me in my shit-kicker boots! Do you think it bothered the princess when I kissed him?"

The tingle of curiosity in that elevator was almost palpable; at least our fellow passengers had something to speculate about all day long.

So we return, after this retrospective digression, to 1976, the year Carter edged out Ford and kept détente alive a few more years, even though Kissinger had warned in the spring that it "could not survive any more Angolas." Since the Cuban troops were there at the Luanda government's request to repel South African/FLNA/UNITA assaults that almost reached the capital, this remark made little sense, unless he assumed the Russians were fomenting all the tribal and regional unrest. (In fact, the Russians assisted but did not press for the Cuban expeditionary force.)

Carter used and then discarded an even more unfortunate French word than détente—malaise, which was meant to characterize America's post-Vietnam mood. But détente did continue to flourish in divided Europe, where trade and travel in both directions were punching more holes in the old iron curtain. A shortage of hard currency rather than minefields was becoming the main obstacle for the average East European wishing to visit the West, while tourism from the West to the East was actively sought.

As a Democrat, I now had more friends in the Washington bureaucracy and got in touch with the designated secretary of state, Cyrus Vance, during the transition about a trip to Cuba. Téofilo Acosta, a Cuban acquaintance and intelligence officer now serving at the Cuban U.N. Mission, had suggested it to me in October, but I said I'd go only on condition we could fly there in a private plane. (Going commercial involved a detour via Mexico City, an arduous route Sim and I had taken in 1969.) Jan was by then engaged to Dick duPont, whose cousin Kip, a Cessna dealer, owned a DC-3. So we decided to assemble an airborne expedition if we could get clearance.

Vance wrote me a note December 20 saying he'd want to see me after I returned from Cuba. I showed it to Acosta a couple of weeks later, and within a few days he reported it was okay for the plane and that we'd also be meeting with Castro. Bill Moyers and Congressman Jack Bingham also made this pilgrimage in the first weeks of the Carter presidency as part of an unofficial probe of Cuban receptivity to negotiations. Cuba's relations with other Latin American countries had been improving: In 1975 the Organization of American States had voted, 16–3 with two abstentions, to lift diplomatic and political sanctions against Cuba—with the U.S. joining the majority. But in October 1976, a Cuban exile named Orlando Bosch, jailed but then paroled in the States, where he had CIA connections, blew up a Cubana Airlines plane taking off from Barbados. All seventy-three people aboard were killed, including Cuba's fencing team, and Castro announced there could be no agreements with us until this "terrorist campaign against Cuba is ended once and for all."

So it seemed like a good time to reestablish contact and see if a fresh start was possible with a new administration in Washington. Already, on February 5, Washington announced it was ready to normalize relations with Cuba, regardless of Angola, thereby reversing the policy laid down by Kissinger just ten months earlier.

There was a personal reason, too, for my wanting to make this trip. Ever since our aborted U.N. negotiations in 1963, I'd had a nagging sense of unfinished business where Cuba was concerned. I'd wanted for years to complete what had been started, however it turned out.

In March, the State Department lifted the seventeen-year ban on travel to Cuba by ordinary U.S. citizens and on spending dollars there, but in February I still had to get our group's passports validated for Cuba. I went to see Phil Habib, now under secretary of state, who told the security officer in charge of such matters to stamp all our passports. No problem—but how? As a certified journalist, my validation was automatic. But the security officer was stumped by my companions. Simone? "My wife—also my secretary." Janet? "My daughter and interpreter." Susan? "Other daughter—photographer." Richard C. duPont? "Pilot." Richard S. duPont "Copilot." How about Caroline duPont? I hesitated. "Stewardess?"

The man finally smiled. "I love it," he said. "One newspaperman with a retinue like the Shah's—and everybody technically legitimate."

We flew to Havana from Palm Beach on February 20. Kip, who had never been allowed inside Cuban air space, was as excited as an astronaut making contact with a Martian when the Cuban controller came on the radio and gave us our flight path.

Two men from the Foreign Ministry and the president's office and two women interpreters met us at José Marti Airport and drove us to a villa on the beach at Santa Maria, east of Havana, where a cook and two cars and drivers were put at our disposal. After a swim with some Canadian and East German tourists, we explored the old city and dined at Las Ruinas, one of Havana's showplace restaurants.

The city had changed only slightly: It was cleaner and there were now more new European cars than old American ones on the streets, but shelves in the shops looked just as bare. There were fewer militant anti-Yankee billboards and signs extolling Fidel; instead people were exhorted to work, study and save. *Venceremos*—we shall overcome—was the watchword. Our escorts said we'd be meeting the boss in due course; meanwhile there was a "program."

It was a pretty good program. We spent the morning at the General Maximo Gomez High School—about thirty miles out of town, which turned out to be both new and different from any I'd seen (twenty-three similar schools, we were told, were in operation nationwide). The students boarded there and alternated a half day's study with a half day's labor on the school farm, raising produce that they both consumed and sold to help support the school. Weekends they went home, most of them to Havana. We lunched in the mess hall, toured the well-scrubbed dormitories, listened to the school band (soft rock and rhumba) and left feeling we'd seen something that worked. Americans were and are still prone to sneer at Cuba—and God knows it's never been a bastion of civil rights or civic affluence—but the government had, by 1977, all but wiped out illiteracy, something the U.S. has yet to accomplish, let alone Latin America.

Later José Fernandez, the Cuban commander at the Bay of Pigs and now minister of education, answered our questions for an hour, and his commitment to scholarship—with scant regard for ideology—was intense, as well as unusual in a self-proclaimed Communist society. Even stalwart Delaware Republicans like the duPonts came away impressed by his dedication to the ideals of a "revolution" he considered peculiarly Cuban.

Ricardo Escartín, our escort from the Foreign Ministry, told us to hang around the beach house in the evening as Fidel might be dropping by. He didn't, so we had a welcome rest, which we made up for the next day by visiting the Alamar Housing Project, a community of 150,000 built in their free time by the workers who would be occupying it; and also Fidel's elder brother, Ramón, a burly, genial farmer who managed a 110,000-acre cattle ranch and dairy cooperative fifty miles away and disclaimed any interest in politics ("I leave that to Fidel"). The dairy made its own yogurt with Bulgarian culture, and Suzy managed to put away four containers of it beneath a wall poster depicting Uncle Sam being decapitated by a Cuban arrow. "Don't mind the poster," Ramón told her. "That's just politics. Have another yogurt." And she did.

Back at Santa Maria, we found tension and agitation: Fidel had been trying to find us, and no one at the presidential palace knew we'd gone to Ramón's. He now expected us at nine, which gave us half an hour to wash up while Suzy, not unsurprisingly, became sobbingly sick and Caroline got trapped in the bathroom. But we roared up to the palace only three minutes late and were greeted by Castro—calm, courtly and only slightly heavier and grayer than when Sim and I had met him nearly eighteen years before.

After introductions, I thanked him on everyone's behalf for his hospitality, and on my own behalf expressed the hope we were now on the path of reason in Cuban-U.S. relations and that I'd be interested in hearing his views. When I ran out of words, Castro took charge. First, he went around the room, asking everyone what he or she did—work, study, hobbies, sports—with some casual but highly appreciated compliments for the women. And did anyone have any questions before he answered mine? Jan asked one, I think about health care in the countryside.

"Es una buena pregunta," he said, looking at me. "Su hija está muy inteligente."

Jan, accustomed to being praised more for her looks and charm than her intellect, became an instant Fidelista.

When he had captivated all his audience, one by one, he turned back to me and said, "As for your question, it raises three points, and the answer to the first may be divided into four parts, as follows."

And he then proceeded to respond, apparently having composed the answers in his mind while we were chatting. Whatever Castro may be—dreamer, tyrant, spellbinder—he's no slouch at organizing his thoughts and words. A few of those he articulated that night bear repeating ten years later:

On relations with the U.S.: "It's up to you. If you want to be friends, we'll be friends. If you want to go on being our enemy, we'll be your enemy. We've grown used to it. You can go on making life hard for us, but we have ways of being disagreable too, if that's what you want. . . . I was for Carter because he'd never made anti-Cuban statements and seemed to be a moral, realistic and sincerely religious man. Now I'm not so sure. Carter sounds more moralistic than moral."

Later, mellowing, he said Carter might still be learning to be a president and that he, Castro, would do or say nothing to upset the applecart for the time being. But he wished Carter would stop telling Cuba how to behave. What if he, Castro, said he'd meet with us only on condition we withdraw our troops from Korea, Europe, Taiwan, Panama and so on? Or even Guantanamo? "And what about human rights in America—for the jobless, the urban blacks, the Chicanos and the Indians?"

On Africa: "Cuba feels an obligation to help other struggling young countries . . . When the Angolans tell us they no longer need us, we shall leave. We now have five thousand civilians working there to maintain public services, and slightly more than that many troops, as a shield against South Africa. But the Cuban presence was not imposed." (He also asked me what it was like to be an American ambassador in Africa and what I thought of Sékou Touré, whom he considered highly intelligent. I told him Touré seemed to have gone crazy—*"Creo que ahora está loco."* No comment.)

On Kennedy: "By 1963 he had learned a great deal. He would have become a great president." (Castro recalled my exploratory talks at the U.N. and felt Kennedy was killed by certain elements, including Cuban exiles, who feared U.S. policy in Cuba and Vietnam was about to change. He mentioned Lee Harvey Oswald's vain attempt to get a Cuban tourist visa as a possible provocation aimed at pinning the murder on Castro ("Was it even Oswald who applied?") and suggested I read the material Cuba turned over to the Warren Commission.

On Vietnam: He thought it was a good thing we exposed Nixon's misdeeds but wondered at the hue and cry over Watergate compared to the relative silence over the war—which he considered a far greater crime. I pointed out that public opinion did eventually stop the war but also that fifty thousand Americans had died and far more were wounded there, and it was hard enough for their families to think they had suffered in vain, let alone that they were criminals. Castro pulled thoughtfully on his beard and then said quietly that he understood.

On Cuba's economy: He admitted the Soviet Union was keeping it afloat by paying inflated prices for Cuban sugar and selling oil to Cuba cheap. But Cubans had learned from their mistakes, and crop diversification plus more trade with Western Europe was making a difference.

There was more, dated now, but when daiquiris were passed around and conversation became general again, his informality was contagious. We certainly felt no compunction about contradicting him. When someone mentioned the book *Roots,* and he said we had killed off many blacks and most of our Indians, I denied this and said his own Spanish ancestors had a much worse record. Well, he said, at least they mixed well with the blacks. I said yes, and usually the black was a girl, and flat on her back.

And he was still curious about everything: *Newsday* and statistics about newsprint, profits and wages; my daughters' activities; the du-Ponts' business ventures; my wife's work as a realtor (it surprised him she held a job at all, as well as the fact that we had no servants); what we did weekends (he'd taken up bowling) and how I commuted. We even argued about the number of New York City's bridges and which ones had toll booths.

Some time after midnight we adjourned because, he said, Suzy at thirteen should not stay up so late. It was obvious he still liked Americans (as most of the world's radical leaders did then—far more than they did the taut and formal Russians), but his political and economic outlook had been deformed by Marxist indoctrination in the last twenty years.

In the memo I wrote later for the secretary of state, I said:

> He's a born leader . . . Now we have another momentary opportunity to get through to him and perhaps influence his actions. He still wants to believe in Carter's intentions and integrity. So I hope we don't fumble this chance, because all we have to do is simply treat Cuba like any other "socialist" country and then sit down and resolve a few unresolved issues, most of them minor.

One way to start, of course, would have been to lift the trade embargo, which was achieving no real purpose other than helping perpetuate Cuba's economic dependence on the Soviet bloc. The Cubans also regarded it, not without reason, as an act of aggression which had to cease before "peace talks" could get under way. A proposal to end the embargo was rejected in the Senate Foreign Relations Committee later in 1977 even though advocated by the U.S. Businessmen's Conference. (A 142-page report by Business International, a New York consulting firm for multinationals, concluded: "Don't let anyone tell you there are no opportunities in Cuba. There are . . . Dismantling the embargo will be an enormous and welcome step forward.") But the Cuban exiles, still dreaming of another invasion, had a more effective political lobby.

After our meeting with Castro, we headed for Varadero, where he had urged the duPonts to visit their former family estate—now a restaurant where Sim and I had lunched in 1969. When Kip said his parents had honeymooned there, Castro slapped his thigh and exclaimed, "That means you were probably conceived in Cuba! It's too bad you don't *look* Cuban, like your cousin here."

Before driving down the coast, we visited a children's holiday camp, where small girls in red scarves and berets led us politely through an exhibit honoring Che Guevara; and later, our friend Roberto Retamar, at the Casa de Las Americas, where we were greeted like fellow revolutionaries. He looked forward to cultural contracts with U.S. Hispanic communities when the long-awaited "normalization" took place. Over the years I'd grown used to the Communist custom of exempting individual Americans—and indeed the American "masses" in general—from the policies and actions of our government. It certainly made for congeniality and I knew it was futile to argue, as I had many times, that foreign policy in our system cannot deviate too far for too long from public opinion; but the duPonts were surprised by the genuine warmth of our Casa hosts as we sipped coffee and discussed the "institutionalization of the revolution" beneath the defiant anti-American posters that adorned the walls.

Of course, Cuban communism has never seemed as stern, at least in demeanor, as the European varieties. One day, when Dick duPont and I were riding in one of the assigned cars with the two interpreters and driver, he jokingly suggested we might all slip away to some isolated beach for some weekend dalliance. Such a suggestion would have met with shocked and reproachful silence in Russia; but our two young women giggled with glee and the driver cheerfully guaranteed to keep the excursion discreet. We pressed on to Varadero, but in a merrier mood.

Xanadu, the duPont mansion, was still an elegant restaurant, and the former golf course, converted to a sheep meadow in 1969, was being restored. But when the duPonts introduced themselves to the manager, he kissed Caroline's hand and seemed about to genuflect. It turned out he'd been an assistant butler in the old household. After showing them the old paperbacks still on the shelves and the family portraits on the piano, he led us upstairs, unlocked a bureau drawer and brought out a pile of old photo albums with snapshots of festive gatherings at the estate with Batista and his bunch. Kip recognized some aunts and uncles.

"You see," said the former retainer, "nothing has been disturbed. You could move back in tomorrow."

Instead, we moved into the hotel, where we found Ben Bradlee of the Washington *Post* waiting for *his* interview with Castro. While the others went fishing, he and I talked shop, and I decided to write up my interview as soon as I got home, even though the Cubans had specified this was to be a "private talk," presumably for transmittal to Vance and Carter only; Castro felt this was not a time for public rhetoric but for quiet diplomacy and mutual gestures of good faith. But on the way back to Havana, Escartín indicated that a quick story just now might be useful since Fidel was getting fed up with Carter's "moralizing" statements implying he was setting preconditions for productive bilateral talks. Escartín feared Castro might retort in anger and wreck the chances for a fresh start.

"He's tired of being told how to behave by Washington," he said. "After being bullied, harassed and invaded by Americans for nearly twenty years, we can take only so much lecturing before telling you to mind your own business."

So I filed a piece that evening from Palm Beach warning that "one more public reference by Carter to Cuba's internal or foreign policies will provoke an emotional response from Havana that would scuttle the first real opportunity in more than a decade for ending the seventeen-year cold war between the two countries."

And I added, "All these years of struggle and austerity have made this generation of Cubans extraordinarily tough, skeptical, disciplined, patriotic and feisty. They are prepared for a settlement of differences, but only if we deal with them as a sovereign nation and not as juvenile delinquents."

Carter did quiet down, and over the next few months we signed agreements on fishing rights and discussed cooperation in rescue operations, drug enforcement and antiterrorism. U.S. reconnaissance flights were halted and all Americans in Cuban jails released. And we opened diplomatic missions in Washington and Havana—"Interest Sections" attached to the Czechoslovak and Swiss embassies, respectively.

Our group left José Marti Airport with only a modicum of confusion. The security office couldn't find our passports, so the officer in charge offered me his chair while he went to look for them. The phone rang a couple of times but I simply answered, *"No está aqui."* Still, it was larkish to be in charge of security at Havana's air terminal, if only for a few minutes. Our plane, with the American flag painted on its tail, was parked next to a huge Aeroflot passenger jet. As we gathered for final *embrazos* with our Cuban companions, the Soviet captain emerged from his aircraft, glanced at our DC-3 and did an old-fashioned double take. An American plane at José Marti was then as unexpected as a Montgolfier balloon, since the Pan American airlift flights used Varadero airport. The Russian must have figured we'd been hijacked.

Home again, I checked with Vance, who asked for my memo. I sent him about 1,500 words and then Brzezinski phoned. He'd heard about a memo I was writing for Vance and wanted a copy "to show the president." I should have suggested he ask Vance for a copy. But a call from the White House usually gets results. So I said okay. "Keep it short," he added.

Years later, I mentioned this to Vance, who just smiled. "Zbig wanted to be in on everything," he said, "even things that weren't happening. Sometimes he would tell me the president wanted something done—and it wasn't true."

Vance, a quiet man who believed in patience, principle and the power of reason, was no match in the end for the man who believed in confrontation and coercion—and who above all had ready access to an impressionable president.

A letter from Bill Moyers a short time later reported on a lunch he'd had with the president, who now agreed that public criticism of Castro served no purpose: "He nodded approvingly when I said progress had to be achieved in private because Castro could no more negotiate with a megaphone in his ear than Carter could. . . . There is a chance of a breakthrough."

Cuban troops in Africa remained the main obstacle to normalization, as State Department spokesman Hodding Carter declared early in 1979, even though the troops were there at the request of countries that were under attack—Angola by Savimbi's rebels and South Africa, and Ethiopia by Somalia. We had dispatched troops for years to many corners of the world to help defend threatened friends, but where Cuba was concerned, it was always understood that a double standard applied.

There was a summit meeting in Vienna in June 1979, at which Carter and an already ailing Brezhnev signed a SALT II Treaty, exchanged friendly toasts and kept détente's flame flickering a little longer. Carter also assured Brezhnev that our establishing formal diplomatic relations with China in March had no anti-Soviet connotation. Meanwhile, Western Europe's once militant Communists had turned tame and sought respectability and perhaps a taste of power by talking up democracy and "Eurocommunism"—a word meaning greater independence from the Kremlin. I'd heard it broached during my stopover in Rome in 1976, and now, soon after our return from Cuba, I received an invitation from the Communist mayor of the city of Florence to participate in its celebration of our bicentennial, never mind that 1977 was the wrong year. The Italian friend who'd taken me to see Bufalini had recommended me to the mayor. It was a weekend affair, and our newly appointed ambassador, Richard Gardner, could not get confirmed in time to attend; so I accepted and agreed to give the speech in his place. The U.S. consular staff, whose instructions had been to view Eurocommunism with alarm, were somewhat discomfited when I played down the threat and told the gathering that Italians had had enough experience with a Fascist dictatorship to prevent Communists from imposing another on them; but if the Communists really wanted to play by the rules, why not welcome the repentant sinners to the parliamentary fold, while naturally keeping an eye on them?

The speech was well received, perhaps because those delivered by Italian academics were incomprehensible, even in translation. But Eurocommunism, as I suspected, had no future. The political alignment then emerging in Western Europe (and now a reality) resembled our own—with a center-left coalition that included socialists vying with a center-right coalition that included conservatives. Extremists, whether Communists or ultra-right, were being relegated to the impotent fringes of the political spectrum. So the totalitarian menace we used to write about so urgently and repeatedly in *Collier's* many years before proved to be no match for the unity, stability, prosperity and hope we Americans, starting with the Marshall Plan, did so much to promote.

As a publisher concerned with administrative and fiscal matters, I could no longer be as directly involved with cold war developments as in the past, yet I kept abreast of them, and on vacation trips even caught glimpses of the continuing action. One such opportunity occurred in November 1977, when I decided to make one more journey to Egypt, this time with Sim and Suzy, to see some of the sights we'd always missed on previous working visits. Cairo was as usual worse than the time before—smoggier, dustier, noisier—and the phones had finally stopped working altogether. Even the once romantic desert road to the Giza pyramids was now engulfed by urban sprawl, and at the now vast and charmless Mena House it was hard even to find a proper camel; everything had been motorized. So as soon as Suzy had seen Giza we boarded a Nile cruise ship at Luxor—on the very day Anwar Sadat made his bold and dramatic flight to Israel. The reporter in me missed not being there, while the middle-aged executive I'd become was content to ruminate in a deck chair. But I did want to see the event, so where was a TV set? Only in the crew's quarters, according to the bartender.

After dark, he led us below, where chairs and coffee were brought out and an English-speaking steward translated the narration for us. The arrival scene at floodlit Lod Airport was exciting, riveting and unforgettable, especially for someone like me who had heard nothing but a steady drumbeat of hostility between Arabs and Jews for thirty-five years. And the Egyptian crewmen with us seemed stirred as well. I asked the steward what they were saying.

"They are very surprised and pleased that the Israelis look just like us and that they are applauding our president."

I had a feeling that night of something happening that would set in motion a gradual but irreversible change in the history of this tormented region. Today, despite Sadat's murder by Muslim extremists in 1981 and Begin's subsequent aggression in Lebanon and illegal infiltration of the West Bank, I still believe that Sadat's trip, followed by Jimmy Carter's valiant mediation at Camp David, will be remembered as a turning point in the blood-drenched sequence of Near East events since World War II.

And I was glad to get a glimpse of it on the River Nile in the company of startled Arab sailors.

My last excursion into diplomacy took place a year later, at the biennial UNESCO conference in Paris. For some time, the Soviets had been pressing for adoption of a "Declaration on the Mass Media," booby-trapped with clauses reflecting their view of relations between government and the press. There were references in their draft document to licensing and "protection" of journalists, as well as to taboo topics (like incitement to war) that were inconsistent with Western concepts of press freedom. So action on the Declaration kept getting postponed to avoid a bruising showdown in UNESCO until now, in 1978, when the Senegalese director-general, Amadou M'Bow, decided he wanted the thing voted on and removed from the agenda. The draft was still unacceptable to us and other free press countries, but approval was likely since it sounded all right to most Third World delegates. We therefore had three options: to try to get another postponement—which we knew was a hopeless endeavor; to try to transform it into an acceptable document—something the State Department didn't believe could be done; or to vote against it and be defeated by a Soviet bloc–Third World coalition. Although the Declaration was unenforceable, such a document could be invoked by police states to restrict the activities of journalists, and its adoption would certainly discredit UNESCO in the eyes of Western democracies. These considerations led some of us to favor a stab at modifying it rather than to accept defeat.

While none of this sounds vitally important in the context of life and death cold war issues, the 1978 UNESCO exercise deserves some space because it provided a case history of how to achieve an objective through negotiation and compromise when you sense that righteous confrontation, while easier and more emotionally satisfying, is sure to fail.

Confrontation is also more popular, as politicians well know. Senator Pat Moynihan weighed in on this issue before the conference opened with a statement urging the U.S. delegation to "thunder our contempt for this contemptible document" and to refuse to listen to any speaker "who did not circulate in advance an editorial critical of his government." He more or less reflected the sentiments of the *New York Times,* whose management has consistently opposed any code of conduct for the press, a stalwart position that can occasionally be carried too far. Well, Pat is a good senator and entertaining companion, and the *Times* an indispensable newspaper.

My own involvement in this controversy came about when some Associated Press executives proposed me as the media representative on the five-person American delegation headed by USIA Director John Reinhardt. The White House approved the appointment, the FBI investigated me for the hundredth time and in October I was flying to Paris once again on a government voucher and an $88 per diem allowance, a sum insufficient to live on in our assigned hotel, the Paris Sheraton, without subsisting on CARE packages and washing one's own clothes. The Department had not changed, frugality-wise. (Ours was the only delegation at the conference that went to work by bus and subway, but sometimes the Togolese ambassador gave me a lift back in his Mercedes.)

A month before, I'd become *Newsday*'s chairman in preparation for my intended retirement in 1979 at age sixty, and could therefore turn over most of my publisher's duties to my successor, Dave Laventhol, that fall, and devote full time to UNESCO intrigue.

And intrigue of sorts it turned out to be. Perhaps the best way to explain it is to quote these excerpts from my daily diary:

October 23—No one here or in Washington seems to think there's much chance of amending the Declaration enough to make it acceptable.

October 25—Somebody heard M'Bow's friend and attorney, Boissier-Palun, indicate willingness to be flexible. Phoned him at home as he was preparing to leave for New York. Borrowed Reinhardt's car and met him in airport lounge in time to express concern we were headed for a confrontation that could damage UNESCO. Boissier agreed and offered to meet me next week to go over Declaration line by line and amend it. Reported to State Department by telegram which apparently revived option of negotiating a new text.

October 26—Delegation agreed we should pursue Boissier channel and coordinate efforts with Information Group consisting of twenty-six Western European nations plus Canada, Japan, Finland, Greece and Turkey. Meanwhile, we appear to be the only delegation instructed to vote no on Namibia admission. Reinhardt asked Department for authority to abstain since problem essentially legalistic and now is when we need Third World support. He also assigned me responsibility for negotiating mass media issue in part because I spoke French and had met Boissier.

October 27—Informed Italian chairman of IG of Bossier meeting and got his encouragement to pursue. Apprised AP's Stan Swinton in New York of developments.

October 30—Got green light from Department on discussions with Boissier and on Namibia vote abstention.

October 31—Informed IG meeting of our intention to seek revisions. Attended meeting of 11-nation subcommittee of Fourth Committee that included Russians and non-aligned and was charged with editing draft Declaration. We decided to use this group, headed by Wagner, a Peruvian, as decoy while negotiating acceptable compromise privately with Boissier. Set up meeting with him for Nov. 2. He had seen Swinton in New York.

November 2—Met M'Bow reps Boissier and Wynter (of Jamaica) with Deputy Asst. Secretary George Dalley and Al Kreczko of State's legal staff, both in from Washington. Worked our way through preamble in empty office near Director-General's suite. Looked in on Wagner committee, then we resumed editing in evening with Boissier. Reached agreement on all but one preambular paragraph.

November 3—Tried to explain our strategy to *Time* and Washington *Post* reporters who don't believe we can produce innocuous text. Convinced them worth making effort to put Soviets in minority position and improve relations with Third Worlders in view upcoming conferences. Met again with Boissier and others, finished preamble and worked human rights into title. Nuances of wording in French text a problem. Attended Wagner committee meeting later which got nowhere as expected.

November 4—Met all morning with Boissier group plus Italian rep and changed first four articles. White House rep arrived and I briefed him. Feel optimistic since clear M'Bow wants our support and just needs text of roughly same length with enough similar boilerplate wording to save face.

November 6—Wynter confirmed their desire wrap this up at almost any cost. Tougher German draft (supported by Swiss) helping us look less rigid. Finally reached accord on our IG compromise text.

November 7—Sent complete new draft to Washington by telegram. Met Wynter to reconcile French and English texts. Called Swinton, who will help out over there.

November 8—Department pleased Boissier outcome, added a few minor changes.

(Over the Armistice Day weekend, I flew to Budapest for some tennis and bridge with Phil Kaiser, my old friend who was now our ambassador to Hungary. On the way, I realized I had no visa. When I discovered these were routinely issued for a fee on arrival, I couldn't help recalling our incessant but always futile efforts fifteen to twenty years ago to penetrate the iron curtain.)

November 13—Boissier said nearly all Africans will support whatever M'Bow wants. Reported this by telegram.

November 14—Filled in IG members on status our draft. Met with Boissier, Germans, French and Swiss, who had some problems with it. All finally came around. French, who had been playing own parallel game with M'Bow, now very cooperative.

November 15—Washington suggested we work for consensus on

Boissier/IG text. Some further improvements made in wording. Australian made point Central Europeans like Germans and Swiss take "rigid, provincial line" with Third World because don't have as much to do with them as British, French and we do. Briefed *Trib* and Los Angeles *Times* reporters, who are best informed here because come to meetings.

November 16—Sat in with Wagner group which now tinkering with preamble but mostly treading water. New committee, including Reinhardt, French, Pole, others now working on consensus resolution.

November 18—Our move to delay consideration of existing Draft Declaration (since all wrinkles not yet ironed out) challenged by Soviet bloc in Fourth Committee and they won on show of hands since few understood what really going on. Peruvian chairman then asked for roll call vote because of "confusion." Vietnamese protested this not democratic, causing even Bulgarians to laugh. Motion to delay then passed, 55–40–16. Later met Boissier, who said Russians now realized our draft would carry but were balking at phrase condemning violations of human rights. Don Cook (of Leipzig days) lunching with me suggested we leave in human rights but eliminate condemnation phrase which Russians always consider aimed at them. French delegate agreed and we three passed idea on to Boissier, who was closeted with Russians. He seemed grateful, thought it might work.

November 20—Telegram from Department proposing virtually same change in human rights reference that we'd given Boissier. And Russians did accept it. M'Bow at press conference said text now 98 percent satisfactory to everybody.

November 21—Incoming telegram raised question about Soviet addition to text citing certain "principles" in another UNESCO document we disagree with. But we got to M'Bow during night and he stopped presses to insert "corresponding" before "principles" (which solved our problem) without bothering to inform Russians. As expected, they didn't notice added adjective.

November 22—Our draft adopted in plenary session by consensus and acclamation. All praised M'Bow. Some quibbling from Chinese, Vietnamese, Filipinos and Swiss—last because Declaration too tough, others because too vague.

November 23—Held background conference for press explaining why U.S. satisfied. Soviet delegate with straight face also expressed satisfaction, saying Declaration corresponded to Article 50 of their constitution guaranteeing freedom of expression.

I flew home the next day, pleased to have played a part in formulating a winning strategy and upsetting Soviet calculations. This was the cold war as I enjoyed waging it, with psychological weapons and no casualties except a few bruised egos. Of course, the fact I was an outsider and regarded as the spokesman for the American media gave me more clout at the State Department than had I been a Foreign Service officer.

Not all the news media back home were pleased with the outcome. In an editorial November 25, the *New York Times* called the Declaration "a triumph of obfuscating" even though "no longer a clear and present threat to news agencies." It added, "We do not negotiate codes of press behavior with our government and should not be negotiating them with any other," and concluded, "One by one, our diplomats eliminated from this UNESCO declaration the most offensive passages sanctioning state control of the mass media. And now they ask whether it does not feel wonderful to settle for this compromise. We feel very crowded still."

In a letter, which the *Times* reprinted in full, I replied we really had only two alternatives—to vote against a Soviet-inspired resolution which would have passed, or to produce a document in cooperation with other delegations and the Secretariat "that would be at worst innocuous and at best helpful to the free flow of information." I used a zoological analogy, saying we had a rattlesnake of a declaration loose in the garden, and the only chance of getting rid of it was to replace it with a harmless garter snake: "It can be argued that we didn't need any snake, but under the circumstances the question was academic."

The *Times* also missed the significance of the "corresponding principles" phrase which I said was put in "to exclude the very stipulation to which all of us object."

The alternative would have been "an unacceptable declaration that could and would have been invoked as a pretext for banning, arresting and otherwise harassing our reporters all over the world; we would have seen support for UNESCO and other international bodies further eroded in the West, and the influence of the Soviet Union on the Third World further enhanced." This, I suggested, would have smacked of "defeatism and isolationism," while what we emerged with should make all free news organizations breathe easier rather than feel "crowded."

In the end, most of the American press endorsed the outcome at Paris.

Sihanouk turned up in January 1979 in New York's Lenox Hill Hospital, recuperating from nearly four years' house arrest in the infamous world of Pol Pot's Cambodia. Several of his children had been killed, along with about a third of his country's population. Now he wanted me to help him write a book. I brought a publisher friend, Mike Bessie, over to see him, but it turned out that the kind of book we both had in mind —a personal adventure story—was not the one he wanted to write. "I must consider my political future," he said, at which Princess Monique burst into tears and hurried out of the room. "Talk of politics makes her nervous," he said, I thought unnecessarily.

So nothing came of the book. But they did come to tea at our house in a Chinese mission car with two U.S. Secret Service escorts, and we dined with them in their hotel suite, which he liked but which was costing the U.S. Mission at the U.N. more than it could afford. Ambassador Donald McHenry finally called me to see if I knew of anyone willing to put up some exotic royal houseguests. I did, on Long Island, but just as the Sihanouks were due to move in, he decided to go to Paris instead, and eventually back to Peking. But I doubt if we've seen the last of each other.

The Soviet trip was a family expedition undertaken in August 1979, a month after my leaving *Newsday,* with Sim, Jan and Suzy. Our intention was to drive a Soviet rental car around the Baltic states, closed to Americans until 1965. "No problem," said Georgy Isachenko, the Washington-based editor of *Soviet Life,* when I broached the idea in February. He or his new deputy, Gennadi Savchenko, would arrange everything, including the car, hotels and meetings with journalists, artists, scholars, anybody.

Weeks passed, so I phoned. Georgy was on leave. What about Savchenko? "Not here. Out to lunch."

"When will he be back?"

"I don't know. Nobody knows."

"Then please leave word Mr. Attwood called."

"Mr. *Attwood?* But *I* am Savchenko!"

Arrangements were eventually made, and we flew to Berlin on August 7 and then on to Moscow via Schoenefeld Airport in East Germany. This time we were lodged in the ancient but still classy National

Hotel with its turn-of-the-century suites; Jan and Suzy even had a grand piano in theirs.

In the morning, while the women wandered around the city, Vitaly Prokoshev, the Novosti man assigned to us, introduced me to his boss, Fedyashin, and I called on the U.S. Embassy political officer, as well as Yuri Zhukov at *Pravda* and Georgy Arbatov, the director of the USA and Canada Institute, and some of his staff. While I'd retired from my last newspaper job a month earlier, nobody ever retires from journalism. I still kept a notebook in my pocket.

Zhukov said the U.S.S.R. was too busy planning for the next century to think of war. Arbatov worried about the price Carter would have to pay to get SALT II through the Senate; he and I both picked him to win in 1980 anyway. (Who could then anticipate the Tehran hostages, the failed rescue mission, Afghanistan and the rest?) The Institute's scholars wanted to know how we would react if OPEC cut off our oil, who made the decisions in the Kennedy family and whether Brzezinski was in or out of favor. The U.S. diplomat I called on thought we should recognize the de facto situation in the Baltic republics, and also in Mongolia. English-speaking Russians we encountered at random were as patriotic as ever and still thought for the most part that Americans were either very rich or very poor—a stereotype as false as ours about the Russians being either Communists or dissidents. In short, not much had changed in what we saw of Moscow, and my daughters managed the impossible: they failed to find Lenin's mausoleum.

We flew to Vilnius, Lithuania, a couple of days later and then took a train to Riga, the capital of Latvia, and eventually another plane to Tallinn and a train back to Russia, to Leningrad. I say "back to Russia" because even after thirty-five years of Russian domination, it was still possible, up to a point, to feel that these small republics were part of the real Europe. The many castles and churches, the cafés and taverns, the cobbled streets, the Germanic architecture and Scandinavian decor, the Latin alphabet, the jeans and stenciled T-shirts and rock music all contributed to the illusion. It could be reinforced by small gestures—an artist kissing Sim's hand at an exhibit of surrealist paintings—and just as quickly dispelled by the dreary reading matter in bookshops and on newsstands or the sparsely stocked grocery stores. Still, in a nation as strictly conformist as the Soviet Union, the differences made the Baltic nations and their 6,000,000 people interesting and explained why Russians sometimes referred to this area as *Sovetskaya zagranitsa*—the Soviet "abroad." It was the next best thing, one woman told us in Riga, to visiting Europe; and you didn't need hard-to-get foreign currency.

Our rental car, as expected, never materialized. There was always a "problem"—none available, mechanical trouble, agent on holiday; the Soviet bureaucracy is skilled at saying "no" in a hundred different ways without ever using the word. Finally, in Tallinn, we seemed all set for the final, sixty-five-mile lap along the coast to Leningrad. Then, the night before, we met Vitaly talking to Novosti's Estonia representative in our hotel lobby.

"Good news!" he cried, handing me a telex. "You have rooms at the Pribaltiskaya in Leningrad!"

"Isn't that one listed as fair to rock-bottom in Fodor?" asked Jan.

"That must be the old one—the Baltiskaya. You are in the new one."

"What's the bad news?" I asked.

"Oh, it will be another ninety-six rubles for the car tomorrow," Vitally replied. "You must have guide and driver."

"Forget it," I said, "we'll take the train."

"That would be better. We have already reserved you a compartment."

The Baltic countries differ in language and culture, but share some history. All were fought over for centuries by Danes, Germans, Swedes and Russians. All briefly experienced independence between the two world wars. All were absorbed into the Soviet Union in 1940 in a bloodless but cynical maneuver engineered by Andrei Vyshinsky whereby Moscow, in the words of the official history, "granted the request" of local Baltic Communists installed by the Red Army to join the U.S.S.R. The "requests" were in fact ordered by Stalin.

After a brutal "liberation" by the Nazis in 1941 and another by the Russians in 1944, all suffered from forcible Russification (something we wrote about in *Collier's* in 1951) until Stalin's death. But by 1979, about 90 percent of the population of Lithuania and 75 percent in Latvia and Estonia were natives, and Russian was taught in schools only as a second language, with English a strong third. The Russians discovered that letting the Balts talk and behave a little differently paid off in political tranquillity and high productivity. All things considered, the Baltic states seemed in custody rather than in bondage. So they worked harder. For example, we were told that Latvia, with one percent of the Soviet Union's population, manufactured one half the country's telephones and motorcycles.

After vainly searching for our baggage at the Vilnius airport, I found a uniformed official and told him in Russian that I didn't speak Russian. "Well, I don't either," he replied in German with a grin, and in a few minutes reunited us with our bags. When Vitaly turned up the next day ("To make sure you have no problems"), Lithuanian Intourist personnel, polite to us, were surly with him. The Russians knew they weren't beloved and surely swallowed hard at the teenagers flaunting T-shirts and tunics embellished with a variety of U.S. Army patches, swatches of the American flag and Disco Fever, Kung Fu and rock star decals. In Tallinn, a young Estonian woman working as an interpreter at an international sailing regatta sported a khaki shirt decorated with a green and purple replica of the Stars and Stripes and patches touting the U.S. Air Force, the Sea Scouts, the "Germany Navy" and the RAF. I asked her where she had found this incredible garment. "They're imported from India," she replied.

Some of the random observations jotted down in my notebook probably aren't yet dated: At the Vilnius Writers' Union, they ask us about modern American authors but have only heard of Vonnegut. . . . In Gedimino Square, a photographer poses kids with stuffed replicas of Mickey Mouse, Kukla and Ollie. I aim my instant camera at the scene. He's excited. "American? I have cousin in Chicago. How much the camera?" . . . In Riga, we go to Handel's *Messiah* sung in Latin at the jam-packed cathedral. . . . At the *Put, Vejinii* (Blow, Wind) restaurant, the ambience is candlelit and intimate, the cold *okroshka* soup delicious, the prices reasonable. . . . In a sun-dappled pine forest by Lake Jurgla, a peasant village of czarist times has been meticulously restored as an "ethnic museum." The elderly caretakers greet us in German while the Uzbek tourists in beaded caps stare at us silently. . . . The flamboyant artist Maya Tabaka pours beer in her studio, ridicules "socialist realism" and talks of her recent fellowship in West Berlin. . . . Up the winding streets of Tallinn's Old City, we follow the tolling bells of an Orthodox church, where we find twenty old ladies at a benediction service and about fifty curious Russian tourists peering through the doorway. All of us get blessed. . . . On the parapet overlooking the harbor, a group of young Soviet sailors pose shyly for Suzy's camera. . . .

On the train to Leningrad, where a polite but initially nervous young Estonian shared our four-berth compartment (Sim having taken the ferry to Helsinki), I reflected that periodic appeals to the U.N. and the Kremlin by audacious Baltic activists for self-determination have about as much impact as would a proclamation by the Hawaiian royal family demanding we return their islands to them. And as I wrote later in a piece for the *Atlantic:* "Life in these republics is likely to remain a shade more drab than in, say, Hungary, but also a shade less so than in Russia. And if you have no choice but to belong to the Soviet Union, that certainly rates at least three small cheers."

Our Leningrad hotel turned out to be indeed new, and also gigantic and way out past the inner suburbs. Our room keys were numbered 11050 and 10038. Could there be more than eleven thousand rooms in this mighty monument to mass tourism? I wanted to believe it, so didn't ask. In any case, the rooms were spotless, furnished in Swedish modern style, and every bathroom fixture was adorned with a "disinfected" label—in English. There was a hangarlike banquet hall where tour groups were marched in, fed to rock music and marched out; the cafeteria was quicker and cheaper, and the Neva restaurant costly and faintly elegant.

Was this a model for future tourist hotels? Apparently so. When I visited Intourist headquarters and had coffee with a Mr. Bazhenichev and a Mrs. Beliakova, they told me the U.S.S.R. was gearing up for a massive influx of foreign visitors and that more Pribaltiskayas were the answer. The advantages are obvious: Since tourists are delivered by the busload, dispatched to clean rooms, group-fed, driven around all day to museums and palaces and eventually shipped off to the next city on their itinerary, the opportunities for possibly disturbing contacts with ordinary Russians are almost nil, the drain on Intourist resources is minimized and the visitor sees only what is officially approved. He leaves with lots of pretty slides and a sense that Russia is, on the whole, clean, courteous and efficient.

"Individuals" like us, who tended to wander off on their own, posed problems for the system, which was why they got charged more. So I think we saw the future at the Pribaltiskaya and, for those who don't mind regimentation, it seemed to work.

We took the train to Finland on a rainy morning. At the border, Soviet officials became inquisitive when they learned I was a journalist. What had I been doing and writing about in the Soviet Union? It was none of their business, so I produced Zhukov's, Arbatov's and Fedyashin's calling cards, and their manner instantly became obsequious. I think they even saluted.

At the first station on the other side, the sun came out as if on cue, and two Finnish friends took us to a "surprise" lunch two miles away —at an Italian-owned pizzeria called the Casa Nostra. Suddenly we were back in *Amerikanskaya zagranitsa—our* abroad.

When we got home on September 1, a pseudo-crisis was under way involving the presence of a Soviet brigade in Cuba. The resulting flap all but wrecked any chance of Senate ratification of the SALT II Treaty and ushered in the twilight of détente. Thereafter, Carter's foreign policy gradually disintegrated, along with his chances for reelection.

Very briefly, what happened was the discovery, or rediscovery, by American intelligence of some 2,600 Soviet troops in Cuba during the summer. The fact that the troops had been there for seventeen years, with our concurrence, was overlooked amid the mounting speculation in Washington that the Soviets were up to something sneaky. A little research might have refreshed the State Department's collective memory and cooled things down before they heated up; but Vance chose instead to take a few key senators and congressmen into his confidence about the existence of this Soviet "brigade." One of them, Senator Frank Church, normally reasonable and even considered dovish, unfortunately was having political problems with Republican hawks in Idaho and therefore decided to burnish his macho credentials by sounding the alarm—which he did with gusto on August 30, denouncing "Russian penetration of this hemisphere." He then postponed the Foreign Relations Committee hearings on SALT II.

The result was a month of rhetorical and diplomatic disorder. The president, Secretary Vance and other administration spokesmen boxed themselves in with statements saying the presence in Cuba of Soviet troops was "unacceptable." The Russians were first perplexed, then suspicious. At one point, Dobrynin asked Vance whether the Soviet military presence in Cuba was a threat to the United States and whether it violated any Soviet-American understandings; Vance had to say no to both questions. Then why the fuss? In retrospect, the only answer is that a kind of mindless momentum took possession of our political leadership.

On September 25, Carter did try to back off some by saying the "combat" status of the Soviet unit, while no threat to us, was the only thing we were really concerned about. And he reiterated our intention to "change the status quo" if the "combat nature" of the unit wasn't modified. Actually there was not a thing we could do or would do.

Two days later, a Thursday, I got a call from Acosta at the Cuban

U.N. Mission saying that Castro wanted to see me right away—and could I leave for Havana the next morning? I had weekend plans and no intention of chartering a plane, but there was now a weekly flight to Varadero from Miami operated by a travel agency. It left on Mondays, and I booked the last available seat on October 1, informed *Newsday* and called David Newsom, the under secretary of state (and a friend from Guinea days) who had originally briefed Frank Church. Like most people who read the papers and watched the TV news, I figured we must have something on the Russians and Cubans to warrant all the tough talk. But Newsom sounded vague when I asked him what I could confront Castro with. "Well, we do have firm evidence the Soviet troops are there," he said. So what else was new? Apparently nothing.

The weekly plane developed engine trouble on the ground. Scouting around, I met a young couple with a Cessna 310 who were going to Varadero and offered me a lift. At the other end, all was informality and confusion. Apparently there was now a good deal of private plane traffic in and out as more Cuban exiles were invited to come and visit their relatives.

I was promptly taken in hand by a Foreign Ministry representative named José Delgado who drove me to Havana and installed me, over my vain protests, in two double rooms at the Hotel Riviera. Dan Rather was there with a CBS retinue and we listened to President Carter's TV address that night on the shortwave radio. He waffled away the great crisis by noting Soviet assurances that the "brigade" was a "training center" and would not be enlarged nor its mission altered—which had been the case since 1962.

To maintain the required tough stance, he went on to reaffirm our commitment to resist aggression in the Caribbean (which no one had committed for generations except for the United States), to increase surveillance worldwide and even, for some reason, to beef up our naval force in the Indian Ocean.

My appointment with Castro was for October 3, so the next morning I decided to start writing a mood piece that could blend in with the interview. Here's how it started:

> The comedy crisis, the Frank Church crisis, the non-crisis—whatever you want to call it—was over. The night before, on the shortwave radio, we heard Jimmy Carter say, in effect, that Fidel Castro was right, that the Soviet brigade had been in Cuba a long time and posed no

conceivable threat to us and that the important thing was to get the SALT II ratification process moving again.

Early the next morning, the American TV network crews and their gear were assembled in the lobby of the Hotel Riviera, heading home by chartered plane. A tour group of animated Cuban exiles from Florida occupied the coffee shop. *Granma*, the Communist daily, carried a straightforward account of the Carter speech, with no comment . . .

But the strange, neurotic, love-hate relationship between Cubans and Americans persists, to no one's credit or advantage. Even in his backdown speech, Carter felt obliged to make ritualistic mention of Cuba's economic dependence and subservience to the Soviet Union; earlier, he had called Castro a puppet—which is about as constructive as calling a hunchback a hunchback. And Castro, in reply, had accused Carter of being "immoral"—a singularly inappropriate adjective for the President.

It was 20 years ago last January—just after Castro took over—that I last stayed in this early-Las-Vegas-style hotel. Sitting now on my balcony, 18 stories above the Malecon drive, I reflected that, while American actions under four Presidents have certainly strengthened Fidel Castro, they have not advanced U.S. interests one inch.

When I met him in his office the next evening, only his aide, Alfredo Ramirez, and an interpreter were present, and he spoke of the mini-crisis more in sorrow than in anger. He seemed disappointed in Carter but intent on exonerating him. ("He is badly advised.") Castro laughed when I suggested that since he had both Soviet troops and U.S. Marines in Cuba, we could stage joint maneuvers at Guantanamo with blank ammunition—and himself as umpire. "But would you trust me to be impartial?" he asked.

We talked for two hours about many things—Carter's speech ("arrogant"), U.S. politics, solar energy, Pol Pot, Nicaragua, Angola, the lunacy of nuclear war, cigars, windmills, Panama ("I helped you by telling Torrijos to be patient"), poverty, newsprint and what he should say at the United Nations ("Don't write yet that I am going") and what kind of trees grew on my land in Connecticut and how was my family?

I decided he'd summoned me to Havana just to talk in a relaxed way with an American he knew and could trust to report what he said accurately.

And we agreed, as usual, to disagree about some things. He seemed stumped when I asked him to give me just one example of American "imperialism" in recent years. But he had no doubt—he *knew*—that Zbigniew Brzezinski tried to sabotage the Non-Aligned Movement conference with the Soviet brigade story. I suggested Washington's real concern was not about a conference or even about the presence of Soviet troops but whether a new attempt at deception was involved. This mattered in the SALT context. After all, I said, the Russians did lie to us about the missiles in 1962. Castro nodded: they "handled it badly" by lying; he, Castro, never would have denied their presence in Cuba.

Castro had not quite and not yet given up on the idea of normalizing relations with the U.S., though he spoke, somewhat unconvincingly, as if it didn't really matter to him. If Carter wanted to see him when he came to the U.N., he'd be willing. But it wasn't up to him to request a meeting.

"Why," he asked ruefully, "do your politicians always speak much more harshly of Cuba than they do of the Soviet Union or of other socialist states? Do we threaten you, as you have threatened us so many times? We are neighbors, natural trading partners, yet you always single us out for abuse. Why?"

In all honesty I had to tell him, as I took my leave, that I didn't know (though I suspect it's because we aren't used to people who defy us and get away with it). And I asked him, for the hell of it, to drop in for a home-cooked meal when he came to the States. (And he remembered. When he got to New York later that month, I got two successive calls from the Cuban Mission asking if we'd be at home on such and such a day if Fidel could get away from the city. I was then running for the town council, and when I divulged my secret at a Kiwanis lunch, I was assured a visit from Castro couldn't hurt my chances, since Democrats where I live don't have any chance anyway.)

At the hotel, I phoned in a brief story, saying Castro was glad Carter finally admitted the truth and considered the incident closed. Then I wrote a memo for Vance and Brzezinski while the interview was still fresh in my mind.

In the morning, I called on Wayne Smith, the head of the U.S. Interests Section, whose staff of thirty occupied the former American Embassy, now flying the Swiss flag. He was a big man who reminded me at first glance of Hemingway, and he shared my views on our Cuban policy and also on Brzezinski's generally negative influence on Carter. I dictated my memo, lunched at the hotel at a table between Soviet officers and American clerks from the Section and grudgingly paid a $400 bill for my two double rooms.

Surprise. When Delgado came by to take me to the airport, he handed me $200 as reimbursement for the extra room. "We had to hold it," he explained, "in case Fidel decided to drop by some evening instead of receiving you in his office. We never know."

I got home October 5. The decade was almost over so far as the cold war was concerned. But not quite.

On November 4, the staff of the U.S. Embassy in Tehran were taken hostage by street mobs acting with the Ayatollah Khomeini's blessing.

And on December 25, Soviet troops moved into Afghanistan to prop up a new Communist leader, the last two having turned out to be loose cannons.

The Russians underestimated both the resistance that their fraternal interference would encounter and Carter's horrified reaction. With respect to the latter, I remember Brezhnev's speechwriter observing later—and not inaccurately—on an ABC news show, "We put détente ahead of Vietnam, but you put Afghanistan ahead of détente."

Chapter 16

Winding Up and Winding Down

Early in 1980, a Washington *Post* writer suggested that future historians might say of this particular winter, "The Soviets invaded Afghanistan, and the Americans stopped thinking." It can be argued that we have not yet resumed thinking, as a nation, preferring instead to react emotionally to events—with the encouragement of a new president, Ronald Reagan, who has been more concerned with making us feel good than face facts.

Carter responded to the Afghan action as though the Russians had done something so unprecedented as to pose "the most serious threat to world peace since the Second World War." Actually they had been doing this sort of thing for decades whenever Communist satrapies on their borders stepped out of line. Having installed a puppet ruler named Taraki, who was murdered by a second puppet named Amin, they were now replacing the latter with one named Karmal (who in turn has since been replaced), for fear Amin's excesses would lead to an Islamic uprising, which might then stir up trouble in the Soviet Union's Muslim republics and even provoke intervention by the Ayatollah's fanatics in neighboring Iran. But in fact the invasion was no more a threat to world peace than our more massive and even less justifiable intervention in Indochina.

So the Soviets, having underestimated U.S. reaction and Afghan resistance, got roundly condemned in the United Nations, as well as bogged down in a frustrating war, while Carter "punished" them by withdrawing from the Moscow Olympic Games and halting grain sales to the Soviet Union. The chief result was to penalize America's farmers and athletes, since the Russians simply bought grain elsewhere and were greatly relieved not to have to cope with the security problem posed by thousands of American sports fans in their midst. This was typical of the impulsive but empty gestures designed to score points in an election year; empty because our boycotting the Games would no more inhibit Soviet actions than their boycotting the 1984 Games in Los Angeles in retaliation had the slightest impact on *our* foreign policy.

In Iran, Carter exhibited more restraint on the hostage issue and yielded to the pressure to "do something" only once—in approving the disastrous helicopter rescue mission in April. It could have been worse: Had the rescue team ever reached Tehran, the fifty-two hostages would probably have been murdered, as Hossin Sheikholislam, their captors' chief spokesman, bluntly warned them. Secretary Vance, who opposed the mission, resigned in protest at not being consulted, a class act in a town where prominent officials generally resign in disgrace rather than on principle. And a combination of quiet but persuasive threats (of retaliation *if,* not *unless*) plus patient diplomacy, with Algerian cooperation, eventually paid off: All the hostages were released unharmed— ironically, just as Carter's presidency came to an end in January 1981 (ironically, because the frustration engendered at home by their imprisonment was one of the principal causes of his defeat in November).

Carter was an inexperienced but well intentioned and hardworking president. (He learned his foreign policy at meetings of the Trilateral Commission, where just staying awake is a triumph of will, and was coached in the cold war by Zbigniew Brzezinski, a Polish-born academic who, like Kissinger, spoke English with an accent but lacked his charm.) Carter never should have admitted the Shah to the United States (which is what triggered the seizure of our Tehran embassy), but it wasn't easy to turn down a very sick man who had been our ally nor to resist the pressure of David Rockefeller and Kissinger, whose support he needed to get the Salt II Treaty ratified by the Senate.

Carter did secure narrow approval of the vital Panama Canal Treaty, which Ronald Reagan assailed as a giveaway, and he did single-handedly get the Near East "peace process" under way at Camp David, though Menachem Begin later stalled it by his defiant rejection of any Palestinian compromise either on the West Bank or in Lebanon.

The Carter Administration also supported the British solution in Zimbabwe against the advice of the Republican establishment, ranging from Kissinger to Senator Jesse Helms; and officially recognized, at long last, the People's Republic of China. In addition, it exerted pressure for human rights wherever they were violated, not only in Communist states but from Indonesia to South America; in Argentina, where Kiss-inger once praised the brutal junta, Carter is still remembered for his stand. And, at least until the Afghan flap, his administration's opposition to trade barriers such as the counterproductive Jackson-Vanik Amend-ment linking trade with the Russians to Jewish emigration resulted in a steady increase in such emigration—up to 30,000 in 1978 and 51,000 in 1979. The resumption of cold war trade policies under Reagan has since reduced it to about a thousand a year.

For these and other reasons—such as the relatively high quality of Carter appointees in policymaking jobs—I found myself lending a hand in his campaign for the nomination against Ted Kennedy. I considered Kennedy a good senator but had a gut feeling he was not electable; and with Reagan clearly the likeliest Republican candidate, Carter, for all his shortcomings, looked a lot better to those of us who feared another upsurge of the cold war and an America progressively alienated from its allies.

I tried to sum up my reasons for supporting Carter in a piece for the *New Republic* that spring, in reply to a scathing attack by Arthur Schlesinger, a Kennedy backer, on what he called "an administration in ruins."

> It's only fair to point out that . . . Carter's weakness—common to many contemporary politicians who watch the polls the way network executives watch the Nielsens—has been to react to public opinion rather than to educate or influence it. He often seems unduly concerned with appeasing the right-wingers, not realizing that it's all but impossi-ble to outflank the Reaganites without coming out for child labor, apart-heid and the Great White Fleet . . .
>
> Reagan's naive and therefore dangerous global view is that there is a Soviet conspiracy behind all of the problems and unrest in the world, when in fact most of what happens is due to circumstances and historical imperatives quite beyond the control of either Moscow or Washington . . .
>
> That's why it's time, high time, for Schlesinger and Ted Kennedy's partisans to join forces with the Carterites to beat back, once again, the crusaders of illusion and nostalgia. . . .

Aside from some memos and speech ideas, my contribution to the Carter campaign was largely confined to a poll I conducted by tele-phone with men and women who had left their jobs in the early sixties to work for John F. Kennedy's New Frontier. Did they now favor Ted

Kennedy, as might be expected, or Carter? I assembled 110 names and phone numbers and in January called a dozen or so every day. The results were encouraging for the president: 53 former Kennedyites were now for him, as against 31 for Ted, 2 for John Anderson and 22 undecided. Only two declined to express an opinion. The resulting news story may have raised Carter's spirits but not his reelection chances.

For Carter, perceived as earnest but bumbling, was no match for Reagan, a lifelong entertainer who knew how to work an audience and took full advantage of camera angles and photo opportunities. Television had helped JFK defeat Nixon in 1960, and it now ensured Reagan's triumph twenty years later. In their debate, Carter's reasonable arguments were dismissed with a good-natured but patronizing "There you go again," to which Carter should have responded affirmatively by reiterating his points—but didn't. And Reagan knew, too, that running against the Russians (by calling the Democrats soft on communism and weak on defense) had been an effective tactic ever since the cold war started, and still was.

Yet the Russians seemed pleased at first that Reagan won. Soon after the election, Andrei Kokoshin, the U.S. domestic politics expert at Arbatov's Institute, came to my house for a visit, purring over his friendly reception at the pro-Reagan Hoover Institute and predicting a revival of Nixon's commitment to détente. "Only hard-line Republicans," he explained, "can overcome the political risks of cooperating with the Soviet Union."

Kokoshin was wrong, of course, since he underestimated Reagan's stubborn ideological streak, a trait that the more flexible Nixon could also exhibit but then discard to suit his purposes. At any rate, Kokoshin's visit did provide our alert local weekly with some speculative copy since I signed him into our country club's guest book just under the name of Jia Dingzhi, an editor of *Peking Daily,* and my luncheon companion the day before.

"A glance at the guest book," said the paper, "might lead some to believe that we are entering a new era in Sino-Soviet relations. Their names are in such close proximity it would be natural to believe they had lunch together . . . [But] no, there is no new cordiality between the two great Red powers."

And there was certainly no new cordiality between the two so-called superpowers either. (I say "so-called" because both the U.S. and the U.S.S.R. had become militarily muscle-bound; indeed, it sometimes seemed that the only superpowers in the world of the eighties—super in the sense they could pretty much behave as they pleased—were Israel, South Africa and Iran.) One reason for the steady deterioration of U.S.-Soviet relations, with the concomitant renewal of cold war attitudes, was that the Soviet Union was virtually leaderless for about seven years. A gradually failing Brezhnev, who died in 1981, was succeeded by an ailing Andropov, who was in turn succeeded by an aged and feeble Chernenko. So the country was administered by sometimes overlapping and often competing baronies—the military, the Party, the KGB and the industrial bureaucracy, to cite the most powerful. But there was no strong central executive power to set national policy or take new initiatives in foreign affairs. Until Mikhail Gorbachev emerged in 1985, the U.S.S.R. was a nation in need of a leader.

The other reason we drifted back into a cold war posture was that our own president was an amiable but stubborn man with at least four simplistic but deeply held beliefs—in small government, low tax rates, a strong defense and Communist perfidy. He was a president who much preferred to entertain the nation than to govern it—a feeling that, for the moment, was reciprocated. He liked to make people feel proud and virtuous, to tell them that "America is back and standing tall" and that the Soviet Union was an "evil empire" masterminding all the world's troubles—even though headed for the "ash heap of history"; that massive defense spending really served the cause of peace; and even that the Vietnam war had been "a noble cause."

For a people who could no longer understand a world where American supremacy was not taken for granted, the combination of fatherly reassurance, genial good humor and a wisecracking cowboy approach to the black hats was bound to be irresistible. Add the soothing if meaningless lilt of Reagan's formal speeches ("Let no one say this nation cannot reach the destiny of our dreams. America believes, America is ready. America can win the race to the future—and we shall"), and you can easily see how he took the country by storm.

Other events contributed to his popularity: Shot by a would-be assassin, he was joking as he entered the hospital. Then the Russians had to show their iron teeth in Poland in 1981 when Solidarity demanded political power. Thanks to General Jaruzelski and the Catholic Church, the Poles kept the lid on by themselves and averted a dangerous and bloody intervention by the Red Army. For this we should have been grateful; instead, we penalized both the Poles and the Russians with commercial sanctions that might also be termed sanctimonious since only twelve died in the military crackdown, compared with the more than twenty thousand killed by "anti-Communist" death squads in U.S.-friendly El Salvador. And when the Polish crisis finally subsided in 1983, the downing of an off-course Korean airliner over Siberia by a Soviet fighter plane slapped a fresh coat of red paint on the image of the "barbaric" Russians. Actually, all it proved was that a trigger-happy pilot and his local headquarters apparently made a mistake, thinking it was one of the U.S. spy planes known to be in the area; but the Soviet High Command, preferring to appear brutal rather than incompetent, insisted the airliner was on an espionage mission even though filled with civilian passengers. Our side, ignoring our own intelligence analyses, insisted the act was deliberate murder. (It's possible that even we Americans, who don't suffer such paranoia as the Russians, would have shot down a North Korean airliner flying over one of our Alaskan bases; but in Reagan's view, the evil empire had once again revealed its Satanic visage.) In short, both sides were back to believing the worst about each other before all the evidence was in.

For me, by now a fairly grizzled newsman, Reagan's half decade provided fewer tales for this memoir—in part because I traveled less, being involved in closer-to-home activities, though most of them still related to the state of the world both as it was and could become. But I was no longer prowling the cold war's trouble spots. The jet lag was getting harder to take, and I became involved in other things than reporting, such as teaching journalism and current events at various colleges and universities; writing one book and translating another; serving in town government, making speeches, helping launch a foreign trade periodical (that sank), chairing the advisory board of a magazine (that also sank), working with organizations like the American Committee on U.S.-Soviet Relations and CARE—in short, keeping busy in areas that were related to my professional, preretirement life.

Sometimes I despaired over the Reagan Administration's policies—not because I was a Democrat, but because I had been a kind of closet patriot all my life (which is to say there's no flagpole on my lawn but I choke up a little when I hear "The Star-Spangled Banner" played abroad); so I hated seeing my country losing respect and influence in the world by reverting to the pious and inept bullying that never did work for us in the past. A great power, which is what we were, does not win support by coercion and bribery but by setting an example. The deterioration of our relations with a country like New Zealand is a case in point.

Meanwhile the doomsday weapons piled up, but halfway through his second term, Reagan was still the first president since Truman not to have negotiated an arms control agreement. (Eight were produced by the Nixon Administration alone.)

I did venture abroad during the Reagan years—three times to France, twice to England and Switzerland and once to Germany, Haiti and South Africa. And each time I went to Europe, I was made aware of a further erosion of American prestige: Our old friends and allies couldn't understand our obsession with tiny El Salvador and Nicaragua, our snubbing of the World Court, our ineffectual pressures against the pipeline sale to Russia and our renewed preoccupation with nuclear supremacy in a world whose problems were less and less susceptible to military solutions.

There's more; let's just say that as a cold war veteran with more than my share of hash marks, I came home from my European trips progressively more dispirited; by 1985, personal friends long sympathetic to America now regarded the United States not only as immature but, worse, as irrelevant to what was happening in the real world.

The extent of U.S. reversion to early fifties ways of thinking under Reagan can be gauged by a quote from *Beyond the Cold War,* a book written in 1966—more than twenty years ago—by Marshall Shulman, a scholar-diplomat and the now-retired director of the Russian Institute at Columbia University:

> The cold war has changed its character not only because Soviet policy has been evolving in response to change in the world environment, but because the U.S. and its Western Allies are becoming aware that anti-Communism is not an adequate response to the total situation in which we live.

This awareness has grown in Europe but shrunk in Washington, and this is the main reason we are in trouble with our allies.

When I hear the resurgent but shopworn anti-Communist rhetoric of some politicians, I recall a talk I had with a young Lithuanian professor about communism in Vilnius in 1979. "Communism as a coherent philosophy or even as a political movement no longer exists," he told me. "Its slogans are still used to justify the seizure or retention of power by national oligarchies. But the communism we decry is like a distant star, millions of light-years away. We think we see it up there in the sky. But it actually died a long time ago, and all we are seeing is the fading light of nothing at all."

I repeated this remark on my return to former CIA Director William Colby, and he agreed with it. But that was in 1980. It's no use telling that today to the Washington zealots in the White House and State and Defense departments (let alone the CIA) who translate Reagan's innocent fantasies into policy. I've tried it. The things that concern them are the things that trouble the boss, like Nicaragua refusing to say "uncle" and posing, as the president said last year, the threat of "a national security disaster for the United States." In an earlier speech, in Atlanta, he vowed to "repel attempts by Communists to impose their will on Central America." Referring to Nicaraguan President Daniel Ortega's trip to Moscow (as well as to Western European capitals) in search of help against U.S. military and economic pressure, Reagan said:

"The little dictator who went to Moscow in his green fatigues to receive a bear hug did not forsake the doctrine of Lenin when he returned to the West and appeared in a two-piece suit."

Such utterances have bewildered our allies, who used to think of us as steady but soft-spoken, as befits a great power. They have generally muted their public criticism of such silly rhetoric for fear of aggravating what a British friend called America's "prolonged fit of the sulks" because things didn't seem to go our way anymore. But in Europe I found myself apologizing, as an American, for U.S. policies and actions no longer geared to reality—something I haven't had to do since Joe McCarthy was stomping around.

Of course, like McCarthyism, this phase of self-righteous bravado won't last. As former Conservative Prime Minister Edward Heath said last year: "Those of us who know the United States intimately . . . know that it is passing through a time of intense and distasteful nationalism. It believes that it walks high and that the rest of the world has to do what it demands. It will get through that in time. It is an unpleasant reaction to the defeat in Vietnam."

So if I prefer to stay home these days, it's not only because the jet lag tires me; it's my country's awareness lag as well.

Renewed U.S. hostility to the Soviet Union (two words that were synonymous among the Reaganites with "Communist conspiracy") surfaced early in the first term. On March 31, 1981, I presided at an informal meeting in Washington for Georgy Arbatov, who said that "the feeling in Moscow is that your government has not got a policy yet. It could go in different directions . . ." In brief, he was already far less sanguine about restoring a semblance of détente than his deputy, Kokoshin, had been three months earlier.

And Arbatov had even less reason to be sanguine a couple of days later, when Secretary of State Alexander Haig blocked his appearance in a TV debate on "Bill Moyers' Journal" April 3 by suddenly canceling his visa. (Arbatov was immediately invited to speak in Canada as a guest of the prime minister.) Moyers commented later: "One hates to see General Haig and his lieutenants infect every transaction between the two countries—journalistic, cultural, educational, scientific—with the fever of the cold war that happened in the fifties and left a poison in our lives which lingers to this day. No Russian anywhere can say anything to damage this Republic as much as we injure ourselves when we forget who we are and why."

I found myself recalling comedian Mort Sahl's one-liner of the late fifties: "Every time the Russians shoot a CIA agent, we get even by shooting a CIA agent too."

But Reagan was accurately reading as well as shaping the national mood. Unilateral, Rambo-like solutions were now certain crowd-pleasers. "We did it all by our little selves," the president exulted when we forced an Egyptian plane to land in Italy without notifying either country. Even after negligent security caused the death of 241 marines on October 23, 1983, in Lebanon (on a mission never clearly defined), random sidewalk interviews back home revealed that most Americans were not so much angry or sad as rather proud of them for "defending their country" and hoped our forces would stay there and shoot back at somebody. (This was a much bigger deal, casualty-wise, than the *Mayaguez* thing.) But when the last marines were pulled out soon after, no one seemed to care, or wonder why the battleship *New Jersey* lobbed 16-inch shells indiscriminately at Druse villages in the hills as a farewell salute to the Near East. ("New Jersey!" cried the TWA hijackers a few months later as they sought out American passengers.) Perhaps our military triumph in Grenada two days after the marine tragedy, when more than seven thousand U.S. troops overcame some eight hundred Cuban construction workers (for which eight thousand medals were awarded) erased Beirut from our collective memory. Or perhaps we were by now standing so tall our heads were in the clouds.

There was more to come. We zapped Libya in high good humor (THIS IS FOR MUAMMAR'S MOM read the inscription on a sidewinder missile aboard the carrier *America*); we mounted our own covert proxy wars in Central America despite the disapproval of our allies; we withdrew from the Law of the Sea Treaty and quit UNESCO, an arena of both cooperation and competition that will grow in importance as war making becomes ever more obsolete. And we boycotted the World Court in The Hague when that body agreed to adjudicate our dispute with Nicaragua—apparently, as President Reagan later told the American Bar Association, because "a confederation of terrorist states" run by "the strangest collection of misfits, Looney Tunes and squalid criminals since the advent of the Third Reich" was trying "to expel America from the world." The assembled lawyers predictably laughed and applauded.

Watching and reading the news these past few years has been like watching the weakening of America—a saddening experience for those of us whose work has so long been entwined with the course and conduct of the cold war.

An example of how American attitudes have changed—to our detriment—struck me recently while scanning the lead of an AP story that read: "Vernon A. Walters, the American delegate to the United Nations, said today that he was warning countries getting American aid that they could expect less money if they voted against the United States in the General Assembly." I couldn't help but compare this confession that we now intend to purchase support with that memorable sentence in John F. Kennedy's Inaugural Address: "To those people in the huts and villages of half the globe, struggling to break the bonds of mass misery, we pledge our best efforts to help them help themselves, for whatever period is required, not because the Communists may be doing it, not because we seek their votes, but because it is right."

Well, why expect Reagan's U.N. spokesman to sound like Kennedy? Knowing Walters as an elegant linguist since my Paris days, I wasn't surprised when he told me at a Palm Beach gathering in 1982 that Fidel Castro suffered from "male menopause" and that Vietnam had been "our noblest cause." He was a logical choice for the U.N. job.

Nor should we blame Reagan for the dilution of American prestige and influence during the eighties. Why should anyone with so little first hand knowledge of the world beyond our shores be expected to understand the needs and aspirations of this revolutionary generation or to appreciate the unprecedented perils of this nuclear age? Without experience to guide him, he could only fall back on ideological certitudes some forty years old and long out of date. If blame must be assigned, there are no better scapegoats than the American voters who chose twice to be led by the candidate who could perform on the tube like the old pro he was.

When not writing, lecturing, politicking and wishing that Reagan were our king rather than our president, I indulged my occasional impulses to travel—not only with trips to Europe but, early in 1984, to South Africa, where the wind was rising. Violence and threats of violence had increased, and still more were predicted. The only questions now were: How would it all end? And: Would the United States manage to alienate black Africa, as the Russians hoped, by appearing to side with the doomed white minority regime while the South African Communist Party backed the sure-to-win African National Congress?

Since I'd acquired some knowledgeable contacts in the white community during my African and U.N. years, I decided to find out how they saw the future shaping up. For company, I chose Sim and Jan, and for recreation, we planned to start our journey among the wildlife in Kruger National Park.

When I applied for our visas at the South African Consulate in New York, I was asked to state in writing that I would not report on my trip. I wrote that I had no assignment nor any intention of reporting at this time. This seemed to satisfy them. And I did keep my word: All I ever wrote after my return was some brief commentary for *Newsday* several months later.

But I could and did keep copious notes on a journey that took us, by car and plane, from Johannesburg through Zululand to Durban, down the coast via Port Elizabeth to Cape Town, and back up north through Bloemfontein and Lesotho. Perhaps the best way to recapture the mood of white South Africa as we observed it in February 1984 is to quote the most relevant excerpts from my notebooks:

> Johannesburg. Joslin and Louw drive me to a private dinner at the prestigious Rand Club with about a dozen publishers and editors, both "English-speakers" and Afrikaners. First we talk of U.S. election year politics, then I'm asked to pose a question. I wonder aloud what this country will be like in ten years. Harald Pakendorf, the editor of *Vaderland*, replies, quickly and cryptically, "More black." We all know the black population is increasing faster than the white—from 71 percent today to probably 75 percent in 2000—not counting the 12 percent of Coloureds and Indians. Does he mean more black power—political and economic? He smiles enigmatically. The conversation takes a different tack: the external situation is "more fluid"; there is less rigidity in Pre-

toria; the "frontline" black states seem more reasonable; Namibia's a tough problem, but still . . . with some face-saving, some give-and-take, "We can buy more time, lower the level of violence—and that's already something."

Johannesburg. Coffee with the editor of *Beeld,* another Afrikaner newspaper: "Yes, we have censorship, but only where internal security is concerned. For example, statements by leaders of the African National Congress are banned as inflammatory. But you must realize the ANC is responsible for most of the 400 incidents of violence we had last year—that's over one a day. Fortunately they are directed mostly against property, not people—yet." I ask if there will be more violence as the blacks, now better educated, demand full citizenship. "Some violence is inevitable. Many people are opposed to what they call 'majority domination.' They say, this is our country, we are staying here and we will make the rules. This is obviously unacceptable to black militants. So the real question is—how much violence?"

Johannesburg. In his penthouse office, an "English-speaker" businessman says: "I think social and political reform is possible only when the white minority feels less threatened. That's why the talks and incremental agreements with Mozambique and Angola are so significant." I ask him about the projected tricameral parliament—which will permit the Indian and Coloured (mixed blood) minorities to have their own legislative bodies. Wasn't it essentially a cosmetic reform since they would always be outnumbered and outvoted by the all-white parliament? "Perhaps, but it does represent change. Remember that even if the clock moves forward very, very slowly, it cannot be turned back, not any longer." So he was an optimist? "We have to be optimists."

Sandton. Barbecue at the home of a U.S. businessman. "This country needs a black middle class with a stake in stability," he says over drinks on the terrace. "And I think there's one in the making. Black wages are rising faster than white wages. American firms here are helping the process—most of them set an example with desegregated facilities, equal pay for equal work and training blacks for managerial jobs." What would disinvestment or economic sanctions accomplish? "That would just stiffen the hard-line Afrikaners. This country is virtually self-sufficient. And any plants we shut down they'd nationalize and reopen. Sanctions have never worked anywhere."

Durban. Reading a paper by the swimming pool on the 32nd floor of the beachfront Maharani Hotel, I reflect on our two-day drive through Zululand—and our perilous shortcut. An Avis agent had recommended it. "Turn left at the new highway just before Barberton—it will save you 80 miles." The road looked good for 15 minutes, then turned to gravel, then became a narrow dirt track rutted by recent flooding and hugging the side of a mountain where our wheels grazed the edge of a 500-foot cliff. Turning back, or even turning, was out of the question. Three hours later, we'd covered 60 miles through forested, sparsely settled hills, stared at by an occasional African farmer. And then were stopped at the border of independent Swaziland, far off our intended course. Two South African frontier guards, one white and one black, came out. "You need a Swazi visa to go through," says the white one. "You'll have to turn back." I told him no way, not over that road. "Sorry about that," he said and returned to his official shack. What could they be doing here? Keeping Swazis out? But why would a Swazi want to leave?

The other guard had a suggestion. "Try taking the left fork back a mile or two. I think it leads into the valley. There must be a better road down there. But if you get stuck, don't expect any help."

In Guinea, more than 20 years before, we drove into the bush on roads that now and then disappeared altogether. This one, choked by high grass, seemed worse, or were we just getting older and less adventurous? Black children, wide-eyed, peered at us from grass huts, as though we were the original Boers on their great trek more than a century ago. At least the track was downhill, and a mining community suddenly loomed in the distance, like a mirage. A white man was watering his lawn. "The tarmac road? Thirty miles, straight ahead."

Amsterdam, Piet Retief, Paulpietersburg—shopping centers in these lush, fertile valleys where Zulu tribesmen once wiped out a British regiment. Whites own the towns and big farms, blacks are the manual laborers. We check in at a faded, deserted spa. Jan, driving to Durban with some friendly park rangers, is worried, with good reason, when we phone her at a Holiday Inn. The spa is depressing, a set for a Fellini or Buñuel movie. We leave at dawn.

Port Elizabeth. We are at a seafood restaurant on the Indian Ocean; outside there are garlands of colored light bulbs along the promenade, like an American resort of the twenties. Our South African companion, who works for an American company, talks to me out on the terrace: "I may sound like a racist to you, but I'm really not. I just hate to think of how this country would deteriorate if the blacks took it over. Didn't you see everything fall apart in Guinea and Kenya after independence?" I tell him there was a decline in efficiency and a good deal of official corruption, but that in time and with outside advice and help, black-ruled countries eventually got back on their feet. He looks dubious. "I hope you're right. Because it's bound to happen here too. I'd prefer some deterioration to a lot of strife and bloodshed. And if enough of us whites were willing to stay on and help out . . ."

Wildernis. Jan arrives in the Holiday Inn taproom with a crew of young "English-speaker" yachtsmen in tow. We buy each other several rounds of Castle beer. One of them asks me, "So what do you think of our country?" Beautiful scenery, I say, but trouble ahead. "You're bloody right! Five years at the most and then me and my chums will sail away—to Australia maybe. Let the Boers circle their wagons and end up like your General Custer. We're getting out—and don't talk about peaceful transition. That's as balmy as Reagan's constructive engagement policy. In Pretoria, 'constructive' just means anything that will keep them in power." I glance at two young blacks taking seats at the bar. "That's no big thing anymore. There's residential and school segregation, of course, but if a black's dressed all right and has money in his pocket he won't get thrown out of places like this."

Oudtshoorn. This is the world's ostrich capital, or, in Afrikaans, *Die Wereld'se Grootse Telers van Volstruise,* but the plume market's been in a 75-year slump. The hotel's Sunday buffet is where the stern Afrikaner burghers and their stout wives congregate after church. Two black couples come in and occupy a center table, but nobody seems to notice. Later, Sim and Jan visit the ostrich farm and the three-star caverns while I nurse a touch of tick fever, and we dine at the Panorama restaurant on—ostrich steak (which tastes like beef).

Laingsberg. Over the door of the only hotel in this town on the Karroo plains there's a sign that says, "Europeans. Blankes." It's the first such sign we've encountered so far. "It doesn't say anything about Americans," I remark, a feeble quip that evokes sighs from Sim and Jan and cold stares from the beer drinkers on the terrace. Laingsberg is a wide place in the road surrounded by a West Texas landscape, and the expressionless Africans crouched on the sidewalk in the shade of the whites-only entrance to the general store remind me of a small-town vignette of the Deep South a generation ago. There, easier voting, fatter paychecks and black emigration northward changed the southern scene forever; nothing seems about to change it here, nothing peaceful anyway.

Cape Town. The American ambassador tells me he thinks (wrongly, as it now seems) that "the government understands that better relations with neighboring countries is linked to peaceful and gradual evolution at home." He also thinks (rightly) that "the big problem is to bring the ANC into the process of accommodation and negotiation before the younger elements become even more radicalized." I ask about U.S. investment in South Africa. "If you include portfolio investment, about $14 billion," he says.

Cape Town. A cable car takes us to a restaurant atop Table Mountain to dine with a "liberal" Afrikaner couple named Van Ryneveld. We talk of their work with the Urban Foundation—a multiracial, privately financed enterprise that concentrates on housing, employment, education and training without regard to race. Our companions see "glimmers of hope but only glimmers." Hope enough, though, to keep them chipping away at the monolith of apartheid. Would they ever consider emigrating? "No, we'll stick it out, no matter what. This is our country after all. Our ancestors settled on the Cape before there were any Africans here. Whatever happens, I'm sure we'll be needed."

Cape Town. We lunch at Parliament with Helen Suzman, the vivacious dowager of white liberalism, who for years was the only elected member of her party—which now has 28 seats (out of 179). "I can't see a happy end," she says. "Improving relations with the black front-line states will buy some time, perhaps curb the ANC and ease some tensions. But real reform, real power sharing—well, I don't see it in the cards. Young whites for the most part are as adamant as their parents, and young blacks more aggressive than theirs." She takes us to the visitors' gallery, where we can watch the proceedings. "At any rate," she adds with a smile, "we can say whatever we please in this chamber, and that's something."

Wynberg. Tea at the estate of a wealthy businessman, also active in the Urban Foundation. He hopes the "inevitable" transition to majority rule will be both measured and peaceful. "But whatever the temporary dislocation, this country will prosper in the long run. It has so many resources. If only there were more compassion . . ."

Maseru, Lesotho. In this hilly, independent kingdom surrounded by South Africa, we check into the plush Lesotho Hilton with pool, casino —and North Korean diplomats. Soviet, Chinese and Czech missions are also here. In the morning we visit a mohair cooperative set up by CARE that now earns about $500,000 a year in foreign exchange. Blacks here are more relaxed and outgoing. (The South African Army had not yet raided Lesotho in search of ANC bases; that would be for next year.)

Johannesburg. On our last evening, we go to a farewell party at the home of an English-speaking editor of Afrikaner descent. "If only the population ratio were reversed—83 percent white instead of 83 percent black, Asian and Coloured—there'd be no racial problem," he says. "It would be like your southern states in the fifties, where the blacks got political and economic equality when they ceased to outnumber the whites." I point out that they also had the law of the land on their side. "True," he says, "and we'll have to change some laws here, too. But we aren't about to, at least not soon enough. How about a refill? We'll drink to South Africa. Beautiful country, isn't it? And also much more complicated than you expected? And maybe a little frightening?" I nod, and he says, "Cheers," and we drink—he to South Africa and I to, I guess, compassion. . . .

On the long flight home, I reflected on the glimpses we'd had of this society in the agony of transition and concluded there could be no orderly outcome since political power, not just apartheid, is and always has been the issue. And power is seldom surrendered, seized or transferred peacefully in a nondemocratic nation like South Africa, which denies the vote to four out of five citizens. Perhaps the ruling whites will experience a sudden change of heart, but I wouldn't bet on it. Perhaps the progressive brutalization of the whites and the radicalization of the blacks will lead to all-out civil war. Or perhaps the final alternative to ever escalating bloodshed will turn out to be partition— one state being a predominantly white Afrikaner republic where blacks would be admitted as foreign workers (as are the Turks, Yugoslavs and Algerians in Western Europe), while in the other—call it the Republic of Azania—majority rule would prevail and whites who chose to remain could, as in Kenya, become citizens.

Meanwhile, more English-speaking whites are emigrating as the storm signals multiply; even white Rhodesians are returning to Zimbabwe. And the optimists have even less reason to be hopeful. Since our trip, more than two thousand people, mostly blacks, have been killed in two years of violent confrontation. The South African government reneged on its agreement with Mozambique and resumed aid to the rebels there. Their troops have invaded the front-line states—Botswana, Zambia and Zimbabwe—looking for ANC camps, and still conduct raids into Angola, one of them aimed at sabotaging Gulf Oil installations in Cabinda. As for Namibia, they maintain their illegal occupation of that former German colony in defiance of U.N. resolutions. And they have imposed strict censorship at home on the pretext of preserving "order."

What is certain, and has been for years, is that the days of white supremacy are numbered. What is different is that the pace of change has accelerated and the United States has lost what little leverage it ever had. Today our national interest will best be served by disengagement. Reagan's "constructive engagement" policy has been a predictable failure that has cost us the confidence of all South Africans, whatever their race. As an American diplomat told me in Johannesburg, "Under Carter, the blacks loved us and the whites hated us. Now the blacks hate us and the whites ignore us."

A year later, I heard from some of our Cape Town friends. Van Ryneveld had managed to remain hopeful: "The Urban Foundation," he wrote, "continues to progress and to have an effect—I feel I can claim a significant effect—on the thinking of our government and the South African community, and continues to achieve improvements. Of course, I do not wish to exaggerate what we have done or what we can do . . ."

Helen Suzman's letter expressed a starker view: "I think we are in for a long period of ongoing unrest, though we are not, in fact, in the midst of a revolution as some journalists would have the world believe. It is very difficult indeed to foment a revolution when one side consists of a fully equipped army and police force, and the other side is armed with sticks and stones and petrol bombs. However it is certainly possible for the enraged black population to make life very unpleasant for South Africans, and I have no doubt that urban violence and internal sabotage is going to increase . . ."

Soon after we got home, Sékou Touré, on whom I'd expended so much time and energy in the early sixties, died (of natural causes), and his cronies were deposed by the army a few days later in one of those uprisings our government should have hailed but barely took notice of. For once, an erratic and brutal tyranny was replaced by a regime that explicitly renounced Marxism, endorsed free enterprise, freed all political prisoners, posted the U.N. Declaration of Human Rights on public buildings and even changed its name from the People's Revolutionary Republic of Guinea to plain Republic of Guinea—a clear sign of progress toward democracy.

The tyranny had prevailed off and on ever since 1970, when an abortive armed raid mounted from Portuguese Guinea inflamed Touré's latent paranoia. In the subsequent backlash, the most talented men and women in his government were arrested, framed, tortured, hanged, shot or confined in the infamous Boiro prison camp in unspeakable conditions. Karim Bangoura, the former ambassador to the United States and one of the most incorruptible Africans I ever met, was deprived of food and water for eight days and then tortured with electric shocks until he signed a "confession" stating I had recruited him for the CIA—at a salary of $400,000 a month *plus* a Ford sedan! Even after this preposterous statement he was sentenced to the *diète noire*—the black diet—a euphemism for being starved to death in solitary confinement. (And while the hidden horrors of Boiro were at full throttle, Andrew Young, our touring U.N. representative, was innocently shouting, "God bless you, Sékou Touré!" in the municipal stadium a few miles down the road.)

Others managed to escape—most of them to France, Senegal or the Ivory Coast. But Diallo Telli, Guinea's former ambassador to the United Nations, minister of justice and secretary-general of the OAU, was seized at his home on July 18, 1975, and never heard of again. Not even the State Department knew of his fate.

On June 29, 1982, when Touré was David Rockefeller's guest at a Council of Foreign Relations luncheon meeting in New York, I called Rockefeller in advance and advised him I'd be asking Touré what had happened to Telli. He asked me to do it privately, after the lunch, so as to avoid possible embarrassment. Despite our long acquaintance, Touré looked at me without expression when we met, for the first time in fifteen years, after his speech, and remained impassive while I posed my question about Telli. Then he replied in a flat voice, "He was tried by a tribunal, convicted of treason and shot."

And we adjourned. Later I found out that Telli, too, had been a victim of the "black diet."

Together with other former U.S. ambassadors to Guinea, I had tried to intervene with Touré during these dark despotic years on behalf of people we knew to be innocent of subversion. But we could never muster the necessary support from the State Department; we were left to infer that Guinea had too much mineral wealth for the U.S. to risk alienating its dictator.

To return, briefly and for the last time, to South Africa: On our return, I was surprised to find so much acceptance of South African assurances that they were really committed to social reform and meanwhile remained the West's dependable bastion against Communist infiltration from the north. Reagan wondered how we could "abandon a country that has stood beside us in every war we have fought"—overlooking the fact that most of the grand old men of the now ruling National Party were interned during the last World War for pro-Nazi sympathies. But I'd become inured to Reaganisms, and they no longer bothered me, even when he said, in 1985, that segregation had been "eliminated" in South Africa or that there were no Germans alive "who were adults and participating in any way" in World War II. Did he mean there were no Germans left who are over sixty? Surely he was joking again; at least I prefer to think so. (Poor Jimmy Carter was more sensitive to Reagan's fanciful attacks on the previous administration and in 1986 phoned him to protest, saying, "Some of his statements are almost more than a human being can bear.")

But what did bother me were columnists like Bill Buckley's protégé Joseph Sobran, who wrote in a March 1985 assault on liberals: "That South African blacks are better off than most blacks (and most Russian whites) is no justification for apartheid. But in light of the liberal record, maybe we should preserve just one reactionary racist regime—as a haven for African blacks fleeing from the fruits of self-government."

When I wrote Bill, a friend since we debated at a meeting in the 1960 campaign, saying Sobran was getting more and more sophomoric, he replied that I "shouldn't dispute the talent of the brightest writer I have cultivated in thirty years" and wished I were "intelligent enough to recognize the wit and profundity of a social critic of seminal importance." One thing about Buckley: He's loyal to his writers and manages to retain the friendship of most of his critics.

On the other hand, Senator Ted Kennedy has expressed the views of what I believe are a growing number of Americans: "No matter what the South African government does, no matter how many innocent people are killed, how many neighboring countries are invaded, how many children are tortured . . . the administration clings to a bankrupt policy that puts the United States on the wrong side of history and human rights in South Africa." All we can hope for is that the White House will eventually heed the pressure of public opinion whether or not Reagan ever learns the truth about our stalwart Afrikaner allies.

Cuba has surfaced in many previous chapters but can be quickly dismissed in this one since the new administration resumed our now familiar David and Goliath relationship despite Cuba's growing acceptance among democratic Latin American leaders, who now feel Castro cares more about them than Reagan does. The diplomatic Interest Sections established under Carter still exist, so at least a channel of communication remains available even though seldom used. What discourse exists today between Washington and Havana consists chiefly of trading childish insults.

The last time I heard from Castro was in November 1981, when he wrote me denying some accusation of Secretary Haig and sending greetings to my family. I've been invited back to Havana, but can't think of a good reason to go. I think I've heard everything Castro has to say, and I also think I understand the root causes of our churlish immobility about Cuba: that Cubans have not been properly grateful for our liberating them from Spain many years ago; that more than 500,000 Cuban exiles in the U.S.—some cowed by terrorist groups like Omega 7—represent a sizable voting bloc; that the status quo, which allows us the use of Guantanamo and costs the Russians about $4 billion a year, isn't all that terrible; that Cuba is a convenient scapegoat for whatever doesn't go our way in Latin America; and finally that years of conditioning produce knee-jerk reactions, like the automatic association of the words "Soviet" and "aggression," however flimsy the evidence (Afghanistan excepted) during at least the last thirty-five years of the cold war.

Mikhail Gorbachev came to power in Moscow on March 11, 1985, and the new look he introduced in Soviet diplomacy was as striking as the contrast between his wife's appearance and, say, Mrs. Khrushchev's. For the first time we were up against an adversary who could be tough but understood the value of charm and the use of public relations. We could no longer count on Soviet ham-handedness to cancel out our blunders. "The change in Soviet style," as Flora Lewis wrote in the *New York Times,* "is a sophisticated challenge." Andrei Gromyko, the new president of the U.S.S.R., described Gorbachev to the Central Committee in even plainer terms: "Comrades, this man has a nice smile but he has iron teeth."

Within months, a summit meeting with Reagan was arranged for November in Geneva. It was clear that for domestic reasons Gorbachev needed détente and arms control. I decided this was a conference not to be missed. Back in 1982, I'd written in *Newsday* that a Reagan-Brezhnev meeting had become imperative: "Never mind an agenda or even a final communiqué. Never mind where it takes place or who issues the invitation. Instead of exchanging stiff formal notes or trying to score debating points, let them just meet alone and talk, not so much as two adversaries as two septuagenarians, each with the power to obliterate all human life and the shared resolution that it must not be allowed to happen. We have reached the point where mankind has nothing to lose from such a meeting and perhaps its own survival to gain."

Today, with a younger, more vigorous leader in the Kremlin, who knew what might happen if the chemistry between him and Reagan was right? Could the deadlock in the drawn-out arms negotiations be broken? Might the meeting produce another thaw—a lasting one in this cold war I'd started writing about nearly forty years before? I had to go.

Newsday accredited me to do some Viewpoints pieces. So I boarded the White House press plane at dawn on November 16 at Andrews Air Force Base and was assigned a seat way back in the 747 with the TV soundmen and the clipboard girls, now that I was an outsider, a has-been no longer persona grata in the first-class section with the likes of Sam Donaldson and Leslie Stahl. But I'd been there, up front, for many years, and I kind of liked the camaraderie of steerage, where nobody pontificated or reminisced and I had a chance to ponder the signifi-cance of what lay ahead. I had missed the 1955 summit but referred to it a few days before in an advance piece whose first two paragraphs surprised *Newsday*'s editors, who thought at first I was concocting some premature reporting:

> The President arrived from Washington on the 16th and was met at Cointrin Airport by Max Petitpierre, the Swiss president. At least 100 U.S. security personnel were in Geneva, along with nearly 1,500 media representatives reporting on this first summit meeting in ten years. On arrival, the President reiterated his pledge to change the "spirit" of mutual distrust: "We are not here to repeat the same dreary excuses that have characterized most of our negotiations for the past ten years . . . We are here to launch fresh negotiations."
>
> Few observers expected a major breakthrough. James Reston of the *New York Times* called the meeting "an effort to re-establish a system of diplomacy that has been suspended . . ." Congress was skeptical, seeing it as a Soviet propaganda show. But it was at least a chance to get acquainted with the new Soviet leadership.

So far, it could be 1985. But then came the paragraph that whisked the reader back thirty years to that other summit:

> The President's plane had made a refueling stop in Iceland. It was 1955, and not even the *Columbine* could fly nonstop to Europe. But Dwight

D. Eisenhower, soon to be stricken by a heart attack, was jaunty and optimistic. His wife, Mamie, was all smiles.

What had not changed, I reflected, sipping my second complimentary drink, was that the Russians were still determined to be treated as equals; that they still worried about our encircling them and that we were still worried about their wanting to break out. And once again, under Reagan, we were competing not with our real rival, a nation-state called the U.S.S.R., but with that venerable chimera of the early fifties, "Godless communism," bent, as ever, on world domination. As Edward Crankshaw, the British Sovietologist, used to point out, the bogeyman image of the Russians that we had conjured up gave us an excuse to stop thinking.

What *had* changed since the other summit was that together we had deployed some twenty thousand nuclear warheads, far more than enough to wipe out all traces of civilization, even though neither side had shown any inclination to use them. (In 1953, when we had amassed —not deployed—only one-tenth that many between us, Eisenhower recorded in his diary his "clear conviction that as of now the world is racing toward catastrophe—that something must be done to put a brake on the movement.") Also, we were now dealing with a new generation of Soviet leaders headed by a man who needed an easing of tensions to achieve stature as a world statesman as well as to push his costly and controversial reforms through his hidebound bureaucracy.

Unfortunately, neither Reagan nor Gorbachev knew very much about each other's country. A week before the conference, the president invited a group of Soviet scholars to the White House to brief him on the summit. Later, one of them said, "He talked a good deal but didn't ask any questions," while Russian historian Suzanne Massie came out saying, "The president doesn't know anything about the Soviet people at all. He's in the same position as other Americans, despite all his advisers . . ."

A foolish cartoon in the Buffalo *News* of October 21 reflected what a lot of "other Americans" thought. It showed Gorbachev telling a group of Americans at a bus stop that the Soviet Union really and truly wanted peace, and his audience walking away saying, "Excuse us while we go throw up."

But when Reagan described Gorbachev before the summit as "a reasonable man" who understood "that if we both want peace there'll be peace," it suggested he'd traveled some distance from his 1981 news conference when he said that while the Russians were on "a starvation diet of sawdust" their goal was "world revolution" and "they reserve unto themselves the right to commit any crime, to lie, to cheat in order to attain that."

As for Gorbachev, the *New York Times* ran a story from Moscow on November 14 that said: "Mikhail S. Gorbachev's America is a land controlled by wealthy capitalists and conservative business interests. Right-wing forces dictate government policy and would never permit a lasting improvement in relations with the Soviet Union. A profit-hungry military-industrial complex is the real force behind the development of space-based weapons."

Wide of the mark, of course, but not *all* that wide of the mark, as anyone familiar with Washington's power politics today would have to concede. Maybe he knew more about us than Reagan knew about them.

It was bitter cold in Geneva. A bus took those of us from the rear of the plane to the most Spartan of the three hotels housing the U.S. newspeople—the Ramada Inn, smack in the middle of Geneva's red light district. Walking around the block and stretching my legs while waiting for my bag to arrive, I passed a stout, matronly woman of a certain age on patrol with the conventional streetwalkers. Surely she had reached retirement age; but no, she was a specialist. *"Chéri,"* she murmured, "wouldn't you like to make love to your mommy?" I know Switzerland well—two of my children were born there—but it has never ceased to surprise me.

I moved into a less tacky hotel near the lake, and in the morning mingled with the thousands of media folk who had gravitated to Geneva from all over the world only to discover they had nothing to write about. A news blackout was mutually agreed upon by both sides—a sensible decision that minimized leaks and damaging speculation, as well as the traditional jousting and jockeying of official spokesmen. As Larry Speakes, the White House press secretary, put it, "The people who know something aren't talking, and the people who are talking don't know anything." Coverage was limited to formal statements and photo opportunities, with the result that the print reporters really had little to do, while the TV people, with air time that had to be filled, resorted to interviewing each other as well as most anybody who looked knowledgeable and strolled by their cameras. So the actual conference, which was scheduled to last two days and was extended to three, seemed much longer, like a play with lots of dialogue but no plot.

The daily U.S. briefings—usually by Speakes or National Security

Council Director Robert McFarlane at the Intercontinental Hotel—mostly chronicled the times and duration of meetings, and the participants; so did the Soviet briefings at the nearby International Conference Center. McFarlane did say at the outset that Reagan would "focus on realism" and stressed that "we don't intend to change their ideology." And we gathered that Reagan and Gorbachev were spending more time holding private talks than in formal meetings with their staffs —supposedly at Nancy's urging.

The day after the first Reagan-Gorbachev exchange, I ran into Malcolm Toon, our former ambassador to Moscow, wandering around the lobby, and he sounded optimistic, predicting that in time the Strategic Defense Initiative would "peter out." So did Paul Nitze, in another chance encounter; he assured me that Defense Secretary Caspar Weinberger's gratuitous message to the president, warning him against any compromises, had *not* been leaked by the Pentagon.

By the end of day two, some reporters were filing stories hinting that the prolongation of the conference was a sign of failure; others were speculating about which side would come out of it the winner.

One of the few advantages of becoming an old hand in journalism is that you can rely on that osmotic aptitude acquired by experience to anticipate and interpret events. For example, I knew this conference would not fail (or be allowed to seem to) because both Reagan and Gorbachev needed to go home proclaiming success; and consequently there would be no winner or loser, at least not in the eyes of the watching world, nor at this particular time.

So I wrote a piece along these lines, figuring I'd earned the right to contradict the younger speculators of my trade. Besides, my equally decrepit contemporaries at the scene—like Don Cook, John Chancellor and Dan Schorr—shared my view.

And of course the proceedings ended in televised harmony, with warm smiles and handshakes, and the Strategic Defense Initiative neatly swept under the rug.

What I wrote about the finale at Geneva may sound starry-eyed at *this* writing, many months later, for the nuclear arms race is still unchecked despite Soviet concessions that led Flora Lewis to write that the United States is a nation "that can't take yes for an answer." And without the prospect of some substantive agreement, there's little chance the Soviet leaders would be interested in a showboat summit just to make Reagan look good in the last years of his presidency. As I heard Arbatov say recently, "We can afford to pull back and wait for talks with a serious American administration. After all, 1989 is not so far away."

Yet I can't discount my impression on that chilly gray morning in Geneva when I joined some three thousand other newspeople at the Conference Center to watch the two principals in this first summit meeting since 1979 perform their cordial farewell ritual.

"I had an irrepressible feeling," I wrote, "that what we were witnessing was the beginning of the end of the cold war." And I continued:

> I know that a good many commentators are calling this a cosmetic conference, devoid of meaningful agreements beyond sending the Bolshoi Ballet over here and the Beach Boys over there. But my intuition tells me a different story . . .
>
> Why? In part because Reagan and Gorbachev . . . spent more time together, starting beside the fireplace in the poolhouse, than in formal sessions with their aides. Here were two men who not so long ago were comparing each other to Darth Vader and Adolf Hitler seeking out each other's company. "We looked at one another straight in the eyes," was the way Gorbachev put it after conceding that these discussions had often been "very, very lively" but also "frank and productive."
>
> "The real report card on Geneva will not be in for months and maybe years," said Reagan cautiously, but he was convinced that after their "fireside summit" the two superpowers are "headed in the right direction."
>
> No, they didn't agree on the Strategic Defense Initiative . . . but Reagan heard the case against "Star Wars" expressed forcibly and quite possibly for the first time—since presidential aides seldom have the nerve to contradict their boss.
>
> So both men may have shed some illusions as well as pondered the consequences of nuclear conflict. And that was a good thing . . .
>
> In the end, the outcome was not as barren as some are depicting it. An array of modest but real confidence-building agreements were signed in the areas of cultural and scientific exchanges, consular representation, civil aviation, risk reduction, air safety and research. The two sides came out for military parity rather than superiority and agreed a nuclear war "cannot be won and must never be fought." . . . And they decided to meet regularly, in the United States next year and in the U.S.S.R. in 1987, to help keep our ongoing competition peaceful. Could we expect much more in two days? . . .
>
> Gorbachev displayed his iron teeth on "Star Wars," just as Reagan

revealed his own stubbornness. But both men kept smiling. And the subject is sure to come up again.

So I'm betting the consequences of this summit will be more lasting than in the past. I'm betting future historians will write about what happened at Geneva in 1985 as a real turning point in the cold war. . . .

Today, I would hedge that bet only by adding, *if* both sides fully comprehend that it is no longer Us against Them, whatever our differences, but Us and Them against It—It being the ever-present risk, in this unstable world, of a nuclear exchange.

And indeed, that is what seems to be happening. There *has* been a winding down of the cold war even as I've been engaged in writing about it. True, the arms race has not slackened, and the 1986 summit meeting in Iceland foundered on Reagan's infatuation with Star Wars; yet the two sides have not retired in surly silence to their igloos, as they might have in the past. No doors have been slammed. The arms talks in Geneva continue. Even the diehard cold warriors speak in more muted tones. Perhaps they sense that an awakening public opinion, worldwide, has now made significant arms reduction inevitable, and that the militarization of space is not a concept likely to survive our 1988 presidential elections.

And now, in 1987, the initiative for greater accommodation has been seized by Gorbachev. In February, he received a high-level delegation of private U.S. citizens—people like Vance, Kissinger, Harold Brown and Jeane Kirkpatrick. A week later, more than a hundred other Americans of various professions and political hues were invited to Moscow—ranging from Ken Galbraith and Don Kendall, chairman of Pepsico, to Gregory Peck, Yoko Ono and me. In two days of roundtable discussions, I was struck by how often our Soviet colleagues stressed the need for "a new way of thinking" in order to "save the world from catastrophe." I was reminded of Einstein's prophetic words at the start of the cold war: "The splitting of the atom has changed everything save our mode of thinking, and thus we drift toward unparalleled catastrophe." Apparently the Soviets had remembered those words too.

Without precisely defining it, they suggested this "new thinking" would draw not only on the teachings of Marx but on those of the golden rule, Buddhism, humanism, Confucius and even the Bible. And when I cited Kennedy's 1963 speech about making the world "safe for diversity" and devoting our resources to solving global problems, the Soviets at the table actually applauded, something they don't do unless author-ized—and a new experience for me.

On our last day in Moscow, Gorbachev addressed the plenary session of our forum—as they described it—at the Kremlin and talked urgently about our mutual interest in a stable and secure peace without ever directly criticizing the United States or President Reagan. In fact, he spoke of the Reykjavik meeting not as a failure but as a basis for future progress. Andrei Sakharov was across the aisle from me, and Dr. Bernard Lown of Harvard was sitting next to Gorbachev on the rostrum. At the reception that followed, Russians and Americans talked about everything from human rights to the population explosion with greater candor and good humor than I had ever encountered on any previous visit.

Something was happening in the Soviet Union. You could feel the loosening of traditional Communist constraints in ordinary conversations. The word "change" was on everyone's lips; even the young woman who guided me from the airport to my hotel mentioned it. And when I shook hands with Gorbachev and exchanged a few words I had the clear impression that here was a man with whom we could negotiate an end to the arms race if only our leadership could disenthrall itself from the past.

Chapter 17

Reflections on an Age of Lunacy

IT WAS A DINNER MEETING like so many others I seem to drift into. The topic was the Strategic Defense Initiative, and the speaker was General John T. Chain, in 1985 the director of the State Department's Bureau of Politico-Military Affairs. His audience, about sixty men and women in all, had been invited to hear him because of their past or present involvement with the study or formulation of foreign policy.

Both the after-dinner speech and the questions that followed were predictable. Subjects dealt with or touched upon included speculation about the Geneva negotiations, strains in the NATO alliance, Soviet adventurism, the importance of maintaining a credible deterrent, the ABM Treaty, the Intermediate Range Nuclear Forces (INF), hardened silos, no-first-use, the role of conventional forces, verification, détente and so on.

One is reminded at these gatherings that the nuclear arms race has spawned a fraternity of experts, many at think tanks and universities and others free-lancing, who understand the jargon of high-tech warfare and treat each other with deference, even while propounding sharply differing points of view about mankind's chances for survival.

And so the general, whose assignment this evening was obviously to win over some converts to the SDI (it's not good form in this kind of environment to call it Star Wars), was not asked any questions to which he did not have an articulate and even plausible answer.

As the discussion droned on about the MX and Tridents and Pershings and throw weight, I began to feel as though I had wandered into the recreation room of a mental hospital where the inmates were playing a silly new game called Kill You, Kill Me. After nearly an hour, no one had raised any really essential matters—such as the rationale for amassing so much costly, devastating weaponry if we aren't planning to use it; or the bases for the assumption that the Russians are preparing to launch a first strike even though they know our undetectable submarines alone are capable of obliterating most Soviet cities with their nuclear missiles; or what Star Wars is sure to accomplish other than to bankrupt us.

Finally I raised my hand as the questions tapered off and was recognized by the general. I started by pointing out that the expenditure of trillions of dollars by both sides since the cold war began had made us not more but less secure with each passing year. Yet we went right on pursuing a course that makes peace more precarious and accidental war more likely. In preatomic times, wars were fought by soldiers for territory, for markets, for glory, for loot, for raw materials, for what Hitler called *lebensraum.* But did anyone on either side today expect to derive any advantage from a nuclear exchange fought by computers? So what, in short, was our quarrel with the Russians all about?

After a pause, the general replied that this was "a philosophical question."

I demurred, pointing out that an accurate estimate of enemy intentions is as important to military intelligence as an accurate estimate of military capabilities. Did we understand each other's intentions?

After another pause, he said with some asperity that while he of course couldn't speak for the Russians, he knew that *our* purpose was to bring the benefits of democracy to every country in the world.

With that, the chairman adjourned the meeting, and I didn't get a chance to suggest that we seem to have moved away from John F. Kennedy's reasonable aim, "to make the world safe for diversity," all the way back to Woodrow Wilson's unattainable one, "to make the world safe for democracy." And even beyond.

On the way out, one of my tablemates said she was glad that I'd raised a "fundamental issue," but the rest of the audience appeared to resent my having slightly disturbed the equanimity of the evening. For the tenor of discussions in the foreign policy community is by tradition conciliatory and rarely confrontational.

But when the emperor has no clothes, someone ought to say so. When we don't know for sure what our feverish dispute with the Russians is about, we ought to be seeking out the root causes instead of merely scoring rhetorical points. And if we are embarked on a global crusade to bring the heathen to democracy or the sword, someone in charge ought to let the American people know, and see if they approve. Otherwise we could be headed, by drift rather than design, toward that long cold winter now called nuclear.

And so I've continued to pose my quarrel question with people who might be expected to have a ready answer. One was Deputy Secretary of State John C. Whitehead, at a lunch in Washington. He seemed at a loss for a reply. So I recalled that back in Stalinist times we were worried about Soviet expansionism, but today . . .

"That's your answer," he broke in. "Our quarrel with the Soviets is that they are expansionist."

There was no reason, not in this setting, to point out that in the past quarter century, the Soviet Union had gained influence in just eight countries, worldwide, and lost influence in eighteen. So I let it pass.

Still another opportunity to ask my question arose at a talk two weeks before the Geneva summit by Vladimir Petrovsky, the Soviet deputy foreign minister. He replied, "The U.S.-Soviet dispute is based more on subjective than objective factors," which I took to mean that our relationship has been affected more by our feelings about each other than by any real conflicts of interest. This interpretation certainly makes sense today and, looking back over the ground covered in this book, has to a substantial degree always made sense. What does not make sense is our choosing to remain prisoners of these feelings regardless of the spiraling costs and risks they entail.

The cold war, as we have seen, started in the forties with the Soviets' effort to consolidate their hold on Eastern Europe, keep West Germany prostrate and cripple Western Europe's recovery with politically motivated labor unrest. This led to a cycle of reactions fueled by emotion: traditional near-paranoid suspicion on their side and anger on ours that our wartime enthusiasm for our Russian allies had been "betrayed" at Yalta—that we'd been suckers about Ivan as well as Uncle Joe Stalin.

So we pumped $30 billion worth of aid into Western Europe and helped our Germany get back on its feet and drove the Russians into a frenzy: in 1948 they snuffed out Czech democracy and tried pressuring us by imposing a blockade on Berlin (even though we had the atomic bomb and they didn't). Their most implacable cold warrior, Andrei Zhdanov, the founder of the Cominform, died in 1948, but by then the policies he had helped set in motion were irreversible.

Then came the Korean War. Intended as a minor operation, it triggered a massive reaction by the West, coming as it did soon after the

Communist conquest of China and the first Soviet atomic explosion. And it militarized U.S. foreign policy once and for all.

And so fear engendered fear, just as actions invited reactions, even though, as Marshall Shulman wrote in 1966, "The specter of international communist revolution is a myth. It belongs in the world of verbal symbols and not in the world of actual behavior." We didn't realize it in the forties and fifties, but our central problem, then and now, was not the Soviet Union but how to survive the cold war without a general war.

For after Stalin's death, a fresh start was possible, and in fact some tentative steps were taken even as Americans built backyard fallout shelters and schoolchildren hid under their desks in civil defense exercises.

But there was an almost uncanny ebb and flow in the level of tension that has prevailed ever since. We have seen how the "Spirit of Geneva" generated by Eisenhower and Khrushchev in 1955 was chilled by the Hungarian revolt a year later; the 1960 Paris summit, by the U-2 incident; the discreet Kennedy-Khrushchev correspondence, by the Cuban missile crisis; the momentum of the Limited Test Ban Treaty, by Kennedy's assassination; the 1967 Johnson-Kosygin meeting at Glassboro, by the Soviet invasion of Czechoslovakia the following year; the Nixon-Brezhnev détente of 1972, by apparent Soviet "adventurism" in Africa, the "Yom Kippur" war and the Jackson-Vanik amendment linking trade policy to Jewish emigration; the SALT II accord signed by Brezhnev and Carter (but not ratified by the Senate), by the phony Cuban brigade flap and the Soviet move into Afghanistan; and early hopes for an accommodation with Reagan, by Poland's crackdown on the Solidarity movement, followed by the downing of KAL 007. It almost seemed as if a deus ex machina was at work, winding up the cold war whenever it appeared to be running down.

And yet, like the barely perceptible ebb of a receding tide, each successive high-water mark of tension looked to many of us observing this era of confrontation as being a little farther down the sand than the one before; except for brief interludes (as in Reagan's first term), the rhetoric became more subdued, the propaganda less virulent, the quest for peace seemingly more earnest and the mutual accusations of bad faith and foul play far less strident than in these glacial early years of the cold war. The iron curtain had been rusting away, and words like rollback, brinkmanship, massive retaliation and unleashing Chiang now sound as archaic as manifest destiny.

Certain policies and attitudes have remained rigid simply because they have been in place so long that generations of bureaucrats have acquired a vested interest in their perpetuation. Changing a policy implies it was wrong, not just that it has become outdated, and the careers of its advocates can be adversely affected. And so inertia normally prevails at the policymaking levels.

We have seen this syndrome during decades of arms negotiations. "You can't trust the Russians" and "Peace through strength" remain the safest and most durable phrases in political parlance. This despite warnings from some of our most revered military leaders, such as General Douglas MacArthur in 1955, General Omar Bradley in 1957 and President Eisenhower (in his 1961 Farewell Address) that the momentum of a lethal arms race prompted by a military/industrial complex and grounded in baseless mutual suspicion posed, in Bradley's words, "the most strenuous challenge to man's intellect today." Yet at this writing we cannot even agree on joining the Russians in a moratorium on nuclear testing, which is like telling the world we would rather continue our tests than stop the Russian ones.

So it sometimes seems as if we like the arms race as much as the giant "defense" contractors do, or at least that we have grown accustomed to it and to the waste, the exorbitant costs and the long-term damage to our economic vitality. Who cares? Piling up the missiles and megatons has brought America back, we've been told, looking lean and mean and standing tall. Didn't we prove it in Lebanon and Grenada and Libya?

Looking back—as I have been doing in this book—at my own involvement in the history of these forty years, I naturally feel impelled to set down some of the most important things I've learned in what was never a nine-to-five, five-days-a-week kind of job. Reporting current events is a demanding profession. You are seldom off duty. Much of our conversation was shoptalk, and much of our reading was job-related, as it is in most professions dealing with evolving and ever-changing subject matter. Sometimes there is no escape even in sleep. My most recurrent dreams are still frantic episodes in far places featuring missed planes, lost baggage and botched interviews.

The total immersion that we chose as well as endured is one reason I can even now be irritated by amateur experts in foreign affairs who are aggressively assertive about things they've neither experienced nor thought very much about, such as: "The only thing the Russians respect is brute force." Like a lawyer confronted by a garrulous layman prattling about, say, promissory estoppel, I quickly distance myself from know-nothings in fields I'm familiar with. Arguing with them is a waste of breath. As a publisher, I must have heard the assertion, "You print bad news just to sell more papers," on the average of once a week. Does *anybody* know that advertising linage and not newsstand sales accounts for three-fourths of a paper's revenues? Or that the New York *Post,* which deliberately falsifies and sensationalizes—proclaiming "15,000 mass graves" at Chernobyl and "crack Soviet commandos" on Grenada —loses about $11 million a year selling those extra papers?

So I've learned to say, "If you want only good news, read *Pravda,*" or, better yet, in all situations, "You may be right." And then walk away.

What else have I learned with the passage of time? The most important lessons can be distilled into a few paragraphs:

• I've learned you do not add to your own security by adding to the insecurity of your opponent. That's why $2,000 *billion* in war-making expenditures under Reagan has not bought us any more safety than we had before.

• I've learned that our enemy is not Marxism-Leninism, nor an assertive but nonaggressive Soviet Union. Our enemy is stupidity. (This did not dawn on me until the late fifties, even though Walt Kelly's Pogo Possum had already said, "We have met the enemy, and he is us.")

• I've learned that good diplomacy is finding out what's most important to the other guy and then seeing how far you can accommodate him without jeopardizing your own vital interests. Two examples from recent times are the restoration of normal relations with China and the resolution of the Cuban missile crisis.

• I've learned that the time when there were victors and losers in wars, whether hot or cold, is now past. It has finally been openly acknowledged by both U.S. and Soviet leaders that a nuclear war is unwinnable and must never be fought. But the cold war had also been a losing proposition for both sides. The Soviets did manage to infect us with their anxiety neurosis, but our overreaction to their spastic actions of the Stalinist years, culminating in Korea, also swept us both into the same debilitating cycle of dirty tricks, bootless intrigue and swollen military budgets. Had we retained our self-confidence, we might have devoted the greatest part of our resources to strengthening our economy—which is the real source of U.S. power and influence—and kept military spending at the minimum needed for deterrence. In short, "strength through peace" is a more sensible if less rousing slogan than "peace through strength," a formula that has never worked, since almost every arms buildup in history has ended in conflict.

• I've learned that imagination—by which I mean the ability to put yourself in somebody else's shoes—is an essential attribute in business, marriage and diplomacy, yet it's not one that Americans often display in dealing with foreigners. Unable to see ourselves as others see us, we are surprised to discover that not everyone thinks of us as compassionate, law-abiding and peace-loving. For example, a 1986 poll of one thousand university students from ten European countries revealed that a majority thought the U.S. was more likely to start a nuclear war, more to blame for the failure to achieve arms control agreements and doing less than the Russians to prevent nuclear conflict. (Both nations were also viewed by a majority of the students as seeking to dominate the world.) I have trouble convincing people that our perception of ourselves has never been shared by the rest of mankind, except perhaps briefly in the first postwar years and in the early sixties. Certainly we have been generous—or used to be. (Our foreign aid now accounts for less than one percent of our annual budget, and one half of that goes to two countries—Israel and Egypt.) But as we should know, the richest man in town is seldom beloved and not always respected. Of course, now that the United States has become the world's leading debtor nation with the world's largest deficit, we may be regarded with more sympathy in the global community.

This question of imagination was highlighted in a letter written by Gerard Smith, the U.S. representative in the first SALT negotiations, to the *New York Times*. It is worth quoting here:

As we hear the Administration's demands that the Soviets correct their arms control behavior, I've been asking myself what we Americans would think if the Soviets had: Failed to ratify the three latest arms control agreements that their Premier had signed; walked away from negotiations for a comprehensive test ban and for limitations on antisatellite systems; announced that they were making an all-out effort to develop nationwide defenses banned by the ABM treaty; announced that that treaty's correct interpretation permitted the development and testing of systems which the treaty by its very terms prohibited; had refrained from starting negotiations about strategic arms for many months, and then made offers which their former minister of foreign affairs had acknowledged to be non-negotiable and "absurd"; while claiming violations, had refrained from making effective use of the Standing Consultative Commission to resolve disputes or was reported to have denied permission for its delegates to raise the issues; announced that it was breaking out of an agreement setting ceilings on missiles and bombers because of bad behavior by the other party.

This is what we have done, and I suggest that it warrants a degree of caution in making judgments about Soviet behavior.

• I've learned the chief motivation of all ambitious people is to gain and cling to power. With rare exceptions, the motivation is neither ideology nor idealism, though these are often invoked as camouflage. Soviet leaders customarily *talk* in Marxist and Leninist jargon but *think* of their own careers and Russian national interests. As an ideology, communism is a shambles, with almost as many squabbling sects as there are Christian denominations. Some imaginative diplomacy on our part in the post-Reagan years could lead, as former Assistant Secretary of State Harlan Cleveland has suggested, to "a non-explosive decomposition of the Soviet empire." For starters, we could avoid calling the Russian people hopeless and incurable barbarians, which only reinforces their feeling of kinship with their rulers.

• I've learned that threats in the tradition of gunboat diplomacy are less and less effective as the yellow, brown and black people of the world become more assertive. They no longer cringe at the crack of the white man's whip, not even in South Africa. The last world war, jet travel, the dismantling of colonial empires, the spread of literacy, radios and television finally roused the wretched of the earth from centuries of torpor. The revolution of rising expectations is now irreversible, and when we tell the Nicaraguans to say uncle "or else," you can be sure they'll choose "or else" every time, just as the Vietnamese did. And then what do we do? Bomb them back to the stone age—or just fade away? Nor will we stop terrorism by dropping a few bombs on Libya or hijacking some hijackers. We can reduce terrorism only by undercutting and eliminating the forces that give rise to it, even at the risk of standing up to Israel when its actions impede the peace process. As Moorhead Kennedy, one of the American hostages in Iran, has written, "In a larger sense, it means real and overdue dialogue with the Third World."

• I've learned that casting our rivalry with the Soviet Union in terms of moral absolutes has always been a mistake. Dulles used to call neutralism "immoral," and Reagan has described our rivalry as a "struggle between right and wrong, good and evil." Like most Americans, I wouldn't want to live in a Communist society, but it's important for us to understand that the living conditions of average citizens in the Soviet Union, Eastern Europe and even Cuba are no longer as grim as the exiles and dissidents make these out to be. In Russia, per capita consumption has tripled since 1949, new housing has burgeoned and life, though dull and regimented, is secure for the great majority of people. I even met Jews in Moscow and Leningrad who did not want to emigrate. Of course, the plight of political prisoners is harsh and sometimes brutal, but these comprise less than one percent of the population in most Communist states. And torture, as practiced in Argentina as late as 1979, seems to be going out of style among contemporary despotisms, including Cuba's.

• I've learned that the words "left," "right," "liberal" and "conservative"—not to mention their "neo" and "extreme" variations—have become useless in defining political attitudes. They are now objectively meaningless and serve only to suggest approbation or opprobrium, depending on the user's point of view. Left and right are especially useless and indeed have been ever since the radical Jacobins and the moderate Girondins convened on opposite sides of the old Parisian indoor tennis court during the revolution of the 1790s. For the past two decades, when the authoritarian tactics and philosophy of the "extreme left" and the "extreme right" have become almost indistinguishable except for their slogans, the linear left-to-right spectrum has become wholly obsolete; it has come to resemble a horseshoe, with the two extremities much closer to each other than to us moderates in the center, which is up where some players hold the shoe for the pitch. And who knows what a "conservative" is anymore? You have to use a lot of litmus paper to see if he or she is *against* handgun control, legal abortion, SALT II, the press, the United Nations, environmental conservation and the Equal Rights Amendment; and *for* capital punishment, aid to the Contras, school prayer, more arms spending, lower taxes, nuclear power and white rule in South Africa. Jerry Falwell's recent reference to "conservative issues" like trillion-dollar funding for Star Wars and big bucks for the Nicaraguan "freedom fighters" camped in Honduras would cause an authentic conservative like the late Senator Robert Taft to moan in his grave. As for "liberal," it has become a label to be avoided, nothing more. Since both words contribute more to imprecision than to clarification, they should be banished from our political vocabulary, along with doves, hawks and owls.

I get called a liberal now and then for criticizing radical policies, such as trying to overthrow governments for ideological reasons, favored by the Reaganites. I oppose these policies because they reflect the

Soviet style of problem solving and usually fail the true conservative test of our national interest. Patrick Buchanan, the leading White House ideologue, expressed what I mean by such failure in a 1984 column that said in part:

> Review the list of the especially despised of the Western liberals in the postwar era—Chiang Kai-shek, General Franco, General Batista, President Thieu, Marshal Ky, Lon Nol, the Shah, General Somoza, General Pinochet, Ian Smith, Botha of South Africa, etc. What all these rulers had in common was that they were militantly anti-Communist, pro-West, and, in the struggle for the future of mankind, they openly sided with the United States.

What they chiefly had in common was that all were or are born losers, out of step with the rhythm of history and out of tune with professed American ideals. But Buchanan wouldn't be in the White House if he didn't say what Reagan feels.

"Are there Marxist-Leninists here and about in the world?" asked Senator Pat Moynihan in a commencement speech that same year. "Yes, especially when the West allows communism to identify with nationalism. But in truth, when they do succeed, how well do they do? And for how long?"

• I've learned those are good questions, based on the evidence of long years of cold warfare. People struggle for nationalism, not ideology. Stalin knew this. When he exhorted his people to repel the Germans on the outskirts of Moscow in 1941, he did not mention communism, only *rodina*—the motherland. "They are fighting for Russia, not for us," he told a colleague on the Politburo. Later, as Edward Crankshaw pointed out, "It was Russia in arms, not communism, which occupied half of Europe in 1945."

• I've learned Americans are more violence-prone than I'd been taught in school or college, where we were never even told of our bloody war of repression in the Philippines; and increasingly so, judging from today's hit shows and movies. Since 1945, we've conducted no fewer than nineteen major military campaigns or paramilitary operations in Third World countries, starting in Greece in 1948 and continuing through Korea, Iran, Guatemala, Indonesia, Lebanon, Laos, Cuba, the Congo, British Guiana, the Dominican Republic, Vietnam, Cambodia, El Salvador, Nicaragua, Grenada and Libya. We certainly have wasted plenty of gooks in our time, to employ the jargon we all used in Okinawa in 1945 and later in Vietnam; and now the hundreds of U.S. military bases that speckle the globe make us seem even more militaristic than we actually are.

• I've learned that civil wars are seldom negotiable—the rebels must either win or surrender—and that revolution or counterrevolution cannot be imported from the outside; the uprising must be spontaneous and homegrown, as in Haiti and the Philippines in 1986, or Guinea in 1984. That is what makes the administration's obsessive support for Nicaragua's feeble and quarreling Contras so unexplainable in terms of U.S. interests and prestige.

• I've learned that humiliation is never forgiven, although killing often is. The Germans don't brood about the savage, senseless firestorms started by British and American bombers in Dresden in the final months of the war. But the humiliation they felt was imposed on them by the victorious Allies in the twenties is what helped pave Hitler's road to power.

• I've learned, finally, that the only meaningful political distinctions are between those people, regardless of partisan or class identification, whose reactions to issues are instinctively rational/pragmatic and those whose reactions are instinctively emotional/ideological. Typical of the latter would be Claire Sterling (remember her as Claire Neikind in Chapter 4?), author of *The Terror Network,* which promoted the wildly irrational and now discredited theory that the Bulgarians, under KGB orders, hired a Turk to kill the Pope. Typical of the former would be George Kennan, seeking to deal with the Russians "as they are—not like us in some ways—but also as a great and proud people" who deserve more comprehension than the perennial outrage (remember Carter after Afghanistan?) that we are so quick to express at their often brutal but, from their perspective, understandable behavior.

Many of these deceptively simple truths, gleaned from the exercise of an exacting profession, are not always expressed in the foreign policy scriptures: the heavy, often turgid volumes—the Ph.D. theses—the think tank reports—the kinds of articles in specialized journals that deal in abstractions and are read as a duty and employ words like "construct" as a noun. Their authors usually have very little mud on their boots; some are dogmatists who write not so much to enlighten their readers as to validate their credentials as pundits or scholars. Old leftists who became neo-conservatives, like Norman Podhoretz, are particularly adept at propounding views that I suspect they are too intelligent to honestly believe.

Irving Kristol is another guru of this intellectual faction who can talk utter nonsense with authority and a certain style. At one meeting I attended in 1985 where he was part of a panel, I heard him say we lived in an ideological world (not true); that the U.S. is an ideological country (not true except for our present leadership); that the European socialists are an anti-U.S. influence (not true—François Mitterand is far more sympathetic to our interests than was Charles de Gaulle); that nothing will come out of Geneva (not true—a dialogue was started that hasn't stopped yet); that it's a good thing our Latin American policy is "abrasive and dynamic" (an argument I was unable to follow); that Europeans are scared of the Soviets (perhaps, but less than formerly and far less than Americans are); that professional diplomats hate Reagan's policies (no wonder, since they don't work); that Europe has no interest in Latin America and shouldn't have (actually they do and why shouldn't they?); and that Soviet foreign policy has been "relatively successful" (though he didn't say where, and I could only think of southern Africa as a place where they could score some points if we go on losing the confidence of the black majority that will eventually prevail).

Yet Podhoretz, Kristol, Jeane Kirkpatrick and the other rigid cold warriors continue to command attention and exert influence, however skewed their analyses and interpretations of history.

One reason for the hearing accorded proponents of policies unsuited to the present day is that American attitudes about the Soviet Union and *its* policies jelled during the Stalinist years and have persisted long after they ceased to be valid. And as we have seen, some Soviet actions since Stalin—in Hungary, Berlin, Czechoslovakia, Cuba, Ethiopia, Afghanistan and at home (against dissidents like Sakharov)—reinforced our stereotype of a brutal, malevolent regime bent on world domination and standing ten feet tall. Strong as we were and are, the Pentagon and those who depend on its largesse propagated the notion that the wily Russians were stronger, or anyway catching up fast, and that we had to spend more money to stay ahead.

And they are still at it, more ardently than ever. In Secretary of Defense Caspar W. Weinberger's Annual Report to the Congress for Fiscal Year 1987, there is a paragraph that states a premise no one actually believes but which might scare some congressmen into approving a heftier budget:

> The net results of these Soviet efforts is to create an overall military posture designed to fight and win a nuclear war. Indeed, the magnitude of Soviet expenditures on offensive and defensive forces combined with the evidence from their military exercises and writings, underlines our strong conviction that the Soviets continue to believe that a nuclear war could be fought and won.

The truth is that the Russians know what we know—which is that a nuclear war is *not* winnable. Yet the quoted paragraph, belied by all serious intelligence estimates, slipped past the State Department, where I was told the officer responsible for reviewing the annual D.O.D. Report to the Congress was away when it arrived. Former Defense Secretary Robert McNamara was with me when we were given this explanation, sheepishly I might add, and he expressed his outrage in no uncertain terms. Nor did any of the Department's top Sovietologists present agree with the Weinberger conclusion.

Fortunately, the Congress no longer takes every Pentagon statement at face value, as it once did.

Yet the stereotype of insatiable, untrustworthy Russians is still widespread, as reflected in newspaper cartoons. I have one before me, from the Washington *Times,* showing a Russian bear, burping and chewing chunks out of the globe as he tells a tiny, bewildered Uncle Sam across a negotiating table, "Keep talkin' . . . I'm listening!" The wonder is that the latest 1986 polls I've seen show that at least two-thirds of all Americans want us to abide by SALT II and oppose giving more money to the Contras. Perhaps American common sense is reasserting itself after six years of Reaganite hokum; nobody can go on believing what ain't so forever. Given the thin gruel of world news displayed on TV and all but about twenty-five newspapers, nationwide, this is reassuring.

Understanding foreign policy is really quite simple if you concentrate on essentials. Its aim, so far as I'm concerned, is clear: the survival of our free democratic system in a habitable planet. Of course the world has become increasingly interdependent, and we must cooperate with other countries in solving global problems—pollution, population growth, renewable energy, famine, war, resource depletion, drug addiction, crime, nuclear proliferation and so on. But our core concern must always be the United States national interest, which is not served by meddling in every barroom brawl on earth.

It's no secret that we have not concentrated our efforts on the aim expressed above. As a people, we seem to have decided to stop thinking, tense up and let the adrenaline flow whenever Russians intrude on our newscasts or conversations. Watching a stern young editorial commentator on "Nation's Business News" on a Providence, Rhode Island, station the other night, I heard him read the teleprompter's message that we must "strike at communism wherever it rears its ugly head"—which is not just an infelicitous phrase but an enterprise so quixotic that you wonder how they go about recruiting editorial talent in the Providence media. Yet he was mild compared to the WABC talk show I heard in a New York taxicab last summer during which Bob Grant, the host, interrupted a caller who pointed out quite rightly that it was safer to walk around Moscow than New York after dark.

"Shut up!" screamed Grant. "I'm hanging up on you Russian fink, you Communist slime!"

The driver cheered me up by changing stations. "The guy is nuts," he said, "but sometimes he's funny."

Why such rage—not just on Grant's part but so quick to flare up among otherwise rational Americans? Habit, I think, nurtured by at least sixty-five years of conditioning, explains much of this fear and loathing of all things Russian. (During the McCarthy period, I remember the owner of the celebrated Russian Tea Room in New York saying, only half in jest, that he might have to change its name to the Anti-Russian Tea Room.) There is also the perceived existence of a perpetual Russian threat, perceived even by high officials like Caspar Weinberger, who last year quoted Lenin's call for the fusion "of all nations of the world into a single, worldwide Soviet Republic." And Weinberger added, "This goal remains unchanged." While it's true that Lenin made the remark, it's not true that his goal remains unchanged so far as the present Soviet leadership is concerned. Many of Lenin's sayings have been overtaken by reality; moreover, he didn't know about nuclear weapons. I have yet to meet a single student of contemporary Soviet policy who thinks the Kremlin hopes to gain control of the entire world, but it does suit Secretary Weinberger's budgetary purposes to say so. Unfortunately he frightens a lot of his fellow citizens in the process.

Then why doesn't the Kremlin explicitly repudiate Lenin? Probably for the same reason we don't repudiate any utterances of the Founding Fathers, who lived in an age when slavery was legal; nor the Monroe Doctrine, even if we only pay lip service to it: we tolerate the presence of British troops in the Falkland Islands, French troops in Guiana and

Soviet troops in Cuba since they pose no threat to us. So the pronouncements of another era by long-gone statesmen are preserved like dusty scrolls in a vault, not to be fished out and invoked in serious argument. Weinberger is smart enough to know this, which makes his scare tactics all the more reprehensible.

We do face a threat, but of a different nature. George Kennan defined it on the eve of the 1985 Geneva summit as follows:

> I see the weapons race in which we and they are now involved as a serious threat in its own right, not because of aggressive intentions on either side but because of the compulsions, the suspicions, the anxieties such a competition engenders, and because of the very serious danger it carries with it of unintended complications—by error, by computer failure, by missed signals, or by mischief deliberately perpetrated by third parties. . . . For all these reasons . . . what most needs to be contained . . . is not so much the Soviet Union as the weapons race itself."

I have heard it argued by Assistant Secretary of Defense Richard Perle and others that the Russians will drop out of the arms race if we keep accelerating it so as to avoid the collapse of their economic system; and that, as we regain nuclear superiority, this will compel them to change their system and their policies. I doubt that the kind of people who endured the 900-day siege of Leningrad, survived a devastating war that killed fifty times as many Soviet citizens as Americans and then rebuilt their country into a superpower are likely to belly up or cry uncle under financial pressure; they are much more likely to tough it out, whatever the cost to us both.

The Perles, Weinbergers and other so-called hawks in Washington do not want a nuclear war any more than the Soviet hard-liners do; they may be wrong, but they aren't crazy or suicidal. By now they know the consequences of a nuclear holocaust. Americans and Russians together peered into the abyss during the 1962 missile crisis; we stopped short, thanks to Kennedy's diplomatic acumen, and they drew back, thanks to Khrushchev's appreciation of reality. It's doubtful that we'll ever get into such an eyeballing confrontation again.

Yet the last two world wars were neither planned nor anticipated. In the summer of 1914, not one European leader believed in the possibility of a general catastrophe. Past Balkan crises had been resolved without major conflict. But this time there were too many miscalculations and uncertainties and ambiguous commitments. War came and bled Europe white. In 1939, Hitler wanted conquest without major war and figured the Allies would back down over Poland as they had over the Rhineland, Austria and Czechoslovakia; they didn't. Two years later, he miscalculated again, figuring the Russians, who had trouble defeating four million Finns, would be a pushover; they weren't.

Miscalculations are still possible today but less likely because of the nuclear factor. Even an impulsive leader will pause before taking an action that could escalate into a conflict with no victors. The chief danger, as Kennan suggested, is in the growing role of machines that care nothing about mankind's survival when plugged into the war-making decision process.

Why then, with about fifty thousand nuclear weapons between them, do the United States and the Soviet Union produce two or three new ones every week? Even a cut of 50 percent in both arsenals, which was agreed upon in principle at Geneva, would leave enough to blow up the world ten times over. Why go on testing them? Why press for the militarization of space?

There being no logical answers to such questions, we can only refer to columnist Art Buchwald's Kill Ratio proposal, which would reduce the nuclear arsenals in both countries to the point where they could kill every American and Soviet citizen only *five* times.

> Cutting the Kill Ratio in half won't be easy [he wrote], but it is possible to persuade the superpowers to agree to it, particularly when it can be argued that you only have to kill a person *twice* to make your point in an all-out holocaust . . .
>
> The U.S. military will argue that the Soviets may sign a treaty agreeing to kill every American only five times, and then cheat, by stashing away enough weapons to kill them seven times . . .
>
> The Soviet military could balk at cutting the KR in half on the grounds that, while the U.S. might reduce its weapons, they are still at a disadvantage because if we refuse to include West European warheads in the count, each Soviet citizen could still be killed eight times. . . .

And so on. Without Buchwald and a few other satirical columnists —like Russ Baker, Art Hoppe and Bob Yoakum—today's newspapers that publish only the "serious" commentators might sound to future generations like house organs of a lunatic asylum. The humorists are the

Scaramouches of our time—"born with the gift of laughter and a sense that the world is mad."

And so it is. Lunacy is not too strong a word for a world—

where $800 billion are squandered annually on military expenditures while one person in four is hungry and one adult in three cannot read or write;

where in this enlightened century alone, 78,000,000 lives have been lost in 207 wars, more than five times as many deaths as in the previous hundred years;

where there is now one soldier for every 43 people, and one physician for every 1,030;

where the Soviet Union alone in one year spends more on its military establishment than all the developing countries spend for education and health care for 3.6 billion people;

where every day the U.S. spends $595,000 to operate one aircraft carrier while 14,000 African children die of hunger-related causes.

Such a list could go on and on. The bottom line is that the total military expense of the cold war now exceeds $3,000 billion, yet we go right on draining the lifeblood out of our economy by diverting resources and talent to design and build devices for waging a nuclear war which everybody agrees cannot be won.

More than thirty years ago, President Eisenhower said, "The problem in defense spending is to figure how far you should go without destroying from within what you are trying to defend from without." Later, in a letter to a friend, he wrote: "Some day there is going to be a man sitting in my present chair who has not been raised in the military services and who will have little understanding of where slashes in their estimates can be made with little or no damage. If that should happen while we still have the state of tension that now exists in the world, I shudder to think of what would happen in this country."

That is where we are today. The ever mounting deficits mean that in effect we are selling our productive capacity to foreigners and borrowing from our children and grandchildren in order to finance the acquisition of high-tech weaponry no sane person would contemplate using, as well as seventeen thousand more nuclear weapons in the next ten years. President Reagan, as I write this, still seems infatuated with Star Wars, a trillion-dollar fantasy, but it's beginning to look as if he may not get his way. As Noel Gayler, a retired admiral who was commander in chief of U.S. forces in the Pacific—and director of the National Security Agency from 1969 to 1972—wrote in 1985:

> If we *look*, we can see two roads into the future: one road perilous to ourselves and all others, the other leading to the peaceful use of space for all mankind. If we *listen*, we can hear the voices of sanity here, in Russia and around the world saying, "Put an end to the arms race in space."

Lunacy. With one exception, there is not a single really vital problem confronting mankind that would be solved by nuclear war—not poverty, not disease, not pollution, not hunger, not crime—to cite just a few. The exception is population growth, which underlies many of the others. Since 1850, when world population finally reached one billion, it has risen to five and now increases by another billion every twelve years or so. Nuclear war might indeed solve the population problem once and for all.

None of the urgent matters on our national agenda are novel; it's just that they have been shoved aside so long most people tend to overlook them. Back in 1969, I remember writing Chief Justice Warren with some suggestions for an article we hoped he would write for *Look*. The topics are as valid today as they were then, eighteen years ago: the population explosion, the computerization of society, the peace imperative, the erosion of the Bill of Rights, the degradation of the environment, the widening gap between the affluent and the poor, the decline in educational standards and the end of ideology.

These questions have not been seriously addressed by the executive branch or the Congress any more than has U.S. policy toward the Soviet Union—which remains our most important short-term domestic and international issue. Do we have a long-term goal? Are we prepared to live at peace and as an equal with the Soviet Union? Do we want to roll back Soviet power? Destroy the Soviet system? Without discussing and answering questions like these we will never develop a coherent policy, and a kind of solemn lunacy will continue to prevail.

By solemn lunacy I mean statements like this excerpt from a background paper sent to me last year by the State Department: "The U.S. has learned from hard experience that moratoriums such as those proposed by the Soviets cannot be counted on to lead to increased security." What hard experience? Has a moratorium such as the one instituted unilaterally by Gorbachev in 1985 ever been tried? If the administration wants to continue testing nuclear devices in an endless pursuit of superiority, it should at least have the honesty to say so to the taxpayers who are footing the bill.

But we are not a thinking nation at this moment in history. "You can't trust the Russians" is usually the opening and closing statement of people with whom I occasionally raise the issue of U.S.-Soviet relations. Sometimes I persist by asking, "Isn't avoiding nuclear war in their interest as well as ours? So why can't we trust them to act in their own interest?" I can't recall anyone ever answering, "Yes, unless they're crazy." Instead, they change the subject.

Yet a tough, patient, lawyerly approach has achieved agreements with the Russians that have been adhered to, as U.S. negotiators have learned during the thirty-odd years we've sat across tables from each other. They will probe the soft spots and loopholes in any agreement (as in the ABM treaty) and stretch the spirit, though not the letter, of whatever has been signed and sealed. But they respect precision.

This is something we really have learned from "hard experience," or should have. Still some Pentagon officials, watching defense contractors lined up at the Star Wars window, prefer to ignore the evidence and stay within the more familiar and politically safe perimeters of make-believe.

Younger people, too, seem to accept the tired clichés of the cold war more readily than their elders. The generation that has lived with these monstrous bombs in their backyards, so to speak, has grown accustomed to them and tends to discount their awful potential.

Younger people also accept the mostly obsolete but easy to grasp slogans of the early cold war because they are taught so little history at school and, from what I have seen as a visiting lecturer at colleges these past few years, are not pressed to think much beyond what they are told in class and need to remember long enough to regurgitate at exam time. The U.S. has now sunk to forty-eighth among the 159 members of the United Nations in literacy levels, and a 1985 survey of seventeen-year-olds by the National Endowment for the Humanities found that one-half did not recognize the names of Winston Churchill and Josef Stalin, while one-third could not point to Britain or France or West Germany on a map of Europe. A random quiz conducted around the country by *USA Today* on abiding by the SALT II Treaty revealed the relatively more casual views of the young about the nuclear threat, compared to their elders. The three respondents between nineteen and thirty-four replied, "I'm not optimistic about there ever being peace between the USA and Russia. . . . It seems that there is no way to regulate what the

Soviets do, so a SALT II agreement is useless. . . . If we did not build up our arms they would just build up theirs. I just don't trust the Soviets."

Conversely, the four respondents between forty-five and eighty all favored our abiding by SALT II and stressed the importance of "doing anything," as one said, "to encourage peace."

In my hometown, a local committee for nuclear arms control has a membership of nearly seven hundred, but at its meetings, no matter how prominent the speaker, the median age of the audience must be at least fifty. I guess the young have decided to let us save their world —they have other things to do. And since the president doesn't seem worried . . . why worry?

Unfortunately, Reagan is so comfortable with unreality and fiction —which is where he comes from—that he seems to have no problem presiding over the general lunacy while exuding confidence and merriment.

As David Broder, the reasonable and highly respected Washington correspondent has written, "Reagan is the living refutation of Francis Bacon's aphorism that 'knowledge is power' . . . The task of watering the arid desert between Reagan's ears is a challenging one to his aides." When Reagan worries, it's about the Nicaraguan army being "two driving days from the Texas border," not about the concerns of men like John Oliver Wilson, chief economist of the Bank of America, who has said, "Ten years from now, we will look back and ask: What happened to the industrial and financial strength of the American economy?"; nor, surely, like former Secretary of Defense Clark Clifford, who told the National Press Club in 1985, "I pray to God that some day the nations of the world will have leaders who can bring to a grinding halt this incredible arms race, which is, to me, the most poisonous insanity ever to afflict the minds of men."

In an earlier chapter, I said the cold war had been fueled by ignorance, fear and greed. Before concluding these reflections, let's reexamine the basis for this statement.

Ignorance of Soviet fears and motivations, for all of our elephantine intelligence apparatus, has caused us to overestimate their appeal and overreact to their every gambit since 1950. And our response has usually been military in nature. Certainly public support for increased military spending rose sharply after the Iranian hostage and Afghan crises; yet not even a budget twice as big would have deterred the Ayatollah or the Kremlin. It would simply have aggravated our deficit.

Henry Rositzke, a retired CIA official who ran our espionage operations against the Soviet Union, explained why in a 1985 interview:

> After twenty-five years of "fighting the Russians" in the CIA, and ten years on a Virginia hilltop watching détente slide into confrontation, it is my conviction that the long-term Soviet threat to the American interest is not military but political and economic.

After pointing out that we have not been using our superior economic clout in the developing world, he dismissed a question about the widespread belief that the Russians want to invade the U.S. and make it a Communist state:

> It's such a ludicrous, stupid affair. In thirty-five years they have never sent their troops outside their border areas. . . . Afghanistan is along their border. In all my years in government and since, I have never seen an intelligence estimate that showed how it would be profitable to Soviet interests to invade Western Europe or to attack the United States. There is no rationale for it. They are mainly concerned with becoming stronger to withstand the American threat, which is obviously greater than the Soviet threat is to us. For thirty-five years we have had bases around the Soviet Union. We encircled the Soviet Union because we were afraid they were going to expand their power by military means. Then why are we so afraid of them? Because we have a leader who has a real deep emotional fear and hatred of the Russians, of communism. It's that little thing in the American stomach that says, "This is the devil."

If we were not ignorant, I wouldn't have to avoid pointless arguments by changing the subject when wealthy, college-educated contemporaries try to provoke me after a few drinks with statements like, "The liberals lost China," "The Council on Foreign Relations is organizing the surrender of the United States to the Russians," or "Watergate was a Democrat conspiracy." Oh sure, I could shoot back, but to what purpose? These people are usually over sixty and as petrified as Jurassic fossils.

Fear is the offspring of ignorance, and if we were not fearful, the administration we elected twice would not run away from the World Court, from UNESCO, from the Law of the Sea Conference, from groups where we can't have it all our way, all the time. This didn't use to matter when we were less afraid. For twenty-five years, from the establishment of the U.N. in 1945 until 1970, the U.S. was able to advance its policies through persuasion, friendship and moral authority. We took pride in pointing out that the Soviets had cast 103 vetoes while we had cast none—a sign of which side had the confidence and respect of the nations of the world.

Then, in 1970, the Nixon Administration cast America's first veto, and in the next fifteen years we cast forty-one more—eighteen of them during the first four years of the Reagan Administration. During this time, the Soviet Union cast only nine. As George Ball has written, "There is an old cautionary French saying that one tends to assume the visage of one's adversary."

Fear. The late British Sovietologist Edward Crankshaw, whom I wrote about earlier, called his last collection of essays *Putting Up with the Russians.* In it he wrote:

> An American President appears to see nothing demeaning in proclaiming to the world at large that the fate of his great, magnificent, rich and so powerful country depends on the outcome of this or that squalid war in Central America—and this after Cuba, 1962!
>
> Many years ago, I wrote that the Kremlin's one great achievement was turning itself into a bogey to give us an excuse to stop thinking. . . . The Soviet Union is a fact of life, like the weather. We have to live with it. Soviet leaders go on about "peaceful coexistence" as though it were an original idea they had dreamed up. It is not an idea at all. We do in fact coexist and will continue to do so whether we like it or not unless and until we blow ourselves off the face of the earth. The adjective "peaceful" simply begs the question. . . . For us it means, or should mean, live and let live.

Otherwise, there's always *Rambo.* As an eleven-year-old boy was quoted after seeing the picture, "It makes you want to go out and kill a Commie." Or as the president said (with a grin), "I've seen *Rambo.* Now I know what to do."

The Russians are scared of us too. But not that scared.

And finally, greed. Waste and profligacy are a permanent scandal in the Pentagon and a topic well documented in other books than this. As I write this chapter, Litton Systems, Inc., a subsidiary of one of the ten biggest arms contractors, has pleaded guilty to 321 counts of fraud involving more than $6 billion of taxpayer money. It neither shocks nor surprises me. When hundreds of billions of dollars are dispensed each year by an overstaffed government agency long accustomed to getting what it wants and spending it as it wants, the taxpayer is bound to be fleeced.

Moreover, not many congressmen with arms industries in their districts and PAC funds available to them if they vote right are going to blow the whistle on waste, especially since their uninformed and fearful constituents have been all too willing, until recently, to support "defense" spending. Of the fourteen senators who got more than $30,000 each from arms industry PACs, thirteen backed production of the destabilizing MX missile. (Reagan has said he wants one hundred of them, which, equipped with ten warheads each, could finish everything off, senators included.)

It has always been so since the cold war started. As early as 1946, *Business Week* was reporting that Washington policymakers were "beginning to think in terms of gearing industry for a quick shift back to a war basis." By 1950, *U.S. News and World Report* could say, "The cold war is the catalyst . . . for almost endless good times. . . . Cold war is an automatic pump-primer. Turn a spigot, and the public clamors for more arms spending. Turn another, the clamor ceases . . . Cold war demands, if fully exploited, are almost limitless."

Of course, a permanently frightened public was part of the scenario. There had to be periodic crises to justify military spending when the economy went into a slump. Imaginary bomber gaps, missile gaps and windows of vulnerability were made to appear, by politicians of both parties, real and frightening.

It's too bad we don't divert a portion of these billions to waging a serious war on the drug barons and criminal underworld who are sapping America's strength far more than—dare I say it?—the Sandinistas. But we don't. Maybe we are getting used to living in a blighted society with a permanent, stunted underclass.

Why do people like me and my closest friends care so much about the madness of these times? Why have some of us become involved with a cold war that historians are certain to look back on as a time of dangerous and turbulent idiocy and even, now and then, tragedy? One reason is that we hope to die knowing that the children we helped bring into this world, and *their* children, will live out their lives in a saner, less frenzied and more humane environment. It is not too wild a dream. We ourselves are too old to suffer the consequences of a precipitous decline in civilization; the dark ages, if they come, are probably some decades away.

Another reason is that my generation, unlike the young who mostly exist in the present, lives also in the past and the future—recalling the former's mistakes and the latter's promise. And over the years, we have developed a kind of esprit de corps about this queer human race. If we believe in God, we must assume we are being tested. Will we pass the test, shove the nuclear genie back into its bottle and accomplish what a probably benevolent deity expects of us on this small planet?

It may take a few nuclear explosions and a hundred million deaths to bring home the enormity of our madness to enough people and to wrench them away from old and familiar habits of thought. If so, these deaths, unlike those in so many other wars, will not have been in vain.

The trend of events in the forty years spanned by this book has not been all bad. Adversaries, for the most part, have moderated their dialogue. Even Reagan, after his first two years, found he could not turn the calendar back to the darkest winters of the cold war and still retain the popularity he treasures. There is less invective and more restraint. There is also creeping democracy in Latin America and creeping capitalism in the countries called Communist. A renewal of détente, with a different label, seems inevitable, given the calamitous economic alternative. The U.S. Congress has become more assertive, as have our European allies, and the more our representatives hear the voices of reason and of protest from the hustings, the sooner we will emerge, as a nation, from this lunatic but transitional moment in the human adventure on earth.

Getting the attention of our leaders is still, thank God, something we can do that the Russians can't, at least not yet.

Will the turnabout come before the arms race spins out of control and the new technology takes charge of our destiny? "Your people don't understand that we're living in a different time," said a *Pravda* editor to one of my friends last year. "I love your country, your cities, New York especially. But I get the feeling your technology has gotten ahead of your understanding of reality."

So much depends on how fast we grow up. As Frances FitzGerald wrote in *The New Yorker* in 1985: "The question left for the next election is what any candidate can say about foreign affairs that will get him elected and at the same time be true. This question, bizarre as it is, may be as profound as any in American political history."

I've quoted a good many people in this book whose opinions I've learned to respect as my own understanding of the cold war has been deepened by experience. One of the wisest, and the first I quoted—in the Foreword—was George Kennan, the eminent scholar and diplomat whose involvement with Soviet-American relations goes back nearly sixty years. In 1983, he wrote a piece called "Breaking the Spell." I can think of no more fitting conclusion to this book than the closing words of that essay:

> At the end of our present path of unlimited military confrontation lies no visible destination but failure and horror. There are no alternatives to this path which would not be preferable to it. What is needed here is only the will—the courage, the boldness, the affirmation of life —to break the evil spell that the severed atom has cast upon us all; to declare our independence of the nightmares of nuclear danger; to turn our hearts and minds to better things. . . . For all their historical and ideological differences, these two people—the Russians and the Americans—complement each other; they need each other; together, granted the requisite insight and restraint, they can do more than any other two powers to assure world peace. The rest of the world needs their forbearance with each other and their peaceful collaboration. Their allies need it. They themselves need it. They can have it if they want it. If only this could be recognized, we could perfectly well go forward to face the challenges that the true situation presents, and to shoulder, soberly but cheerfully, and without all the melodramatics of offended virtue, the burdens it imposes.

Index

ABOUT THE AUTHOR

William Attwood was born in Paris of American parents and educated in the United States, graduating from Princeton in 1941. He enlisted in the U.S. Army and after four years' service in the Middle East, Europe and the Pacific, he joined the New York *Herald Tribune* and was sent to Paris in April, 1946 as a foreign correspondent.

In 1949, Attwood left the paper to freelance with two other reporters—writing a syndicated column and scores of magazine articles from Europe and Asia. He became *Look*'s European editor in 1951, accompanied Adlai Stevenson on his world tour in 1953, and returned to the United States in 1955 to become national affairs editor and later foreign editor.

In 1959, Attwood took a leave of absence to work on the 1960 presidential campaign and was a speechwriter for John F. Kennedy, who appointed him ambassador to Guinea in 1961. After serving with the U.S. delegation to the United Nations in 1963, he was named ambassador to Kenya by President Johnson.

Attwood came home in 1966 to be editor-in-chief of Cowles Communications, a publishing conglomerate that included *Look*. Four years later he became president and publisher of *Newsday*, the nation's eleventh largest newspaper. He retired in 1979 to lecture at universities, travel, take part in local politics and write numerous articles and two books, as well as translating a French novel. He is the author of four previous books.

Attwood married Simone Cadgene in 1950. They have three children and two grandchildren and live in New Canaan, CT. and Block Island, RI.